❻ ✶✶ Medina Azahara
The ruins of the caliph's 10th century palace bear witness to one of
the world's most magnificent seats
of power, which Abd al-Rahman III
named »the flower« after his favourite wife Al-Zahra. **page 335**

❼ ✶✶ Córdoba
The former »Constantinople of the
West« boasts the Mezquita, one of
the greatest monuments to Islamic
architecture on western European
soil and a highlight of any trip to
Andalucía. **page 204**

❽ ✶✶ Coto de Doñana
Lynx still hunt in Europe's largest
nature reserve; the bird sanctuary
is home to 360 species in pine
forests, swamps and lagoons.
page 227

❾ ✶✶ Ronda
A breathless location above a
gorge, the small town of big
bullfighters – Ernest Hemingway
and Orson Wells were here too.
page 371

❿ ✶✶ El Torcal
The park offers an exciting natural
drama with its wild, craggy landscape. **page 162**

W9-CPF-792

⓫ ✶✶ Granada
The city at the foot of the
Sierra Nevada is reminiscent of A
Thousand and One Nights: the
magnificent Alhambra and the Al-
baicin, the picturesque old Moorish
quarter, are the heritage of the
caliphs. **page 245**

⓬ ✶✶ Sierra Nevada
The highest peaks on the Iberian
peninsula are part of this often
snow-covered mountain range.
page 430

⓭ ✶✶ Cueva de Nerja
The famous, bizarre dripstone cave
has fairytale-like illumination and
is the setting for a festival with
ballet and music in the summer.
page 351

⓮ ✶✶ Gibraltar
The rocky peninsula attracts with
its exotic location, pubs and
duty-free shopping, for Girbaltar
has belonged to the English since
1704. **page 240**

⓯ ✶✶ Jerez de la Frontera
Jerez offers classic Andalucía with
flamenco, sherry bodegas and
the royal Spanish riding school.
page 303

⓰ ✶✶ Costa de la Luz
Sun-spoiled coast with long
beaches, fine sand and clear water.
page 224

Do You Feel Like ...

... architectural wonders, peaceful places, restaurants and tapas bars, culinary specialties, beach fun on the coast? A few ideas for Andalucía just the way you like it.

IMPRESSIVE BUIDLINGS

- **Alhambra in Granada**
  Most magnificent Arab palace complex in Europe
  page 250
- **Mezquita in Córdoba** ▶
  One of the largest and most impressive mosques in the world.
  page 267
- **Cathedral in Seville**
  World's largest Gothic church
  page 399

»WHITE VILLAGES«

- **Arcos de la Frontera**
  One of the most beautiful »white villages« with an old city full of nooks and crannies
  page 167
- ◀ **Júzcar**
  This little village has completely laid off its white colour
  page 386
- **Vejer de la Frontera**
  This city also clings to a cliff
  page 440

TOP ADDRESSES

- **Mirador de Morayma**
  Romantic venue in Granada with a
  view of the Alhambra
  page 248
- **Tragabuches**
  Luxury restaurant in Ronda with
  creative cooking
  page 372
- **El Rinconcillo** ▶
  Classic Andalusian tapas bar in
  Seville
  page 398

CUISINE

- **Alfajores**
  The haven of sweet creations is
  Medina Sidonia.
  pages 100, 338
- **Olives and olive oil**
  In the Museo de la Cultura del
  Olivo you will learn that there are
  712 different varieties of olives.
  page 181
- ◀ **Sherry**
  For sherry lovers visiting a bodega
  is a must.
  pages 306–311

FANTASTIC BEACHES

- **Cabo de Gata**
  The Playa de los Genoveses on the
  east coast is more than 1km/0.6mi
  page 182
- **Sanlúcar de Barrameda** ▶
  Broad and fine-sanded beaches on
  the Atlantic
  page 387
- **Tarifa**
  The beaches here are 10km/6mi
  long and a paradise for windsurfers.
  page 433

BACKGROUND

12　Facts
13　Nature and Environment
14　🔛 Infographic: Facts and Figures
24　Population · Politics · Economy
26　🔛 Welcome to Everyday Life!
30　🔛 Infographic: Europe's Hothouse

34　History

46　Art and Culture
47　Art History
60　Andalusian Festival Culture
62　🔛 Special: In Search of El Duende
65　Moorish Life in Andalucía
66　🔛 Infographic: Civilisation for Europe

72　Famous People

ENJOY ANDALUCÍA

84　Accommodation
85　Pure Variety
87　🔛 Special: Showpieces

88　Children in Andalucía
89　Theme Parks and Splashing Fun

92　Festivals · Holidays · Events
93　Ferias – the Original Fiesta

96　Food and Drink
97　Andalusian Soul
100　🔛 Typical Dishes
102　🔛 Special: ¡Vamos al tapeo!

106　Shopping
107　Arts, Crafts and Culinary Gifts

110　Sports and Outdoors
111　True Paradise

TOURS

118　Tours Through Andalucía
120　Travelling in Andalucía
124　Tour 1: Andalucía in Three Weeks
127　Tour 2: White Villages
128　Tour 3: Tour of the Caliphate
130　Tour 4: Through the Sierra Nevada

An absolutely contagious dance with fire, passion, rage and pride

SIGHTS FROM A TO Z

134 Los Alcornocales
135 Algeciras
138 Almería
148 ◨ *Infographic: The Sun's Energy*
150 Almuñécar · Costa Tropical
153 Las Alpujarras
156 Andújar
158 Antequera
164 Aracena
167 Arcos de la Frontera
171 Baeza · Úbeda
182 Cabo de Gata
186 Cádiz
196 Carmona
201 Ceuta
204 Córdoba
212 ◨ *3D: Mosque and Cathedral*
224 Costa de la Luz
226 Costa del Sol
227 Coto de Doñana
233 Écija
236 Estepona
238 Fuengirola
240 Gibraltar
245 Granada
258 ◨ *3D: Alhambra, the Red Fortress*
274 Guadix
276 Huelva · Ruta Colombina
284 ◨ *Infographic: A Mistake Makes History*
286 Itálica
289 Jaén
296 ◨ *Special: Land of Olives*
300 ◨ *Infographic: Versatile Fruit*
303 Jerez de la Frontera
306 ◨ *Infographic: The Secret of Sherry*

308 ◨ *Special: Wine in Andalucía*
316 Linares
318 Málaga
328 Marbella
335 Medina Azahara
337 Medina Sidonia
340 Melilla
344 Mojácar
346 Montilla
351 Nerja
354 Niebla
356 Osuna
360 Priego de Córdoba
364 El Puerto de Santa María
367 El Rocío
368 ◨ *Special: Three Days of Commotion and Devotion*
371 Ronda
380 ◨ *Special: The Corrida – Last Bastion of Machismo*
384 ◨ *Infographic: Bloody Relict*
387 Sanlúcar de Barrameda
392 Sevilla
404 ◨ *3D: Largest Gothic Cathedral*
424 Sierra de Cazorla, Segura y Las Villas
427 Sierra de Grazalema
430 Sierra Nevada
433 Tarifa
437 Torremolinos
439 Utrera
440 Vejer de la Frontera
443 Vélez Blanco

Granada: garden in the Alhambra

The most important Semana Santa processions are held in Seville

PRACTICAL INFORMATION

446 Arrival· Before the Journey
450 Drugs
450 Electricity
451 Emergency
451 Etiquette and Customs
452 Health
453 Information
454 Language
464 Literature
465 Media
466 Money
466 Post · Telecommunications
467 Prices · Discounts
467 Time
467 Transport
469 When to Go

470 Index
475 List of Maps and Illustrations
476 Photo Credits
477 Publisher's Information
480 ⚠ *Andalusian Curiosities*

PRICE CATEGORIES
Restaurants
(price of a main dish)
€€€€ = more than €20
€€€ = 15 – 20 €
€€ = 10 – 15 €
€ = up to 10 €
Hotels (price of double room)
€€€€ = more than 200 €
€€€ = 150 – 200 €
€€ = 100 – 150 €
€ = up to 100 €

Note
Billable service telephone numbers are marked with an asterisk: *0180…

Ronda sits enthroned high up on a cliff.

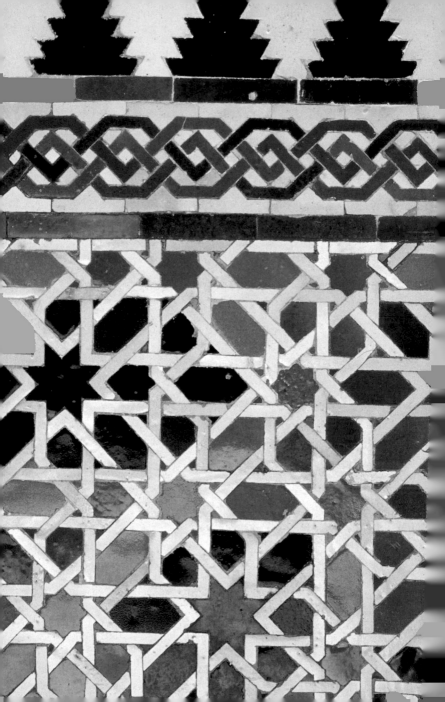

BACKGROUND

Brief and concise, clearly written, and quick and easy to consult: facts worth knowing about Andalucía and its Moorish legacy, about the country and its people, its economy and politics, its society and everyday life.

Facts

Nature and Environment

Large parts of Andalucía are still agricultural, even if tourism is one of the main pillars of the economy. While the roots of an ancient farming culture can still be felt, expanses of olive plantations, fields of sunflowers and seemingly endless seas of plastic sheeting beneath which vegetables are cultivated dominate the landscape.

GEOGRAPHIC DIVISIONS

Andalucía is divided into two natural environmental zones: **Upper Andalucía** with a small strip of the Costa del Sol, and **Lower Andalucía** in the north. Andalucía also shares a part of the Castilian plateau bordering Sierra Morena.

Upper Andalucía is made up of two mountain ranges that run parallel forming a west-east axis, the inner Penibetica range (Cordillera Penibética) and the outer sub-Betica range (Cordillera Subbética). These are separated by the Betic intermountain basin running in the same direction. They are the result of over-thrusting and basal folding processes during the Lower Triassic **approximately 37–38 million years ago**, a geological event which also created the Pyrenees. Steppes, pastureland, and maquis scrubland cover the detritus-strewn mountain regions; cork-oak and chestnut-tree woods thrive in lower areas.

Upper Andalucía

The mountains of the inner range **Cordillera Penibética** stretch from Río Guadiaro that flows into the Mediterranean about 20km/12mi north of Gibraltar to Cabo de Palos on the coast of Alicante. The limestone and clay slate mountains of the Málaga Mountains dominate in the west, reaching their highest point with the Sierra de Tolox at 1,919m/6,296ft above sea level and possessing **one of Spain's most impressive mountain landscapes**, the Jurassic limestone landscape of Torcal de Antequera. The Valle de Lecrín marks the cleft behind which there is a rise northeastwards to the Sierra Nevada all the way to Pico de Veleta and to Mulhacén (3,481m/11,421ft above sea level), **Spain's highest peak on the mainland** (highets peak: Pico del Teide, Teneriffa, 3718 m/12,269 ft). They continue in the Sierra de Baza and Sierra de los Filabres, which rise no higher than

A common sight: sunflower fields characterise the Andalusian landscape, along with olive plantations

Location: **southern Spain**
Language: **Spanih**

Area:
87,268sq km/33,690sq mi

Length of coastline:
836km/519mi

Population: **8.4 Mio.**
(17.8 % of Spain's pop.)
Largest cities:
Sevilla (pop. 704,000)
Málaga (pop. 568,500)
Córdoba (pop. 328,500),
Granada (pop. 239,000)

Population density:
96 per sq km/255 per sq mi
By comparison UK: 255 per sq km/662 per sq mi

37° 22' 58"
east longitude

■ Madrid

392km/
243mi

Lisbon
■
312km/
194mi

Sevilla

5° 59' 47"
north latitude

150km/93mi

■ Gibraltar

©BAEDEKER

▶ Population

Andalucía has the largest population of the 17 autonomous regions of Spain. 600,000 Gitanos (Roma; 1.5% of the Spanish population) and about 200,000 Africans live here.

▶ Provinces

Andalucía is divided into eight provinces. The two Spanish enclaves on the coast of North Africa -- Ceuta and Melilla – are autonomous cities. As a dominion Gibraltar is part of the United Kingdom.

▶ Administration

Government: »Junta de Andalucia« is responsible for culture, education, health and infrastructure policy. The PSOE (Partido Socialista Obrero Español), which is social-democratica oriented now, has been ruling since 1982; in the March 2012 elections it did not get an absolute majority, so formed a coalition with the IU (Izquierda Unida, United Left).

Provinces:

A: Huelva   E: Córdoba
B: Sevilla   F: Jaén
C: Cádiz   G: Granada
D: Málaga   H: Almería

▶ Tourism
7.8 mil visitors in 2013
(total Spain: 60.6 mil.)

▶ Religion
Catholics

Muslims,
jews and
protestants

94 %
6

▶ Economy
Per capita GDP (2013):
€17,600 (Spain: €22,663)

Unemployment rate (2013):
35 % (Spain: 25 %)

Economic structure
(share of GDP, 2011):
Services **73.9 %**
Industry, construction **1.7 %**,
Agriculture **4.6 %**

▶ Climate in Córdoba
Average temperatures

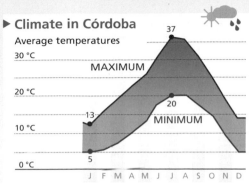

Precipitation and sunshine

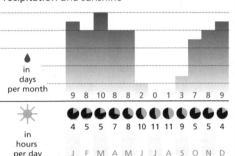

in
days
per month

9 8 10 8 8 2 0 1 3 7 8 9

4 5 5 7 8 10 11 11 9 5 5 4

in
hours
per day

J F M A M J J A S O N D

▶ »Boat People« across the Straits of Gibraltar
Every year thousands of people risk their lives to cross the Straits of Gibraltar in
small boats. They paid smugglers large amounts of money to be able to do this.
The EU organization Frontex heads the boats off – obviously successfully as
the statistics of the last years show.

Number of illegal border crossings
»Western Mediterranean Route« (Straits of Gibraltar)

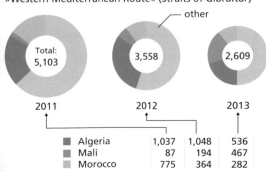

	2011	2012	2013
Algeria	1,037	1,048	536
Mali	87	194	467
Morocco	775	364	282

The peaks of the Sierra Nevada can be seen from the Andalusian Mediterranean coast, here at Nerja

2,300m/7,500ft above sea level. To the south, a strip of lower coastal mountains walls off the Mediterranean coast. It stretches from Sierra Bermeja in the west across the Sierra de Gádor to the Sierra de Alhamilla (highest point 2,242m/7,356ft), Europe's only natural desert. The valley of the Río Guadalfeo cuts between the coastal mountains and the Sierra de Gádor and forms the **terraced landscape of Las Alpujarras**.

The Andalusian Mediterranean coastline is characterized by relatively short, sandy beaches, occasionally with shingle, which are repeatedly interrupted by cliffs, as well as by the towering mountains only a few miles behind the coastal strip – the **snow-covered peaks of the Sierra Nevada**, for example, can be clearly seen from the beach. It is divided into the universally known Costa del Sol that reaches from the tip of Gibraltar to the eastern parts of the province of Málaga and the eastern Costa de Almería that passes around Cabo de Gata in the west; the Costa Tropical has become the accepted name for the short section that lies in between in the province of Granada.

Starting with the distinctive Jurassic limestone rock of Gibraltar (425m/1,394ft), the ridge of mountains of the outer sub-Betica range, **Cordillera Subbética**, runs north of the inner chain of Campo de Gibraltar, rising sharply from the north toward the south around the Málaga Mountains, and reaching its first point of culmination in the **rugged Sierra de Grazalema**. It continues on with the peaks of the

Sierra de Cazorla y Segura, which are almost as sharp and rise to above 2,000m/6,500ft, **where the Río Guadalquivir has its source**. The Betic intermountain basin lies nestled between these two main mountain ranges and rises from west to east from approx. 400m/1,300ft to a final 1,300m/4,250ft. It consists of the basin landscape of the Serranía de Ronda, where the Río Guadelevín **breathtakingly breaks through** to join the Río Guadiaro, the high-altitude basin of Antequera, the fertile central countryside of Granada's Vega and finally the Guadix and Baza basins.

The second natural environmental zone, Lower Andalucía, is essentially comprised of the Guadalquivir river basin that extends in a stretched-out triangular form between the Sierra de Morena in the north and the Upper Andalusian mountains to the south. The Atlantic coast in the west, the **Costa de la Luz**, dominates the landscape. The up to 100m/328ft-wide strips of sand dunes with seemingly endless beaches are characteristic of the region, as are the »marismas«, the wetland region north of the Río Guadalquivir which reaches the Atlantic here near Sanlúcar de Barrameda. Another marsh area is to be found near Huelva around the mouths of the Río Tinto and Río Odiel rivers flowing out of the mining region of Aracena, as well as at the Bay of Cádiz in the south into which the Río Guadalete flows. Adjacent to the coastal strip is Campiña, undulating hill country on either side of the Guadalquivir, in summer **one of the hottest zones in Europe** with temperatures often exceeding 40°C/104°F. The still extensive pastures grazed by fighting bulls and Andalusian horses are being increasingly squeezed out by artificially irrigated fields of wheat and vegetables, vineyards and citrus tree plantations. Lower Andalucía is bordered to the northeast by the nearly 250km/150mi-long Loma de Úbeda plateau that rises from 900m/2,950ft to 1,300m/4,265ft. This landscape in the eastern part of the Jaén province is marked by **gently rolling hills** with fields of grain and olive plantations, bounded in the distance by **sheer mountain peaks**.

Lower Andalucía

? | MARCO POLO INSIGHT

Guadalquivir

Andalucía's longest river is the Guadalquivir with a length of 650 km/404 miles. It is also Spain's only navigable river. In Roman times it was navigable up to Córdoba, today it can only be travelled up to Seville – by ocean-going vessels as well.

The Sierra Morena mountains rise up to the north of the Guadalquivir Plateau as a natural border to the Castilian Meseta or central plateau. The thinly populated mountain range, **bedecked with woods of cork and holly oak**, stretches across the provinces of Huelva, Córdoba and Jaén, reaching a top altitude of 1,323m/4,341ft. From

Sierra Morena

time immemorial, the most important route between Castile and Andalucía was the 1,009m/3,310ft-high Desfiladero de Despeñaperros pass (»Pass of the Overthrow of the Dogs« – so called because in a battle between Christians and Moors many were thrown from the cliffs to their deaths). The journey through this remote landscape was once feared because of its bands of robbers.

Water Andalucía is not blessed with water. The water level in the major rivers is below average for six months of the year while many smaller rivers dry up completely in the hot summers. The main watershed between the Atlantic and the Mediterranean runs along the inner Betic mountain range. The **Río Guadalquivir** (from the Arabic »great river«), Andalucía's major river, flows into the Atlantic. It has its source at an altitude of 1,369m/4,492ft in the Sierra de Segura; after Seville it spreads out into a delta that forms the »Las Marismas« of the **Coto de Doñana** and then empties into the Gulf of Cádiz near Sanlúcar de Barrameda in a 3km/2mi-wide estuary. The estuary up to Seville – where the tides are still noticeable – is navigable even for ocean-going ships. In the province of Huelva, the Río Tinto and Río Odiel rivers flow into the Atlantic, while the Guadalete ends near Cádiz. The major Mediterranean rivers are the Río Guadiaro and the Río Guadalhorce, whose mouth is situated near Málaga. **Reservoirs**, primarily those of the Guadalquivir, play an important role in irrigation and as a source of energy. The reservoir system on the river's upper course and the tributaries flowing out of the Sierra Morena (including Laguna de las Yeguas near Andújar and Embalse Puente Nuevo north of Córdoba) and the Sierra Nevada (Embalse de Iznájar / Río Genil) hold several thousand million cubic feet of water. Large reservoirs have also been created with dams along the Río Guadalete and the Río Guadalhorce.

Water shortage Water is a precious commodity in Andalucía, but also an especially limited one. Green golf courses and tourist facilities, inefficient irrigation systems in the farming sector and especially the turbo-growth of cucumbers, tomatoes and other kinds of vegetables cause water shortages every year. Summers are often so dry that there is hardly a drop of rain and the plastic coverings of the vegetable fields reflect the light and drive away any clouds that might develop, especially in the province of Almería. Between May and September the water level of the valuable dams sinks and rivers dry out. Andalusians still shudder at the memory of the 1995 drought when the Guadalquivir was just a trickle and water was often shut off in the cities for hours at a time. Out of fear of a further drought the government has invested in desalination plants along the coast. The largest one in Europe is currently in Carboneras on the Cabo de Gata in the extreme south-east of Spain.

Climate Andalucía

CLIMATE

Andalucía, like all of Spain, has a characteristically Mediterranean climate that is generally marked by hot, dry summers and damp, mild winters, as well as – once away from the coasts – by temperatures that vary greatly according to the time of day and the season. The good news for tourists is the **high number of hours of sunshine**, reaching a Spanish peak on the Costa del Sol and the Costa de la Luz with 3,000 hours annually. Thanks to the powerful wedge of **Azores highs**

Land of the sun

that keep the Atlantic low pressure areas at bay, the sun shines almost without interruption from May to the middle of October. From mid-October until the end of April, when the highs shift to the south in the autumn, areas of rain are more often able to reach Andalucía. But even in the dampest months, November and December, the duration of sunshine still reaches up to 60% of the amount of time astronomically possible, greater than in northern European summers.

Temperatures in summer Andalucía isn't called »the frying pan of Europe« for nothing. The temperature during the day in the interior exceeds the 30°C/86°F mark on over 100 days in the year. On average, between June and September, the mercury reaches 32 to 36°C/90 to 97°F; such temperatures are even typical in July and August for 700m/2,300ft-high Granada. On individual days it can even get decidedly higher, especially in Lower Andalucía, where the Guadalquivir river basin, the **hottest region in Europe**, averages ten days of temperatures of 40°C/104°F or higher between mid-July and mid-August. Only along the coast is it somewhat cooler because there the sea breeze blows during the day, bringing relief from the summer heat.

Spring and autumn are much more pleasant, but winter is particularly mild too, thanks to the sheltering effect of the Sierra Nevada and the Sierra Morena blocking off the cold northern winds. This is above all true for the coasts, where the Atlantic and the Mediterranean, whose temperatures do not fall below 14°C/57°F, act like a hot water radiator. For this reason daytime temperatures there, even in the coldest month of January, usually still reach 16 to 18°C/61 to 64°F; at night it hardly ever cools down below 9°C/48°F. It is different inland: with daytime temperatures similar to those of the coast, the thermometer in the lowlands of the interior drops down on average to 5°C/41°F; in the central hill country it approaches 0°C/32°F. Authentic **winter weather** can be found above 2,000m/6,560ft. In the higher regions of the Sierra Nevada up to 50 days of snowfall are recorded annually, and from the end of October to the beginning of June the highest peaks are crowned by a solid blanket of snow or at least snow patches.

An **unexpected climatic characteristic** of the extreme south of the European mainland between Tarifa and Gibraltar, of all places, is that the summers are the coolest there, averaging 22 to 24°C/72 to 75°F, and the winters the mildest, with an average of 12°C/54°F. The reason is that the moderating influence of the very evenly tempered Atlantic waters (max. 20°C/68°F; min. 15°C/59°F) is particularly strong in this section of coastline which protrudes far out into the ocean. At the same time, strong winds blow from the east (»**Levante**«) or the west (»**Poniente**«) that are additionally fanned by the jet-like effect of the strait, building down-draughts in the Bay of Gibraltar that can become dangerous for smaller boats.

Cabo de Gata is the driest part of Europe

The water temperature is influenced by the Atlantic, whose cool currents have an effect through the Strait of Gibraltar all the way to the eastern Costa del Sol. As a rule of thumb, **the sea gets warmer moving eastwards**. The water is warmest in mid-August when temperatures average 21°C/70°F on the Gulf of Cádiz, 22°C/72°F on the Costa del Sol near Málaga and 23°C/73°F on the beaches of Almería. The sea is coolest at the beginning of March with temperatures between 14 and 15°C/57 and 59°F.

Water temperatures

The Cordillera Bética is a prominent **rain trap** for the moisture-bearing west winds. As a result, many of the regions lying on the leeward side of the mountain range are particularly dry and feature **steppe-like landscapes**. Precipitation is extremely low on the eastern Costa del Sol, where downright desert-like conditions reign, as well as on Cabo de Gata, where **Europe's driest climate station** is located. Moving southwest, precipitation rises. July and August, the drought months, are practically precipitation-free, while the most rain falls from November to January and in April. Even then, the risk of rain is still very low with 10–20% on the coasts and a maximum of 30% inland and along the Strait of Gibraltar. Periods of pronounced bad weather are rare; however, individual storms with strong rainfall, especially in autumn and winter, are more frequent.

Precipitation

Effects of climate change

Spain is suffering more and more from the consequences of global climate changes. Since the 1980s, little or the complete lack of winter precipitation has led to a worsening **drought**. But the real danger comes from the mountains. The failing winter precipitation is causing the snow cover on the peaks of the Sierra Nevada to shrink, which has severe consequences for the water supply in the dry areas of East Andalucía. Until now, the melting snow has supplied enough drinking and industrial water to meet the needs of the major cities, tourist centres and irrigated agriculture, which are partially in totally arid climate zones. Modern horticulture and irrigation techniques involving cultivation under plastic sheeting and the growing of fruit trees with avocados and chirimoyas revolutionized agriculture in the 1980s (►MARCO POLO Insight p.29). With the continuing trend toward aridity which the climate experts predict for the whole Mediterranean area, all of this is at risk.

FLORA AND FAUNA

Flora

The immense forests that once covered Iberia fell victim to merciless campaigns of deforestation in ancient times. The flora characteristic of the lower terrains consists of woods of holly oak and cork oak and the »dehesas«, areas of pasture grasslands grazed by goats, cattle and pigs and scattered with holly oak and cork oak. Exotic plants such as **agaves**, which develop metre-high inflorescences, also thrive in these zones. Higher up, stands of red and black pine are to be found with an undergrowth of aromatic shrubs and herbs such as rosemary, juniper, hawthorn and gorse. A rarity is the **Spanish fir**, an endemic fir found only in the Sierra de Grazalema. The upper regions of the Sierra Nevada are dominated by robust types of shrubs with the occasional sprinkling of alpine grasses and foliage, forming the so-called »hedgehog heath«.

Alpha and esparto grasses dominate in the province of Almería in eastern Upper Andalucía and are used in traditional wickerwork. Maquis shrubland consisting of typical Mediterranean foliage and shrubs also thrive on the mountainsides, as do Indian fig cacti, often planted to mark off parcels of land. Another endemic variety often seen is the **European fan palm**. Mediterranean varieties of palms can be seen growing along the Costa del Sol. Crops requiring intensive irrigation such as citrus fruits and vegetables such as bell peppers, tomatoes, aubergines and so on are cultivated over wide areas. The sugar cane and banana plantations to be found primarily on the Costa Tropical are smaller. Although located at a high elevation, the climatic conditions in Alpujarras are very favourable and citrus fruits, vegetables and grapes thrive in large terraced gardens.

The flora found in **Lower Andalucía** includes forest communities of holly oak, cork oak and Lusitanian oak. These formations were once typical for the hill country lying beyond the coastline, but have visibly degenerated to Maquis shrubland of rockrose, pistachio, myrtle, arbutus and a variety of herbage. Grape vines for sherry thrive behind the sand dunes along the Atlantic coastline, along with pine and eucalyptus trees, which, however, are the product of afforestation measures. Plants that survive in salty soil like the sea holly are characteristic of the »marismas«. Extensive areas of Lower Andalucía are covered with endless rows of olive trees that reach into the regions of Upper Andalucía and make up the **largest olive-growing area in the world**.

Wolves and lynx find a habitat in Andalucía in the foothills of the Sierra Morena. It is only in the fertile river marshlands of Coto de Doñana that the extraordinarily rare **Iberian or pardel lynx** and the ichneumon, a variety of civet cat, have managed to survive. Also among the endangered animals are genets (a viverrine), otters and the Iberian ibex. An animal that is not rare but whose absence from this landscape is impossible to imagine is the ancient breed of half-wild **fighting bulls** (»toros bravos«), mainly bred in the southwest of the province of Cádiz in the ancient countryside of the big landowners. The imperial eagle, golden eagle and the booted eagle have withdrawn to the lonely mountain regions. The monk vulture and the

Fauna

Original and copy: »Toros bravos« and the popular Osborne bull

griffon vulture are also frequently observed there. **Innumerable sea-birds and water fowl** live in the wetlands of the »marismas«, among them the only European breeding colony of purple swamp hens; there are also herons, and rare varieties of duck such as the white-eyed pochard and the white-headed duck, as well as the ruddy shel-duck. In addition there are flamingos, and, in the Coto de Doñana, imperial eagles and short-toed eagles, and occasionally also ospreys and azure-winged magpies. A lot of white storks are to be seen, as well as cranes; much rarer, though, are the black storks.

The **world of the reptiles and amphibians** is represented by varieties of snakes (snub-nosed vipers, the Montpellier snakes), geckos, aquatic turtles and swamp turtles, as well as fire salamanders.

Nature conservation areas   154 ecologically valuable areas are under protection in Andalucía – close to 20% of its total area, the highest in Spain. Two regions – ►Coto de Doñana and the ►Sierra Nevada – can claim to be national parks; 24 are designated as »parques natural« (nature parks), in which restricted agricultural exploitation is still possible.

Population · Politics · Economy

Andalucía is an economically poor region. Tourism is the main source of income. Many stretches of land are being abandoned because young people are going to the cities to look for work.

POPULATION

Population structure and religion   The majority of the Andalusian population is concentrated around the provincial capitals, in the tourist centres and in the areas intensively used for agriculture. Accordingly, the **areas of high population density** are Greater Seville (approx. 1 million), the Mediterranean coast around Málaga (approx. 650,000) and the industrial area around Cádiz (approx. 600,000). Most sparsely populated are the Sierra Morena, the Betic Cordillera mountain ranges and the desert regions of East Andalucía. The age pyramid in the villages has gradually been turned on its head as the youth have left their homes and headed in the direction of Málaga, Seville or Madrid to secure employment in the big cities. The majority of Andalusians are **Catholics**. There are a small number of Muslims, Jews and Protestants. Islam plays a bigger role in the North African enclaves of Ceuta and Melilla; the Islamic community is also growing in Granada.

Andalucía Provinces

The Gitanos (**Roma**) originally came from **northwest India**, migrating from there as early as the Middle Ages. They came by way of North Africa with the Moors to Spain, where today approx. 600,000 individuals live. Despite popular preconceptions, only a few actually still move about the country. Many have settled in the province of Granada. High unemployment, no vocational training, widespread illiteracy, low life expectancy and high infant mortality characterize the situation of this people, to whom Andalucía in particular owes a debt of thanks for flamenco, a significant contribution to its culture and folklore. Integration into society is hampered by the persistent antipathy of the population on the one hand, and the resistance of the Gitanos on the other, who – through a lack of social recognition – cling to their traditions and their pronounced common identity and sense of solidarity.

Gitanos

In recent years, the number of illegal immigrants being brought across the Strait of Gibraltar for huge amounts of money by people traffickers has risen sharply (►p,14). Not a few of these from Morocco, but also from sub-Saharan Africa, Pakistan, Iraq and Palestine have lost their lives in the attempt. Without valid residency papers, they have no chance of finding regular employment in Spain, so in

Illegal immigrants

Welcome to Everyday Life!

Let specialists in their field show you Andalucía away from the tourist bustle!

WITH MARY CARMEN IN THE WORLD OF OLIVES

Mary Carmen Segovia Ruiz is an experienced tour guide. And the best part: she is unique in the northern Andalusian province of Jaén for the are gets few visitors and thus has few guides. Touring the olive groves with her means seeing everyday Andalucía at its greenest. She will take you to rural haciendas, along old trade railway lines and to local olive oil tasting opportunities. Wonderful!

mcarmensevovia@hotmail.com

MORNINGS IN THE MARKET IN MÁLAGA

Andalusian men love this joke. At least Malagueños do. It goes like this: »Málaga has three famous sons: Pablo Picasso, Antonio Banderas and me!« Mario, 50 years young, is only one of the market sellers in Málaga who love to talk to visitors with hands and feet, starting with this joke. And of course sampling is allowed: shrimps, olives, the best ham...

Atarazanas market: daily 8am – 2pm

TALK LIKE AN ANDALUSIAN

Starting a conversation with an Andalusian, understanding the babble in a tapas bar: a little small talk will get you a peek into the real Andalusian soul. The Academia Hispánica Córdoba offers great courses all year round, also combined with cooking and flamenco lessons (▶Enjoy Andalucía, Accommodations).
www.academiahispanica.com

ACTION IN FRONT OF THE CAVE

Riding Andalusian thoroughbreds, motocross on four wheels, hitting the bull's eye with bow and arrow. The holiday resort Tío Tobas in the shadows of the Sierra Nevada has lots on its programme, including visits to ancient ruins and beautiful bodegas. This is far away from the Robinson Club and right in modern Andalucía.
www.tiotobas.com

TAPAS TOUR IN ALMERÍA

Whoever wants to mingle with Andalusians had better go on a tapas tour. Almería is a real highlight; here you can just flow with the crowds through the old city from tavern to tavern, pick a tapa with every drink and get into conversation with the locals quickly at the bar, with hands and feet as well (▶Almería).

Religious devotion and enjoying a party are not mutually exclusive during Semana Santa

order to earn a living the best they can do is find jobs as day labourers on vegetable and fruit plantations. In the province of Almería, for example – as even tourists can see – they are forced to exist under the **most wretched of working and living conditions**. The Spanish authorities are trying to gain control of the situation by patrolling the strait more frequently. The border fences between Ceuta and Melilla and Morocco were raised from 3 m to 6 m (10 ft to 20 ft) after several thousand illegal immigrants tried to storm the border in 2005.

POLITICS

Government Since October 1981 Andalucía has been an autonomous community. The seat of the »Junta de Andalucía« is in Seville. Although the powers of the Spanish central government in Madrid are more comprehensive than those of the German Federal government, it is still possible to compare the autonomous communities with the German states.

ECONOMY

A poor region Andalucía is among the less developed regions of Spain. There are still large numbers of landless seasonal workers, who find work only as day labourers (»jornaleros«) during harvest time and thereby also find themselves facing the strong competition of African immigrants – a cause for xenophobic antagonism. There is no government support for the times without work; no wonder that **illegal employment** is flourishing. Although Andalucía is indeed getting aid – a large part of all EU aid funds for Spain flows into Andalucía – **structural problems** stand in the way of a real upswing. Among them remains the ownership situation in agriculture in particular, where 270,000 operations with half of the developed land are in the hands of about 9000 big landowners. Naturally, they profit from the blessings of EU funds: 6% of the monies from Brussels are divided among the 200 largest agrarian enterprises.

The **main products** of Andalusian agriculture are wheat, olives, vegetables, fruit, and wine. Predominantly wheat, oats, barley, beans and chick-peas, as well as maize, are found where only dry farming can be conducted. Olive tree cultivation covers about a third of the arable land of Lower Andalucía. The regions around Jerez de la Frontera, Málaga, Montilla-Moriles and Huelva are the focus of wine growing. Cork is produced primarily in Sierra Morena.

Agriculture

The fact that extensive areas of Andalucía is farmland at all is thanks solely to **large-scale irrigation**, the areas under cultivation in the Guadalquivir basin and in the provinces of Huelva and Almería being of major importance. Citrus fruits, sunflowers, potatoes, sugar beet, cotton and even rice are grown there. Thanks to irrigation under transparent plastic sheeting, the provinces of Almería (tomatoes, cucumbers, beans, peppers, melons) and Huelva (strawberries) are able to reap **multiple harvests per year**, which has made them the major centre of Spanish vegetable farming that supplies large parts of Europe with its products – Germany is Andalucía's most important customer. With an average annual production of 300,000 tons on 7,500ha/18,500ac, Spain is **Europe's largest producer of strawberries** and indeed, after the USA, the second largest producer in the world. 95% of the Spanish production comes from Huelva. The production methods, however, are ecologically questionable because of the wide use of pesticides. They are also socially dubious because the major part of the workforce are Africans who have immigrated – either legally or illegally – and who live in third-world conditions. Finally, the landscape is ruined. The farmland around Almería is not called »**Mar de Plástico**« for nothing: the plastic hothouses stretch for mile upon mile (▶MARCO POLO Insight, p. 30).

Animal husbandry now only has relatively little significance in the total economy. Large herds of sheep graze the Sierra Morena in summer. Dairy farming and the breeding of horses and fighting bulls are carried out on the pastures of Marismas. Traditional goat keeping still occurs in Upper Andalucía; pig breeding, especially fattening pigs with acorns, is traditionally at home in the Sierra Morena and Sierras Béticas. Up until the 1950s, **fishing** was practised in every settlement on the coast, but today the spread of tourism, over-fishing

Europe's Hothouse

320 sunny days a year means that not only tourism blossoms in the province of Almería, but also tomatoes, paprika and cucumbers. Thanks to the gigantic fields under plastic sheets in Andalucía Spain can keep pace with the large producers and can supply Europe with vegetables during the winter months. But the pickers in the »mar plástico« mostly live and work under miserable conditions; about 50% of them are in the country illegally.

▶ **The world vegetable market**

Annual production in mil Tonnes

* China is the largest producing country

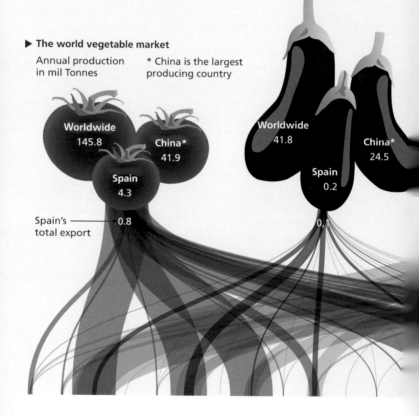

Worldwide 145.8

China* 41.9

Spain 4.3

Spain's total export — 0.8

Worldwide 41.8

China* 24.5

Spain 0.2

0.1

BELGIUM

DENMARK

GERMANY

ESTONIA

FINLAND

FRANCE

GREECE

GREAT BRITAIN

IRLEAND

ITALY

CANADA

LATVIA

▶ **Growing vegetables under plastic**

Growing area	350 sq km/135 sq mi
Businesses about	about 15,000
Annual production	about 3 mil. T
Workers	abou 80,000
Earnings	about €36 a day
Seasonal labourers from	Morocco, Romania, Bulgaria, Sub-Saharan Africa, Latin America, Poland, Ukraine

Almeria

El Ejido

■ Hothouse areas

20km/12mi

©BAEDEKER

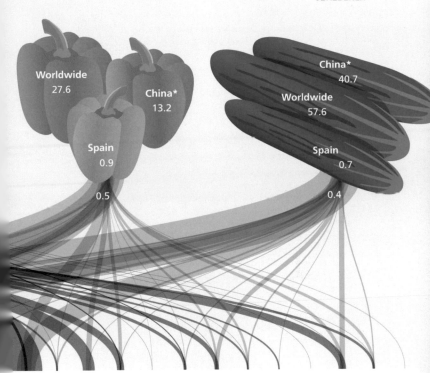

Worldwide
27.6

China*
13.2

Spain
0.9

0.5

China*
40.7

Worldwide
57.6

Spain
0.7

0.4

NETHERLANDS

AUSTRIA

POLAND

PORTUGAL

ROMANIA

RUSSIA

SWEDEN

SWITZERLAND

SLOVAKIA

SLOVENIA

CZECH REP.

UNGARN

USA

of the traditional fishing grounds and restrictive quotas have led to a sharp decline. The most important fishing locations are Huelva, Cádiz, Algeciras, Málaga, Almuñecar and Motril. The catch includes sardines, anchovies, tuna and octopus. Fish and shellfish farming in aqua-farms have now taken the place of traditional fishing, above all in Cádiz province.

Mining Although Andalucía is rich in mineral resources, the situation on the world markets has plunged Andalusian mining into a **crisis**. The cupriferous pyrite deposits in the provinces of Seville and Huelva are still of particular importance, above all in the regions of Río Tinto.

Solar and wind power Economic prospects for Andalucía are being created from the **use of renewable energy**, for which there are favourable climatic conditions such as those enjoyed by the Tabernas solar power station near Almería. The generation of wind energy in the mountains between Tarifa and Algeciras has gained special significance. Andalucía supplies more than 20% of the total amount of energy produced by wind power in Spain (▶MARCO POLO Insight, p.148).

Industry Industry remains relatively weak in Andalucía. Seville is developing into the most **important economic centre**. Not only are the food, beverage and tobacco industries concentrated here, but Seville is also home to iron and steel works and the metalworking industry. The chemical and petrochemical industries have established themselves in Algeciras and Huelva, and shipbuilding takes place in Cádiz. Added to that are the traditional industrial sectors such as sea salt production – above all in Almería province – and the reprocessing of ores. Until now, the high-tech era has as good as passed Andalucía by; the hopes of creating a Spanish Silicon Valley in Seville as a result of the World Exposition of 1992 were not fulfilled.

Andalucía profited from the construction boom for a long time, until the real estate crisis brought it to an end in all of Spain. Today most of Spain's construction workers are unemployed or abroad.

Tourism Tourism is by far the most important economic factor in Andalucía. The figures speak for themselves. Tourists annually spend about 14 thousand million euros; directly or indirectly, tourism provides close to 258,000 jobs. The rise to becoming a **holiday paradise** was tentatively initiated in the 1950s with the first charter flights, and in the 1960s tourism began developing into the most important source of revenue. The core area is, as it always was, the Costa del Sol on either side of Málaga, where holiday centres like Torremolinos, Fuengirola, Marbella, Estepona, San Roque, Almuñecar, Motril, Castell de Ferro, Roquetas de Mar and Aguadulce are lined up one after the other – every one of them once a sleepy fishing village that was transformed

As if the artist Christo had covered it up – »Mar de Plástico« in the province of Almería

within a short time into a conglomeration of hotels for tens of thousands of holidaymakers. This development triggered, on the one hand, a great migration of job hunters to the coasts and, on the other, eventually resulted in **80% of all Andalucía's beaches becoming built-up and spoiled**. An attempt was made in 1988 to counter this with the coastal law (»Ley de Costa«), according to which it was no longer allowed to build within 100m/328ft behind the beach and 1km/0.6mi distance from a river estuary. Andalucía experienced its first **tourism crisis** in the 1990s as a result of unimpeded expansionism that placed more emphasis on quantity than quality and, for example, hardly provided for sewage treatment plants. That has been made up for in the meantime: in 1990, 33 beaches had to be closed because of poor water quality, but since 1997 there has not been one closure.

The future of tourism in Andalucía will very much depend on whether environmentally sustainable development can be brought about and whether the efforts of the government aiming at a qualitatively better, individual holiday experience are successful, which also include the hinterland.

History

Influenced by Many Peoples

Many peoples have influenced Andalucía: Phoenicians, Greeks, Carthaginians, Celts, Romans, Visigoths. The influence of the Moors on Andalucía proved to be the most sustained. They brought Andalucía to a cultural flowering – during the period of their reign, al-Andalus was economically, artistically and academically vastly superior to the rest of Christian Spain.

FROM PREHISTORY TO THE ARAB INVASION

8th–6th century BC	Tartessos Culture
237 BC	The Carthaginians advance into Spain.
27 BC	The province of Baetica is established under Augustus with about the same boundaries as today's Andalucía.
AD 507–711	The Visigoths rule from Toledo.
711	Landing of the Arabs

The **first pieces of cultural evidence** of human settlement are cave paintings dating to the Palaeolithic (2000–10,000 BC), found, among other places, in the Cueva de la Pileta near Ronda and the Cueva de Nerja on the Costa del Sol. The first town-like settlement was built by the Los Millares culture, considered to be part of megalith culture (3000–2000 BC). The large **burial complex near Antequera**, dating from a thousand years later, is also considered to be their work. The beginnings of the Bell-Beaker culture also occurred in this time period (approx. 2000–1500 BC); one of its largest settlement centres was in today's Almería province.

First cultural witnesses

The ancients viewed the world as ending at the Strait of Gibraltar with the »**Pillars of Hercules**« – Jebel Musa on the African side and the Rock of Gibraltar on the European. The **Phoenicians** were the first to dare to venture beyond this point and in around 1100 BC founded the trading settlement of Gadir (Cádiz), **Europe's oldest city**. Malaka (Málaga), Sexi (Almuñecar) and Abdera (Adra) followed.

Phoenicians

Burial mounds provide evidence of the legendary Tartessos culture that has been located by most historians in the area of the Guadalquivir estuary and whose flowering is dated from about the 8th to the

Tartessos

Moorish arches in the Mezquita of Córdoba

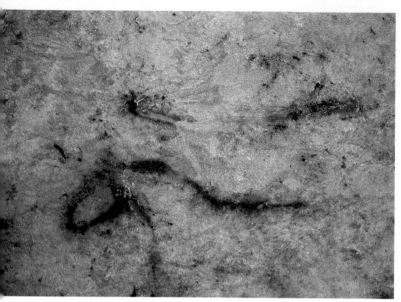

Prehistoric cave paintings in Cueva de la Pileta

6th century BC. The most important reports of this culture, which has been equated by some with Atlantis, are from later Greek (Herodotus) and Roman sources, which agree that the Tartessos supplied the Phoenicians and Greeks with ore. The later, mainly Asia Minor Ionians from the Phocaian colony of Massalia (Marseille) established a few ports on the Mediterranean coasts as early as 700 BC, including Mainake near today's Torre del Mar.

Carthaginians The Greeks lasted for only a century. They were ousted by the Carthaginians around 600 BC, whose conflict with Rome spread out to include Iberia. After the loss of Sicily in the First Punic War (237 BC), Hamilcar Barcas, Hasdrubal and Hannibal concentrated on Iberia and pushed up from the south to Ebro. This border was recognized by Rome. At the beginning of the Second Punic War (219–206 BC), Hannibal destroyed Sagunt, which was allied with Rome. The Romans then advanced ever deeper into Carthaginian territory and in 208 BC reached the Guadalquivir River near Baecula (Bailén). Carthage's defeat was ensured two years later with Publius Cornelius Scipio's victory near Ilipa (Alcalá del Río). In Spain Scipio settled his veterans not far from the battlefield in what became **Itálica**. In the peace settlement with Rome in 201 BC, Carthage relinquished all its Iberian possessions.

The Romans divided Iberia into two providences, »Hispania citerior« in the northeast and »Hispania ulterior« in the southwest. In 45 BC during the Roman Civil War, Julius Caesar defeated the sons and supporters of Pompey near Munda (southwest of Córdoba) and became the dictator of the Roman Empire. When the Iberian Peninsula was reorganized under Augustus in 27 BC, **Baetica province** (named after the Guadalquivir, called by the Romans »Baetis«) was created, which had approximately the same boundaries as today's Andalucía. Major centres were Hispalis (Seville), Corduba (Córdoba) and Itálica. The Christianization of the Iberian Peninsula began around AD 100.

Romans

Over a period of a little more than 20 years during the great migration at the beginning of the 5th century, the Vandals moved out of eastern Germany and settled in southern Spain. In 429, led by Geiseric, they moved over to North Africa and founded a kingdom there. They left practically nothing behind in Andalucía except the name – it comes from the Arabic »al-Andalus«, a derivation of the Gothic **»landahlauts« (= landless)** used to denote the Vandals.

Vandals

King Euric (466–484), ruler of the Visigothic Kingdom in Toulouse founded by Theodoris, spread Visigoth rule to Spain. After their defeat at the hands of Clovis I in 507 at Poitiers, the Visigoths withdrew completely back into Spain and ruled there in Toledo until 711. From 551 on, they had to fend off the Byzantines, who had taken the southern coast of Spain, until they were able to force them out again in 624. Under Reccared I, the Third Council of Toledo dissolved the Visigoths from Arianism (that recognized only a God-like Christ) and professed Catholicism (that postulated a Christ equal to God).

Visigoths

The Arab general **Tariq Ibn Ziyad** crossed over the Strait of Gibraltar with his 7,000-strong army in the year 711 and landed in the vicinity of today's Tarifa.

Landing of the Arabs in 711

AL-ANDALUS

July 711	Tariq defeats Roderic in the Battle of Jerez de la Frontera.
732	Charles Martel defeats the Muslims as they advance into France near Tours and Poitiers.
756–929	Emirate of Córdoba
929–1031	Caliphate of Córdoba
1086–1147	Rule of the Almoravids, a Muslim sect from Morocco
1147–1212	Reign of the Almohad dynasty, which was also Moroccan

Tariq's troops met an opponent weakened by internal disputes. In July 711, they decisively defeated the Visigoth army led by King

Conquest of Iberia

Important Battles between Moors and Christians

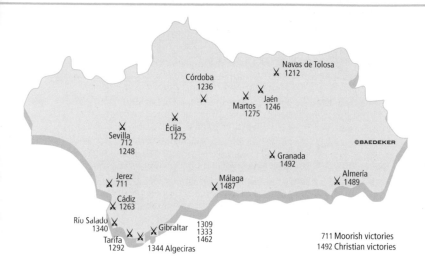

Córdoba
1236
✗

Navas de Tolosa
✗ 1212

✗ Jaén
Martos 1246
1275

✗
Martos

✗ Écija
1275

✗
Sevilla
712
1248

✗ Granada
1492

Almería
✗ 1489

Jerez
✗ 711

Málaga
✗ 1487

Cádiz
✗ 1263

Río Salado ✗
1340

✗ Gibraltar 1309
1333
1462

✗ ✗
Tarifa
1292 1344 Algeciras

711 Moorish victories
1492 Christian victories

©BAEDEKER

Roderic in the seven-day battle of Jerez de la Frontera. In the following three years, the Muslim army conquered almost the whole of the Iberian Peninsula up to the mountains of Asturia, Galicia and the Basque Country. Named »al-Andalus«, the region was made a **province of the Umayyad Caliphate** in Damascus. Increasing numbers of Muslims poured in, among them many North African Berbers from the former Roman province of Mauretania, which is why one generally speaks only of the »Moors«. The triumphant progress of the Muslims was finally halted by Charles Martel's victory at the Battle of Tours.

756 – 929
Emirate of
Córdoba
The Umayyad Abd ar-Rahman I, the sole survivor of his family in the fight against the Abbasids of Baghdad, fled to al-Andalus and in 756 founded the **Emirate of Córdoba**, which encompassed the whole Pyrenean Peninsula. New crops (including rice and sugar cane), artificial irrigation and the increasing production of silk and weapons facilitated a great economic and cultural flowering. In general, the Moors practiced religious tolerance towards the Christians (Mozarabs) and Jews living among them. Many Christians converted to Islam and adopted the Arab language and customs. In 785, Abd-ar-Rahman I began the construction of the **Mosque in Córdoba** as a visual symbol of his rule. He died in 788. From the beginning, however, there was a stirring of Christian resistance to the Moors that

originated in the non-occupied regions in the mountains of Asturia in the north of the Iberian Peninsula, and the emirate found itself constantly on the defensive.

Abd-ar-Rahman III declared himself caliph in 929. This was **a tremendous event**, because in the Islamic world the only recognized caliph – and as such the legitimate successor to the Prophet – was the caliph of Baghdad. Despite that, Moorish culture reached its zenith in Andalucía, most clearly expressed in the **palace complex of Medina Azahara** that was begun in 936. The caliph was also successful in his fight against the advancing Christians. In 930 he conquered Toledo; a year later he even reached out into Northwest Africa (to Tahert), which was lost again in 979. Under Almansur (»Victorious by Grace of God«), the grand vizier of Caliph Hisham II, Spain experienced the **peak of the development of the Moors' military might**. One after another, Almansur conquered Barcelona (985), León (987) and Santiago de Compostela (997). With his death in 1002, the end was in sight, which was sealed with the overthrow of the last Umayyad caliph, Hisham III, in 1031. The caliphate broke up into more than 20 **independent emirates** (»Taifas«), which mostly warred against each other.

929 – 1031 Caliphate of Córdoba

The Christians took advantage of the disunity of the Muslims. Alfonso VI of Castile retook Toledo in 1085 and threatened Seville. In 1086, the local emir sent for help from Yusuf ibn Tashfin, the leader of the fundamentalist Berber sect, the Almoravids, based in North Africa. Within a short time, they had forced back the Christians and united the Islamic southern part of Spain with their North African kingdom.

1086 – 1147 Almoravids

The Almohads, led by Abd al-Mum, were also Berbers, and conquered the Almoravid kingdom. They were incessantly forced to fight against the Christian kingdoms and in 1195 gained the last great Muslim victory over the Christians in the Battle of Alarcos. Nevertheless, they displayed lively building activity – the Alcázar and the mosques, of which the Giralda still stands today, were built in their capital Seville.

1147 – 1212 Almohads

THE RECONQUISTA

1212	Battle of Las Navas de Tolosa; the beginning of the Reconquista with the victory of the Christian armies over the Almohads
1238–1492	The Nasrid Emirate of Granada
2 January 1492	Catholic monarchs enter Granada.

2 January 1492: the Moors hand Granada over to the Catholic Kings

The advance of the Christians

The Almohad caliph, Mohammed ibn Nasr, suffered a crushing defeat in 1212 against the allied armies of Castile, Aragón and Navarre at the Battle of Las Navas de Tolosa. That signalled the downfall of Islamic rule and the final re-conquest by the Christians (»**Reconquista**«). Again, smaller states emerged that were, however, unable to stop the disintegration. The losses of the Moors against Ferdinand III, called the Saint, and Alfonso X the Wise included Córdoba (1236), Seville (1248) and Cádiz (1263).

1238 – 1492 Nasrid Emirate of Granada

The last Moorish state able to survive over a longer period of time was the Emirate of **Granada** founded in 1238 by Mohammed ibn al-Ahmar of the Beni Nasr dynasty. It stretched from Gibraltar to Almería. Its capital was the richest city of the peninsula and, at the same time, its cultural centre. The Nasids left behind a unique legacy of their reign, the **Alhambra**, built in the 14th century. A fragile peace was bought with the Christians in 1246 by submitting to Castile, to whom the Nasrids were required to pay tribute. Granada even went into battle on the side of the Christians in the conquest of Seville in 1248. The Christians continued a policy of pin pricks. Although King Mohammed II defeated the Castilians with the help of the Marinid sultan of Morocco, Abu Yûsuf, in 1275 at Écija and Martos, Granada lost Tarifa in 1292 and Gibraltar in 1309 (which was regained in 1333 and remained Moorish until 1462). In 1340, Yûsuf I, in alliance with the Moroccan sultan, suffered a severe defeat at Río Salado north of today's Vejer de la Frontera. The Castilians entered Algeciras in 1344. The unification of the two great Christian kingdoms of Spain began with the marriage of Isabella of Castile and Ferdinand of Aragón (the »**Catholic monarchs**«) in 1469. The couple was determined to drive out the Muslims, and they became overpowering adversaries of the Moors.

> **?** MARCO ● POLO INSIGHT
>
> *Origin of the name*
>
> Many place names have the suffix »de la Frontera« (on the border), because during the course of the Reconquista, which ended in 1492 with the conquest of Granada, they were located on the constantly shifting and contested frontier between the Moors and the Christians.

In 1481, open war between Castile-León and Granada began, with Granada weakened internally by disputes over the throne between Muley Hassan (ruled 1464–1482) and Abu abd-Allah (Boabdil, ruled 1482–1492). In 1487, the Spaniards stood in Málaga, cutting Granada off from the sea. In 1491 the city was besieged.

On 2 January 1492, the Catholic monarchs entered into Granada. The **last Moorish ruler, Boabdil**, withdrew to Africa, ending almost eight hundred years of Islamic culture in southern Spain. The subsequent expulsion of several hundred thousand Moors and Jews meant a grave setback for Spain's cultural life and further economic development.

2 January 1492

THE ERA OF THE HABSBURGS AND BOURBONS

1492	Columbus lands in the New World, thus founding Spain's colonial empire
1496	Spain falls to the Habsburgs.
1700–1873	Reign of the Bourbons
1808	Napoleon's troops occupy Spain, except Cádiz.
1834–1876	Carlist Wars

Even before entering Granada, Isabella of Castile concluded a contract with Christopher Columbus enabling him to seek a western route to India. Andalusian ports were used as the starting points for his four **voyages of discovery**. In 1492, he set sail from Palos de la Frontera, in 1493 from Cádiz, in 1498 from Sanlúcar de Barrameda and in 1502 again from Cádiz (▶MARCO POLO Insight, p.284). The marriage of Isabella's daughter, Joanna the Mad, to Philip the Handsome in 1496 gave Spain to the **Habsburgs**.

Columbus discovers the New World

The **discovery of the New World** founded the Spanish colonial empire. Communication with the colonies was maintained from Andalucía, where their immense wealth would first arrive, resulting in a great blossoming of trade, industry and, in their wake, also art – for this reason the 16th century is referred to as Andalucía's golden age. Seville, where the galleons laden with gold and silver landed after crossing the Atlantic, profited the most. In 1503, the city became the seat of the Casa de la Contratación, the chamber exclusively responsible for trade with the new colonies. It was from there that in 1519 the Portuguese mariner Magellan set sail on the first circumnavigation of the globe. The Habsburg Empire reached its greatest extent under Charles I of Spain (ruled 1516 – 1556), who was at the same time Holy Roman Emperor Charles V (In the Sights section, only the name **Charles V** will be used). He immortalized his reign with the construction of his palace on the Alhambra in Granada and the erection of a cathedral in the middle of the Great Mosque of Córdoba.

Jews and Moriscos

In 1492 the Catholic Kings had the Jews driven out of the kingdom and for the Moors who stayed in Granada after its conquest, the so-called **Moriscos**, the age was anything but golden. Many retreated to the Alpujarras. Constantly under pressure from the Church, even threatened with forced baptism in 1502, they tried to improve their conditions through revolts, as in 1568 to 1570 in the Alpujarras, which Philip II had brutally crushed. Beginning in 1609, the last Moriscos were **driven out** once and for all.

1700 – 1873 Bourbons

Charles II, the last Habsburg, died in 1700 without designating a successor. With Philip V, the Bourbons ascended to the throne of Spain. This ignited the War of the Spanish Succession – Philip V and France on the one side, Charles of Habsburg and Great Britainon the other – during the course of which in 1704 the British **conquered Gibraltar**, which was awarded to them in the Treaty of Utrecht in 1713. In return, they accepted the Bourbons on the throne. Andalucía became appreciably poorer under their reign. The gap between the big landowners and the landless peasants became ever greater. The wealth from the colonies was scarcely still flowing; the Guadalquivir was silting up and the ships could no longer reach Seville. In 1717, the Casa de la Contratación was transferred from there to Cádiz. An attempt, begun in 1767 by Charles III who was influenced by the Enlightenment, to revive agriculture by settling German farmers in the Sierra Morena failed.

Napoleon and the consequences

On 21 October 1805, the English fleet under the command of Admiral Nelson destroyed the combined French and Spanish fleets in the **Battle of Trafalgar**. The French-controlled politics of the monarchy elicited a revolt in 1808; Napoleonic troops occupied Spain and suddenly found themselves facing a guerrilla war. Only Cádiz in Andalucía remained unconquered. The French were defeated for the first time in Europe in July 1808 at the Battle of Bailén. The parliamentarians who had fled from Napoleon to Cádiz passed a **liberal constitution** in 1812, which among other things guaranteed free speech and freedom of the press, and established a separation of powers. However, after the French had been ousted in 1814 and the Spanish throne reinstated, Ferdinand III threw it out and restored **the old absolutist order**.

The Liberals, however, did not accept defeat. In 1820, Rafael de Riego Nuñez instigated a popular uprising in Cádiz, which at first forced the king to accept the constitution again. French troops sent by the »Holy Alliance« crushed the revolt in 1823. **Mariana Pineda** from Granada, who was executed for her avowal of liberty, became a folk heroine. While the **Carlist Wars** flared up over the throne (1833–1840, 1847–1849, 1872–1876) **Spain failed to become involved in the industrial revolution**. Economically, Andalucía fell further and further behind. In particular, the position of the farm workers worsened dramatically. For this reason, socialist and anarchist ideas won increasingly more followers among the farm workers in the last quarter of the 19th century, who became vocal about their dire situation in revolts and strikes.

On the path to the First Republic

FROM THE FIRST REPUBLIC TO FRANCO

1873–1874	First Spanish Republic
1936–1939	Spanish Civil War
1939–1975	Franco's reign

The First Spanish Republic lasted only from 1873 to 1874. After it was crushed by General Pavía, the monarchy was restored. The situation in Andalucía did not improve. In 1910, Andalucía's first anarcho-syndicalist trade union was founded. At the same time, intensified emigration to North America began. With King Alfonso XIII's approval, **General Primo de Rivera** governed dictatorially between 1923 and 1930.

Republic and restoration

The Second Republic was formed following Alfonso XIII's abdication. In 1936, on the eve of the civil war, the People's Front won the parliamentary elections in Andalucía. During the **Spanish Civil War (1936 – 1939)**, Andalucía was the deployment area for the insurgent army under General Franco that advanced from Morocco. Franco set foot on Spanish soil again near Barbate. Morón near Seville was one of the most important bases of the German Condor Legion (air force) that supported Franco. The west of Andalucía was on the side of the Nationalists, while the east defended the Republic. His victory in the civil war brought »Caudillo« Francisco Franco **unrestricted power to rule** over Spain. Efforts to move toward democracy and autonomy

Under Franco

were suppressed. Politically, Franco turned to the West. Through agreements signed in 1953, Spain was able to gain millions in **economic aid** in return for hosting American military bases. The Americans were given Morón air base and the harbour of Rota, which they developed into a huge marine base. In 1954, »Marbella Club« was opened in Marbella and with it began **Costa del Sol's rise to become a holiday region**. Its immense popularity in the 1960s only increased in the 1970s.

NEW DEMOCRACY

1975	Franco's death and Spain's return to democracy
1992	EXPO World's Fair in Seville
2005	Several thousand immigranst storm the border fences around Ceuta and Melilla

The path to autonomy
Spain's return to democracy began after Franco's death in 1975. **Juan Carlos**, a Bourbon, became King of Spain and persistently supported the process of democratization. On 15 June 1977, **democratic elections** were held for the first time since 1936. As early as 1978, Andalucía experienced its first demonstration for autonomy. In 1981, the majority of the Andalusians voted in a referendum for a statute of autonomy. The Socialists won the first election for an Andalusian regional parliament in 1982, and the same party emerged as winners in the overall Spanish elections as well, with Felipe González, an Andalusian from Seville, becoming prime minister.

World's Fair
Seville hosted the World's Fair, EXPO '92, on the occasion of the 5th centennial of Columbus's first voyage. A portion of the funds were used to improve Andalucía's infrastructure. Among other things, the east-west motorway from Seville to Almería and a stretch of track for the high-speed train AVE from Madrid to Seville were built. However the hoped-for lasting economic boom, and in particular the establishment of hi-tech industry, failed to materialize.

Economy
At the beginning of the 1990s, tourism suffered a setback – there had been too much reliance on unbridled growth. Since the turn of the century tourist numbers have started rising again thanks to the construction of well-tended beach promenades and sewage treatment plants, as well as a **reorientation** toward high quality, environmentally friendly tourism.

Domestic policies
Andalucía has increasingly had to deal with the problem of illegal immigrants. After several thousand people tried from Morocco to breach the border fences of the exclaves Ceuta and Melilla in 2005,

On the Málaga Front during the Spanish Civil War

these were fortified considerably. In spite of this many desperate people have tried to break through them in the recent past or try to cross the Straits of Gibraltar by boat; these are being stopped more and more often by patrol boats (▶MARCO POLO Insight, p. 15).

Art and Culture

Art History

Remarkable artistic and architectural monuments from the Phoenician, Roman, Moorish, Jewish and Christian past have survived and provide an insight into an authentic aspect of Andalucía.

EARLY HISTORY AND ANTIQUITY

The oldest forms of artistic expression of the former inhabitants of today's Andalucía have been found near Málaga and near Huelva, as well as in the interior near Ronda. For the most part, these people left behind drawings and petroglyths that have survived for **20 to 25 centuries** on the underside of overhanging cliffs and in caves. The favourite subject of these hunters was animals, but there are also hand prints and symbols whose meanings still remain uncertain today. As the pictures were found in rather remote parts of the caves, it is assumed that they did not have a decorative but rather a ritual function. The caves of Pileta and Nerja, both in the province of Málaga, have most of these drawings.

Cave paintings of the Stone Age

The remains of Los Millares in Sierra de Gádor are, if not in their state of preservation then in their extent, the most important evidence of the megalith culture of the 3rd millennium BC, at least a millennium before the burial mounds or dolmens of Antequera were built.

Megalith culture

At the end of the 3rd and the beginning of the 2nd millennium BC, a culture which was to extend throughout the whole of Europe began on the Andalusian coast. The early inhabitants of the Iberian Peninsula laid decorated bell-shaped ceramic beakers in the graves of their dead and, additionally, often a bone or stone vambrace that served as protection against the snapping back of the bow string. These people, or at least their cultural technology, quickly conquered the **whole of the central European area** – such beakers have been found in England, across France and Germany and into Hungary.

Bell Beaker culture

Large deposits of copper, along with tin the basic raw material for bronze, were present in Andalucía. At the beginning of the 2nd millennium BC, trade relations based on these commodities were estab-

Copper ore and Mediterranean trade

During Moorish times pleasantly warm water splashed in the currently restored baths of Jaén

The Museo de Cádiz has a collection of Roman sculptures

lished between southern Spain, Egypt and the Aegean. At that time, the **»El Argar culture«** (2200–1500 BC), evidence of which was discovered in the province of Almería, were a people engaged in mining, metalworking and agriculture, who developed their own language of forms with their sparsely decorated tools, weapons and pottery.

Cádiz, Spain's oldest city, was founded in the 11th century BC by the **Phoenicians** in their westernmost colony of the time and named »Gadir«. Málaga and Córdoba also date back to this time. The local museums, especially in Cádiz, and in particular the archaeological museum in Madrid, show the historical cultural evidence of this period. In the 7th century BC the **Greeks** and **Carthaginians** began to establish further cities on the Mediterranean coast. Southern Spain became an important source of metal and ore and also a trading base for the world powers of the time. Their influence is strongly displayed in the Iberians' pottery and sculptures; their most significant legacy is the head of the Lady of Baza.

Romans   In the peace settlement with the Romans after the Second Punic War, the Carthaginians were forced to relinquish to Rome all of their territory on the Iberian Peninsula – this was an event of the greatest significance for the Andalusians, as well as Spanish culture as a whole. From then on, Roman culture shaped the country. The most obvious legacy of the Romans is, naturally, the **Spanish language** itself. Moreover, at least for today's autonomous community of Andalucía, the borders have remained similar; its territory corresponds approximately with the Roman province of Baetica. The introduction of Roman culture above all meant the **advancement of the technologies of civilization**. Roads, bridges, aqueducts, temples, theatres and baths were built and irrigation systems laid out. An important archaeological excavation site close to Seville is **Itálica**, founded in 207 BC. There, the Roman occupiers formed the political and social upper class and orientated their tastes strongly along »Roman Empire« lines, so that the so-called provincial Roman »mixed style« did not develop in Baetica as in other Roman provinces. Further important excavations have been carried out in Bolonia near Tarifa and in the necropolis of **Carmona**.

EARLY CHRISTIANITY

In the year 325, the year of the Council of Nicaea, Christianity was already widely spread in Baetica. The famous sarcophagus of Écija, which serves as an altar in the church there in Santa Cruz, dates from that time. Later, tribes moving through Baetica primarily influenced arts and crafts. The Vandals, however, who plundered Baetica on their way to North Africa, left next to nothing of artistic or cultural value.

Migration

The Visigoths (Spanish: »visigodos«), at first allied with the Romans, dominated the region of southern Spain for close to 300 years (418–711), but stimulated no new artistic achievements. It was mainly churches that were built under their early feudalistic rule. Along with the Roman elements already found there, they primarily used Byzantine, Coptic and Syrian construction details such as horseshoe arches and stone vaults. The **Visigothic calendar pillar** in Santa María church in Carmona is of some importance.

Visigoths

MOORISH ART AND CULTURE

From the conquest of southern Spain in 711 by Tarik to the handing over of the keys to the city of the last Moorish bastion in Granada to the Catholic monarchs in 1492, the **Moorish-Islamic Culture** had determined the production of art in Andalucía for 780 years. Its influence lasted much longer, however: the later art of the region also clearly referred to and cited the Moorish era, and this applies to some extent even up to the present day.

Centuries long influence

Although Islam was hardly 100 years old at the time of the Moorish invasion of Andalucía, it had already developed its own, in part synthetized, artistic features. There are no devotional images in Islam, for example, so therefore no contrast was drawn between art that served ritual purposes and profane art. Primarily, art had a decorative role, and space-filling ornamental decorations were therefore predominant. Ornamentation created as sculpture or as plaster relief dominated the architecture of the façades. Plaster work was either carved or, where the pattern is repeated, formed with moulds. A third decorative technique consisted of rhombic patterns laid with bricks, the »ajaracas«. In the interior, ornaments were used on the ceilings and above all in the colourful wall tiles typical of the country, the »azulejos«. Depictions of humans and animals are very rare; the ornamentation principally takes its themes from plants and geometric designs. Often Arabic characters expressing praise to Allah or individual rulers were also integrated into the ornaments.
An essential feature of Moorish construction, however, is the **multi-**

Characteristics of Moorish-Islamic art

Types of arch

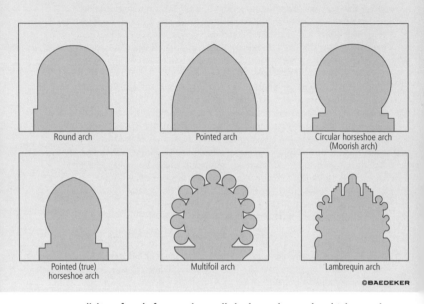

Round arch

Pointed arch

Circular horseshoe arch
(Moorish arch)

Pointed (true)
horseshoe arch

Multifoil arch

Lambrequin arch

©BAEDEKER

plicity of arch forms, above all the horseshoe arch, which was already known in Iberia in Visigoth times. The typical twin windows (»ajimez«), for example, were developed from the basic form of two horseshoe arches. Columns, often old Roman **spolia**, divide the interiors of mosques, private homes and palaces or separate covered promenades from the inner courtyard. The artistic design of the ceilings likewise led to a specific type of ceiling, the richly carved coffered ceiling (**»artesonado«**). The art of the stonemason, plasterer and gilder reached their peak in the stalactite vaulted ceilings that still can be marvelled at, primarily in the **Alhambra** in Granada, but also in the Capilla Villaviciosa in the **Mezquita** of Córdoba.

Umayyad Emirate Córdoba was made the **seat of the Moorish emirs** as early as 712. The outstanding flowering of Moorish-Andalusian culture began with the arrival from Damascus of Abd ar-Rahmans I, the last survivor of the Arab Umayyad dynasty, in the year 756. He had work begun in 785 on the first section of the **Mezquita**, which after the Grand Mosque of Mecca is the largest (former) Islamic place of worship still in existence today. The building followed the Umayyad tradition with a square ground plan and forecourt. In contrast to the

popular image of pencil-shaped minarets, the towers for the Muezzin in Andalucía had a basic square form and
were adorned with brick patterns, following the manner of construction in
the North African Maghreb. The most
important spot in the mosque was the
Mihrâb, the prayer niche orientated toward Mecca. The Friday prayers were
held from the pulpit-like Mimbar.

In the year 929, Emir Abd ar-Rahman   **Al-Andalus**
III, who had by then both in political and economic terms optimally   **Caliphate**
consolidated his Spanish emirate, declared himself caliph in Córdoba. Under his government, Moorish Spain with Córdoba as its centre
achieved its **cultural zenith**. Medicine, poetry, astronomy, mathe-
matics, as well as luxuries, conveniences and lifestyle experienced a
blossoming unknown to the rest of the world of that time. The **Medina Azahara**, the palace-city close to Córdoba, was founded in this
period and today its remains provide an extremely impressive picture
of the caliph's need to demonstrate his power and wealth.

The last Umayyad caliph was overthrown in 1031 and the caliphate   **Almohads**
disintegrated into more than 20 independent minor kingdoms, some
of which, however, were united again in 1039 by the North African
Berber dynasty of the Almoravids, who took their seat in **Seville**.
Their successors, the Almohads, erected a magnificent mosque there
in 1172 under Emir Abu Jacûb Yûsuf, probably comparable to the
one in Córdoba. A cathedral stands on its former site today. Only a
minaret, the Giralda, today the city's landmark, has survived with
slight changes and is an outstanding example of the form of western
Islam's minarets.

A ruling dynasty also declared itself independent in Granada, name-   **Granada**
ly the Zirids in 1031. Though they resided on Alhambra hill, it was
not in today's palace but in an earlier building. The palace that stands
today was first constructed by the Nasrids. Mohammed I, who came
to power in 1232, began with the first section in the eastern part. By
that time, the Reconquista had already made great advances. Mohammed saw the writing on the wall and allied himself with Ferdinand III. Though this alliance contributed to Seville also being taken
by the Christians in 1248, it also ensured that the Islamic kingdom of
Granada was able to coexist with the Christian kingdoms for almost
250 years, and a separate artistic development – represented today
above all by the Alhambra – was able to take place there. The **Patio
de los Leones**, created under Mohammed V in the second half of the

14th century, shows this development toward a more filigree language of form in architecture and decoration and, through the Fountain of Lions, toward more figurative representation, which also demonstrated an opening toward Christian art.

WESTERN CHRISTIAN ART BEFORE 1492

Romanesque

Evidence of Romanesque art and architecture that dominated Christian Europe of the 11th and 12th centuries can hardly be found in al-Andalus, though some buildings and stonemasonry in areas that were re-conquered early do exist. In Cantillana, in a little town in the vicinity of Carmona, the small Romanesque Ermita San Bartolomé still stands. A few monasteries also continued to exist in Muslim al-Andalus and along with the Carolingian script and the greatly influential Beatus Commentaries (commentary on the apocalypse by the monk Beatus of Liébana from the 8th century), they also adopted Arabic graphic elements in their illumination workshops. This individual language of form of Christian-influenced art mixed with Arab elements was named after the so-called **Mozarabs**, the Christians under Muslim rule.

Star and network vaulting decorate the Cathedral of Seville

The Andalucía of today, with the exception of the kingdom of Granada, was conquered by the Christian kings in the first half of the 13th century. The building of churches, frequently on the sites of destroyed mosques, took priority in the construction plans of the new regents. But monasteries were also specifically established to make the dominance of the »new« religion visible in their urban development.

From the 14th to 16th centuries, Gothic cathedrals were built in all the major cities, including the **largest Gothic church in the world**, the **Cathedral of Seville** with its nave and double aisles, begun in 1402 on the site of the mosque which was just 200 years old and essentially completed around 1500. As a monument to the victory of the cross over the crescent, it was provided with a gigantic sculpted doorway on the west side. The former minaret of the Almohad mosque (»Giralda«) remained standing with little change. A characteristic feature of the interiors of all Spanish cathedrals is the freestanding choir in the nave in front of the chancel.

»Estilo mudéjar« is taken from the Arab word »mudejalat« (»con-   **Mudéjar style**
quered«), the **style of the conquered Moors**. The Catholic conquerors, after centuries of battle, were primarily proficient in the art of warfare. They did not have a sufficient number of their own craftsmen, artisans and master builders and so in large part the subjugated Moorish master craftsmen were entrusted with the new building projects. The result, a successful merging of Gothic and Arab elements of form, later also incorporating those of the Renaissance, can be admired in Andalucía and **particularly in Seville**. This style is tangible most notably in architecture and arts and crafts and seen at its most beautiful in Alcázar, begun around 1360 for Pedro the Cruel. The craftsmen from Granada given the job brought with them their experience from the building of the Alhambra and within a few decades built the palace for the Christian ruler using spolia from Córdoba and Medina Azahara. Casa de Pilatos is an example of the use of this style in the private residence of a rich Sevillian.

The Catholic monarchs, Isabella and Ferdinand, entered Granada in   **Isabelline**
1492. The New World had just been discovered, the rejection and rac-   **style**
ism against the Moors and Jews had escalated and as a consequence more and more **French and Flemish masters** were being brought into the country. An influence from the North became noticeable, particularly in sculpture. This development is discernable even before 1492 in the terracotta sculptures of the west façade of the Cathedral of Seville created by the Breton sculptor Lorenzo Mercadante and by Pedro Millán. Lavish filigree embellishments are characteristic for this »Isabelline Gothic style«.

FROM THE RENAISSANCE TO CLASSICISM

Pedro Machuca, a student of Bramante and Michelangelo, built a pal-   **Architecture**
ace in pure Italian Renaissance style (Spanish: »renacimiento«) in 1526 for **Charles V** on the grounds of the Alhambra. The wealth of the New World had also helped the Spanish royal house to gain great political clout. Accordingly, a new thrust came in the production of

art that was mostly reflected in secular construction. Examples of this are the Renaissance palaces in Úbeda and Baeza, particularly the Palacio de Jabalquinto there.

The structuring elements of the Renaissance together with the dense and highly complex ornamentation of the Mudéjar style are denoted as **»Plateresque = in the manner of a silversmith«** (Spanish: platero). The town hall of Seville (1527–1564) and the chapter house and sacristy of the local cathedral are examples of this language of form used in architecture and wall decoration; the architect of the Capilla Real in Granada, Enrique de Egas, and Diego de Siloé, who constructed the cathedrals in Granada and Málaga, are its most famous representatives. However, there were still some resemblances to Gothic style in the construction of churches.

In the famous group portrait *Las Meninas* **Velázquez immortalized himself in the left part**

It was not only the last Christianized Moors (**»moriscos«**) and Jews that were driven out by Philip II and the Holy Inquisition, inflicting great injury to the cultural diversity; changes had also occurred in the politics of art and the zeitgeist. The consciousness of being a world power paired with asceticism and religious fanaticism banished the lavish ornaments for some decades in favour of a plain **deornamentation** of the façades (»desornamentado«). In the painting of the time, the mythological themes otherwise so popular in the Renaissance were no longer to be found. Luis de Morales (approx. 1505 – 1585), for example, strictly preferred **Christian subjects** stressing suffering, such as *Pietà*, *Mater Dolorosa* or *Ecce Homo*. His works are represented in the art collection of every provincial town in Andalucía.

Painting in the 16th and 17th centuries

The spirit of this era was expressed above all in the dark, serious faces of the portrait paintings. The Greek **El Greco**, who painted the test-piece *The Dream of Philip II* in 1579, failed to gain favour with the king with his subsequent work for El Escorial near Madrid because of its garish colours and received no more commissions. This did not prevent him, however, from giving form to his deeply mystical images and visions of light in the service of the Church thus enabling **Spanish Mannerism** to flourish. El Greco, however, worked for the most part in Toledo. In Seville, the only place in Andalucía where a politically significant middle class had formed, other foreign Mannerists were also working, including the Dutchman Pedro de Campaña (Pieter de Kempeneer).

The demand for art from the court and the aristocracy shifted more and more, however, to the young capital of Madrid, at the latest after the construction of El Escorial. The history of art in Andalucía from this point on can hardly be separated from Spain as a whole.

The 17th century is known as the »Golden Age« of Spanish art, even though the country was experiencing a political and an economic decline. The gold supply from America inflated the domestic market and famine among the needier in the population was the result. On the other hand, the royal family, the aristocracy, the Church and in turn the arts profited from colonialism. The painting of the time was predominately orientated toward Caravaggio and Correggio.

Golden Age

The artists' order books were full. **Francisco de Zurbarán** (1598 – 1664), the »painter of monks«, and **Bartolomé Esteban Murillo** (1618 – 1682) are the important representatives of the styles that made up the **Seville School**. Zurbarán had led Spanish painting, after José de Ribera (worked in Naples) and Francisco de Herrera the Elder, up to the point when Velázquez gained international standing. What was new, beginning in the 1630s, was his abandonment of chiaroscuro, the bold contrast between dark and light. The Carthusian Order, his main source of commissions, was not alone in recog-

The churrigueresque altar of the virgin of El Rocío

nizing his qualities. In 1632, he was named court painter to the king, given state commissions and remained successful until around 1645 or 1650 when Murillo outshone him as court painter. The Museo de Cádiz owns the most important collection of Zurbarán paintings in Andalucía. Murillo, who in his delightful genre paintings and scenes of everyday life painted commoners' children just as charmingly and warm-heartedly as he did saints and is therefore considered to be Spain's most demotic painter, came from Seville, as did the somewhat older Diego Velázquez de Silva (1599 – 1660).

Madrid School **Diego Velázquez** landed in Madrid soon after his training with Francisco Pacheco, among others, which he completed while still in Seville. Working at the Spanish court from 1623, he became the most important Spanish painter of the 17th century. His talent and his independent position at court made it possible for him to revolutionize whole genres, to introduce new subject matter and to pursue new paths with his more strongly realistic perception of images. He worked primarily in Madrid and in Italy. Some of his paintings hang in the archiepiscopal palace and, naturally, in the Museo de Bellas

Artes in Seville, Spain's second largest art gallery; but the most important ones such as *Las Meninas*, the famous picture of the Spanish royal family, which includes his own portrait, are to be seen in the Prado of Madrid (▶p.54).

Sculpture

Andalusian Sculpture produced notable artists who restricted themselves solely to **religious themes**. Alonso Cano (1601–1667) stands out among them. He produced the façade of the Cathedral of Granada and left behind numerous portrayals of Mary. The choir stalls in the cathedral in Málaga are by Pedro de Mena (1628–1688); Martínez Montañés (1568 to 1646) specialized to a certain extent in processional figures.

Baroque architecture

Baroque architecture, which replaced desornamentado style, is named **Churriguerism** after its most important proponent, **José de Churriguera** (1665 – 1725). The figured decoration became more and more opulent, reaching its peak in altar retables usually inundated with putti. Luis de Arévalos' design for the sacristy of Cartuja in Granada is regarded as an outstanding example of Churriguerism. With the spreading of the Order of the Jesuits, the effort to provide the masses with an impressive spectacle became popular; magnificent altars, retables adorned with gold and silver and luxuriously clad »virgen«, the Virgin Mary, who today still retain their importance in processions in Semana Santa and other places.

Rococo and Classicism

In the second half of the 18th century, the absolutist monarchs made much use of foreign artists. Along with **Tiepolo** and his son, both of whom worked for only a few years in Madrid, it was principally **Anton Raphael Mengs** who embodied academic Classicism in the newly-founded Academy of San Fernando.

Goya

Against this backdrop, Francisco de Goyay Lucientes (1746–1828) occupies a unique position. In a period when the academic and court art of Spain was no longer in any way setting the tone Europe-wide, he began working on a »modern« version of art. At first, Goya also pursued a career at the Academia San Fernando, but was soon able to win over the heir to the throne, Charles IV, and became court painter. His contact with Andalucía was of a significant nature: he travelled to Cádiz in 1792, was seized by a severe illness and from then on was deaf. This fateful event is generally judged as the impetus for his individual, new conception of art. A second trip soon followed in 1796, which took him to Sanlúcar de Barrameda, where he stayed in the country residence of the Duchess of Alba, with whom he is said to have had an affair – although this is disputed among art historians. Sketchbooks exist from the time and are preserved in the Prado in Madrid. Goya's significance primarily lies in his **new, realistic point**

of view, a view of the world that – after the French Revolution – became pivotal, questioning the distribution of power as a God-given absolute, and which he was the first to express in his work. His most important works in Andalucía are the paintings of the patron saints of Seville, Justa and Rufina, in the Cathedral of Seville.

MARCO ❓ POLO INSIGHT

Andalusian clichés

Probably one of the most beautiful Andalusian clichés, namely that of Carmen, the vivacious gypsy from the Sevillian tobacco factory, was created by two Frenchmen: Prosper Mérimée, who wrote the literary work in 1845, and George Bizet, who immortalized it in his world-famous opera in 1875.

FROM THE 19TH CENTURY TO THE PRESENT

Although an enormous amount of building took place in Andalucía in the 19th century, classic and historical architecture barely achieved any greater significance in this period. Things were the same in the field of sculpture. Even painting hardly reflected the politically troubled times – but perhaps the **sugar-coated folklorism** was precisely a reaction to the uncertain times, projecting a romanticized image of Andalucía, an Andalucía of »majas«, of »bandoleros« and of »toros«. The real situation – not represented in the arts – was that through the ever-increasing loss of colonies in the 19th century, the country was economically bankrupt. The Spanish philosopher Ortega y Gasset formulated it thus: »Art is not capable of bearing the gravity of our lives«. It wasn't until the turn of the century that a painter, Rodríguez Acosta (1878 – 1941), appeared in Granada who represented a new realism.

Julio Romero de Torres Julio Romero de Torres (1885 – 1930) was highly famous in Córdoba. As a painter, he was a unique figure at the beginning of the 20th century and his idealized, sensuous images of Andalusian women are still being used today on bullfight posters and in advertising. Even during his lifetime, he was so popular with his contemporaries and particularly the female ones that, according to legend, hundreds of women lined the streets crying at his funeral.

Picasso Naturally, this account would not be complete without mentioning the most famous painter and Andalusian of all: Pablo Picasso (▶Famous People). Picasso was born in Málaga and lived mostly in France, making world art history there.

Ibero-American Exhibition Seville 1929 In 1929, 31 years after the loss of the last Spain's colonies overseas, the **Ibero-American Exhibition** was held in Seville. The Parque de María Luisa was laid out for it and huge buildings were erected, in front of which even today almost every wedding party has its picture taken. Aníbal González (1876–1929) was the architect of the **Plaza de España**, a semi-circular enclosure surrounding the eclectic Palacio Central. Every historical style from Spanish history is supposed to have been used in this building; regional historicism with an Arab touch and a clear debt to the Renaissance was intended to convey the nation's continuing great importance.

The architecture of some of the buildings for the EXPO '92 in Seville were very innovative; for example, the Santa Justa train station by the architects **Cruz and Ortiz** or the extravagant Puente de la Barqueta by **Santiago Calatrava** – in Spain, bridge architecture is associated with modernity.

EXPO architecture

During the Second World War, as also under the Franco regime, Spanish artistic work was concentrated in the industrial regions of the north and in the capital Madrid. Only since the 1970s have Andalusian sculptors and painters tried to regain access to the international scene. Various groups of artists have formed, mostly in Seville. The political transition to democracy that took place in the 1970s and 1980s brought forth a wide variety of directions in art, which are now – without political or ideological functions – relating to social development. Because contemporary art was seen as a synonym for progress and modernity, it was not only tolerated, it was supported. New exhibition centres were created all over Spain, such as the **Centro Andaluz de Arte Contemporáneo in Seville**.

Most recent past

Calatrava's Puente de la Barqueta in Sevilla is a suspention bridge without any supports

In the 1980s and 1990s, it was almost exclusively painters and sculptors that set the scene. They worked in the most diverse directions, from Expressionism to Conceptual Art. Better known names today are Guillermo Paneque (born 1963), Guillermo Pérez Villalta (born 1948), Luis Gordillo (born 1934), Ferran García Seville (born 1949) and Miquel Barcélo (born 1957). With his synthesis of figuration and abstraction, Gordillo greatly influences younger Spanish painters.

Andalusian Festival Culture

»A people that suffers a lot, sings a lot.« This Andalusian saying may provide an explanation for the Andalusians' proverbial enthusiasm for »fiestas«. When and where these festivals take place can be found in the events calendar on p.93 (»Enjoy Andalucía).

SEMANA SANTA

Incense and orange blossoms

Viewed from the outside, Semana Santa, **Passion Week**, is both surprising and confusing. Two fragrances dominate the towns and villages during these days before Easter and introduce an apparent incompatibility of opposites: incense and orange blossoms. The first symbolizes the Passion of Christ; the second expresses the character of festivals and the awakening of spring. **Compassionate suffering** and repentance merge to some extent with an extremely secular **zest for life** and wild abandon.

A procession from every church

The streets of many villages, and naturally of the big cities, are transformed into one great stage for the most magnificent processions. In many places, usually toward the end of Semana Santa, thousands of **»nazarenos«** parade past with their conical hoods and monk's robes at all hours of the night and day. By now, there are over 50 processions in Seville. The processions are each conducted by a **»cofradia«**, a **religious brotherhood** of the parish. At the centre of the procession is the **»paso«** with sculptures of Christ, whole scenes from the Passion and often figures of the Virgin Mary (»virgen«) carried on a platform which usually weighs over a ton. Up to thirty bearers, the »costaleros«, are required for a single »paso«. During the hours-long procession, concealed beneath cloths, they become welded together into a rhythmic body. The skill of the »costaleros« is the focus of everyone's attention – particularly at the beginning of the **procession**. The shrines are carried out through the church portals, some of

Dancing a »Sevillana« in a flamenco dress attracts admiring looks

which are very narrow, and the bearers are applauded when they succeed in not bumping into anything. The Nazarenes then begin to move along with their candles. The beating of drums and Easter hymns (»marchas«) accompany the processions.

Things change when the Madonna, portrayed as a queen, emerges. These shrines (»paso de palio«) are decorated all over with burning candles, flowers and chased silverwork, also often adorned with a majestic canopy. The Madonna figure is enveloped in an up to 3m/10ft-long train of costly fabrics embroidered with precious items, and, with all the luxury, literally presents a counterpoint to the suffering Christ. The Mother of God is fashioned as a child-like figure of a girl (Spanish: **»virgen«**), with a realistic Baroque face, which is emphasized through glass eyes and tears. The crowds celebrate their »virgen« at the top of their voices with calls of »bonita«, praise her beauty and drink wine in her honour.

La Virgen

In Search of El Duende

In Jerez de la Frontera there is a professorial chair for »Flamencologia«; the specialist literature on the subject fills whole bookcases, and everyone in Andalucía has something to say about flamenco. Nevertheless, it is almost impossible to get a clear answer to the question of what flamenco is, what constitutes the »arte« of a dancer or singer – it is easier to find out what flamenco is definitely not.

Flamenco is not »merely« music, dance and singing. For the connoisseur it is the expression of an attitude to life. The **sources that formed the character of flamenco** are as varied as the history of Andalucía itself. Moorish influences, elements of Byzantine liturgical

For the Gitanos, the Gypsies, castanets are taboo. A »bailaora«, a real dancer, would never accept them as a substitute for the rhythmic clapping of the hands of her musicians, the »toque de palmas«.

music and the structures of medieval romances have all been traced. One thing is certain: the Andalusian gypsies, the **Gitanos**, have had the greatest influence on flamenco. To this day the best flamenco artists come from gypsy families. About 200 years ago they established the original form of modern flamenco, which was danced and above all sung in family circles in those times. In the early 20th century flamenco moved out beyond its ethnic base, was performed at festivals and spread in the 1920s through the **cafés cantantes**. There are flamenco schools in all Andalusian cities, and even abroad – including in Japan! – where enthusiastic learners discover how to express its rhythms and movements in song and dance.

Flamenco is Not Folklore

It would be wrong to regard flamenco as a folk dance, as folklore, even though **commercialization** has produced more and more music and dance rhythms that are borrowed from flamenco – and have hardly anything in common with its original character. Flamenco is more than this; it is an art form, at which few attain perfection.

El cante jondo

There are no less than **30 types of song**, not all of which can be danced to, but which all originate in the provinces of Andalucía: the bulería comes from Jerez and the alegría from Cádiz, while the malagueña is mainly sung in Málaga. Whether they tell of joy or pain, all of these forms have one thing In common: **el cante jondo**, the intensity of feeling of the music and song. The themes are taken from everyday life: love, pain, a lost son, a failed harvest, happiness, finding a friend, subjects that are sung in a language rich in imagery but at the same time simple and intense. The same applies to dance. The **staccato of boots** expresses anger and pride, the beguiling **movements of the hands** and fingers tenderness and courtship. Just as the listeners are at one with the emotions of the singer and sometimes feel a tremor or run through them that is released at the end of the song with a liberating, many-voiced »**olé!**« onlookers experience of the movements of the dancer in their own bodies. When this happens, flamenco transcends the boundaries of song and dance and finds its »**duende**«, its demon, as the writer Federico Garcìa Lorca put it.

Performance in a flamenco bar

»ROMERÍAS« – A FESTIVE PROCESSION OF CHEERFUL PILGRIMS

A »romería« in every village

A »romería« is celebrated at least once a year in almost every Andalusian village. This pilgrimage named after Rome usually leads to a »santuario«, a small chapel or church set in the open countryside that had been erected there because of an apparition of the Virgin Mary or another miracle. The pilgrimage to ▶El Rocío has gained renown outside Spain.

Pilgrimage, worship and festival

Having arrived after the pilgrimage at the »santuario«, camps are set up and paella prepared over an open fire. Usually on the same evening, Mass is celebrated as the religious climax, during which the pilgrims devote themselves to worship and the adoration of the figure of the Virgin Mary. For the rest of the night, however, it is »fiesta« time. Then there is plenty of sumptuous eating, drinking and dancing until the early hours.

THE »FERIA« – THE MAJOR SUMMER FESTIVAL

Origin

Andalucía's »ferias« almost always have their origins in the cattle markets held since the 19th century. Once a year the farmers in the towns and villages gathered to offer their animals for sale. Today though, this reason for the »ferias« has almost disappeared. The »fiesta« character is foremost, even if the festival costumes and the »señoritos« on horseback still reflect the colourful atmosphere of bygone days. While in smaller places only one large colourful tent is set up, whole **tent quarters** spring up in the large cities. Many of the »little houses« are not open to everyone. In these, members of the upper crust mingle amongst themselves.

A stage for self expression

The great Spanish thinker, Ortega y Gasset, spoke of the »tendency of Andalusians to dramatize themselves and to be actors playing themselves«. The »ferias« are the perfect stage for this phenomenon. In the morning, the members of the »great families« of Andalucía promenade down the lanes between the rows of tents on their elegant, highly bred horses: the men with wide-brimmed »sombreros« and in short bolero jackets and, behind them on the horses' croups, the ladies in flamenco dresses laden down with frills and flounce bring to life the world of the big landowners.

Bullfighting

Andalucía is hard to imagine without bull fighting and no »feria« is complete without it (▶MARCO POLO Insight p.368) – unlike Catalonia and the Canaries, where bullfighting is prohibited.

Moorish Life in Andalucía

The Moors were present in Spain for almost eight centuries and produced one of the most flourishing cultures, which also had a significant influence on the history of European civilization.

MOORISH URBAN CULTURE

Moorish culture, for the Middle Ages, demonstrated an amazing tolerance. Muslims, Christians and Jews lived together in al-Andalus without any great conflict. Although Islam was the dominant religion, the new rulers forced neither the Christians nor the Jews to convert – a special tax was merely levied on them. In the first years after the invasion, the Muslims and Christians even shared the same places of worship. In a certain way, this culture, which was far superior to the Christian West in terms of the thirst for scientific knowledge, state organization, way of life and civilized refinement, was in fact the result of the close exchange between precisely these three religious and cultural circles. The scholars of Moorish Spain had assimilated the philosophies of ancient Greece, produced the best mathematicians of their time, developed complicated irrigation systems and succeeded in perfecting the production of paper. The legacy of this unique culture lives on today, above all in Andalucía, in the big cities as in the smallest villages – not only in the monuments there, but also in the alleyways of the old towns, in the »patios« of the houses, in the small »plazas« of the city districts and even in some of the habits the Andalusians have which are obviously Moorish in origin.

Tolerance as the basis of an advanced culture

It's cooler in the narrow alleys on the Albaicín in Granada

Civilization for Europe

The Moors ruled Andalucía for almost 800 years. They brought technical and civilizational innovations that are still being used today, left their marks on the cities or the language and in part even advanced all of Europe ⊠ like the use of knife and fork ...

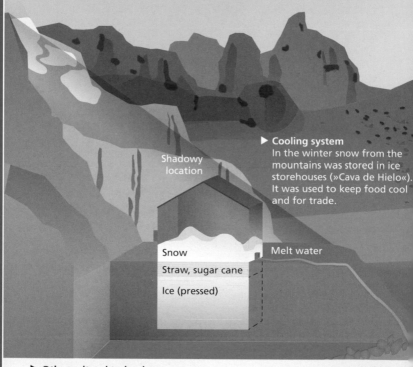

Shadowy location

▶ **Cooling system**
In the winter snow from the mountains was stored in ice storehouses (»Cava de Hielo«). It was used to keep food cool and for trade.

Snow

Melt water

Straw, sugar cane

Ice (pressed)

▶ **Other cultural technology of the Moors**

Bathing
Cleanliness was of utmost importance to the Moors. Numerous bath houses already existed in the 10th century.

Architectur
Until today there are man
»patios« in Andalucía
A large part of life took plac
in these shady courtyard

▶ »There is no god but Allah«

▶ **Irrigation system**
Dams and wells supplied
the water. Canal systems
and giant irrigation wheels
brought it to the fields.

▶ **Water supply**
Water was rationed to the
farmers depending on the
size of the fields and the
dryness (»Almena«).
Taking more water from
the »Azequias« was punished

Main canal
»Almatriche«

Side canal
»Azequia«

Cooling
Cooling food and drinks was especially important
to the Moors in the hot and dry parts of Spain.
Porous ceramic jars let the liquid »sweat«,
and the evaporation kept it cool longer.

Scoop wheels
Numerous scoop wheels (»norias«),
most of them driven by donkeys,
drew the water from the wells
or to fields at higher locations.

Early urban architectural culture
The Moors in Spain built their cities similarly to those in North Africa and in the Near East. The centre of the city was the walled-in »medina« with the main square, the Alcázar that served as the residence of the caliph, and the central mosque. The outer districts were situated beyond the walls that were locked at night. Such was the case in Córdoba. The paved main streets led from the inner city to the city gates. The rest of the public lanes formed a labyrinth of small squares and alleyways that altered in size and direction every few yards, or ended abruptly. A city's importance was measured by the number of its city gates. The »medina« of Córdoba had seven of them and no less than 21 suburban districts enveloped the city core. There were a total of almost 500 smaller mosques in the city. The big cities had enclosed sewage systems, an abundance of wells with drinking water and public baths. Córdoba, during the time of the caliphate with its 300,000 inhabitants, had almost 800 wells – at the time it was Europe's most densely populated and most modern city. Industries and trade were organized into guilds and these usually grouped together in one street or district. Many lanes in the old towns of Andalucía are named after guilds: for example »Calle Lineros« – the street of the linen weavers; and »Calle Armas« – the street of the armourers.

> **!** *Bathe like a caliph* **Insider Tip**
>
> MARCO ⊕ POLO TIP
>
> ... in Córdoba's Hammam, which is set up like a Moorish bath and can be found between the Mezquita and Plaza del Potro. Reservations are necessary (Corregidor Luis de Cerda, 51; tel. 957 48 47 46)

House building
The lanes were built narrow so that the unbearable hot summer sun could not shine in. From the outside the houses looked plain, almost poor, and provided little information about the social status of the people living in them. They were built with two floors and even the poorer houses had a **patio** that allowed light and air to enter and that was the **centre of the family life**. The bedrooms were on the lower floor and only a narrow staircase led up to the floor above – which was reserved for the women. Niches used to store household articles were built into the cooling walls that were up to 1 m/3 ft thick. Cabinets, chairs and tables were unknown to the Moors. Everything took place on the carpets upon the tiled floors. Clothing was stored in trunks.

It is known from the poetry and songs of the time that life slackened during the summer months around midday. The oppressive heat forced the people to withdraw to »patios« shaded by cloths and plants. Public life first began to pulsate again after sunset, but then lasted late into the night. The summer days were divided in two in al-Andalus and it is still so today – this is the natural and historical explanation of the oft quoted Spanish »siesta«. Despite the mild climate, a source of warmth was necessary in the winter. In the finer houses that had baths, hot water was channelled under the floors through ceramic pipes. The poorer people had large bowls of metal or clay (»brasero«), in which charcoal glowed.

»Siesta« and »Brasero«

MOORISH-ARAB BATH CULTURE

The Moors treasured cleanliness in the house, clothing and body. Undoubtedly, one of the reasons for the **great cultural value placed on hygiene** was the ritual washing before prayers in the mosques. In the finer houses, the »bathroom« was an extremely important, aesthetically and opulently decorated room often containing a bath tub carved from a block of marble. The palaces, on the other hand, had their own baths, as can be seen today, for example, in the Alhambra in Granada. Finally, there were **public bathhouses**. It is estimated that 10th-century Córdoba had 600 hundred such facilities, which were available to all levels of the population – this is equal to a bathhouse for every 500 inhabitants. The structure of the bathhouses was imitative of the **Roman baths**. In the morning, the men were allowed in; in the afternoon, the women. First of all came the immersion in a pool of hot water, then in one with warm water and finally cold water. Soap, »ále«, and towels were available. Masseurs offered their services. The walls and floors were often lined with colourful tiles or even marble, and frequently they could be heated with hot-air pipes. There were even reports from Córdoba of a »beauty institute«. The distinguished Cordobans were able to practice handling blades, pastes and waxes to remove body hair and were introduced to the use of toothpastes and »toothbrushes« fashioned from plant roots – in the 10th century already! After a restorative bath, the body was heavily perfumed.

Washing as a ritual

The restored baths in Jaén give an impression of how highly regarded bodily hygiene and culture were in al-Andalus. In contrast, in the Christian West water was an element that, for moral reasons, only seldom came into contact with the human body; this applied far into the modern age. In re-Christianized Spain, church officials immediately set themselves against the »immoral« use of the bathhouses.

Christian prudery

MOORISH SCIENCE AND TECHNOLOGY

The consistent support of science led to a **wealth of discoveries and knowledge**, which in part was only again taken up in the Renaissance.

Irrigation technology and windmills

The country's valley basins were very fertile, but water was scarce. The Moors perfected the Roman technique of agricultural irrigation by boring deep wells and channelling the water to the fields through underground canal systems. Huge bucket-wheels driven by the flow of the rivers conveyed the water to the higher-lying areas, where it was then channelled through canals to the fields. If the power of a river was unusable, mules were used to drive the bucket-wheels. Some such wells, called »norias«, are still to be seen today on the Castilian plateau. Wind was used for windmills that could be adjusted to the wind direction. In Vejer de la Frontera some of them still exist. The constant perfecting of the manipulation of water led to some absurd inventions, such as **hydraulic robots**; figures of clay and bronze with a system of cables, counter-weights and valves inside that were installed in some palaces as »dumb waiters«. By pressing on a lever, they poured out drinks, offered towels or made other movements.

> **?** *al-Andalus*
>
> **MARCO POLO INSIGHT**
>
> The name »Andalucía« comes from the Arabic »al-Andalus«, a derivation of Gothic »landahlauts« (= landless) as the name for Gemanic Vandals or their short-lived kingdom in the southern Spanish Peninsula.

Cooling of drinks

But the mosttechnologically difficult problem to overcome was the heat. There was a type of »refrigerator« for food. Ice dealers would collect snow in the winter in the mountain regions near Granada, compress it in deep rock crevices and sell the **ice** in the cities. Bulbous jugs of porous fired clay were used to cool drinks. Some of the water was able to »sweat« through the porous walls of the filled vessel and evaporate, producing the cold necessary for cooling.

Weapon technology

A chapter in the dark side of human inventiveness also goes back to al-Andalus. During the century-long fight against the Christians, the armies of Moorish Spain were the **first in Europe to use cannons** on the battlefield.

Progressive medicine

One of the mostadvanced sciences was medicine. Diagnostic procedures, based on Hippocrates, were improved and **surgical operations** performed. Anaesthesis, disinfection and the suturing of wounds with strands of gut were widely practiced procedures. Doctors such as **Averroes** dissected corpses and so formulated theories about the human organism.

An extensive paper industry and a high regard for the written word produced libraries, some of whose books are still extant.

Libraries

THE OTHER SIDE OF THE COIN

It is deceptive however to concentrate only on the high level of civilization. Seen as a whole, the living standards of the simple classes in society were lower than in the Near East. Wheat was the basic foodstuff and only through the consumption of lentils, chick-peas and beans was it possible to meet the required amount of protein. Meat was a luxury item.

Meagre diet

The slave trade also flourished. Boys and women were carted off as spoils of war from the attacks on Christian territories and sold in the markets. Galician women were especially popular as concubines for the harems. Black Africans were coveted for their physical strength as slave labourers.

Slave trade

Despite a generally constituted jurisdiction based on the Qu'ran, the people were frequently at the mercy of the judges' arbitrary use of power. During his reign, Abd ar-Rahman II was forced to dismiss no less than eleven of the highest judges (»qádí«) for being guilty of violating the Qu'ran.

Judicial insecurity

Repeatedly, there were fundamentalist movements that restricted liberal thought or considered the living standards of the elite to be »illegal« according to the Qu'ran. The end of the reign of the Caliphate of Córdoba was brought about by a civil war fomented by fundamentalist Berber groups. The library of over 400,000 volumes that Al-Hakam II had built up was censored and thousands of books went up in flames, long before the Christian Inquisition.

Fundamentalism

Famous People

ABD AR-RAHMAN I (731 – 788)

Abd ar-Rahman I was born in Damascus, but was forced to flee from the city in the year 750, the sole survivor of the massacre of the Umayyads at the hands of the Abbasids. Travelling by way of Morocco he came to al-Andalus, where in 756 he founded the Emirate of Córdoba which was independent of the caliph of Baghdad; the emirate later became the caliphate. As Emir of Córdoba, he ordered the construction of the magnificent mosque there.

Emir of Córdoba

ABD AR-RAHMAN III (889 – 961)

Al-Andalus experienced its political and cultural flowering under Abd ar-Rahman III who was from 912 the Emir, and from 929 the self-proclaimed Caliph of Córdoba, and thus a rival of the Caliph of Baghdad. He drove the Christian kingdoms of León and Castile back across the Ebro and in 951 forced them to pay tribute. He defeated the Fatimids in North Africa and ruled over northwestern Maghreb.

Caliph of Córdoba

ALMANSUR (940 – 1002)

Almansur, whose whole name was Abu 'Amir Muhammad ibn Abi 'Amir al-Ma'afiri, was for over twenty years the **sovereign ruler** in al-Andalus, although his formal position was »only« that of grand vizier of Caliph Hisham II. His title, Almansur bi-llah (Arabic for »victorious by grace of God«), and his epithet, the »Scourge of Christianity«, characterize this man, who again spread the domination of Islam over almost all of the Iberian Peninsula more than two hundred years after the Moorish invasion. Almansur was born near Tolox in what is today the province of Almería. He became grand vizier in 979 and soon reduced Hisham II to insignificance. He ruled the caliphate from **Medina Azahara** and expanded it once again far into the north in over 50 military campaigns. He conquered Barcelona in 985 and Santiago de Compostela in 997. He died during one of his campaigns in the fort of »Medina Selim«, today's Medinaceli.

Grand vizier

AVERROES (1126 – 1198)

Averroes (Abu l-Walid Muhammad; also Ibn Rushd) was born in Córdoba, the scion of a Muslim family of legal scholars, and was a **judge** in Seville and a **personal physician at the court of the Al-**

Scholar

Paco de Lucía revolutionised flamenco guitar-playing

mohads in Morocco. Besides writing legal works and a general medical encyclopaedia, he gained importance as the quintessential **commentator on Aristotle** of the Middle Ages and as founder of Averroism, philosophical teachings named after him that permanently influenced Latin-Christian and Jewish philosophy. Averroes interpreted the Aristotelian teaching of the existence of a prevailing intuitive reason (»nous«) in all mankind and of the eternity of the world as a »thinking intelligence« independent of human existence. This view of the world was effective for him in terms of the Qu'ran. Following his lead, numerous Christian and Jewish theorists attempted to prove the compatibility of their religion with philosophy. Among the opponents of Averroism were Albertus Magnus and Thomas Aquinas. Averroes died in 1198 in Marrakech.

BOABDIL (AROUND 1459 – 1536)

King of
Granada

It is not known when the **last king of Granada**, Abu 'abd-Allah Muhammad XII, known to the Christians as Boabdil or »el rey chico« (»the Little King«) was born. It is certain that he was the son of King Muley Hassan and his wife Aisha. His adolescence was marked by the disputes between his father and his father's lover, the Christian Soraya, on the one hand, and his mother and the Abencerrage family on the other. They wanted to raise Boabdil to the throne, but Muley Hassan learned of the conspiracy and had his mother and son imprisoned in Comares tower on the Alhambra. They were able to escape, however, and flee to Guadix. A short time later, a revolt ended Muley Hassan's reign and in 1482 Boabdil ascended to the throne. After he had defeated the Christians at Loja and Ajarquía, he besieged Lucena in 1483 but was captured and taken to Córdoba. The Catholic monarchs forced him to accept subjugation. His uncle, Abu abd-Allah Muhammad el Zagal, attempted to unite the Moors against the advancing Christians and forced Boabdil to side with him. The Catholic monarchs interpreted this as a betrayal and as a consequence they attacked Loja in 1486. Once again Boabdil was taken prisoner and once again he was forced to accept subjugation and, in addition, stand against El Zagal, whom he defeated with the support of the Christians. Despite that, in 1490 the Christians demanded the forfeiture of Granada. When Boabdil rejected this, they accused him again of breaking their agreement and the siege began. On 2 January 1492, the **Catholic monarchs** entered into the city. Boabdil left his homeland on 6 January and withdrew to the Alpujarras, but he was driven out again in 1493 and found refuge with the King of Fez in Morocco. The year of his death is not known. A 16th cent. Spanish chronicler wrote that Boabdil fell in battle in 1536 in the service of the king of Morocco.

CHRISTOPHER COLUMBUS (1451 – 1506)

The seafarer Christopher Columbus originally came from Genoa and **Maritime** in 1476 moved to the Portuguese capital of Lisbon. There he investi-**explorer** gated the possibility of reaching India by sea that had been spoken of since antiquity, but the crown showed no in-terest. So he went to Spain where, in the **monastery of La Rábida**, he was given a let-ter of recommendation by the father confes-sor of the Spanish Queen, Isabella. He sealed a contract with her that ensured the planned sea voyage, bestowed on him the rank of grand admiral, and made him viceroy of any territories discovered; in addition, he was guaranteed 10% of the proceeds of the en-deavour. On 3 August 1492, the caravels the Niña, the Pinta and the Santa María left the harbour of **Palos de la Frontera** on the An-dalusian Atlantic coast. On 12 October, sail-ors sighted the island of Guanahani in the Bahamas; later they reached Cuba and Haiti.

This was followed by three further voyages from Andalusian ports: from **Cádiz**, Colum-bus sailed to the Lesser Antilles, to Puerto Rico and Jamaica (1493–1496); sailing from **Sanlúcar de Barrameda**, he reached the north coast of South America (1498–1500); and again from Cádiz he sailed to Honduras and Panama (1502–1504). That he had not reached wealthy India but rather a supposedly uncultivated land in-habited by savages that held no prospects of economic exploitation, however, caused disappointment in Spain. As a consequence, Colum-bus was denied success during his lifetime – even the lands he dis-covered were named after someone else, the Italian Amerigo Vespuc-ci. Not even his place of burial is certain – although both Seville and the capital of the Dominican Republic, Santo Domingo, claim to have his grave (▶MARCO POLO Insight, p. 284).

CAMARÓN DE LA ISLA (1950 – 1992)

José Monge Cruz was a slight, blonde, seemingly nondescript Gitano **Flamenco** from Isla del León, San Fernando, in the province of Cádiz, which is **singer** why his uncle called him »Camarón«, after the almost transparent little crabs that are fished out of the Atlantic off the coast of Cádiz. The son of a blacksmith first performed as a flamenco singer at the age of eight and as early as this first performance the experts recognized that he could bring expression to the »duende« like no other. He began an unparalleled career that made him the **greatest »cantaor« of this day and age** and earned him the national prize for singing of the Jerez de la Frontera School of Flamenco Art in 1975. At first he stuck to traditional singing, especially during the congenial collaboration with the guitarist **Paco de Lucía**. Later he allowed elements of jazz and rock to be incorporated into his music and created what he called »flamenco rock gitano«. He was one of the few Gitanos also to gain recognition in the world of the »payos«, the non-Gitanos, but he always remained true to his roots. 50,000 people followed the coffin at his burial in his native village.

MANUEL DE FALLA (1876 – 1946)

Composer   The composer Manuel de Falla was born in Cádiz and lived from 1914 in Granada. His roots in Spanish folk music clearly shape his most important works, the opera La Vida breve (1905) and the ballet El Amor brujo (1915). He additionally wrote numerous songs and pieces for the piano. In 1939, Manuel de Falla moved to Argentina, where he died in Alta Gracia. He is buried in the **cathedral** of the city of his birth, Cádiz.

FEDERICO GARCÍA LORCA (1899 – 1936)

Poet   Federico García Lorca, along with other poets of the »Generation of '27«, strove to raise **modern Spanish poetry** to a last high point be-

fore the outbreak of the civil war. He was born in Fuente Vaqueros in the province of Granada, studied philosophy, literature and law, stayed in New York and Cuba from 1929 to 1930 and in 1931 took over the direction of the »La Barraca« touring company, which brought Spanish classics to the stage in the provinces. His own dramas – the best known are *The House of Bernarda Alba* and *Blood Wedding* – are often set in Andalusian surroundings. A major theme of his poetry was also his **native Andalucía**, its landscape and culture, its myths, and the passion of its people, especially that of the Gitanos, expressed above all in *Romancero gitano*. Federico García Lorca was murdered by Falangists in Viznar shortly after the start of the Spanish Civil War on the 19th of August 1936.

WASHINGTON IRVING (1783 – 1859)

It is only thanks to the American writer Washington Irving, born in New York, that the interest in the **Alhambra** in Granada, and with it Spain's Moorish legacy, was awakened in Europe at all. After several years in Scotland – visiting Sir Walter Scott – as well as in Germany, Irving came to Spain in 1826 where he stayed for three years. In 1829, he undertook a journey from Seville to Granada and lived there for four months on the Alhambra in the chambers of Charles V. He wrote down his impressions in the account of his journey *Tales of the Alhambra*, which was published in 1832 and which sold very well. Irving returned to Spain as his nation's ambassador once again from 1842 to 1845.

Writer

ISIDORE OF SEVILLE (AROUND 560 – 636)

Isidore, born in Cartagena, was named Bishop of Seville in the year 600. He is regarded as one of the last Western Church Fathers who was influential down into the high Middle Ages through his writings such as Sententiarum libri tres, a textbook about ethics and dogmatics. Furthermore, he wrote chronicles and historical works such as Historia Gothorum, a history of the Visigoths, and an encyclopaedia of knowledge with his 20-volume Etymologiae. But he also showed himself to be anti-Semitic and sowed the seeds of the pogroms with his sermons and his work De fide catholica contra Iudaeos.

Church scholar

JUAN RAMÓN JIMÉNEZ (1881 – 1958)

Juan Ramón Jiménez is considered the most significant representative of Spanish modernism and had a determining influenced on the direction taken by the subsequent generation of writers. He was born the son of a wine dealer in Moguer. His life was marked by depressive phases and illnesses that appear in his work as strong emotional impressions. He often drew on the landscape and motifs common to his native land. His first great success was the novel published in 1917, *Platero y Yo* (Platero and I), the story of a little donkey in his hometown of Moguer. In 1951, Jiménez moved to Puerto Rico. In 1956, he received the **Nobel Prize in Literature**.

Writer

BARTOLOMÉ DE LAS CASAS (1474 – 1566)

»Apostle of the Indies«

The Dominican monk Bartolomé de Las Casas, the »Apostle of the Indies«, was born the son of a merchant in Seville. He travelled to Cuba in 1502, where he witnessed such terrible treatment of the Indians that he championed them from then on. He undertook fourteen voyages to the New World to study the situation of the indigenous peoples. He converted the impressions he gained into practical suggestions that he presented to Charles V, among others. Tragically, he prompted the importation of slaves from Africa because he considered them to be physically more robust – which he later bitterly regretted. When all of his efforts were to no avail, he withdrew in 1523 for ten years to the Dominican monastery of La Hispaniola (Cuba) and wrote two treatments of the history of the West Indies. After he had instigated Spanish soldiers in Nicaragua to desert in 1539, he was ordered back to Spain. He wrote what is probably his most famous work in the following four years, Brevísima relación de la destrucción de las Indias occidentales (A Brief Account of the Destruction of the Indies). He achieved the promulgation of the **»New Laws«** in 1542, which were supposed to ensure extensive protection for the Indians but which were recalled shortly afterwards in 1545. In 1543, he returned to America as bishop of Chiapas, Mexico. By 1547, however, he was back in Spain. Bartolomé de las Casas died in Madrid without ever seeing America again. The site of his grave is unknown; there is also no monument in remembrance of him in Spain. In Central America, however, he is greatly revered to this day.

PACO DE LUCÍA (BORN 1947)

Guitarist

Paco de Lucía, born Francisco Sanchez Gomez in Algeciras, is justifiably described as the **most important flamenco guitarist of the present day**. Possessing a magnificent playing technique, he is equally impressive as guitar soloist or accompanist of singers, most of all the legendary **Camarón de la Isla**. Pushing his musical boundaries, he has also worked together with jazz greats like Al DiMeola, Larry Corryell and John McLaughlin. He wrote the music for Carlos Saura's film *Carmen*.

MOSES MAIMÓNIDES (1135 – 1204)

Born in Córdoba, Moses Maimónides (Rabbi Mose ben Maimon, called Rambam) was the intellectual and for a time also the official **head of the Jewish community** in Egypt. He studied astronomy, philosophy and medicine. In 1148, he was forced to flee the persecution of the Almohads in Andalucía. In 1167, he arrived in Egypt where he became the personal physician of the son of Sultan Saladin and five years later the head of the Jewish community. Maimónides wrote medical treatises, but his chief work is a commentary on the first record of Jewish religious law, the Mischna, which he codified in his Mischne Tora (Repetition of the Torah), which has been binding for centuries. His major work, *More Nevuchim*, in which he refers to the deeper meaning of revelation being ascertainable only through philosophy, influenced Christian scholasticism, namely Albertus Magnus and Thomas Aquinas.

MANOLETE (1917 – 1947)

Manuel Rodríguez Sánchez, known as »Manolete«, scion of a bull-fighting family from Córdoba, was the **most popular torero of his day**. Beginning in 1940, after having trained for ten years, he triumphed in all of the great arenas of Spain and Latin America and was lauded by the »aficionados« for his calm fighting style. He invented a new pass that was named »la manoletina« in his honour. His career and indeed his life came to an end in ▶Linares during a fight with the bull »Islero«, when he was impaled on the bull's horns during a corrida. Many of Manolete's personal effects are on display in the bull-fighting museum of Córdoba.

Torero

PABLO PICASSO (1881 – 1973)

Pablo Picasso, a painter, sculptor, graphic designer and ceramicist born in Málaga, is considered the **most important artist of the modern age**. After his first years of training with his father, he studied at the academies of Barcelona and Madrid, moving to Paris in 1904. His early work, at first defined by seemingly melancholy pictures, was divided into blue and rose periods according to the dominantly used colours.

Artist

With his epoch-making key work, *Demoiselles d'Avignon*, completed in 1907, he created the prerequisites for **Cubism**. He returned to depicting figures after the First World War and moved closer to the Surrealists. The main subjects were now cycles of illustration following antique texts, works that dealt with the Spanish Civil War – for example, *Guernica*, one of his most famous paintings – as well as pictures of bullfighting and portraits. After the Second World War, Picasso worked intensively with ceramics and graphics. His work in total exhibits a sense of sovereignty in dealing with art history, with his own history and with the greatest variety of artistic media and techniques. He died in Mougins, France.

MARIANA PINEDA (1804 – 1831)

Liberal revolutionary

She is considered a folk hero in Spain, honoured in many songs, poems and pictures. Federico García Lorca immortalized her in his drama of the same name. Mariana Pineda came from a mésalliance between an aristocratic naval captain and a farm worker. At the age of 14, she met and fell in love with a much older man, a supporter of Liberalism. Being an adherent of liberal ideas and voicing the related demands during the time of the Restoration under the reign of the absolutist ruler Ferdinand VII was extremely dangerous. When Pineda's husband died after a few years, she was left alone with two small children. Despite that, she hunted down the injustices in her country, exposed suppression and force and got herself into great difficulties. In 1828, she helped a convicted revolutionary to flee and from that point on was under surveillance by the police. She was finally arrested and after steadfastly refusing to give in to the judge's sexual demands or reveal the names of her liberal conspirators, she was sentenced to death and strangled with the garrotte.

SENECA (AROUND 4 BC – AD 65)

Poet and philosopher

Lucius Annaeus Seneca was born in Roman Córdoba, the son of the rhetorician Seneca the Elder. After being trained in rhetoric, he was made quaestor under Caligula. Empress Messalina had him exiled to Corsica in 41 BC, from where he was called back by Empress Agrippina to tutor her son Nero. During the initial years of his reign, Seneca was Nero's closest confidant, but Nero turned more and more away from him until finally the emperor suspected Seneca of being involved in the Pisonian conspiracy and forced him to commit suicide. The manner of the Stoics was for Seneca the ideal form of human existence; his major philosophical works are Epistulae morales ad Lucilium and the Naturales quaestiones with scientific discussions and moral reflections. As a tragedian, he was basically interested in showing the fatal consequences of human passion.

TRAJAN (53 – 117)

Roman emperor

Marcus Ulpius Traianus, born in Itálica in the Roman province of Baetica, was the first emperor of Rome to come from a province. In the year 98, he assumed power over the world empire that reached its maximum extent through his campaigns in Dacia (which approximates to today's Romania), in Arabia in the year 106 and, in war against the Parthians from 114 to 117, with the conquest of Armenia, Assyria and Mesopotamia. Trajan's column still proclaims today the conquests of Dacia in Rome on the Forum Traianum. Trajan died in Selinus in the province of Anatolia.

DIEGO DE SILVA Y VELÁZQUEZ (1599 – 1660)

Velázquez, a student of Pacheco de Río born in Seville, was the most important Spanish painter of the 17th century. His artistic development can be divided into three periods. Influenced by Caravaggio, he painted religious subjects and Andalusian stereotypes in his early Sevillian period. In 1623, he was summoned to Madrid, where he painted a portrait of Philip IV and soon rose to be **court painter**. The impression made by the art of Titian and Tintoretto during his first stay in Italy from 1629 to 1631 changed his painting, producing often less flattering portraits of the royal family in bold colours, and one of his major works, Las Lanzas (*The Surrender of Breda*; 1634/35). His second trip to Italy from 1649 to 1651 again influenced his style through his development into one of the precursors of Impressionism, who captured the fleeting impressions of light and colour on canvas. But he didn't give up portrait painting. One of his most famous works was created in 1656, Las Meninas (*The Maids of Honour*), in which he portrays the members of the royal family posing for the painting and above all himself, peeking out from behind the canvas. The **Museo de Bellas Artes in Seville** possesses the most important collection of his paintings in Andalucía.

Painter

ENJOY ANDALUCÍA

What are teh specialities of Andalusian cuisine? Which crafts are worth buying? What are the best hotels? You'll find answers here.

Accommodation

Pure Variety

Be it in a whitewashed cave or in a Moorish palace or on a campground with an ocean view. Andalucía's accommodations show pure variety.

Living like cavemen? No chance! In the whitewahsed cave apartments owned by »Uncle Tobas«, the Cuevas del Tío Tobas, the rooms and bathrooms have modern furnishings, TV and telephone are standard. The cave homes with their unusual chimneys lie on the way from La Calahorra to Alcudia de Guadix picturesquely in the shadows of the Sierra Nevada. Surrounded by pine forests guests find themselves in an altogether different »hotel« experience. The 19 whitewashed rooms are not square but formed organically as with Gaudí.

Living in a cave

One night for two people costs between €60 and €120, and because the caves are a little way off the beaten path there is a myriad of recreational opportunities. Be it archery, moto-cross or horseback riding on Andalusian stallions, there is something for everyone. The owners also organize tours in the area to old castle ruins and overgrown railway tracks for trips on converted rail-bikes. And like any normal hotel, there is a restaurant and Internet connection (Ctra. de Almería, km 1, Alcudia de Guadix; tel. 958 69 83 50; www.tiotobas.com ►Welcome to Everyday Life).

Spain's hotel industry distinguishes between hotels (H, with restaurant), Hoteles-Apartamentos (HA, with cooking facilities in the rooms, often also with a restaurant or café), Hostales (HS, basic and often without restaurant), and guesthouses (P). The showpieces of Spanish hotel industry are the **paradors**, (►MARCO POLO Insight, p.87).

Hotels and paradores

The hotels are rated with stars: 1 star stands for accommodation with at least a sink in the room, 2 stars for rooms with bathroom, 3 stars for telephone and TV in addition, plus hotel restaurant, 4 stars for convenience and luxury, 5 stars for luxury. The highest category is 5 stars with the addition GL (»Gran Lujo«). As this classification has limitations as a clue to pricing, only the price range is given here. Prices vary considerably according to season. They can climb to twice the normal amount during festivals or for instance during the Easter week, however, they can also be adjusted downwards in less well-frequented periods, if one asks about it before booking. As a rule, the price does not contain breakfast (€2.50 – €12)

The patio in the parador of Úbeda is designed for daydreaming

Information

PRICE CATEGORIES
Hotels (Price per double room)
€€€€ more than €200
€€€ €150 – €200
€€ €100 – €150
€ up to €100

PARADORES DE TURISMO
www.parador.es/en (in English)

AGROTOURISMUS
Red Andaluza de
Alojamientos Rurales (RAAR)
www.raar.es

CAMPING
Federación Andaluza de
Campings
www.campingsandalucia.es

YOUTH HOSTELS
In Spain:
Red Española de Albergues
Juveniles
www.reaj.com
In Andalucía:
Inturjoven
www.inturjoven.com

Agrotourism Those wishing to spend their holidays in a rural environment can choose from nearly 500 officially approved »casas rurales«, offering a kind of tourism that is gentle and close to nature. The generic term **»turismo rural«** covers small and larger holiday homes, hostels, plus smaller and larger countryside hotels, most of which use historic rural buildings that are furnished in a simple but snug fashion and lie in scenic countryside.

Camping The approximately 100 Andalusian camp sites are heavily frequented during the peak tourist season. They are concentrated on the coast in particular. Booking in advance is recommended. The Federación Española de Campings publishes the four-language **camping guide** »Guía Oficial de Campings«, which can be purchased at petrol stations and bookshops or ordered from the address below.

Wild camping is generally forbidden, yet spending a night at a car park or lay-by is usually allowed; it is advisable, however, to enquire beforehand whether a local or regional prohibition exists. The filling of gas cylinders brought into the country is prohibited in Spain. Campers should therefore have their equipment fitted for Spanish connections.

Youth hostels Many larger and medium-sized towns have youth hostels where younger tourists can find accommodation at little cost. In general, the hostels are available from July to September to members of national youth hostel organizations affiliated with the International Youth Hostel Federation. In most cases, Spain's youth hostels are open from 7am to 11pm.

Showpieces

They are located in Moorish palaces, on elevations overlooking olive groves, in medieval castles and a few in highly modern facilities: Andalucía's paradores.

The showpieces of Spanish hotels state-owned and characterized by trained personnel, very comfortable facilities and a surprisingly fair price. Anyone who wants to stay there can pay as little as €100 and can also enjoy excellent cooking. Here star chefs spoil their guests with everything the region has to offer. It is mainly the Spaniards who stay here. So guests should know: meals are late and Spanish (lunch from 2pm, dinner from 9pm) and filtered coffee or English breakfast are simply no-goes ...

Living Well

In Andalucía a few state-owned facilities have cult status. These include the typically Mediterranean **Parador de Mojácar** right on the beach with the same name with its broad view of the ocean, just like the isolated **Parador de Cazorla** in the middle of the beautiful nature park Sierra de Cazorla. While this one is as quiet as no other and located in Andalisian country-house style on an elevation, the **Parador de Málaga Gibralfaro** is located in a Moorish palace near the city of Málaga and very popular among golfers. Even more famous is the **Parador de Ronda**, which has modern architecture inside despite the town hall façade from 1761. It thrones 120m/400ft above a rcok gorge and competes with **Parador de Jaén** (picture above), situated in a medieval castle overlooking end-

less olive plantations, and with **Parador de Carmona**, which occupies the place of a Moorish castle on a rock peak. The latter had to be stabilized by engineers in 1996, incidentally, as the complex threatened to crush the peak under its weight. But the danger has passed. While it's easy to get a room here the situation in **Parador Nacional de San Francisco** is completely different. What many consider to be the most beautiful parador is located in a Franciscan monastery right in the Alhambra of Granada and only has 39 rooms, which are sometimes booked months ahead.

New Showpiece

The newest of the Andalusian paradores is **Parador Hotel Atlántico** in Cádiz. The newly opened hotel (2012) in the coastal town gleams white and stands out for that which is the trend in paradores anyway: sustainable tourism. Water is collected, filtered and reused; the solar collectors are especially effective. No wonder since sumlight is almost always to be had under Andalucía's skies ...

Children in Andalucía

Theme Parks and Splashing Fun

Children are welcome in Andalucía, be it in a hotel, café or restaurant. While here at home people might be irritated by a crying baby, in the usually much louder taverns they can hardly be heard anymore. Children stay up much later in southern Spain, too, because of the heat and the legendary siesta at noon.

Many museums do not charge admission for children, most restaurants have seats for children available. One thing that is missing is unsweetened baby food; this needs to be brought along from home. Children especially like the beaches, water parks, zoos and animal parks as well as children's museums.

On the island Isla de la Cartuja in ▶Seville the high-tech park Isla Mágica is a brilliant attraction for large and small. It leads into a world of knights and circus artists, into the Amazon jungle and to the most adventurous pirate's lairs. »Discoveries« is the theme of the »magic island«, kitsch trumps and speed is guarantied. The roller coasters are as spectacular as the (almost) real battles of the galleons in an artificial sea.
For the smallest children there is a separate, especially safe play area with slides and carousels.

Isla Magica

Great excitement is guaranteed during a visit to Mini Hollywood near ▶Almería, where Westerns are filmed.

Mini Hollywood

The beaches on the Spanish Mediterranean coast, especially along the Costa del Sol, are especially attractive for children. Unlike the Costa de la Luz in the east with surfing areas the rocky bays here with small playas make for much gentler waves.

Beaches

Riding schools (picaderos) can be found everywhere in horse-crazy Andalucía. They go from the royal riding school in Jerez de la Frontera to private stables.
Real rides into the country, however, are only available for children from the age of 10 accompanied by adults. Local tourist information offices will have information on riding. There are especially beautiful trails around Ronda.

Riding with children

Little señoritas and señores

Addresses

THEME PARKS AND WILDLIFE PARKS
Reserva Natural
in Castillo de las Guardas
60km/37mi northwest of Seville
Opening Hours: daily from
10.30am to 7pm
Visitors can see lions, tigers, monkeys, elephants, rhinoceroses and other animals during a tour on foot, by car or with a small train.

Crocodiles Park
In Torremolinos: C/Cuba, 14
Opening hours: daily from 10am until late afternoon
As the name implies – a park full of crocodiles. Behind the monumental entrance styled like a North African palace »Crocodiles Lake« is the main attraction. More than 300 crocodiles live there, from babies to the adult Nile crocodile Paco, whose 5 m (16 ft) in length and more than half a ton in weight make him the largest Nile crocodile in Europe..

Selwo Aventura
Autovía Costa del Sol, at km 162.5mi
At Estepona

Opening hours: daily from 10am, closed Jan; irregular hours Nov, Dec.
Admission from 10 years €24.50; up to 9 years: €17.
www.selwo.es
Selwo Aventura is an accomplished blend of fun fair and zoo. Penguins, dolphins and seals live here, who are the stars especially during feeding time.

Bioparc Fuengirola
In Fuengirola:
Camilo José Cela 6-8
Daily from 10am
Admission from 10 years: €16.20, up to 9 years: €11.20
www.bioparcfuengirola.es
Spain's model zoo sets great store by natural animal care and breeding. The stars are the wild cats and since April 2011 a pair of white tigers from Sumatra.

Selwo Marina
In Benalmádena:
Parque de la Paloma,
daily from 10am; not open every day in the winter
Admission from 10 years: €18, up to 9 years: €13
www.selwomarina.es
Park with penguins and reptiles from the Amazon Basin. There is also a popular dolphin show and a live show with tropical birds.

AQUA PARKS
Aquopolis
In Sevilla: Avenida del Deporte
Mid-June – early Sept. daily from 12 noon
Admission: €21.95

The theme park »Isla Mágica« in Seville has many surprises

children: €15.95
www.aquopolis.es
Situated in the east of Seville;
along with many different pools
there are also spectacular water
slides.

Aqua Tropic
In Almuñécar:
Paseo Marítimo at Playa de Velilla
June – Sept daily from 11am
Admission from 16 years: €15,
12-15 years: €12, €4-11 years:
€11, children under 3 years free
www.aqua-tropic.com
Situated right at the beach, with
artificial waterfalls, a children's
lake and slides with names like
kamikaze.

MUSEUMS FOR CHILDREN
Parque Minero de Ríotinto
In Minas de Riotinto

Plaza Ernest Lluch,
Daily from 10.30am
Admission from 13 years:
€10, up to 12 years: €9
www.parquemineroderiotinto.
com
A walk through the mining
museum, a visit to Europe's
largest open pit, and a train
ride along the Río Tinto are
all part of a vist.
(▶Aracena, Around).

Parque de las Ciencias
Avda. del Mediterráneo
Granada
Tue – Sat from 10am
Hands-on science museum:
natural sciences for touching
and trying out. Parque de las
Ciencias is the most-visited
museum in Andalucía (▶Granada,
p.272).

Festivals · Holidays · Events

Ferias – the Original Fiesta

The ferias of this southern Spanish region offer wonderful in-sight into the soul of Andalucía. Andalusians celebrate them with lots of music, traditional costumes and proud thorough-bred horses. It is simply the original fiesta.

Malagueños celebrate their annual fair in mid-August with Sevil-lana dancing and live music until dawn, but with much less crowd-ing than the city of Seville. Even the actor Antonio Banderas, who was born here, can be seen occasionally in one of the festival tents if he happens to be visiting his hometown.

Feria de Málaga

The fair grounds are the **Recinto de la Feria** a little outside of the city centre. Many buses run back and forth between the centre and the Recinto, but things only really get going at 9pm. It's fun just go-ing from tent to tent, if you dare, and just watching a band, eating a rice dish and dancing along. Visitors should be aware of two things: there's hardly a hotel room to be had from mid to late Au-gust, so book early. And: since everyone is on the Recinto de la Fe-ria, the old city of Málaga is astonishingly quiet. Even bars and tav-erns are closed, which is usually a no-go in such a typically Andalusian city.

Probably the most spectacular Spanish festivities take place in Se-ville: the Semana Santa (Holy Week) and the Feria de Abril.

Semana Santa and Feria de Abril

Semana Santa begins on Palm Sunday when the brotherhoods (co-fradías or hermandades) start their processions in the individual city quarters, in which they carry extravagently decorated holy shrines (pasos) through the streets. The bearers (costaleros) have to work hard – the pasos weight several hundred pounds and the streets are narrow. Part of every procession are the robe and point-ed hat wearing penitents (nazarenos or penitentes). The main pro-cession including all 58 brotherhoods takes place in the night be-fore Good Friday and the morning of Good Friday and ends in the cathedral (▶p.60).

During **Feria de Abril** (after Easter) families, friends and organisa-tions put up tents and pavilions on the huge festival grounds in the quarter of Los Remedios, where – privately! – they sing and dance until dawn. But the daily magnificent horse and carriage parades, and the bullfights in the Arena La Maestranza are open to the public.

Feria is celebrated especially extravagantly in Seville

You can't suffer more beautifully during Holy Week than in Seville.

PUBLIC HOLIDAYS

1 January: Año Nuevo
(New Year)

6 January: Reyes Magos
(Epiphany)

28 February: Día de Andalucía
(Andalucía Day)

19 March: San José
(St Joseph's Day)

1 May: Día del Trabajo
(Labour Day)

24 June: San Juan
(St John the Baptist's Day)

29 June: San Pedro y San Pablo
(St Peter and St Paul's Day)

25 July: Santiago
(St James' Day)

15 August: Asunción
(Assumption of the Virgin)

12 October: Día de la Hispanidad
(Discovery of the Americas)

1 November: Todos los Santos
(All Saints Day)

6 December: Día de la Constitución
(Constitution Day,
Spanish national holiday)

8 December: Immaculada Concepción (Immaculate Conception)

25 December: Navidad
(Christmas)

MOVEABLE FESTIVALS

Viernes Santo (Good Friday)
Corpus Christi (Corpus Christi)

CALENDAR OF EVENTS
JANUARY
Granada

Granada remembers the final expulsion of the Moors in 1492 with
»Día de la Toma« (2 January).

Almerímar

Romería de la Virgen del Mar:
sea pilgrimage (first Sunday
in January).

FEBRUARY/MARCH
Cádiz / Málaga

Carnival is celebrated exuberantly
with processions, floats, and bull
runs.

HOLY WEEK
(SEMANA SANTA)
Holy Week is marked throughout Andalucía.

EASTER
Arcos de la Frontera
Encierro de Aleluya: bull run in the street on Easter Sunday

Vejer de la Frontera
Fiesta del »Toro Embolao«: popular bull run in the street on Easter Sunday

APRIL
Andújar
Romería de la Virgen de la Cabeza: pilgrimage on the last Sunday in April

Seville
Feria de Abril: begins two weeks after Easter

MAY
Córdoba
Cruces de Mayo: on the first weekend in May; altars with May crosses are set up in the streets, in front of which dances and celebrations take place in the evening
Festival de los Patios Córdobéses: in the week following the first weekend in May; patios are opened to the public and the most beautiful is chosen.

Granada
Cruces de Mayo: May Crosses; first weekend in May.

Sanlúcar de Barrameda
Feria de la Manzanilla: sherry festival; last week in May.

PENTECOST
El Rocío
Romería del Rocío: One of the most significant pilgrimages in Spain (▶MARCO POLO Insight p.368).

JUNE
Granada
At the end of June (until July) the **International Festival of Music and Dance** begins with concerts in the palaces of the Alhambra.

Ronda
Romería de la Virgen de la Cabeza: pilgrimage, 14 June.

JULY
Cabra
Romería Nacional de los Gitanos: gypsy pilgrimage; on a Sunday in July.

Insider Tip

Nerja
Summer festival: 2nd half of July; music and ballet in the Cuevas.

AUGUST
From August on, most of the **Ferias** begin, originally cattle-market days that are always coupled with bullfights.

SEPTEMBER
Carmona
Romería de la Virgen de Gracia: pilgrimage, first Sunday in September.

Granada
Romería del Albaicín: pilgrimage, 29 September.

Food and Drink

Andalusian Soul

The slices that the waiter in black trousers and a brilliant white shirt cuts from the leg of ham are paper-thin. So thin that he can see the knife through them.

The stage: a tavern in the old city of Málaga, tiled walls with naive bullfight scenes, a aisle with a long bar, tapas of sardines, spicy meatballs and olives in brine under glass, the simple dining room in the back that is full to bursting after 2pm. Where everything is served that the region has to offer: tasty gazpacho, juicy veal, fried fish and plain salads. Nothing fancy, the TV is on and the murmur of voices drowns out the music of the slot machines.
That's what a typical Andalusian tavern looks like – away from the beach promenade with chips and filtered coffee. Whoever enters here looks into the Andalusian soul.

Typical tavern

Andalucía's rich historical heritage is »responsible« for the **wonderfully varied cuisine**. The spices, such as pepper, cinnamon, coriander, nutmeg, cumin and saffron date from Moorish times as well as almonds, honey and oranges.
After Columbus discovered the Americas in the late 15th century heavily laden ships brought potatoes, paprika and tomatoes from Central America to the ports of Cádiz and Seville. This was the birth of the refreshing vegetable soup called *gazpacho* as well as the nourishing potato omelette called *tortilla*; simple dishes but still very popular.

Historical heritage

Of course, the region has its top chefs, like the prize-winning superstar Dani García, who prepares the most delicate fish, like perch or turbot filet, in his luxury restaurant Tragabuches in Ronda. But the simple huts called *chiringuitos* at the sea, which entice with fried *pescaíto frito* and show again how much Andalusians admire seafood. The best crustaceans and shellfish on the Andalusian coast are available in the province of Cádiz. *Gambas de Huelva* are especially good and fresh as they are not caught using a driftnet.

Fish

Another highlight is the meat, which is often marinaded (en escabeche) or steamed slowly in a broth made with oil and garlic. Braised beef (estofado de ternera) is just as popular as bull tail (rabo de toro), rabbit or lamb. And what would Andalucía be without its ham, a mong the best it has to offer, be it *jamón serrano* or the even more

Meat

Many taverns in Andalucía serve only delicious tapas

MARCO⊕POLO TIP

Salmorejo **Insider Tip**

If you like gazpacho, definitely try the delicious Córdoban variation called Salmorejo, a thick soup that is garnished with ham and egg, and served refreshingly cool in many restaurants.

refined *jamón ibérico*. The addition »jamón ibérico de bellota« guarantees that the ham originates from free-range pigs of the »cerdo ibérico« race, which feed on **acorns**, a practice that comes at a price. *Jamón serrano* is indeed also air-cured, yet may also originate from pigs from feedlot operations. The hams from **Jabugo** (province of Huelva) and **Trevélez** (province of Granada) are unsurpassed. They are eaten in proper style, thinly sliced and above all, sliced by hand.

Olive oil   The **cooking is down to earth** especially in the countryside and olive oil becomes the measure of all things there. It comes from the northern Andalusian province of Jaén and has such a good quality that it is in demand with international top chefs (►MARCO POLO Insight, p.296–301).

Soups and   Hot soups (sopas) and stews (cocidos) are more popular in the inte-
stews   rior of Andalucía than along the coast, where a cool gazpacho is preferred. The reason is mainly the colder weather in the winter in mountains like the Sierra Nevada. There people will often treat themselves to a tasty stew named *Habas de Jamón*, made with thick white beans and pieces of ham. The regionally popular *Olla de Trigo* is made with chick peas and stewed pork.

Sweets   Andalucía's monasteries have a long tradition of producing *dulces*; they use almonds, dates and honey to turn their sweets into artistic delicacies. While the origins might be Moorish, the names are all the more Christian. Sugar and melon go into *caballo del angel* (angel hair). *Tocinos de cielo* (heavenly bacon bits) consist of almond oil, lemon, sugar and lots of egg yolk.

EATING IN COMPANY

Late hours   In the coastal towns restaurants have adapted and serve pizza and pasta at northern European times. But when travelling in the interior or in less frequented coastal communities will soon discover: Andalusians eat lunch at 1.30pm, and not before 9pm in the evening. Dressing for meals is important, even in simple tabernas, where people in shorts and flip-flops are simply called »sandalitos«, even though Andalusian hospitality is legendary and visible at any time of the day.

The culinary day begins with breakfast, of course. While it is more simple away from the hotel buffet and in bars consists of toast, a piece of cake or churros (fritter), the variation in coffee is respectable. The choice includes café solo (espresso), café con leche (coffee with milk), cortado (café with a splash of milk) or in port taverns it can be carajillo (coffee with a splash of whisky). At noon, but especially the evening is time for tapeo. Then people meet for a glass of dry Málaga wine, a glass of beer or sherry (►MARCO POLO Insight, p.306–311) and picks what's available on the bar: olives, cheese, Venus clams (conchas finas), whether as a small tapa or a somewhat larger ración. More generous than breakfast is lunch (comida bzw. almuerzo) and especially supper (cena). And Andalusians love taking time for it – three or four courses are usual.

Meal times

A rule of thumb when several people go out to eat together: one person pays the bill. That makes things simpler for the waiter, who has more time then – and can go back to expertly cutting paper-thin slices of ham.

Cutting Jamón Ibérico is an art form

Typical Dishes

Andalusian chefs rave about their olive oil, regional sherry and ham.
But Moorish influences can also be seen.

Pescaíto frito: Be it sardine skewers on an open fire, river trout, langostinos or tuna, Andalusians especially love to have their fish fried. They are the hit in *freidurías* (grills) and *chiringuitos* (beach bars). Fried fish Andalusian style is just as popular in Cádiz as in Seville or Málaga, where they are called *fritura malagueña*. Order them to take away or sir at table to eat them, also in a mixed platter of different kinds of fish (*fritura mixta* or *fritura variada*).

Alfajores andaluces: Andalusians love to eat this spice cake at coffee time. It consists of, as many products with Moorish tradition, honey, almonds, cloves, cinnamon and figs – and a little sherry has to go in too.

Gazpacho andaluz: But the soup is cold! Anyone who says this about the gazpacho in an Andalusian restaurant is guarantied to make the other guests laugh. It's intended to be cold; in hot months it's even served with a pitcher of ice cubes. The nourishing vegetable soup consists of pureed tomatoes and paprika, cucumbers, garlic, white bread crumbs and a little wine vinegar.

Jamón: Andalucía is a centre for the production of ham, and anyone who does not have a stand in his bar or tavern holding a leg of ham that has been cut into – is probably running a Japanese restaurant. Hams even by the dozen hang from the walls and ceilings of more rustic restaurants. Jamón Serrano is the classic mountain ham, the ones with the best reputation coming from the area around Tréverez. It is salted and dried and then ripens for at least another twelve months. Jamón ibérico de bellota has even better quality. The pata negra pigs feed on acorns for three months before being butchered, which gives the ham a nutty flavour. The jamón ibérico from the Andalusian province of Huelva has the best quality and is the most expensive.

Tortilla: Andalusians love their tortillas and cook them, as other Spaniards do, all year round. Potato pieces are fried in lots of oil in a pan, eggs beaten separately in a pot, the potatoes added and mixed in. Then the mixture goes back into the pan, where it is turned after a few minutes. As a tapa it is best to order a *pincho de tortilla*, that is a skewer with a piece of a tortilla.

Rabo de Toro: Bull tail is an Andalusian classic, prepared with onions, potatoes and tomatoes, garlic and saffron threads. While it is poular all over Andalucía, but the cooks in Córdoba and Málagas especially are sure that no one in the world can cook the rustic dish as wonderfully as they do.

¡Vamos al tapeo!

When people think of tapas, bars immediately come to mind. Some bars offer at least five specialities of the house with ingredients fresh from the market, from strips of cheese and pickled olives on air-cured ham and little fried squid to small kidneys in sherry and baked mushrooms.

The people come and go in Andalusian bars, ordering in leisure under a roof of hams, engage in a little small talk and usually do not linger for long. Tapas are traditionally eaten standing at the bar, not seated. Small dishes with two to three savoury and **tasty appetizers** are displayed in a long row on the bar counter to be served with beer, sherry or wine. They cannot fill you up nor are they meant to, they sim-

Luxury tapa with crabs

ply make the drink, the conversation, life, more enjoyable and help keep a clear head. Tapa thus denotes not the kind of food but the amount. They can also be ordered as a ración (portion) for several persons, however, or as a media ración (half a portion) for one person. Where the term tapa comes from is not undisputed. More than likely it denotes the piece of bread or slice of sausage that was set on wine glasses as a **lid (tapa)** to protect against dust and flies in the 18th century in Andalusian bodegas, originally in Seville. But one thing is certain; tapa means a dish that accompanies a drink. The **tapeo**, the tradition of eating tapas, is a matter for the whole family. The Andalusian tapa culture spread over all of Spain in the 1920s after the dictatorship of General Primo de Rivera, who was a confirmed tapa-lover.

What's on Offer?

Going out for tapas is a way to bridge the gap before the actual meal, which comes later – at the earliest around 9pm, often not before 11pm. By going from bar to bar and trying a different tapa delicacy each time, it is possible not only to become acquainted with their great variety but in the end to do without the main meal quite

Awaiting hungry guests

easily. Now and then, as is the ancient custom, they are served with the drink without asking and free of charge. The moderate consumption of alcohol, drinking as a social ritual for becoming acquainted and for relaxed togetherness, is closely connected to tapas. Tapas are offered in innumerable forms – depending on the imagination of the kitchen. There are egg and pastry dishes in which lamb's brains and ram's testicles are baked as in tortilla al Sacromonte. Tapas are equally well served in the form of vegetables, fruit and salad; for example, coliflor al ajo arriero (cauliflower mule-driver style) or skewered banana, date and prune. Or as meat dishes like cabrito a la pastoril (kid shepherd style) or callos a la andaluza (tripe pot) and fish dishes like rape al vino blanco y naranja (anglerfish in white wine and orange) and shellfish such as

almejas en Jerez (clams in sherry). **Friends meet in a bar** and hardly ever invite anyone home, but rather move along together from bar to bar. The tab is always paid by the round, which is added up in chalk on the wooden bar counter.

Toast and anchovis

The best restaurants

PRICE CATEGORIES
Restaurants (main course without drinks)
€€€€ = over €20
€€€ = €15 – €20
€€ = €10 – €15
€ = up to €10

ALMUÑÉCAR
Horno de Cándido €€€
This restaurant in an old bakery belongs to the hotel trade school of Almuñécar. What the students create here is a real pleasure at affordable prices (▶p.151).

TREVÉLEZ
La Fragua €€
In the small mountain village of Trevélez this rustic and relaxed restaurant is not specialized in pork for no reason. The most famous legs of ham in all of Spain come from here (▶p.154).

CÁDIZ
El Faro €€€
One of Andalucía's most famous restaurants is known far beyond its borders in all of Spain, but it is still a small family-run business. The best fish and seafood are served in the tavern in Cádiz, the tapas at the bar are less expensive (▶p. 191).

CÓRDOBA
El Caballo Rojo €€€
Moorish flair, a great terrace on the second floor. The »red horse« is known for lamb kidneys and delicious rice dishes, and is a regional classic anyway (▶p. 209).

GRANADA
Mirador de Morayma €€€
The view of the Alhambra is unique, the restaurant with many nooks and corners in Granada is a top tip as a romantic setting, so that the good Andalusian cooking is almost overlooked. Southern Spanish classic and good wines (▶p.248).

HUELVA
Las Meigas €€€€
In the eastern part of the old city of Huelva this excellent restaurant serves, along with Andalusian cooking, the best octopus and monk fish from Galicia. The name comes from there, too: Las Meigas means »the witches« (▶p.277).

JEREZ DE LA FRONTERA
La Mesa Redonda €€€€
Anyone who needs a good base in Jerez de la Frontera before visiting a sherry bodega: this restaurant is a classic and has mainly game and fresh seafood on its menu (▶p. 305).

MÁLAGA
Antonio Martín €€€€
Typical, very popular fish restaurant on the beach promenade of Málaga. Anyone who likes grilled sardines and monk fish with a nice view of the ocean is in the right place here (▶p.320).

NERJA
El Refugio €€€€
Whether couscous, lamb, paella or fish, this top restaurant in Nerja

El Rinconcillo in Seville has been in business since 1670

serves a large selection of tasty dishes, organic vegetables and authentic Andalusian atmosphere on top (►p. 352).

RONDA
Tragabuches €€€€
The best cuisine. This luxury restaurant surprises again and again with its creative cooking; it is decorated in a simple but contemporary style and, of course, has its price (►p. 372).

SEVILLE
El Rinconcillo €€ **Insider Tip**
Classic Andalusian tapas bar, the guests are spoiled for choice because everything from olives to air-cured ham is available here (►p. 398).

Sol y Sombra €€
Wonderful tapas bar in the centre, specialized in bull tail (cola de toro) and a variety of tortillas (►p. 398).

Shopping

Arts, Crafts and Culinary Gifts

From a ham rack to unusual ceramics Andalucía has a lot to offer. Sherry-lovers should buy directly from one of the bodegas around Jerez de la Frontera.

The mercadillo (weekly market) is the best shopping venue in all of Andalucía. In large cities and in small towns, villages on the Mediterranean Sea or in the mountains: the stalls around the churches and main squares groan under the weight of from pomegranates, sausages, clothing and housewares. Farmers bring their own produce and the neighbours stock up for the next few days. The colourful mercadillos are a real experience especially early in the morning. Anyone who misses market day (usually Wednesdays) and still wants to shop should visit the covered market hall, like in Málaga, where Mario, tall and lanky in his white coat, has a colourful stall and tells every visitor right away: »I have the best olives, the best cheese and the best Serrano ham in the universe.« Aha, Andalusian pride at the shop counter. Incidentally, while the markets are open from Monday to Saturday, unlike other shops they close already around 1.30pm. **Mercadillo**

Most shops are open from Mon–Fri 9am or 9.30am to 1.30pm and from 4.30pm or 5pm to 8pm; Sat 9am–1pm. As Spain has no fixed closing times, some supermarkets and shops open outside the opening hours given above, including Sundays, particularly at tourist centres. **Opening times**

Even if the way to someone's heart is through the stomach, traditional arts and crafts from Andalucía are fascinating. Every Andalusian province has its own centre of pottery production. In Almería province it is Albox, Níjar, and Vera, in the province of Córdoba Bujalance, La Rambla, Lucena, and Montilla, in Granada province Cúllar de Baza, Granada, and Guadix, in Huelva province Aracena and Cortegana, in Jaén province Alcalá la Real, Andújar, Arjonilla, Bailén, Martos, and Úbeda an in Seville province Triana quarter in Seville is the best place. **Arts and crafts**

Granada is the measure of all things as far as crafts are concerned. The Moorish heritage thrives here, and apart from valuable wood, ivory and flamenco guitars, the white, glazed **dishes** with a geometric pattern are the hit. In Níjar and Vera the plates and cups are more rustic and in stronger colours. In Cádiz, Arcos de la Frontera, Sanlúcar de Barrameda and Jaén craftsmen produce **metalwork** (forja), from window grating to chandeliers to bed frames. A little hard to

Shopping in the market hall of Jerez de la Frontera

MARCO ⊕ POLO TIP

! *Sampling*

It goes without saying that the olive oil in Baena should be sampled. The right place to do this is the oil mill of the Nuñez de Prado family on the Avenida Cervantes, which has been in existence since the 18th century. Visitors here can learn about the manufacture of cold-pressed oil at anytime, and then purchase the wonderful liquid gold. Opening hours: summer: Mon–Fri 8am–1pm; winter: Mon–Fri 9am–1pm and 4–6pm, Sat 9am–1pm; Tel. 957 67 01 41

transport? True.

Other products, like baskets from Alhabía and Níjar in the province of Almería or from Medina Sidonia and Jerez de la Frontera, are not much easier to transport. But Andalucía also has other items of traditional workmanship to offer. Ornate **lead glass lamps** are a speciality of Granadan craftsmen. Tin lamps, also from Granada, are a more traditional type. Shoppers looking for **leather** products will always find something in Andalucía: Cordovan leather can be found in Belalcázar, Córdoba province; products of morocco leather and shagreen from Ubrique, Huelva province; shoes from Valverde del Camino. **Flamenco guitars** are manufactured in Granada, for example in Cuesta de Gómerez, and also in Málaga and Córdoba. Beautiful silver jewellery can be found in Córdoba.

Fashion   Mantillas from Granada and the Mantones de Manila (Seville), beautifully embroidered silk fringed shawls, are popular, as well as woven textiles: handwoven woollen blankets from Grazalema, Cádiz province; handwoven rugs from Níjar, Almería province; and colourful bedspreads from the villages of the Alpujarras, where for centuries the best woollen blankets and jumpers have been from sheep's wool. For that matter, as far as fashion is concerned, it doesn't have to be Marbella's sinfully expensive luxury shops for the wealthy Russians, more reasonable Spanish designer labels like Cortefiel, Zara or Desigual are available, especially in the larger stores or the gigantic hipermercados (shopping centres) along the city limits of Andalusian metropoles like Sevilla, Córdoba and Granada.

Food items   Culinary gifts are welcome and popular, like **wine**, **sherry** and **brandy** from Jerez de la Frontera and Sanlúcar de Barrameda (Cádiz) as well as from Montilla (Córdoba) and from Málaga (►MARCO POLO Insight, p.306–311) or olive oil (►MARCO POLO Insight, p.296–301). The best **hams** of Spain are made in Trevélez in Granada province, and in Jabugo in Huelva province. The term »Jamón Ibérico de Bellota« denotes the especially fine and very expensive ham produced from pigs fed on acorns. Some people even take a whole leg of Andalusian ham home with them. This can be taken on aeroplanes in hand-luggage, incidentally, (but the ham rack and the sharp knife have to go into the suitcase!).

Don't forget the **sweets**: tortas, cabello de ángel (angel hair), polvorones and other sweet temptations are a deeply **Moorish heritage**, which are made not only in many pastelerías, but also often by nuns.

SOME ADDRESSES
Alfarería Tito
Úbeda,
Plaza del Ayuntamiento,12
Novel ceramics on the town hall square

Espaliu
Córdoba
C. Céspedes, 12
Oriental-looking silver jewellery

Casa del Jerez
Jerez de la Frontera,
C. Divina Pastora, 1
Sherry of all brands, plus arts and crafts

Artesanía Textil
Seville,
C. Sierpes, 70
Stoles, shawls, table linens – all hand-knotted

Granada is known for its guitar-makers: Bellido in Calle de Molinos 18

True Paradise

Andalucía can offer its guests many activities: starting with the fabulous beaches, which allow for the most varied kinds of water sports, through riding, hiking and biking to winter sports. But flamenco courses are also very popular.

Flamenco courses

Raise the arm slowly, extend it. And then the hand turns slowly as if you were standing under an apple tree and turning an apple hanging from a branch. *Coger la manzana*, picking the apple, is one of the first movements learned in a flamenco course in Andalucía.

Whether in Seville, Málaga or Jerez de la Frontera, there are many flamenco schools, some with English-speaking teachers (current information at the local tourist office). It might sound difficult at first and you should set aside some time for it, but no type of movement is as southern Spanish as this one. But in the end: if you can dance along at a village festival or a feria, you're halfway there.

Hiking and biking

Olive groves as far as the eye can see. **Via Verde del Aceite** is a 55-km -long hiking and biking trail along an former, 19th century railway track. It goes through two tunnels and across nine iron bridges. The **»Green Paths«** are a Spanish trademark for the rejuvenation of old transport routes. Here in the province of Jáen it refers to the longest, immobilised, traditional railway track between Jaén and the lake Laguna del Conde to the west.

In the past crop pickers used to load the olive harvest onto rail wagons here, which then ran over the iron bridges and a narrow track to the west and back. The train chugged along here until into the 1980s.

As a half-day excursion the trail is an experience, especially on a bike. The route starts in the west of the provincial capital of Jaén at Ronda de Juan Ruiz (km/mi 0) and follows the tracks to old, tiny station houses, across bridges and especially along the endless olive groves. At km 22 the town of Martos is interesting, with its pretty old city, where the residents chose their olive princess in early September. And at km 50 is the apparently huge viaduct across Río Guadajoz. Information on bike rentals can be obtained from the tourist information office in Jaén, which can also recommend English-speaking guides.

»Coger la manza/picking the apple« – like in this bar – can be learned in a flamenco course in Andalucía

BEACHES

Beach holiday | The Andalusian coast stretches for 836km/520 mi along the Mediterranean Sea (**Costa del Sol**) and the Atlantic Ocean (**Costa de la Luz**). An enjoyable beach holiday is guaranteed, especially as many beaches have showers and beach bars.

Mediterranean coast | The western Costa del Sol (Costa de Málaga) is characterized by **large tourist centres** such as Torremolinos, Marbella, Fuengirola and Estepona, where the beaches are well-kept, yet often overcrowded.

The beaches of the eastern Costa del Sol, between Rincón de la Victoria and Castell de Ferro, lie partly in rocky bays and consist mostly of fine gravel sand. The coast of Almería has about 45 beaches. Whereas mass tourism prevails to a large extent at the bay of Almería, delightful, little-frequented natural beaches can be found, especially to the east of Cabo de Gata.

Atlantic coast | The **coast of Huelva** possesses with the Playa de Castilla, among others, a large beach of fine, white sand. However, the water quality in the proximity of Huelva leaves much to be desired. Far better are the beaches of the Costa de la Luz (▶MARCO POLO tip, p.224).

Beach warning service | The most important beaches are supervised; and their current status is shown with coloured flags: green = bathing is unrestricted, yellow = bathing is dangerous, red = bathing is prohibited.

Quality of the beaches | The beaches are kept clean by the communities along the entire Costa del Sol, and at the larger resorts of the Costa de la Luz. In the 1990s, following growing complaints, beach resorts along the Costa del Sol in particular took measures to regenerate the beaches and improve the environmental situation. For example, new promenades were built, and the construction of sewage plants was enforced.

> **!** *Atlantic Coast* **Insider Tip**
>
> **MARCO POLO TIP**
>
> **Costa de la Luz** has outstanding, expansive sand beaches in sometimes untouched dunes. Between Tarifa and Sanlúcar de Barrameda there are around 40 beaches, among the most beautiful along the Andalusian coast.

The **blue flag** of the Foundation for Environmental Education in Europe (FEEE) flies at many beaches, indicating clean water and a good infrastructure. It is awarded to the communities upon application, a procedure that environmental associations criticize. Thus the absence of a blue flag by no means implies that the beach is bad. Information in the Internet: www.banderaazul.org.

Summer, sun and beach – sweet holiday experience on the Costa del Sol near Nerja

Andalucía's Mediterranean coast possesses 22 marinas, some of them very modern. Up to now, the Atlantic coast has taken second place – it makes different demands on **yachtsmen** – but in recent years steps have been taken to establish mooring facilities for **pleasure craft** there as well. There are now 18 marinas and buoy mooring locations. The Mediterranean coast, for its part, has more than two dozen modern sports marinas, which have long since been a popular destination for sailers.

Sailing / boating

Windsurfers and surfers find good conditions off the Atlantic coast in particular. The surfing area at **Tarifa** off the coast of Cádiz is internationally renowned.

Windsurfing

OTHER ACTIVITIES

Anglers find rich fishing grounds both on Andalucía's coasts and in the rivers and lakes of the Sierra Nevada and Sierra de Cazorla. A fishing licence is required. This is issued by the Andalusian ministry of the environment and is available for a fee at every branch of the Caja Rural de Andalucía savings bank. Handling time is at least a week, but the paying-in slip is normally accepted by the fishing clubs, as well.

Angling

The exclusive golf course with a sea view in Sotogrande is one of the best in all of Europe

Mountain climbing and hiking	**Climbers and hikers** will love the Sierra Nevada and the more remote Sierra de Cazorla near Jaca. Follwoing the signs there through the mountains will lead to a »casa rural« to stay in.
Golf	With over 60 golf courses Andalucía provides optimum conditions for **golfing**; the Costa del Sol alone accounts for 30 facilities, and has meanwhile acquired the byname **»Costa del Golf«**. The tourist offices have information.
Horseback riding	Andalucía is of course an ideal place for **riding holidays** of a special kind all year round: on Andalusian thoroughbreds. Riding stables are equally available all through the region, be it along the coast or in the interior. Even the famous riding school in Jerez de la Frontera offers riding courses for large and small.
Skiing	**Europe's southernmost skiing area**, the Sierra Nevada, offers ample opportunities for skiing, sledding and hiking from November to the end of May. Sol y Nieve (sun and snow) is the most important stop.
Tennis	There are numerous tennis courts all along the Costa del Sol. Many hotel resorts have their own courts.

Some sport addresses

ANGLING
**Federación Andaluza de
Pesca Deportiva**
Tel. 956 18 75 85
www.fapd.net

BIKING, HIKI NG
»Green Paths«
www.viasverdes.com

CLIMBING / HIKING
**Federación Andaluza de
Montañismo**
C. Santa Paula
Edificio Atalaya
E-18001 Granada
Tel. 958 29 13 40
www.fedamon.com

GOLF
**Real Federación Española de
Golf**
Tel. 902 20 00 62
www.golfspainfederacion.com

Real Federación Andaluza

de Golf
Sierra de Grazalema, 33
E-29016 Málaga
Tel. 952 22 55 90
www.fga.org

RIDING
Escuela de Arte Ecuestre
C/ Río Padrón Alto
E-29680 Estepona
Tel. 952 80 80 77
www.escuela-ecuestre.com
Riding schools and arenas.

Equiberia
E 05635 Navarredonda de Gredos
Tel. 689 34 39 74
www.equiberia.com
Equiberia organizes riding trips
lasting several days, following in
the tracks of the pilgrims of El
Rocío, and around the Coto de
Doñana.

SAILING AND
MOTOR BOATING
**Real Federación Española de
Vela**
Luis de Salazar, 9
E-28002 Madrid
Tel. 915 19 50 08
www.rfev.es

**Real Federación Española de
Motonáutica**
Avda. de América, 33
E-28002 Madrid
Tel. 914 15 37 69
www.rfem.org

TOURS

Along the sun coast or through olive groves into the interior? To the white villages or the craggy mountains? Our suggested tours will take you to the most beautiful places in Andalucía – like here in Ronda!

Tours Through Andalucía

Are you wondering where to go? Our suggestions for tours reveal some particularly beautiful and exciting routes and tips for the best destinations.

Tour 1   Andalucía in Three Weeks

This tour, which can be reduced to two weeks, touches the sites in Andalucía that must be seen!
►page 124

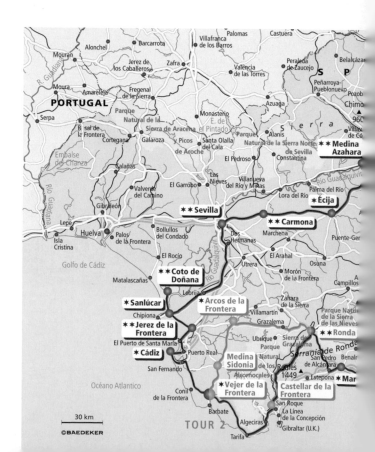

Tour 2 White villages

Immerse yourself in the fascinating hill and mountain countryside of southwestern Andalucía – picturesque villages just waiting to be discovered.

▶page 127

Tour 3 Tour of the Caliphate

Discover Andalucía's Moorish element on a tour that combines Granada and Córdoba.

▶page 128

Tour 4 Through the Sierra Nevada

Andalucía's highest point, Europe's only desert, volcanic land-scapes, and terraced countryside will thrill you on this tour!

▶page 130

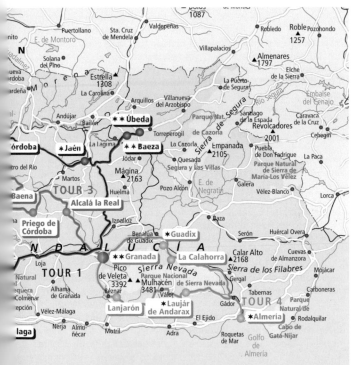

Travelling in Andalucía

Fun at the beach, enjoyment of nature and cultural delights of the highest order; in Andalucía you don't have to do without anything, because it can all be nicely packaged together. In the morning, an excursion into the **Moorish past**, in the afternoon, a hike in **secluded countryside** and in the evening, a **dip in the ocean** to cool off – this is certainly possible if you pick the right place as a base. It depends to no small extent on how you travel to Andalucía. Because most holidaymakers arrive by air, which are downright cheap and take only about three hours from the UK and most other parts of Europe, it makes sense to present Andalucía's holiday regions according to the airports; travel by car takes two to three days, and the rail journey is equally long (►Practical Information, Arrival).

? MARCO ⊕ POLO INSIGHT

Brilliant sunshine

The southern Atlantic coastline of Spain between the estuary of Río Guadiana on the Portuguese border and the headlands of Tarifa on the Straits of Gibraltar is called the »Coast of Light«, because it is almost always inundated by brilliant sunshine.

Arrival in Málaga: Costa del Sol

Málaga, Andalucía's second-largest city, is the traffic hub of the Costa del Sol. The »sunshine coast« reaches from Tarifa in the southwest to the province of Málaga's eastern border. Its nucleus, the coastline from Málaga to Estepona, is **Europe's largest continuous resort area**. If you are neither a beach-lover nor a partygoer but are seeking peace and quiet, this coast is not for you because the **night life** is just as important as the **beach life**, and there is no lack of discos, nightclubs, restaurants, bars, fiestas and every conceivable kind of beach entertainment. It gets quieter further away from the coast into the mountainous hinterland. Just a few miles from the beach there are pretty little hotels or holiday cabins perfect for a **relaxing holiday with excursions** to towns like Ronda or Antequera. Granada is not to be missed; an overnight stay there is recommended. The Costa del Sol is also **Europe's golfing paradise**. Many hotels have their own golf courses and offer golfing holidays (►Practical Information, Sport and Outdoors). The strip of coastline east of Málaga belonging to the province of Granada is called **Costa Tropical**. Building eyesores have been avoided here for the most part, and this is still the **most beautiful and pristine** part of the sunshine coast, even though the coastline is steep and the beaches therefore smaller. Tourism around the main city, Almuñécar, is on a smaller scale.

A ride on horseback along the beach at Tarifa

Jerez de la Frontera is **the most convenient airport** for a holiday on the southern Costa de la Luz, a destination for everyone who wants to enjoy sun, sand and sea **without disco and entertainment hype**. **Fantastic beaches** (totalling 265km/165mi) with fine sand are inviting places for a swim in the Atlantic. Water-sports enthusiasts, mainly surfers, consider the isolated coves to be unmatched. **Nature lovers** are attracted to the Coto de Doñana National Park and the Sierra de Grazalema. **Culture fans** will find what they are looking for in Cádiz on the coast and inland in Jerez de la Frontera, in the »pueblos blancos« and above all in Seville, which is not far from the sea. The hinterland is the country of the big landowners, who cultivate sherry, Manzanilla and olives, as well as breeding fighting bulls and horses – which makes it ideal for a **holiday on horseback** (▶Practical Information, Sport and Outdoors). When looking for a place to stay, it is best to remember that although the beaches north of the Guadalquivir are great, they are located inconveniently if you want to get to the southern Costa de la Luz because there is no bridge over the river mouth, necessitating very long detours by way of Seville.

Arrival in Jerez de la Frontera: southern Costa de la Luz

Arrival in Sevilla: northern Costa de la Luz and Guadalquivir Basin

Anyone who gets out of an airplane in Sevilla has many choices. The northern Costa de la Luz is not far and even if there are a few new resorts like Matalascañas or Novo Sancti Petri, it is fortunately still a far cry from the conditions on the western Costa del Sol. Coto de Doñana is right next to it Jerez de la Frontera is also within easy reach. Toward the east the Guadalquivir Basin extends from Sevilla – not exactly inviting as this place is not called »**Andalucía's frying pan**« for nothing. It is not unusual for the thermometer to climb over 40°C/104°F here between June and September! But **Córdoba**, the old capital of the caliphate, is a must.

Arrival in Almería: Costa de Almería

A holiday on the Costa de Almería is **pretty much off the beaten track** (170km/106mi from Almería to Granada). Instead, there is **countryside like nowhere else** and some of **Andalucía's best beaches** because they are not overcrowded – particularly around Cabo de Gata. Nowhere else in Andalucía is the presence of Africa felt more strongly than here, where it rains just about 25 days a year. The brown and occasionally rugged rocks punctuated by volcanic hills have but a sparse covering of vegetation. This countryside is protected by law. The tourist infrastructure is accordingly relatively undeveloped – no huge concrete hotels or tourist resorts, but rather smaller hotels and isolated bungalow parks on the edge of villages. Only San José has grown a little larger, but is still a pleasant place to stay. Things are a lot different on the coastline west of Almería. It is a **major destination of package tourism**, which means that hotel and bungalow complexes tower over the usually well-tended beaches, and behind the hotels there is often a sea of plastic: the greenhouses. Costa de Almería does not offer much culturally, but all the more of

White villages jumbled together on mountain ridges

the great outdoors. Wonderful day trips can be taken from every coastal town into the Sierra de Alhamilla or the mountains of the Alpujarras, where the climate is so mild that the Moors already cultivated citrus fruit there. Sierra de Alhamilla looks **like the Wild West** – literally, because there are three Wild West movie towns that draw the crowds today with shows like ▶bank robbery with shooting" and Western films are occasionally still shot here.

One region remains where a **seaside holiday** is not possible and no airports are close. The part of northeast Andalucía that essentially encompasses the region of Jaén is well worth discovering. The **largest olive-growing area on earth** is something for people who enjoy **wide, archaic-looking landscapes,** who seek outdoor adventure (in the Sierra de Cazorla) or who have a taste for **magnificent Renaissance cities** like Baeza or Úbeda.

Northeast Andalucía

If you don't want to spend your whole vacation on the beach but also want to experience something of Andalucía, then there is no good alternative to **hiring a car** (from €120 per week, ▶Practical Information, Transport) or having your own car. On the other hand, the bus network is so dense that all the interesting sites can be reached without a problem. In most seaside resorts, the local organizers offer **bus trips** into the interior, for example, to Granada. Andalucía by rail **cannot be strongly recommended** because the railway network is not very dense. It is more than likely that the train station is located miles outside the village you want to visit. One exception is the **Al-Andalus Expreso** (▶ MARCO POLO Tip p.469).

Mobility

To see a lot of Andalucía, allow 14 days for a grand tour (▶Tour 1). A three week stay would be ideal in every respect. Then it is possible to plan a week or more at the **seaside** and have a week or two to **explore the country**. A tour from the Costa del Sol could then include three of Andalucía's main attractions with two nights each in Granada, Córdoba and Seville. Cádiz, Seville, and Jerez de la Frontera can be reached comfortably from the southern Costa de la Luz. A **tour of the white villages** of Sierra de Grazalema is an absolute must. If you feel like undertaking something after a week on the beach at Costa de Almería, begin the following week with a trip to Granada in the Alpujarras (one day), spend a day there and on the third day, after visiting Jaén, Baeza and Úbeda, stay overnight in Jaén. On the return trip to Almería there is still time to see the cave-dwellings in Guadix. If you have just a week's time, choose between a beach holiday and culture. In the latter case, there are two main alternatives; after arriving in Málaga, the tour already mentioned above to Andalucía's three main attractions or a leisurely tour through the white villages (▶Tour 2).

Travel time and tours

Tour 1 Andalucía in Three Weeks

Length of the tour: 995km/620mi
Duration: 3 weeks

This tour touches the sightseeing highlights of Andalucía and can be covered in three weeks. If only two weeks are available, leave out Jaén and the surrounding area, northern Costa de la Luz and Coto de Doñana.

From Málaga to Granada

The starting point is ❶*Málaga, where a day can be spent seeing the cathedral, the Alcazaba and the Picasso sites. Drive north on the A-45 from the metropolis on the *Costa del Sol to *Antequera for a tour of the prehistoric megalith burial sites and a hike in the **El Torcal mountains as well. (Antequera's parador is comfortable, inexpensive, conveniently located accommodation, but not particularly stylish.) The A-92 motorway crosses through the Vega of Granada to

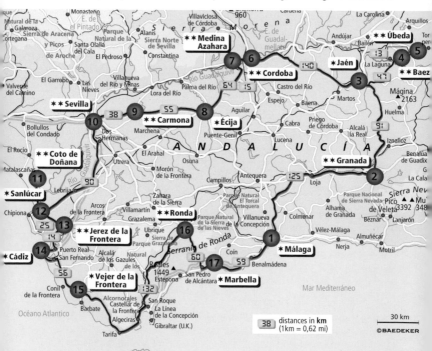

the old Moorish city of ❷****Granada**, the first highlight of the trip. Try to stay here at least two days – three would be better – in order to enjoy the Alhambra (order tickets ahead! ▶ p.252), the cathedral and the old town in a leisurely manner and perhaps undertake an excursion into the ****Sierra Nevada**.

Plan to stay the next couple of nights in Jaén – perhaps in the splendid parador in the fortress – which can be reached from Granada by going north on the N-323. Just the trip there through the endless groves of olive trees is an experience. Once in Jaén, tour the cathedral, the Moorish quarter and the imposing castle. Do take a day trip to the Renaissance cities of ❸**Jaén**, ❹****Baeza** and ❺**** Úbeda** (105km/65mi round trip). Nature lovers will find a side trip from Úbeda into the ****Sierra de Cazorla** (55km/35mi) rewarding.

Jaén and the northeast

Now head from Jaén to Córdoba, either first to the north by way of Andújar and from there in a westerly direction on the A-4, or – even better – straight through the land of olives on the N-432 and the

From Jaén to Seville

Giralda and Torre del Oro light up the Sevillan night

A-306, which joins the N-IV a few miles outside Córdoba. ❻**Córdoba** is also worth a stay lasting a couple of days. It has the Mezquita, one of the largest mosques on earth and the largest old town of any Spanish provincial city. The old caliphs' town can be used as a base for excursions into the wine-growing district of Montilla-Moriles around Lucena (about 75km/47mi) and above all to the once-forgotten residence of the caliphs, ❼**Medina Azahara**, (15km/9mi).

The A-4 runs right across the Guadalquivir plain, passing through ❽**Écija**, the city of Baroque bell towers, and ❾**Carmona**, with its old town and Roman necropolis, to ❿**Seville**, the capital of Andalucía. This city on the Guadalquivir offers magnificent attractions; sights to see of the first order like the cathedral and the Alcázar, the old town and the Triana quarter with its pulsing nightlife, the gardens and parks on the river and Isla Mágica amusement park on the former EXPO grounds. There are also worthwhile destinations in the surrounding area, including the ruins of the Roman town of **Itálica** (10km/6mi), the castle of Alcalá de Guadaira (20km/12mi), the northern part of the **Costa de la Luz** with its beaches strung out around Huelva; and Moguer, the **La Rábida monastery** and Palos de la Frontera, which are closely associated with the voyages of Columbus (91km/57mi to Huelva); and finally a one-day trip into ⓫**Coto de Doñana** National Park (90km/56mi to El Acebuche visitor centre).

From Seville back to Málaga via the Costa de la Luz and Ronda South of Seville, **Jerez de la Frontera**, the capital of sherry and Andalusian horsemanship, can be quickly reached on the AP-4 motorway. ⓬**Sanlúcar de Barrameda**, the city of Manzanilla, is only a few miles out of the way, while the attractions further south are the city of sherry, ⓭**Jerez**, followed by the clear light of the old port of ⓮**Cádiz**. The stretch of the A-48 and N-340 south of Cádiz along the Costa de la Luz with its coves and beaches swept by the eternal wind is the refreshing part of this tour after the trip through the interior. Recuperate in ⓯**Vejer de la Frontera**, a »white village« close to the coast, or in the surfers' mecca of **Tarifa** with its lively nightlife – where a side trip to **Gibraltar** can be taken – before starting the somewhat taxing drive along the A-405 through San Roque, Castellar de la Frontera and Jímena de la Frontera into the **Serranía de Ronda** (alternative route: take the A-382 and A-372 out of Jerez via **Arcos de la Frontera** to Ronda). It is worth spending two days in ⓰**Ronda**, perched breathtakingly above a deeply carved out gorge, to explore the town and the surrounding mountain countryside. The last leg is on the A-397, which crosses the Sierra Bermeja and runs along the Costa del Sol back to Málaga, passing through the holiday resorts of ⓱**Marbella**, Fuengirola and Torremolinos.

White Villages

Tour 2

Length of the tour: about 250km/155mi
Duration: 3 days

The »white village« route (»Ruta de los Pueblos Blancos«) touches the hill country and mountain landscape of south-west Andalucía. Outstanding cultural monuments take second place to the colourful combination of beautiful scenery sprinkled with villages of white-washed houses, each inviting visitors to stroll through narrow lanes. But don't be fooled by the term »village« – many have long since grown into small towns.

The journey begins in ❶*Vejer de la Frontera, high on a hill in the vicinity of Cabo de Trafalgar. The A-396 heads north here to ❷Medina Sidonia, an old noble seat in the middle of Andalucía's bull-breeding region. Take a detour into the interior to experience another typical village, Alcalá de los Gazules (40km/25mi round trip). Leaving Medina Sidonia, continue north to ❸*Arcos de la Frontera. Majestically enthroned on a rock above the Río Guadalete, it is often called the most beautiful of the »white villages«.

From Vejer de la Frontera to Arcos de la Frontera

One of the most pleasant legs of the tour begins here; on the A-372 across the *Sierra de Grazalema through fields of sunflowers, grain, olive groves and copses of oak. Lying at the foot of this mountain is El Bosque, the popular centre for hiking tourism in protected countryside. The narrow road winds up to the pass of Puerto del Boyar, where there is a spectacular view, and down again to Grazalema, nestled on the slopes under the towering El Reloj crag. An alternative to the drive over the pass is the equally beautiful

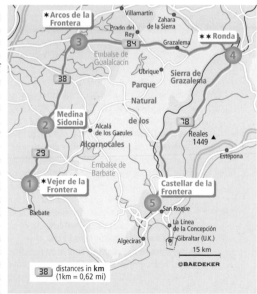

but somewhat longer detour on the A-373 from El Bosque to Ubrique in the south and from there via Villaluenga del Rosan to Grazalema (about 40km/25mi). To see a really attractive »white village«, take a side trip to Zahara de la Sierra north of Grazalema (about 50km/30mi round trip). The next destination after Grazalema is ❹****Ronda**, sensationally built around the Río Guadiaro gorge. Before the town, a small, narrow road branches off at La Quinta to ***Cueva de la Pileta**, a cave lying high in the mountain with fascinating prehistoric paintings. It is worth staying a little longer in Ronda to also undertake excursions to two »white villages« captivatingly set in the rocky countryside: ***Setenil** and ***Olvera**. More than a few people live there in perfectly comfortable cave dwellings.

From Ronda to the Costa del Sol

After touring Ronda, head out to the south on the A-369. The road passes by groves of olive trees and oak and through picturesque villages before it reaches Jímena de la Frontera, from where it heads directly south. A narrow cul-de-sac branches off near Almoraima to the quaint fortified village of ❺**Castellar de la Frontera** with its 13th century Moorish fort. The coast of Africa is visible from here on a clear day. After taking this detour (about 15km/9mi round trip), continue south. The junction with the A-7 / E-15 presents the choice of either going west to ****Costa de la Luz** on teh Atlantic Ocean or east to ***Costa del Sol** on the Mediterranean Sea.

Tour 3 Tour of the Caliphate

Length of tour: about 180km/112mi
Duration: 2-3 days

This route runs west on the N-432 from Granada to Córdoba, combining all the most significant Andalusian Moorish cities. It goes through the heartland of the caliphate, and time and again includes impressive side trips to smaller places where, upon closer inspection, much Moorish heritage remains to be discovered.

Through the heart of the Caliphate

This is the case with the first stop after ❶****Granada**, **Moclín**, on a side road out of Puerto Lope. Here the proud border fortifications of the Nasrid rulers of Granada and the Casa del Pósito, a Renaissance granary, can be visited. It is worth taking yet another detour from here to see a Mudejar-style parish church in the smaller fortified village of **Colomera** (20km/12mi). ❷**Alcalá la Real** on the N-432 has many old churches and the next impressive castle, Cas-

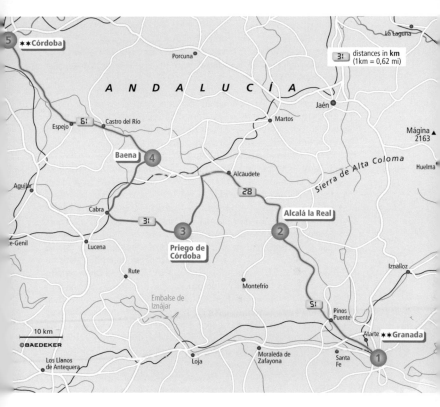

tillo de la Mota, which, together with the destroyed castle of Castillo de Locubín, once dominated the pass over the rugged sierras. The castillo of Alcaudete is also worth seeing. Before driving directly on to ❹**Baena** with its Gothic parish church, it is worth taking a trip on the A-333 into the **Sierras Subbéticas** Nature Park (80km/50mi) with its many caves and springs. ❸ **Priego de Córdoba** is also worth a visit and an overnight stay. Then continue on the A-339 through Cabra and along the A-318 past **Zuheros** (with the Cueva del Cerro de los Murciélagos), whose castle has the most beautiful setting on this excursion.

The N-432 can be reached again from there and not far down it is **Castro del Río** with its picturesque lanes and churches. Besides the Moorish-inspired cuisine, on this leg of the journey it is worth taking note of the famous olive-wood furniture. Finally, after travelling by way of Espejo through wide **fields of sunflowers and olive groves**, the tour ends in ❺**Córdoba**.

Tour 4 # Through the Sierra Nevada

Length of tour: about 400km/250mi
Duration: 3-4 days

This is the route for nature lovers. It leads to Spain's highest peaks, through bleak volcanic tuffstone landscape, to Europe's only desert and finally to an old region of terraced countryside cultivated by the Moors in the Alpujarras.

From Granada to Almería

It is possible to go on a day trip from ❶**Granada** along Europe's highest mountain pass road (A-395) through the ski areas and get right up close to Pico de Veleta (3428m/11,247ft), the highest peak of the **Sierra Nevada** and Spain (round trip 88km/55mi). For the actual tour, turn off about 9km/5.5mi outside Granada into a small connecting road that runs along the Río Aguas to Dúdar and Quéntar. There is a fantastic view of the summit of the Sierra Nevada all along the drive from La Peza to ❷**Guadix** with its interesting cathedral, but in fact the **cave dwellings**, typical of this area, are the real attraction. If the more arduous way was chosen to get here instead of the A-92, then an overnight stay in Guadix is recommended. Continue the next day along the A-92 across the Marquesado de Zenete plateau where there are tempting side trips to pretty villages – don't miss the Renaissance fortress of ❸**La Calahorra**. In Huéneja the **Arab baths** are worth stopping for; in Fiñana a small mosque has survived in almost its original state.

Then the A-92 leads to ❹**Almería**. Plan an overnight stop here to allow time for a drive into the Sierra de Alhamilla or to Cabo de Gata through the **Alpujarras**.

Devotional singing

The brotherhood of the parish church of La Aurora in Priego de Córdoba (► Tour 3), located in a wonderful mountainous landscape, processes every Saturday around midnight through the streets to honour the patron saint of their church with songs.

MARCO ⬡ POLO TIP

Through the Alpujarras

The Río Andarax accompanies the drive back to Granada through the **Alpujarras**. This is the region of the Morisco revolt of the 16th century. It retained a **Moorish character** long after the Reconquista. Mulberry trees were cultivated in its mild climate and today the people still grow vegetables, citrus fruits and wine in **terrace gardens** here. The route leads along the A-348 from Gádor to Alhama de Almería and ❺**Laujar de Andarax**. A side trip to see the source of the Río Andarax river is possible from there. Further on, are **Juviles** with its stunningly beautiful Mudejar church, **Trevélez**, at

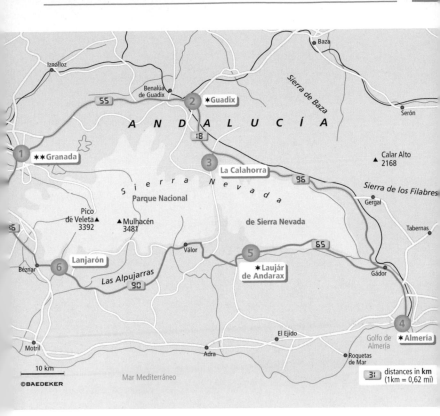

1480m/4,855ft the highest settlement, known for its delicious »jamón serrano« (air-cured hams), and **Capileira**. Then descend deep into the valleys of the southern slopes of the Sierra Nevada and back to Granada through Órgiva, then ❻**Lanjarón** – a good place to stay the night – and Durcal.

SIGHTS FROM
A TO Z

The pearly white iridescence of the cathedral in Cádiz welcomes
the traveller approaching from the sea. Let Andalucía enchant you!

✳ Los Alcornocales
(Parque Natural de los Alcornocales)

──────────────── ✳ **D 8/9**

Province: Cádiz

The Los Alcornocales nature reserve that stretches between the rock of ▶Gibraltar and the ▶Sierra de Grazalema is well worth a visit for nature-lovers because of its diverse vegetation and its rich variety of bird species.

Flora and fauna The mountainous nature reserve covering 1700 sq km/660 sq mi in the westernmost foothills of the Betica Cordillera is **one of the world's largest cork oak forests**. Some truly majestic specimens grow at higher altitudes. The forests form the basis of the region's cork industry. Once a tree's layer of cork bark is 7 to 10 cm (3 to 4 inches) thick, which occurs about every 9 or 10 years, it is ready to be har-

Los Alcornocales

GETTING THERE
Jimena de la Frontera, near ▶Algeciras, and the village of Alcalá de los Gazules are the best gateways into the nature reserve. The park can be explored by car from the A 2304 that runs right across the middle of it from Alcalá de los Gazules into the Sierra de Grazalema in the direction of Ubrique. The A 405 between Castellar de la Frontera and Gaucí is the road to take for a look at the eastern edge of the reserve.

INFORMATION
Asociación Turismo Sostenible de los Alcornocales
Calle los Pozos, s/n
E-11180 Alcalá de los Gazules
Tel. 956 41 32 52
www.alcornocales.org

Oficina del Parque Natural Los Alcornocales
Carretera Alcalá-Benalup km 1
E-11180 Alcalá de los Gazules
The information offices can provide information about hiking and accommodation in the region.

WHERE TO STAY
La Almoraima €
In Castellar de la Frontera
Tel. 956 69 30 02
A good tip for wild game dishes and traditional cooking. Provides hotel accommodation at the edge of the Los Alcornocales nature reserve.

Hotel El Alcázar €€
In Castillo de Castellar, Plaza Salvador,
Tel. 956 69 31 50
www.tugasa.com; 9 rooms
Exclusive hotel with spacious rooms and a restaurant. All of the rooms have beautiful views.

vested and processed. In addition, the acorns serve as the main diet of the Iberian wild boars that roam free in the forests.

Besides cork oak, other plants that thrive here include holly, wild olive trees, hawthorn and bracken. One species of oak is **unusual** in that it is related to the Portuguese oak that grows on shady and moist slopes and tends to be strongly overgrown with epiphytic plants. The wild animals of the Alcornocales include not only wild boar, but red deer, roe deer, otters, mongooses, griffon vultures and booted eagles, lizards and fire salamanders, plus many other reptiles and amphibians.

On the A 405, which runs from Algeciras to ▶Ronda, about 23km/14mi north of Algeciras lies Castellar de la Frontera. From Almoraima, a village further to the south, a small side road branches off to the northwest towards **Castillo de Castellar**, a walled and fortified village in rocky landscape, which is also incorporated into Castellar de la Frontera. Many of the families living there were forced to move to Nuevo Castellar in the 1970s because the new Embalse de Guadarranque reservoir had a disastrous effect on harvest yields. Subsequently, the abandoned village was discovered by artists and dropouts. But the times of a picturesque and secluded paradise behind ancient defensive walls are over as it is attracting an increasing number of holidaymakers with money to spend.

*Castellar de la Frontera

Algeciras

— ✦ E 9

Province: Cádiz
Altitude: 15m/49ft
Population: 116,400

Algeciras lies near the southern tip of the Iberian peninsula on the western side of the bay of Algeciras across from ▶Gibraltar. The city is highly important as a ferry port to ▶Ceuta and Tangiers in North Africa. It is used annually by more than 3 million travellers, particularly during the summer months when Moroccans working in Europe cross the strait to spend their holidays at home.

Algeciras is anything but beautiful, so that most people only take it in as a stop-over on the way to North Africa. The proximity to Morocco also lies behind the fact that the rate of drug offences in Algeciras is higher than anywhere else in Spain. Do not under any circumstances bring drugs (**»chocolate«**) in any form or amount back from Africa and do not procure any in Algeciras – the punishments for this are severe. And the Spanish police check very closely!

Gateway to North Africa

Algeciras

INFORMATION
Oficina de Turismo
C. Juan de la Cierva, s/n
E-11207 Algeciras
Tel. 956 57 26 36
www.algeciras.es
www.campogibraltar.com

WHERE TO EAT
❶ *Montes* €
Juan Morrison, 27
Tel. 956 65 42 07
Far from sophisticated, but authentic
and always full. Tapas from the same
kitchen are served in the accompanying
bar at the corner of C. Castellar.

WHERE TO STAY
❷ *Hotel Reina Cristina* €€
Paseo de la Conferencia, s/n
Tel. 956 60 26 22
www.reinacristina.es; 168 rooms
Romantic, colonial-style hotel south of
the harbour, set in the middle of a park.
The hotel has had a series of illustrious
guests including Franklin D. Roosevelt
and Orson Welles.

❶ *Al Mar* €
Avda. de la Marina, 2
Tel. 956 65 46 61
Fax 956 65 45 01, 192 rooms
The hotel is next to the harbour and the
view across the Bay of Algeciras with its
refineries and oil tanks is not exactly idyllic.

History It was the Moors who re-established the Roman port of Portus
Albo in 713 and named it Al-Gezîra al-Khadrâ (»Green Island«).
It was conquered in 1344 by Alfonso XI (Alfonso the Just) but was
retaken by Mohammed V of Granada in 1368 before being wiped
out by the Christians a year later. When Gibraltar was captured by
the British in 1704, Spanish emigrants from there began to resettle
the town.

WHAT TO SEE IN ALGECIRAS

Plaza Alta In the 18th century, the city began to spread out from around Plaza
Alta, the city's main square, lined with palms and decorated with
fountains. The churches Nuestra Señora de Europa and Nuestra Señora de la Palma date from that time.

Casa In 1906, the conference of Algeciras was held in the Casa Consisto-
Consistorial rial (the old town hall built in 1897), a result of the First Moroccan
Crisis (1905/1906), in the course of which **Kaiser Wilhelm II**, Emperor of Germany, made a point of visiting Tangiers. The Germans
were trying to frustrate French colonial policies in North Africa and
gain influence in Morocco. Despite that, the treaty of Algeciras eventually gave joint control over Morocco to France and Spain.

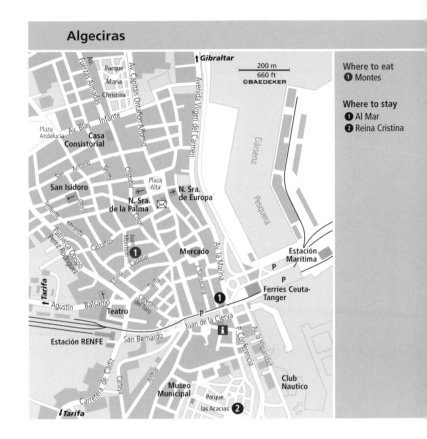

Parts of the **Merinid baths** dating from the 13th or 14th century were found in the city centre in 1996 and have since been moved to the Parque María Cristina. The remains of walls and floors as well as parts of a sewer system can be seen.

Parque María Cristina

The centrally located market hall in C. Nuestra Señora de la Palma is ideal if you are shopping for a picnic. It features an interesting steel structure designed by the engineer Eduardo Torroja

Mercado

The city museum in the Parque las Acacias offers information about the history of the city. Do not miss room IV where the Merinid baths on display illustrate the **domestic hygiene of the time**.

Museo Municipal

ⓘ Winter: Mon – Fri 9am – 2pm, 5pm – 7pm, Sat 10am – 1pm, summer: Mon – Fri 9am – 2pm; free admission

AROUND ALGECIRAS

La Línea dela Concepción
La Línea de la Concepción is the border town leading to the British dominion of ►Gibraltar. The village has a museum featuring works by the local-born artist Cruz Herrera, und exhibits in the Museo del Istmo include archaeological, historic and scientific items.

*Castellar de la Frontera
On the A 405, which runs from Algeciras to ►Ronda, about 23km/14mi north of Algeciras lies Castellar de la Frontera. From there a small side road branches off to the west towards Castillo de Castellar, a very pretty fortified village (►Los Alcornocales).

> **!**
> **MARCO ⊕ POLO** TIP
>
> **Trip to Morocco** *Insider Tip*
>
> The proximity to Africa is evidenced by the lively activity in the harbour and it might just arouse the urge to take a trip to Morocco. The crossing to Tangiers takes only about two hours. Among the companies offering day-trip excursions, including a tour of the city, is Viajes Transafric, Avda. la Marina 4 (tel. 956 65 43 11; remember your passport) and the price is around €45.

To the east of the ►Los Alcornocales nature reserve and 12km/7mi north of Castellar on the A 405 lies **Jimena de la Frontera**, a sleepy village clustered around the ruins of a Moorish castle. The present tourist office is in the restored, 15th-century Iglesia de la Misericordia. Information is available from there regarding tours of the **Cueva de Laja-Alta** to the northwest of Jimena de la Frontera, where cave paintings some 3,000 years old have been discovered.

* Almería

✳ **L 8**

Province: Almería
Altitude: 16m/52ft
Population: 190,000

The broad Gulf of Almería with its long, enticing beaches spreads along the southeastern corner of Andalucía – and not far from a modern, lively provincial capital.

Friendly provincial capital
Only a few kilometres away from the coast the bare pinacles of the Sierra de Gádor rise up in the west and the Sierra Alhamilla in the north-east; in the south-east the ►Cabo de Gata marks the southeatsernmost point of Spain
Almería, the capital of the province, is lively and friendly but not spectacular. Its greatest attraction for tourists is the beautifully restored Alcazaba, **Andalucía's largest Moorish castle**.

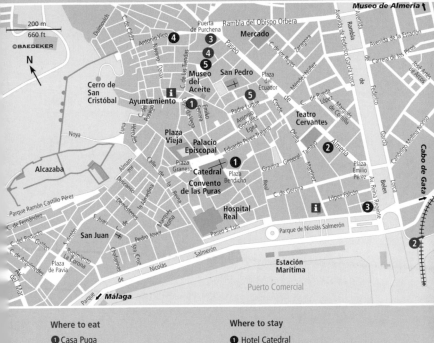

Almería

200 m
660 ft
©BAEDEKER

N

Where to eat

❶ Casa Puga
❷ Club de Mar
❸ El Alcázar
❹ Restaurante Valentín
❺ Bodeguilla de Ramón

Where to stay

❶ Hotel Catedral
❷ Costasol
❸ Citymar Gran Hotel Almería
❹ La Perla
❺ Nuevo Torreluz

The province of Almería is one of the richest in Spain – even though there is little industry. On the other hand, the sun shines 320 days of the year on average, so that vegetables can be grown under plastic on a major scale across the plains around the provincial capital. First-time visitors may be put off by the plastic foil cloches stretching endlessly into the distance. The wretched housing of the day labourers – mostly North African immigrants – does not leave a good impression either. Nevertheless, the province is continuing to win more and more fans thanks to the fabulous, and not yet overcrowded beaches, along with the pristine natural landscape that can be found in the eastern part of the region around the cape. The coast westwards of Almería, on the other hand, has surrendered to mass tourism. The airport lies 8km/5mi east of the city and is Andalucía's second busiest for charter flights after ►Málaga.

History The southern tip of the Iberian peninsula is an area with a culture that dates back to ancient times, since it is a **nexus of sea routes** from North Africa to Europe and from the eastern Mediterranean to the Atlantic. One of the most significant archaeological sites for the Beaker people culture is at Los Millares, 25km/16mi north of Almería. The Phoenicians also settled here, followed by the Greeks, the Carthaginians and after them the Romans, who built up an important harbour by the name of Portus Magnus. After the Visigoths came the Moors, under whom the city flowered and gained the name Al-Mariyya, which roughly means **»mirror of the sea«**. Under Abd ar-Rahman III, it was an important port for the caliphate after AD 955. After that regime disintegrated, it became the capital of a taifa that was mightier than Seville and included Murcia, Jaén, Córdoba as well as parts of Granada. However, this too was short-lived and Almería deteriorated into a nest of pirates. Alfonso VII succeeded in conquering the city in 1147, but ten years later, the Christians had to pull out again and it was not until 1489 that an uncle of the last ruler of Granada handed over Almería to the Catholic Monarchs. In 1492 it was made bishopric. In the 16th century Almería suffered at least four earthquakes. One of them destroyed major parts of the city in 1522 and in 1567 expelled Moslems once again appeared before the gates, but they were defeated. As of the 19th century, ore mined in the surrounding area was shipped from here. The cultivation of vegetables began after the decline of mining in the 1980s.

✳✳ ALCAZABA

Second largest Moorish structure in Europe On the summit that towers above the Barrio de la Chanca to the west of the town, hardly visible from the town centre but well signposted, is the enormous Alcazaba, Europe's second largest Moorish building after the Alhambra in ►Granada. It was built in the 10th century under Abd ar-Rahman III, enlarged by Almansur, further expanded between 1014 and 1028 by Jairán, the first ruler of the taifa, and finally extended once again by the Catholic Monarchs. The rebuilt area of the fortress encompasses more than 35,000 sq m/9 acres and more than 20,000 people could take refuge within its walls. **Tours** Three walls crowned with battlements follow the contours of the hill and enclose three castle compounds at varying heights. A steep, zig-zagging ramp leads up from the ticket box and through the Puerta de la Justicia into the first compound area, which once sheltered refugees during sieges or concealed defenders readying to break out. It has been transformed nowadays into a very pretty park traversed by

Almería

INFORMATION
Oficina de Turismo
Plaza de la Constitución
E-04001 Almería
Tel. 950 21 05 38
www.turismodealmeria.org
daily Sept–June 9am–5pm
July/Aug 9am–2pm, 4pm–7pm

ALMERÍA CARD
The Almería Card enttiles you to discounts in many establsishments: certain buildings and museums, restaurants, tapas bars, hotels, shops etc. The card can be bought at the Oficina de Turismo. 1 week for €5, 2 weeks for €10.

ENTERTAINMENT
Peña El Taranto
Tenor Iribarne, 20
Authentic flamenco

SHOPPING
C. de las Tiendas is the main shopping zone along with the many little side streets around it. A morning market is held in C. Aguilar de Campo at Paseo de Almería.

EVENTS
Feria
Celebrations for 10 days and nights at the end of August with music and bull-fighting.

WHERE TO EAT
❶ *Casa Puga* €€
Jovellanos, 7
The bar is legendary for its tapas, both in terms of quality and quantity.

❷ *Club de Mar* €€€€
Muelle de las Almadrabillas

Tel. 950 23 50 48
Gourmet restaurant in the marina with fish specialities and a classy atmosphere.

❹ *Restaurante Valentín* €€€€
Tenor Iribarne, 19
Tel. 950 26 44 75
Fish dishes in myriad variations.

❸ *El Alcázar* €
Tenor Iribarne, 2
Tel. 950 23 89 95
Typical marisquería offering fried fish and seafood.

❺ *Bodeguilla de Ramón* €
C. General Segura, 17
A good place for a tapas break. Always packed at lunchtime from 2 to 3pm when the people from the surrounding offices come for lunch.

WHERE TO STAY
❸ *Citymar Gran Hotel Almería* €
Avda. Reina Regente, 8
Tel. 950 23 80 11
www.granhotelalmeriacitymar.com
105 rooms
Hotel next to the marina. Rooms with balcony and a sea view. Reaturant with traditonal cooking. Swimming pool.

❺ *Nuevo Torreluz* €
Plaza Flores, 10
Tel. 950 23 43 99
www.torreluz.com, 98 rooms
Modern hotel near the Alcazaba that is also linked with a three-star hotel and an apartment hotel.

Portomagno €
In Aguadulce Paseo Marítimo, s/n

Tel. 950 34 22 16, 383 rooms
Beach hotel with pool, restaurant and all
the extras including a golf course.

❶ Hotel Catedral € €
Plaza de la Catedral, 8
Tel. 950 27 81 78
www.hotelcatedral.net; 20 rooms
Pretty hotel in a city palace from 1850
next to the cathedral. The delicious food
in the restaurant includes tapas.

❷ Costasol €
Paseo de Almería, 58, tel. 950 23 40 11
www.hotelcostasol.com, 50 rooms
The hotel, which was remodeled in
2008, is located between the harbour
and the city centre and provides a great
breakfast but also spacious bathrooms.

Some rooms have a small balcony. Everything is very clean here.

❹ La Perla €
Plaza del Carmen, 7
Tel. 950 23 88 77
The best rooms face the plaza. The
oldest hotel in the city has maintained
its charm.

Playacapricho €
In Roquetas de Mar
Avenida de las Gaviotas
Tel. 950 33 31 00, 331 rooms
www.playasenator.com
Three building tracts with large rooms
and generous doublebeds. There is a
swimming pool area with whirlpool and
a sun terrace in the garden.

streams. Here stands the Torre de la Vela, erected under Carlos III.
Its bell was used to sound alarms but also announced curfew and
watering times. There is a **fantastic view** from here of the Saliente
bastion in the east jutting out from the town like the bow of a ship.
The oldest part of the grounds is in the second castle yard. This was
where the palace of the Moorish rulers once stood, accompanied by
a mosque with a cistern beneath it, although little remains today except for the foundation walls. It is still possible to take a tour inside
the cistern. There are a few modest items of the Islamic past on display. The Christians built the upper enclosure as a self-contained fortress. Three mighty towers are grouped here around the parade
courtyard; the four-sided Gothic Torre del Homenaje with the coat
of arms of the Catholic Monarchs, the Torre de la Noria del Viento
(windmill tower) and, on the west point, the Torre de la Pólvora
(powder tower) with some of the old cannons.

❶ Tue – Sun Nov – Mar 10am – 6.30pm, April – Oct 9am – 8.30pm;
free admission

City wall From the junction between the first and second castle compounds,
the fortified city wall built under Jairan descends down into the la
Hoya valley and climbs back up to the Cerro de San Cristóbal across
from the Alcazaba. The Knights Templar built the **Castillo de San
Cristóbal** on the adjoining hill and four large towers of the castle are
still standing. The giant statue of Jesus was put up in 1928.

Alcazaba of Almería

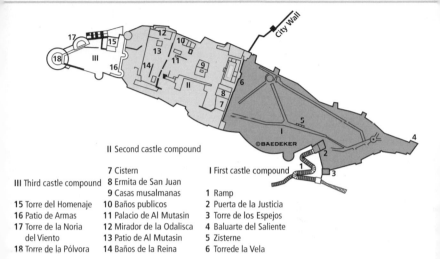

II Second castle compound

III Third castle compound

15 Torre del Homenaje
16 Patio de Armas
17 Torre de la Noria
del Viento
18 Torre de la Pólvora

7 Cistern
8 Ermita de San Juan
9 Casas musalmanas
10 Baños publicos
11 Palacio de Al Mutasin
12 Mirador de la Odalisca
13 Patio de Al Mutasin
14 Baños de la Reina

I First castle compound

1 Ramp
2 Puerta de la Justicia
3 Torre de los Espejos
4 Baluarte del Saliente
5 Zisterne
6 Torre de la Vela

The barrio of La Chanca (Arabic: »tuna net«) beneath the castle is home to many gitanos or gypsies. They are unlikely to appreciate it if their impoverished living conditions are taken for a tourist attraction or snapshot.

La Chanca

TOWN CENTRE

The palm-covered Parque de Nicolás Salmerón extends alongside the ferry harbour. At the far eastern end, the old ore-hauling railway crosses high over the street at a dizzying altitude.

Parque de Nicolás Salmerón

Just before the bridge, the Rambla de Belén forks away and a little further along, the Paseo de Almería turns off it. This is a good place to stroll, shop or visit one of the street cafés. Among the conspicuous buildings in the street are the seat of the civil government, once a casino, and the magnificent buildings associated with it, the Teatro Cervantes and the Círculo Mercantil.

Paseo de Almería

Behind them is the **Basílica de la Nuestra Señora del Mar**, dedicated to the city's patron. An appearance of Our Lady is said to have taken place on the beach in 1502. The market hall is located to the right of the Paseo.

From the Alcazaba there is an attractive view of the city
and the harbour

*Cathedral The grand Plaza de la Catedral can be reached by going to the left of
the Paseo. The cathedral is a **typical fortified church** with four formidable corner towers, tower-like apses and a fringe of battlements.
It also served to protect against pirate attacks. Diego de Siloé built it
after the earthquake of 1522 between 1524 and 1543 on the site of a
mosque known as the Friday mosque. The main portico and the Puerta de los Perdones, both by Juan de Orea, appear less bulky with
double columns richly decorated with statuary and finished off with
the coat of arms of Charles I.

The **choir stalls**, once again carved in walnut by Juan de Orea (1558),
are an outstanding work of art in the interior. Their unusual relief
figures depict, alongside clergy und saints, a worker, an official and a
female Moor as well. Also notable are the »Listening Christ« in the
axis chapel of the choir (Bishop Villalán, the founder of the church,
is also buried there), an Annunciation by Alonso Cano in the Capilla de la Piedad to the left, as well as a statue of Saint Indalecio – the
patron saint of Almería – a work by Francisco Salcillo, to the right of
the choir crest.

A little way past the archbishop's palace is the pretty, arcaded Plaza Vieja (Plaza de la Constitución) where the city hall is situated. C. de las Tiendas, formerly the main axis of the city, goes all the way to Puerta de Purchena at the northern end of Paseo de Almería. Just before it is the 16th-century **Santiago el Viejo** church with its 55m/180ft-high Romanesque tower and a magnificent portal with the figure of St James as a slayer of Moors, again created by Juan de Orea. The church furnishings were destroyed in 1936 during the civil war. A little further up beyond the church, some 11th-century **Moorish cisterns** can be viewed.

Plaza Vieja

❶ Mo. – Fri 9am – 2pm, Sat 10am – 12.30pm

The Museo del Aceite de Oliva in C. de las Tiendas (no. 15) off C. Real is dedicated to all aspects of **olive oil**. For a small fee, some of the different kinds can also be sampled.

Museo del Aceite de Oliva

❶ Mon–Fri 10am–1pm, 5.30–8pm, Sat mornings only; admission €3

It is only a stone's throw from the olive museum to Plaza San Pedro. The church was built on the foundations of the walls of a mosque in 1494. The present structure with frescoes by Fray Juan García dates from 1795.

San Pedro

The Archaeological Museum has a new home at Carretera de Ronda No. 91. It was named one of the best museums of the year in 2008. From pre-history to Moorish rule local finds are presented in excellent exhibits.

Museo de Almería

❶ Tue 2.30pm – 8.30pm, Wed – Sat 9am – 8.30pm, Sun 9am – 2.30pm

AROUND ALMERÍA

The western Costa de Almería (eastern part ►Mojácar) is the **prime destination for the package tour industry**, which means numerous hotels and bungalow complexes tower up behind long and mostly excellently tended beaches are. More often than not, directly behind them is a plastic sea of greenhouses. There is no dearth of pools, parks, sports centres, supermarkets and discos in Aguadulce nor in neighbouring Roquetas de Mar.
Almerímar aims at a different clientele with its luxurious complex built where nothing stood before, almost a city in itself, and its large golf course. Weekend sailors are welcome to anchor here at one of the 1,100 berths in Andalucía's second-largest yacht marina.

Western Costa de Almería

The archaeological site at Los Millares to the northwest of Almería, accessed via the A-92 and A-348, is **of such major importance** that the cultural era between the Stone Age and the Copper Age is named

Los Millares

after it. Here, high above the valley of Río Andarax in the desert-like Sierra de Gádor, between 2,500 and 1,500 BC lived a people who produced pottery beakers of a distinctive bell-shaped design and buried their dead in megalithic tombs.

From Los Millares, continue travelling on the A-348 down into the **green, fertile terraced countryside** of ▶Alpujarras.

Los Millares: Wed – Sun 10am – 2pm; free admission

✳ SIERRA ALHAMILLA

Europe's only natural desert The bare hilltops of the Sierra Alhamilla rise to the northeast of Almería up to a height of over 1,500m/5,000ft. Europe's only natural desert can be explored as part of a day trip by car. Buses also go to the western theme towns.

Wild west towns The sandy brown landscape with its sparse vegetation is instantly reminiscent of the southwestern USA. This fact did not escape the

Showdown in Mini-Hollywood – the public is up close

attention of some film producers, and in short order the sierra became a location for shooting wild west films, since production costs were relatively low here and there were plenty of potential film extras available. It was not only a host of spaghetti westerns that were filmed here; soon major U.S. productions were also coming to Spain and bringing with them stars like Clint Eastwood, Lee van Cleef and Burt Lancaster. Even scenes from **Lawrence of Arabia** (the storming of Aqaba by the Bedouins) and **Indiana Jones** were shot here. After film production rolled back, the Western town sets were opened as tourist attractions. The largest and most professional among them is – as part of the »Oasys Theme Park« (safari park, zoo and water park) – **»Mini Hollywood«**, north of Almería, just after the N-340a forks off from the A-92S. Every day a **bank robbery and a gunfight** are played out between the saloon, bank, hotel, jail and gallows, etc. The can-can is also performed in the saloon, and there is also a parrot show. The more modest »Fort Bravo« is further along the road to Tabernas and, on the A-92S in the direction of Guadix, lies »Western Leone«, where scenes for »Once upon a Time in the West«.

❶ **Mini Hollywood:** June - Sept daily 10am – 9pm, May - Oct until 7pm, otherwise usually only on weekends; admission €19.90
Bankrobbery with shooting: daily 12pm and 5pm, June – Sept also at 8pm
Cancan in saloon: daily 1pm, 4pm, June – Sept also at 7pm
Parrot show: daily 11am, 3pm, 6pm

A little way beyond the sleepy village of Tabernas with the ruins of a Moorish castle enthroned on the hill above it, the N-340a branches off from the A-370 northward towards the solar power facility of the International Energy Agency, IEA (signposted »Plataforma solar«). Some 4km/2.5mi along the road, hundreds of mirrors can be seen to the right, following the course of the sun, focussing the light and reflecting it onto an 80m/260ft-high receiver, where it is transformed into energy (►MARCO POLO Insight, p.148). ***Solar power plant**

Further along the N-340a comes Sorbas, a village known for its red **pottery** with a very lovely and cosy plaza screened by acacias. The eastern edge of Sorbas plummets precipitously down into the Río de Aguas – the houses clinging to the rock at a height of 40m/130ft over the gorge. For cavers, the Karst de Yesos de Sorbas east of Sorbas include a **subterranean labyrinth of caverns**. ***Sorbas**

❶ Natur Sport Sorbas provide guided tours with the necessary equipment provided. Tel. 950 36 47 04, admission: €13; www.cuevasdesorbas.com

The motorway to Almería has a junction at Sorbas. However, a much more attractive return drive follows the N-340a back another 9km/5.5mi and then the AL-102 across the Sierra. A narrow, winding stretch, but amid **stunning scenery** that leads through the former ***Over the Sierra to Níjar**

The Sun's Energy

Thanks to its geographical location and the excellent climatic conditions Andalusia is the ideal location for producing renewable energy. The Andalusian government has also realized this and for this reason it promotes the construction of solar technological facilities. Every new job is welcome in the structurally weak region.

▶ **Solar power tower PS10**
Europe's first commercial solar power tower is located about 10km/6mi north of Sanlúcar la Mayor (Sevilla province); arrive via Los Ranchos del Guadiamar.

200m/660ft

▶ **Technical data**

Number of mirrors	**624**
Height of tower	**115m/380ft**
Contsruction costs	**€35 mil**
Output	**11 MW**
Electricity production annually	**23 GWh**

©BAEDEKER

Solar power towers

tower with absorber

sun's rays

mirrors (Heliostat)

▶ **Solar thermic power plants**
… are not based on photovoltaic, rather they use the warmth from the sun to produce steam by heating an absorber liquid. The steam drives a turbine and a generator converts this movement to electricity.

Solar power plants in Andalucía
With 425 GWh Andalusia is the world's largest producing region for solar energy.

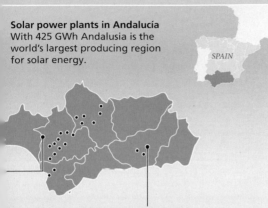

SPAIN

Parabolic through power plant Andasol 1
Europe's first parabolic trough power plant and currently the world's largest solar power plant. It is located near Aldeire/La Calahorra (Granada province).

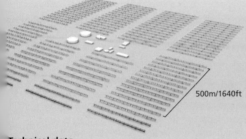

500m/1640ft

Technical data

mber of parabolic mirrors	209 664
lektorfläche	510,120 sq m/5,490,886 sq ft
gree of effectiveness	15 – 28 %
tput	150 MW
ctricity production annually	180 GWh

abolic trough power plant

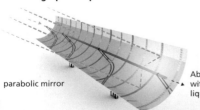

parabolic mirror

Absorber pipe with heat-transfer liquid, e.g. thermal oil

▶ **Energy mix in Spain**
in per cent

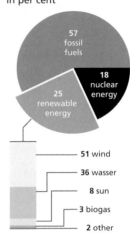

57 fossil fuels

18 nuclear energy

25 renewable energy

51 wind
36 wasser
8 sun
3 biogas
2 other

▶ **Solar electricity advancing**
Development of available solar electricity in Spain

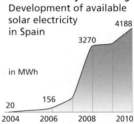

4188

3270

in MWh

20   156

2004   2006   2008   2010

▶ **Collector surface comparison**
in hectares

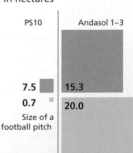

PS10   Andasol 1–3

7.5   15.3

0.7   20.0

Size of a football pitch

Herm (Channel Islands) as a comparison

mining village of Lucainena de las Torres , where old ore-smelting furnaces can still be seen.

The road finally ends up in **Níjar**, high above the sea of plastic that covers the plains of Almería. The village is widely known for its **pottery and woven carpets** offered for sale in many shops along the main road. The small plaza with the village church is at the highest point of the village.

Sierra de los Filabres During the drive along the N-340a, the Sierra de los Filabres mountain range is constantly visible to the north. There, atop the 2168m/7113ft **Calar Alto** are the five domes of the German-Spanish **observatory, the largest of its kind in Europe**. The clear air at that high altitude allows a clear view of the starry cosmos virtually all year round, but only for the astronomers. Normal tourists can nevertheless enjoy the **fantastic view** of the mountains and coastline.

Almuñécar · Costa Tropical

✳ H 8

Province: Granada
Altitude: 24m/79ft
Population: 27,700

Almuñécar is the chief city on the Costa Tropical, as the stretch of the Costa del Sol that lies within the province of Granada has come to be called in recent years. Here, the »sun coast« is still at its most beautiful and natural. Architectural eyesores like those on the coastline around ▸Málaga have been avoided for the most part until now.

Capital of the Costa Tropical Sugar cane, avocados and mangos thrive in this precipitous coastal landscape with its almost tropical climate and the cultivation and processing of these crops, along with tourism, form the major sources of income for the population. As is the case with many places along the Costa del Sol, Almuñécar was also founded by the Phoenicians (Sexi). The town has a very important place in the history of Andalucía – it was here that Abd ar-Rahman I, the **founder of the Emirate and later Caliphate of Córdoba**, landed in 755 after his flight from Damascus.

WHAT TO SEE IN ALMUÑÉCAR

Castillo de San Miguel The remains of a Moorish castle built on Roman foundations are, as always, impressive. It was captured by the Christians in 1489, ex-

Almuñécar · Costa Tropical

INFORMATION
Oficina de Turismo
Palacete de la Najarra
Avda. de Europa, s/n
E-18690 Almuñécar
Tel. 958 63 11 25
www.turismoalmunecar.info
daily 10am – 2pm, 5pm – 8pm

EVENTS
Jazz en la Costa
Two-week jazz festival in mid-July
www.jazzgranada.es/jazz_enlacosta.html

WHERE TO EAT
La Última Ola € € € €
Puerta del Mar, 4; tel. 958 63 00 18
www.restauranteultimaola.es
Two dining rooms and the terrace;
House specialties are fish and seafood.

Horno de Cándida € € €
Orovia, 3; trel. 958 88 32 84

A real bargain! The restaurant belongs
to the school of hotel management
and is situated in an old bakery. It offers
exquisite cooking.

WHERE TO STAY
Casablanca €
Plaza San Cristóbal, 4
Tel. 958 63 55 75
www.hotelcasablancaalmunecar.com
35 rooms
The fancifully Moorish-looking hotel
with its large balcony is very conveniently situated across from Playa de San Cristóbal in the vicinity of the ornithological
and botanical gardens.

Helios €
Playa San Cristóbal de las Flores
Tel. 958 63 06 36
www.helios-hotels.com; 232 rooms
The hotel is on the sea and features
comfortable rooms and a pool.

panded in the 16th century and in 1808 suffered major damage at the
hands of Napoleon's soldiers. A tour leads through the baths, cisterns, the remains of the Nasrid palace.
❶ April – Sept Tue – Sat 10.30am – 1.30pm, 5pm – 7.30pm, Sun 10.30am
– 2pm; admission €2.35

Not far from the castle is the archaeological museum in the »**Cave of
the Seven Palaces**«, a multi-chambered, vaulted complex of Roman
origin. Along with burial objects from the necropolis of the city, the
Egyptian urn of Pharaoh Apophis I (16th century BC) is a valuable
rarity.
❶ Opening times like Castillo

***Cuevas de
Siete Palacios**

The highlight of the aquarium north-west of the museum is the glass
tunnel, which sharks, mantas, turtles and other sea creatures swim over.
❶ Plaza Kuwait; daily 10.30am – 6.30pm, longer on weekends and during
the high season; admission €12

**Acuario de
Almuñécar**

Parque Ornitológico	A number of tropical birds are housed below the castle in a shady bird park. ❶ Daily 11am – 2pm, 5pm – 7pm; admission €5
Parque del Majuelo	Close to the ornithological park in the Parque del Majuelo botanical gardens there are also remains of a Phoenician fish factory from the 5th century BC that was famous in antiquity for its »garum«, a fish paste widely used as a condiment.
Beaches	The Peñón del Santo projects out into the sea and beaches stretch out on either side of it, the most beautiful being Playa de San Cristóbal, west of the rock.

AROUND ALMUÑÉCAR

La Herradura West of Almuñecar lies the crescent-shaped bay of La Herradura, sheltered by the rocky promontories of Cerro Gordo and La Punta de

Well protected: the marina in the Bay of Herradura

la Mona. A **mountain road offering one fabulous view after the other** winds its way to Marina del Este, where there is a pebble beach that is a meeting place for many scuba divers. A small yachting marina has also been established there.

Nearly 14km/9mi to the east along the coast road is the resort of Salobreña, picturesquely set on a mountainside and dominated by a Nasrid castle. It is popular with the residents of Granada who like to meet in the beach restaurants Casa Emilio and El Peñón on Sundays for some tasty fish dishes.

Salobreña

Motril follows just a few miles further to the east. It is worth seeing the churches of La Encarnación and Nuestra Señora de la Cabeza. The latter stands in the ruins of a Moorish castle that was home to the mother of Boabdil, the last king of Granada. The sugar cane processing plant Nuestra Señora del Pilar with its fully preserved steam engines, and which was in operation until 1994, is **Andalucía's most important industrial monument**.
A sidetrip toward Alpujarras leads to Vélez de Benaudalla to the pretty olive oil museum, where tasting is also possible.

Motril

Passing through La Calahonda, a fishing village transformed into a resort with fantastic beaches, the road eventually reaches Castell de Ferro, dominated by a Moorish tower. The village lives from fishing, vegetable cultivation and, in the summer thanks to its long beaches, also increasingly from tourism.

Castell de Ferro

＊ Las Alpujarras

✦ J 8

Province: Granada, Almería

The Alpujarras, lying south of ▶Granada and the ▶Sierra Nevada boast a mountain landscape stretching across the provinces of Granada and Almería.

The Berbers settled here as early as the 8th century and built up a lucrative silk industry in the 10th and 11th centuries. After losing Granada in 1492, all of the Moors withdrew to remote villages until they were finally driven out in 1568 after several bloody revolts. A couple of families, though, were forced to stay by the new Christian settlers to maintain the **cleverly devised irrigation systems and terrace gardens**, in which grain, olives, citrus fruits and vegetables grew and which are still farmed to this day. The low-ceilinged stone houses of the Alpujarras with their cylindrical chimneys are typical of Moorish

Mountain landscape rediscovered by writers

Las Alpujarras

INFORMATION
Oficina de Turismo Nevadensis
In Pampaneira, C. Verónica
Plaza de la Libertad
Tel. 958 76 31 27
www.turismopampaneira.com
This is the place for information about
hiking trails through the mountains.
They can also arrange for guides for
treks, excursions on horseback and
climbing tours.

WHERE TO EAT
La Fragua €€
In Trevélez, San Antonio, 4
Tel. 958 85 85 73
www.hotellafragua.com
Pork specialties are of course served in
this restaurant in a village famous for its
ham, but tasty lamb dishes feature on
the menu as well. There is a wonderful
view from the dining room.

Ibero €
In Capileira, Parra, 1
Tel. 653 93 50 56
Family-run hotel near the church with
low-priced traditional fare, but also couscous and vegetarian dishes like vegetable
omelettes. Good wine selection as well..

WHERE TO STAY
Villa Turística de Bubión €€
In Bubión, Barrio Alto, s/n

Tel. 958 76 39 73
43 rooms
This recently renovated hotel combines a
traditional Alpujarras style of living with
modern amenities. The owner offers an
attractive tour and recreation program.

Las Terrazas €
In Bubión, Plaza del Sol, 7
Tel. 958 76 30 34
www.terrazasalpujarra.com
As the name promises, this simple hotel
has three terraces, as well as a salon
with TV and rental bikes. Pretty mountain panorama.

Finca Los Llanos €
In Capileira, Ctra. de Sierra Nevada
Tel. 958 76 30 71
www.hotelfincalosllanos.com
40 rooms
Pleasant hotel on the edge of town,
with restaurant and beautiful views.

Alcazaba de Busquistar €€
In Busquistar, Crta. Orgiva-Laujar, km. 37
Tel. 958 85 86 87
www.hotelalcazaba.com
53 rooms
The large, rustic mountain hotel has
an outdoor and indoor pool and will
organize rides with horses. There are
also a fitness room. Guests love the
two restaurants.

architecture. The houses are first covered with wooden laths and reed
mats, then by flat stone slabs. A mass of grey clay is then spread over
them providing them with a waterproof, all-purpose terrace.
The Alpujarras were rediscovered by writers and hikers at the beginning of the 20th century and the book **»South from Granada«** by
the British writer Gerald Brenan was instrumental in making them
known to a wider public.

DRIVE THROUGH THE ALPUJARRAS

Head south from ►Granada, initially along the A-44. After 39km/24mi, the A-348 branches off to Lanjarón, a mountain health resort where **one of Spain's best-known mineral springs** bubbles up to the surface.

Lanjarón

From there, a narrow, winding road branches off after Lanjarón at Órgiva and descends deep into the Valle del Poqueira. Three charming villages are lined up here in the shadow of the Veleta, any one of which is a good starting point for hikes. Many weaving mills producing colourful blankets and rugs (»jarapas«) are sited here too.
On the edge of the mighty Poqueira gorge lies ***Pampaneira** with its delightful Plaza de la Libertad, where the tourist office has detailed hiking maps at the ready. At the parish church in ***Bubión** there is an Alpujarran house on display furnished with numerous objects typical of the region (Casa Alpujarreña). Above Bubión is **Capileira**, at an elevation of 1436m/4711ft, it is the village at the highest elevation in the Valle del Poqueira region. It even has a museum of popular art.

*Valle del Poqueira

The A-4132 climbs through Pitres, Pórtugos and picturesquely nestling Busquístar up to an altitude of 1476m/4842ft to Trevélez, the **highest village in Spain**. Some of the best ham in the country is produced in the shadow of the giant Sierra Nevada mountains – on sale in more than just a few stores.

Trevélez

The Alpujarras near Bubión with cinema-quality mountain panoramas and picturesque villages

Yegen	The A-348 can be reached again near Narila and the road then leads on to Yegen. A plaque there marks the house where **Gerald Brenan** lived from 1920 to 1934 and wrote about the life of the villagers in his book *South from Granada*. Then the route leads via Mecina Alfahar to Ugíjar and back to the A-348, which then meets the A-347 after 20km/12mi. It leads southward through Berja down to the coast.
La Alpujarra almeriense	Going north, the road gradually gains height via some sweeping hairpin bends and crosses the »Alpujarra almeriense«. The main town in the region is **Láujar de Andarax**, at one end of which is the source of the Río Andarax. Other sights to be seen include the remains of an alcazaba and the La Encarnación Church, built on the ruins of a mosque burned down during the Moriscan uprising. After his defeat of 1492, the last Moorish king, **Boabdil**, is said to have settled here initially, but he was soon forced to move on to Morocco. From Laujar de Andarax the road mostly follows a route high above the valley of Río Andarax, from Ohanes through a **delightful terraced landscape** and through villages in wonderful settings to the thermal spa of Alhama de Almería. From there, it is another 30km/19mi to ▶Almería.

Insider Tip

Andújar

✶ **G 5**

Province: Jaén
Altitude: 211m/692ft
Population: 39,170

The town of Andújar, located in the north of the province of Jaén on the right bank of the Guadalquivir, is the centre of Andalusian olive oil production and known for its earthenware, »alcarrazas« or »jarras«, that feature motifs of flowers or shapes of grotesque figures. Fighting bulls are also bred here.

History	Not far from the present town, near Los Villares, there was once an ancient Iberian settlement called Illiturgi, the actual origin of Andújar. The Moors set up strong fortifications around Andújar and after the Christians conquered it in the 13th century, they made it their first outpost in Andalucía.

WHAT TO SEE IN AND AROUND ANDÚJAR

Plaza de España	At the peaceful centre of the town is Plaza de España that is separated into two parts by a yellow and white painted gatehouse. Around

Andújar

INFORMATION
Oficina de Turismo
Torre del Reloj
Plaza de Santa María s/n
E-23740 Andújar
Tel. 953 50 49 59
www.andujar.es

EVENTS
Romería de Nuestra Señora de la Cabeza
On the last Sunday in April many pilgrims make a pilgrimage to the shrine of Andújar's patron; along the way there are many fabulous views of the countryside.

WHERE TO EAT
Los Pincelines de Andújar €€€€
Escritor Alcalá Venceslada, 36
Tel. 953 51 11 54
One of the best restaurants in town. Meat, fish, seafood - attractively presented. Attentive and pleasant service.

it there are some pretty houses, the town hall and the church of San Miguel, which has some beautiful carvings inside.

Andújar's most important attraction is the church of Santa María la Mayor, slightly to the north of the plaza. It is a Renaissance building with a Plateresque façade that is somewhat plain but does contain two valuable masterpieces; Christ on the Mount of Olives by **El Greco** in the second chapel off the left-hand aisle and the The Immaculate Conception by Pacheco. A choir screen by Master Bartolomé and a manuscript by Juan de la Cruz are also among its treasures. The Mudejar bell tower is not attached to the church, which may support a theory that it was fashioned out of the minaret of a former mosque.

Santa María la Mayor

The Parque Natural Sierra de Andújar spreads out to the north and east of Andújar, unspoiled **nature amid the wild and romantic Sierra Morena**. The Río Jándula runs through it and opens up into two lakes. Wandering through the oak and pine forests are fallow deer, wild boar, lynx and even wolves. Eagles and vultures still nest in the most remote areas. A good starting place for a hiking tour is the village of **Las Vinas**, 15km/9mi northeast of Andújar, where there is a visitor centre (Information office in Andújar, Cercado Bajo de Ciprés, Camino de los Rubiales s/n).

Parque Natural Sierra de Andújar

Amidst the **quiet solitude of the mountains** lies the ***Santuario de la Virgen de la Cabeza**, which venerates a martyr said to have been sent to »Illiturgi« by Saint Peter. This veneration peaks during the pilgrimage on the last Sunday in April. According to legend, the virgin is said to have appeared to a shepherd in 1227 and ten years later the construction of the chapel began. The former Gothic church was totally destroyed in the Spanish Civil War and rebuilt afterwards. From these heights there is an **awe-inspiring panoramic view**.

* Antequera

$\star$ F 7

Province: Málaga
Altitude: 577m/1893ft
Population: 40,200

Antequera is the main town on the plateau of the same name where the Río Guadalhorce has its source and lies between the rugged Sierra del Torcal and areas. The urban hinterland is dominated by agriculture.

Churches and megalithic tombs

Even though Antequera's architecture may create a somewhat random impression, there are a surprising number of Renaissance and Baroque churches in the old town, often mixed with Mudejar ele-

**At the foot of the Sierra del Torcal
lies Antequera with its proud Moorish castle**

ments. This and the evidence of prehistoric settlement make the town of Antequera a very worthwhile place to visit, although it remains largely devoid of tourists. The burial chambers in the immediate locale are evidence that there were once megalithic settlements there. Under the Romans it was called Anticaria and was of quite some importance, but it was the Moors who built the site up into a great fortress until it was captured in 1410 by Ferdinand »of Antequera«, king of Aragon.

WHAT TO SEE IN ANTEQUERA

The 14th-century alcazaba, thought to have been built on top of a Roman fort, towers atop a hill overlooking the eastern part of town. The entrance is through the Arco de los Gigantes, erected in 1585 to honour Philip II and adorned with the town's coat of arms. Two sections of wall and the great Torre de Papabellotas with its Baroque topping have survived from the castle.   **Alcazaba**

The castle garden offers a beautiful view of the **Peña de los Enamorados**, »Lovers' Rock«, with its distinctive profile that is reminiscent of a Red Indian. Its name is derived from a legend about the daughter of a Moslem city governor and her Christian lover who threw themselves from there to their death when her parents would not agree to a marriage.

Opening times: daily 10.30am – 5.30pm; admission: €6

The church of Santa María la Mayor was built to the east of and below the fortress in the 16th century. It is a Plateresque church with a Renaissance façade that imitates a Roman triumphal arch, while the interior was finished off with a Mudejar artesonado ceiling. Next to it, the remains of a Roman baths have been excavated.   ***Real Colegiata de Santa María la Mayor**

The 17th century church, El Carmen, can be reached by leaving the fortress and turning to the right, then bearing left and right again. It was built between 1583 and 1633 and was once part of a Carmelite convent. The simple façade is in contrast to the Baroque interior and the Churrigueresque wooden retable of red pinewood bearing scenes carved by Antonio Primo.   **Nuestra Señora del Carmen**

From the Arco de los Gigantes head downhill to the left through the Cuesta de Judas to Plaza San Sebastián with its fountains. Here stands an 18th-century brick church of the same name. The nave dates to the 16th century; the main façade is richly decorated in the Plateresque style. Backed against it is the whitewashed **Iglesia de la Encarnación** dating from the 16th century with its beautiful artesonado ceiling.   **San Sebastián**

Antequera

INFORMATION
Oficina Municipal de Turismo
Plaza de San Sebastián, 7
Tel. 952 70 25 05
http://turismo.antequera.es
Mon – Sat 10am – 7pm, Sun
10am – 2pm

Area de Turismo del Ayuntamiento
C. Infante Don Fernando, 90
Edificio San Luis
E-29200 Antequera
Tel. 952 70 81 42 / 38

EVENTS
Real Feria de Agosto
Harvest festival in August with bullfighting and fair.

WHERE TO EAT
La Espuela €€€ **Insider Tip**
C. San Agustín, 1
Tel. 952 70 30 31
open daily
Excellent Andalusian tapas are served here. For main courses the cooks take their inspiration from innovative cuisine. No wonder that the restaurant is always busy.

El Escribano €€€€
Plaza del Escribano, 11
Tel. 952 70 65 33
Closed Mon
The restaurant opposite the Colegiata de Santa María serves typical Andalusian dishes. The Porra Antequerana, a kind of gazpacho, which is also served cold, is worth trying. The guests will also enjoy the wonderful view and the pleasant service.

WHERE TO STAY
Parador de Antequera €€
Paseo García del Olmo, 2
Tel. 952 84 02 61
 www.parador.es, 58 rooms
Modern, but very pleasant and quiet parador in an impressive white building surrounded by an attractive park. Many of the rooms have a terrace, and there is a swimming pool for hot days. A beautiful view of the Antequera plain from the restaurant.

Hotel Convento La Magdalena €€€
Urb. Antequera Golf; Tel. 902 54 15 40
www.hotellamagdalena.com; 21 rooms
Luxury hotel opened in 2009 in a former monastery (1584) outside of Antequera and right next to a golf course. Beautiful spa area with a window wall facing the garden.

Castilla €
Infante Don Fernando, 40
Tel. 952 84 30 90
www.castillahotel.com; 18 rooms
Inexpensive and very clean hotel, centrally located below the castle. The restaurant serves Andalusian dishes. A popular and well attended tapas bar is attached.

Museo de la Cíudad de Antequer From San Sebastián, C. Encarnación descends slightly to Plaza del Coso Viejo, which opens up to the right and includes the Baroque Palacio de Nájera, which contains the Museo de la Ciudad de Antequera. Standing out among the objects on display are the marble head of the Venus of Antequera and a bronze ephebe, a Roman copy of a Greek original from the 1st century AD. (opening hours: Tue–Fri 10am–1.30pm, 4–6pm, Sat 10am–1.30pm, Sun 11am–1.30pm).

❶ Tue–Sat 10am–2pm, 4.30pm–6.30pm, Sun 10am–2pm; admission: €3

Museo Conventual de las Descalzas

Plaza des las Descalzas lies to the north-east and is the location of the convent of the Discalced Carmelite nuns. The convent now houses the Museo de las Carmelitas Descalzas, which is dedicated to **sacred art**. Among the art works that are particularly worth seeing are the sculptures by Pedro de Mena and Pedro de Roldán, as well as a painting of St Theresa by Luca Giordano.

❶ Tue–Fri 10.30am–1.30pm, 5–6.30pm, Sat 10am–12 noon, 5pm –6.30pm, Sun 10am–12.30pm, admission €3.30

Palacio Consistorial

C. Infante Don Fernando, the main shopping street of the city, begins at Plaza de San Sebastián. On the right hand toward its northeastern end lies the Palacio Consistorial with its gorgeous inner courtyard, formerly a monastery cloister, with columns made of marble from the Sierra del Torcal.

Adjacent to the palace is the church of **Nuestra Señora de Los Remedios**. It contains a magnificent retable by Antonio Ribera.

More churches

The Iglesia San Zoilo (Plaza de Abastos) belongs to the monastery complex founded by the Catholic Monarchs. The late Gothic church has a wooden Mudejar ceiling and elaborate plaster work was added in the 17th century. The inside of the Iglesia de Belén (1628–1709; C. Belén) is a prime example of the exuberance of Andalusian Baroque.

**Dólmenes de Antequera

Insider Tip

With the megalithic tombs of Cueva de Menga, Viera and El Romeral, Antequera possesses three prehistoric grave sites that are among the best preserved and most impressive of their kind.

In the Cueva de Menga

The **Cueva de Menga and Cueva de Viera** passage graves are built right into the hill. The entrance is on the left-hand side, right next to a petrol station on the main road leading out of town toward Granada. The first grave has been dated to be from the 3rd millennium BC and is aligned to the course of the sun on an east-west axis. The whole grave has a total length of 25m/82ft and is up to 3m/10ft high. A passage supported by three pillars opens up into the oval burial chamber that consists of 15 megalith blocks. These blocks support immense stone slabs, one of which is thought to weigh 180t. One of the blocks of the left-hand wall has symbol-like drawings on it. The Cueva de Viera dates back to about the same time but is considerably smaller. A passage formed by stone slabs leads to an almost cubical burial chamber.

The **Cueva del Romeral** can be found by travelling a little further from the town in the direction of Granada as far as the N-331 junction and then turning left toward Córdoba. It is also from the 3rd millennium BC and consists of a 24m/80ft passage leading to two chambers.

❶ Opening times: Tue – Sat 9am – 6pm, Sun 9.30am – 2.30pm

AROUND ANTEQUERA

**Parque Natural de El Torcal

About 10km/6mi south of Antequera on the C-3310 in the direction of Villanueva de la Concepción is the entrance to the El Torcal Nature Reserve. The jagged mountains are a **fantastic karst mountainscape** that the processes of upfolding, storm and rain have created out of the porous limestone over the course of millennia. Teo marked circular trails run through the area. The green route is 1.5km/1mi long and takes 45 min. The yellow route is 2.5km/1.5mi long and at an elevation of 1200m/4000ft offers a fantastic view of the valley of Málaga.

Insider Tip

❶ Information centre: daily 10am – 7pm, winters until 5pm

Thousands of years in the making: the craggy rock formations in El Torcal

Southwest of the Torcal mountains, the Río Guadalhorce slices from the north down through the mountain range in a 3km/2mi-long gorge that is up to 400m/1300ft deep. This **spectacular rocky landscape**, the Garganta del Chorro, otherwise known as the Desfiladero de los Gaitanes, is a big attraction to hikers and climbers. North of the gorge, the river has been dammed to create four reservoirs; the most beautiful of them being the Gaitanejo reservoir. Griffon vultures and the occasional golden eagle also make their homes in the gorge.

*Garganta del Chorro

A good starting point for any exploration is **El Chorro railway station** (trains to and from ►Málaga), which can be reached from Antequera via the A-343 and MA 226. It is not advisable to try crossing over the gorge because the only route, the so-called Caminito del Rey, a stomach-churning walkway built at a dizzying height into the rock wall, has partially collapsed and is officially closed. Sneaking through the train tunnel in the gorge is illegal and yet still popular. A section of the gorge can be accessed from the El Chorro camp site.

A hike around the reservoir lakes affords some **good views of the gorge** and it is also possible to look down into the gorge from the higher altitude of the Tajo de la Encantada that can be reached via Bobastro. There is an information centre at the southern end of the Guadalteba-Guadalhorce reservoir that offers further information. The **ruins of Bobastro** (narrow road out of El Chorro) are evidence of a Mozarabic hill fort constructed in the 9th century by the rebel Ibn Hafsun, who had converted to Christianity. This was his headquarters during his resistance against the Umayyad and he had himself buried in the church there when he died in 917. Abd-ar Rahman III captured Bobastro in 927 and had the whole place destroyed.

Laguna de la Fuente de Piedra, near the village of the same name 18km/11mi northwest of Antequera, is **one of the last major breeding grounds for pink flamingos in Europe**. The birds gather in their thousands in spring on this salt lake that covers 13,000 ha/50 sq mi and stay to raise their young until August/September. The lagoon itself is fenced in, but there is a 20km/12mi path leading around the lake that provides observation points at regular intervals (bring binoculars). Besides flamingos, it is also possible to catch sight of Kentish plovers, black-winged stilts, cranes, gull-billed terns, storks, herons and perhaps even an osprey (information centre on the northeast corner of the lake.

*Laguna de la Fuente de Piedra

❶ Tue–Sun 10am–2pm, 4–8pm, Oct–March 4–6pm

Archidona, 15km/9mi northeast of Antequera, served the Carthaginians as a base during the Punic wars. A must to visit is the **Ermita de la Virgen de Gracia** with its lovely view of the surrounding countryside. It was once a mosque that was remodelled into a church at the end of the 15th century and possesses a baptismal font that was

Archidona

a gift from Isabella the Catholic. The centrepiece of town is the unusual octagonal Plaza Ochavada that was laid out in the 18th century by Francisco Astorga and Antonio González following a French model.

✳ Aracena

✦ B 6

Province: Huelva
Altitude: 732m/2402ft
Population: 7700

The mountain village of Aracena nestles in the midst of olive trees, fig and almond orchards amid the Sierra de Aracena at the extreme northwest tip of Andalucía.

Climatic health resort
Due to its climate, Aracena is a popular climatic spa. Local artisans typically create pottery but the processing of cork also provides many here with a livelihood. Sculptures from contemporary Andalusian artists are displayed everywhere throughout the centre of village.

History
The Romans were already taking an interest in the natural resources of this area in the first century. In the Middle Ages, Sancho of Portugal took the town from the Moors, but was forced to relinquish it to Castile in 1267. Alfonso X turned over Aracena to the Knights Templar, who erected a castle. Only the ruins of it remain today.

WHAT TO SEE IN ARACENA

Iglesia del Castillo
On the castle hill amidst the ruins, which the Portuguese controlled for a short time in the mid-13th century, stands the late Gothic Iglesia del Castillo (Nuestra Señora del Mayor Dolor), a church of the Knights Templar, who disbanded in 1312. It was built upon a mosque and the plinth of the minaret (12th century) today supports the bell tower. There is a terracotta tomb inside the church from the 16th century where the prior Pedro Vázquez is buried.

On Plaza Alta beneath the castle is a 15th-century storehouse, the **Cabildo Viejo**, that houses an exhibi-

> **!** *Taking a break in Alájar* **Insider Tip**
>
> **MARCO ⊕ POLO TIP**
>
> One place that is perfect for a short break along the A-470 is Alájar, 12km/7mi west of Aracena, with its central plaza and various small bars. Peña de Arias Montano, a few miles north, with the Virgen de los Angeles hermitage from the 16th century, offers a really fantastic view.

Aracena

INFORMATION
Oficina de Turismo
C. Pozo de la Nieve
E-21200 Aracena
Tel. 663 93 78 77
www.aracena.es
daily 10am – 2pm, 4pm – 6pm

Centro de Interpretación del Parque Natural
Plaza Alta
www.sierradearacena.org
Information is available about the Sierra de Aracena y Picos de Aroche nature reserve half-way up to the fortress.

EVENTS
Feria de Agosto
Music, dancing, bullfighting and fireworks in the third week of August.

Romería de Nuestra Señora de los Angeles
Pilgrimage around 7 – 9 September.

WHERE TO EAT
La Despensa de José Vicente €€€€
Avda. Andalucía, 53
Tel. 959 12 84 55
This restaurant is considered one of the best in town, specializing in pork and mushrooms. Usually only open for lunch, except for July/Aug.

Montecruz €€€€
Plaza San Pedro
Tel. 959 12 60 13
The speciality of the house is dishes with mushrooms. A nice view of the castle can be had from the upper room of the restaurant.

WHERE TO STAY
Finca Valbono €€
Crta. Carboneras, km 1
Tel. 959 12 77 11
The ideal place for a holiday in the country. This finca outside the town offers holiday cottages and a hotel with six rooms and 20 apartments, including a restaurant, sports facilities, a pool and a riding stable.

Los Castaños €
Avenida de Huelva, 5
Tel. 959 12 63 00
A hotel located near the caves with a restaurant and a nice view. The modestly furnished rooms have air conditioning and TV.

tion about the region as well as the tourist office. Taking pride of place opposite is the **Iglesia Nuestra Señora de la Asunción** that dates back to the 16 and 17th centuries.

The Gruta de las Maravillas extends over 1200m/4000ft inside the castle hill; an absolutely beautiful limestone cave with stalactites and stalagmites featuring twelve chambers and six lakes, in which the stone and crystal formations are reflected in glorious colours. The entrance to the cave can be found together with a modest mineral museum at the Ermita de San Pedro.

*Gruta de las Maravillas

❶ Tours: daily 10.30am – 1.30pm, 3 – 6pm; admission €8.50

Convento de Santa Catalina The convent of Santa Catalina, the church of which was once a synagogue, is attractive because of its portal and its most impressive late Gothic interior.

AROUND ARACENA

Jabugo Although Jabugo, 16km/10mi west of Aracena, possesses no tourist attractions, it is known far beyond Spain's borders. It is the **centre of the ham industry** , where the delicious air-cured hams that bear the name »pata negra« are produced from the semi-wild pigs living in the oak forests of the Sierra. Although the countryside round about Jabugo was declared a national park in 1989 (Parque Natural de la Sierra de Aracena y Picos de Aroche), most of the area is in private hands and is off-limits to hikers.

Almonaster la Real Almonaster la Real lies 27km/17mi west of Aracena. The **castle complex is of Moslem origin** and includes a mosque from the 10th century, which has integrated the remains of an earlier Visigoth structure, such as the lintel in the entrance area. It is noticeable that the church of San Martín includes some typical elements of the Manueline style of nearby Portugal; columns twisted like strands of rope and ornamentation richly decorated with shells and crabs. For a splendid view of the Sierra and the village, go to Mirador de San Cristóbal (outside the eastern entrance to the village).

Aroche Located 42km/26mi west of Aracena is Aroche. It was »Aruci Vetus« in Roman times. The Moors built a defensive wall on the Roman foundations. The Castillo de las Armas, also dating back to that time, has an inner court that serves as a bullfighting ring and houses an archaeological museum. For something more curious, visit the **Museo de Rosario** at the entrance to the village. It has 1,300 rosaries on display.

Río Tinto copper mines The mining district of Río Tinto begins south of Aracena, a desolate, scarred landscape, barren of vegetation. The Río Tinto river lives up to its name in that it really is tainted red from the metabolism of a unique ecological system in the river. For a long time it was incorrectly assumed that the river had been polluted by mining in the area. Meanwhile large parts of the region have been placed under protection. Even NASA is doing research along the Río Tinto since the same minerals can be found there as on Mars.

Minas de Ríotinto and Nerva are the main centres of the copper mining district that was mined as early as Iberian and Roman times. From 1873 to 1954 it belonged to the British Río Tinto mining company. A great deal can be learned about its history in the **Museo**

Jewel of the Spanish food industry: Jabugo ham (jamón ibérico)

Minero. The main attraction is a reconstruction of a Roman mine and a luxurious railway carriage that belonged to a maharajah, although it was originally built for Queen Victoria in 1892 in Birmingham on the occasion of a royal visit to India. It was transported to Ríotinto for a visit by Alfonso XIII. On the edge of town is the Barrio Bellavista with its Victorian houses and a Presbyterian cemetery and church built for the British employees of the mining company. Two miles north of Río Tinto is a Roman burial site, the **Necrópolis de la Dehesa** from the 2nd century, that is open for tours.

At the giant ***Parque Minero near Aracena** it is possible to see at how ore was mined up until the end of 2001. Two **railway excursions** of various lengths travel along the Río Tinto in Victorian cars to Corte Atalaya, which is **Europe's largest opencast mine** and descends to a depth of 330m/1100ft.

❶ Information and tickets at the ticket office in the Museo Minero; museum opening times: daily 10.30am – 3pm, 4pm – 7pm, July 16 – Sept until 8pm; museum admission: €4; www.parquemineroderiotinto.com

* Arcos de la Frontera

✦ D 8

Province: Cádiz
Altitude: 185m/607ft
Population: 31,400

Arcos is without a doubt one of Andalucía's most beautiful »white villages«. To find out why, just take a walk through the maze of steep, winding lanes in the old part of town, the layout of which is obviously Moorish.

**Picturebook
white village**
For the best view of Arcos de la Frontera, approach it from the east. Houses like little white cubes cling in a semi-circle to the rock wall **160m/525ft above the Río Guadalete**, and out of the tangle of houses jut the towers of the main churches.

History
The Carthaginians and later the Romans, who called their settlement Colonia Arcensis, made use of the strategic location on the top of the rocks to keep a watch over wide swathes of the countryside. As of the 11th century the town was called Medina Arkosh and had become the capital of a taifa. After 1250, the town came to be called Arcos and was part of Ferdinand III's Christian kingdom; but the population remained Moslem until 1264 when, under Alfonso X, they were driven out after a revolt against Christian domination.

WHAT TO SEE IN ARCOS DE LA FRONTERA

***Plaza del
Cabildo**
Plaza del Cabildo is the town's highest point and at the same time the centre of the old part of town. The observation terrace on the plaza offers a **breathtaking view of the landscape far below**. The town hall stands at the southwest corner alongside a castle of Arab origin that was completely rebuilt in the 15th century (now under private ownership). The Casa del Corregidor opposite, a 16th-century magistrate's residence, is now given over to Arcos' own parador, and to the right of the entrance is its bar offering a splendid view. The most impressive building on the plaza is the ***Basílica Menor de Santa María de la Asunción** with its massive square tower that soars above all the neighbouring buildings. The tower and the portal zone were created in Baroque, whereas the nave is primarily 16th-century work that replaced an earlier church, which was itself erected on the foundation of the original Friday mosque. The finely worked west portal is a **splendid example of the Plateresque style** of the 16th century. In the sanctuary, take a look at the late Gothic fan vault as well as the 17th-century high altar retable with the theme of Mary's assumption. The oldest part of the structure is the apse behind it with elements in the Mudejar style. In the second chapel to the right stands a statue of the town's patron, the »Virgen de las Nieves«.

San Pedro
Santa María's neighbour, San Pedro, was built on the remains of a Moorish fortress. The members of both communities spent decades feuding with each other in a most unchristian manner. The squabble was only settled by a papal dictum in the 18th century. The Gothic interior holds a fine high altar retable from the 16th century and shows Saints Peter and Jerome. Saint Ignatius and the Virgin Mary are to the left and right of them, as depicted by Francisco Pacheco, the tutor of Diego Velázquez.

Arcos de la Frontera

INFORMATION
Oficina de Turismo
Cuesta de Belén, 5
E-11630 Arcos de la Frontera
Tel. 956 70 22 64
www.arcosdelafrontera.es
Winter: Mon – Sat 9.30am – 6.30pm
Summer: 9.30am – 2pm, 3pm – 7.30pm
Sun always 10am – 2pm

EVENTS
Semana Santa
With a bull run on the open streets on
Easter Sunday.

Feria de San Miguel
Dance competition and bullfighting in
honour of the town's patron saint on
29 September.

WHERE TO EAT
The best way to have an inexpensive
meal: stroll through the tapa bars in
Calles Espinosa and Marqués de Torresoto.

Taberna de la Viuda €
Plaza Rafael Pérez de Álamo
Tel. 956 70 12 09
The legs of ham hanging from the ceiling make quite a picture; underneath
the whole spectrum of Andalusian tapas
is available. With flamenco music in the
background Chef Alonso also like to
serve larger portions of meat or fish.

WHERE TO STAY
*Parador de Arcos
de la Frontera* €€€
Plaza del Cabildo
Tel. 956 70 05 00
www.parador.es, 24 rooms

A stylistically authentic reconstruction of
the Casa del Corregidor offers a wonderful view of the old town. The best
rooms have a balcony

Marqués de Torresoto €€ **Insider Tip**
Marqués de Torresoto, 4
Tel. 956 70 42 56
www.hotelmarquesdetorresoto.com,
15 rooms
The former palace of the Marqués de
Torresoto, dating from the 17th century,
offers reserved, stylish rooms and an
unforgettable breakfast in the patio
arcade.

Arcos Gardens €€
Crta. Arcos – Algar, km 3
Tel. 956 70 41 31; 44 Zi.
Elegant Andalusian 17th century country
house with lots of atmosphere, surrounded by olive trees and bougain-
villea, as well as a golf course

El Convento €
Maldonado, 2; Tel. 956 70 23 33
www.hotelelconvento.es; 13 rooms
Hotel in the centre of town, in a former
monastery. A few rooms are named
after famous people, including poets.
Terrace with a beautiful view.

La Casa Grande €
C. Maldonada, 10
Tel. 956 70 39 30
www.lacasagrande.net
Family hotel in a house from 1729 in the
old part of town with a view as fine as
that from the parador as it is located
right on the cliff. Wonderful roof
terrace, whitewashed inner courtyard
and individually furnished rooms.

Arcos de la Frontera rises up on the north side of the Guadalete

Old town   A walk through the old town reveals several aristocratic palaces from the 16th and 17th centuries including the Renaissance façade of the Palacio de Mayorazgo right next to the church of San Pedro, the Convento de la Encarnación with its Plateresque portal and the Palacio del Marqués de Torresoto which has a patio in the street of the same name. The Gothic-Mudejar façade of the Palacio del Conde de Aguila from the 15th century in the Cuesta de Belén is the oldest in the town.

AROUND ARCOS DE LA FRONTERA

Bornos   Bornos, about 10km/6mi northeast of Arcos alongside the reservoir of the same name, grew around a Moorish castle that gained its current appearance primarily in the 15th and 16th centuries. The church of Santo Domingo de Guzmán with its late Gothic and Baroque features is also worth seeing. Beyond the town centre are the remains of the Roman settlement »Clarissa Aurelia«. The CA-6102 leads from Bornos to **Espera**, where there is a very well-preserved Moorish castle.

Villamartín   Villamartín, 9km/5.5mi east of Bornos, was spaciously laid-out in the 16th century with churches and palaces of nobles. That there were settlements here already in prehistoric times is shown by the dolmen of Alberite, 4km/2.5mi south of the village, dated at around 4000 BC.

★★ Baeza · Úbeda

 J 5/6

Province: Jaén

Almost hidden in the northeast of Andalucía and some miles apart, two architectural pearls of the Renaissance slumber practically untouched by mainstream tourism: the towns of Baeza and Úbeda. The drive there is certainly worthwhile because the once prosperous citizens had magnificent palaces built for themselves that have survived almost unchanged, creating a unique, wholly Renaissance townscape. The architect Andrés de Vandelvira was especially active in this region. Both towns are listed as UNESCO world heritage monuments since 2003.

BAEZA

Altitude: 790m/2592ft
Population: 16,360

The Visigoths expanded the former Roman settlement Beatia to the extent that it became a bishopric. Under the Moors it was for some time the capital of a taifa, until Ferdinand III entered it victorious in 1227 and made the place **one of the most important bases for the Reconquista of Andalucía**. Baeza gained a university in 1542. Its first rector was Juan de Ávila, and Juan de la Cruz also worked there. Baeza experienced its greatest flowering in the 16th century when it was a border town and trading centre between Mancha in Castile and Andalucía.

History

Baeza lies surrounded by fields of olives and grain and by vineyards high above the valley of the Río Guadalquivir. The **Plaza del Pópulo**, Baeza's meeting place and the site of its most beautiful Renaissance ensemble, can be seen on the right directly at the edge of the old town. The **Fuente de los Leones** fountain in its centre is adorned with four lion figures from the Roman ruins of Cástulo near Linares and an Iberian-Roman statue of a woman. She is said to represent Imilce of Castillo, the wife of the Carthaginian general Hannibal.
The **Antigua Carnicería** stretches away to the left of the fountain. The former meat market was built in the middle of the 16th century and is now an historical archive. In today's terms, its **features are astounding** for a building with such a mundane purpose. It has a gallery and an unusually large and magnificent coat of arms belonging to Charles V.

Western old city

Baeza

INFORMATION
Oficina de Turismo
Plaza del Pópulo, s/n
E-23440 Baeza
Tel. 953 77 99 82
http://turismo.baeza.net

SHOPPING
Casa del Aceite
Paseo de la Constitución, 9
www.casadelaceite.com
Various varieties of olive oil are available
here, including oil from organically
grown olives.

EVENTS
Romería del
Cristo de la Yedra
On the first weekend in September,
music, dance and the friars' parade
accompanied by decorated carts and
riders on horseback.

WHERE TO EAT
❶ *Andrés de Vandelvira* €€€€
San Francisco, 14   **Insider**
Tel. 953 74 81 72   **Tip**
www.vanddelvira.es
The finest regional cuisine is served in
the gallery around the cloister of the
Iglesia de San Francisco. Baeza's culinary
specialty comes from the sea, but dried
due to the distance; and is called Bacalao (dried cod) al estilo de Baeza.

❷ *La Almazara* €€€€
Pasaje Cardenal Benavides, 15
Tel. 953 74 16 50
www.restaurantelaalmazarabaeza.com
Goof Andalusian cooking, including pasta dishes that can be enjoyed on the terrace in the summer. Attentive service.

❸ *La Góndola* €€€
Portales de Carbonería, 13
Tel. 953 74 29 84
www.asadorlagondola.com
Beef from the grill, tasty fish and shrimps
served in nicely furnished rooms beneath
the Paseo de la Constitución arcades.
Also very popular among the locals

WHERE TO STAY
❶ *TRH Baeza* €
Concepción, 3
Tel. 953 74 81 30
www.trhhoteles.com
Modern hotel with a Renaissance patio
in a former convent from the 16th century. The rooms are arranged around the
cloister of the former convent.

❷ *Hospedería Fuentenueva* €
Carmen, 15, tel. 953 74 31 00
www.fuentenueva.com, 13 rooms
Lovingly decorated, the design hotel is in
a house from the 19th century, which is
also a former women's prison. It is in the
tallest building in town, with a library,
cafeteria, Japanese garden, exhibition
hall.

❸ *Juanito* €
Puché Pardo, 57
Tel. 953 74 00 40
www.juanitobaeza.com, 37 rooms
Family business with a garden terrace on
the edge of the city. The cooking in the
restaurant is authentic to the Jaén province. The perdiz (partridge) and cabrito
(baby goat) are especially delicious.

❹ *Puerta de la Luna* €€
Canónigo Melgares Raya
Tel. 953 74 70 19

www.hotelpuertadelaluna.com; 44 Zi.
Luxury accommodation in a 16th century house near the cathdral. Beautiful
rooms with all modern comfort. The hotel also offers its guests a very good restaurant and a bar. There is an outdoor
pool and on warm days the food is
served on the pretty patio.

❺ *La Casa del Seise* €
Conde de Romanones, 9
Tel. 953 74 08 23
www.lacasadelseise.com
3 apartments
Simple accommodation in an 18th
century house with room for up to
6 people. Suitable for families

The Plateresque **Casa del Pópulo** on the east side of the plaza is by
no means overshadowed by the meat market in terms of beauty. Behind the six double doors on the ground floor, chamber clerks once
produced documents for the court that sat in session on the upper
floor. Today, Baeza's tourist office occupies the building.

Next door to the right of the Casa del Pópulo are the **Puerta de Jaén
city gate** and the **triumphal arch, the Arco de Villalar**, that was
erected in 1521 to commemorate the crushing of the revolt of the
»comuneros«. These were several Castilian cities that had joined together under the leadership of Juan de Padilla and demanded more
rights from Emperor Charles V.

Up the steps to the left of Casa del Pópulo and then on further to the
left is Plaza Santa Cruz. Almost the whole length of C. Beato Avia
along the way to Plaza Santa Cruz is taken up by the front of the **Antigua Universidad**, which was founded as a university in 1542 and
converted into a grammar school in 1875. A portal crowned by a
medallion depicting the Holy Trinity forms the entrance to the inner
court where there stands a simple monument to the poet **Antonio
Machado**, who was a French teacher at the school from 1912 to 1919
and died in exile in France in 1939.

**Plaza Santa
Cruz**

The most impressive building on the plaza is the ****Palacio de Jabalquinto** constructed at the end of the 15th century by Juan Guas
and Enrique Egas for the Countess of Jabalquinto and Benavente. The
Isabelline façade is without parallel. Its dressed blocks like cut dia-
monds and its Gothic buttresses are flanked by two large columns
that broaden towards the top into small pulpits at the apex, a feature
characteristic of Andalucía. The palace encloses a pretty patio and
possesses a monumental Baroque stairway.
❶ Mon – Fri 9am – 2pm

It is worth taking a look at some of the late Gothic frescoes in the late
Romanesque **Santa Cruz** church across from the palace that gives the
plaza its name. Next to the church is the museum of the Santa Cruz
friars whose order was founded in 1540.

Santa Cruz

A purely Isabelline façade on the Palacio de Jabalquinto

Plaza Santa María   It is only a few paces from there to Plaza de Santa María, dominated by the cathedral, although a fairly weathered fountain in the form of a triumphal arch bearing the coat of arms of Philip II also stands out. The Gothic ***Santa María cathedral** was erected on the foundations of a former mosque on the south side of the plaza and remodelled in 1567 and 1593. The Puerta de la Luna in the west is still Moorish while Puerta del Perdón, spanning a lane in the south, exhibits a Gothic style. Andrés de Vandelvira helped to fashion the interior and it is worth looking at the **Capilla Mayor** with its stellar vault and the elaborate, fully gilded retable with its spiral columns. The masterly rendering of the choir screen is by Bartolomé de Jaén, who also fashioned the screen in the Capilla del Sagrario to the right of the Capilla Mayor. The six-sided, wrought-iron pulpit was made in 1580 and shows the apostles Paul and Andrew as well as four former bishops of Baeza. Some arches from the former mosque are included in the cloister.

Connected to the cathedral are the **Casas Consistoriales Altas**. They were built at the end of the 15th century and bear the coats of arms of Joanna the Mad and Philip II. Across the way, the seminarians immortalized themselves in bull's blood on the façade of the former Seminario Conciliar San Felipe Neri – today the international Antonio Machado University.

Baeza

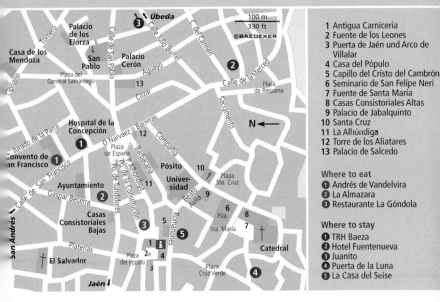

1 Antigua Carnicería
2 Fuente de los Leones
3 Puerta de Jaén und Arco de Villalar
4 Casa del Pópulo
5 Capillo del Cristo del Cambrón
6 Seminario de San Felipe Neri
7 Fuente de Santa María
8 Casas Consistoriales Altas
9 Palacio de Jabalquinto
10 Santa Cruz
11 La Alhóndiga
12 Torre de los Aliatares
13 Palacio de Salcedo

Where to eat
❶ Andrés de Vandelvira
❷ La Almazara
❸ Restaurante La Góndola

Where to stay
❶ TRH Baeza
❷ Hotel Fuentenueva
❸ Juanito
❹ Puerta de la Luna
❺ La Casa del Seise

Head back from the cathedral past Plaza del Pópulo to Paseo de la Constitución, the centre of Baeza. Its northern end is marked by Plaza de España with the Torre de los Aliatares clock tower, named after a Moorish tribe.

Paseo de la Constitución

La Alhóndiga can be seen on the east side of the paseo, the former grain market hall with its triple-arched gallery. It is connected at the back to an old, beautifully decorated granary (el pósito), which directly supplied the market hall.

On the west side of the paseo is the **Casas Consistoriales Bajas**, which was built at the beginning of the 17th century as a town hall and was specifically provided with a balcony so that high-ranking guests could follow the festivities on the plaza below.

There are also **beautiful palaces** along the Calle de San Pablo that leads off to the north from Plaza de España: first the Gothic Palacio de los Condes de Garcíez with an inner courtyard and a double portico, then the castle-like Palacio Cerón and Casa Acuña, and finally Casa Cabrera with its Plateresque façade.

Calle de San Pablo

To the west of Paseo de la Constitución the main place of interest is the town hall (Ayuntamiento) on Paseo Cardinal Benavides. It was

Ayunta-miento

built in 1559 as a courthouse and prison and is captivating with its lovely balconies, decorative rosettes and magnificent coats of arms including that of Philip II.

Santa María del Alcázar y San Andrés The church of Santa María del Alcázar y San Andrés a bit to the west of the town hall is is consecrated to the patron saint of the city. Its chancel was designed by Vandelvira, and the **nine Gothic panel paintings** that depict themes from the New Testament in the local folk tradition are particularly worth seeing. It was in this church that Ferdinand III brought into being the order of the »200 Archers of the Lord of Santiago« that, despite its name, especially venerated Saint Andrew and Saint Isidor. They were feared enemies of the Moors. Only nobility from around Baeza were admitted to membership.

ÚBEDA

Population: 36,000
Altitude: 748m/2454ft

The Andalusian Salamanca Baeza was impressive enough, but Úbeda, 9km/5.5mi further to the northeast, definitively surpasses its sister city with the harmony of its old town and the number of its Renaissance buildings, which has earned it the nickname »The Andalusian Salamanca«. Add to that the fact that the city is ideally suited as the starting point for an excursion into the ▶Sierra de Cazorla and that extremely beautiful pottery and objects fashioned from esparto grass can be purchased in the barrio of San Millán in the old town, for example, and Úbeda is clearly not to be missed.

History The Moors called the place »Obdah«, fortified it and developed it to a first period of prosperity. Following the Christian conquest in 1234, some noble families living there, like the Los Cobos and the Molinas, rose to be among the most powerful families in Spain. They reached the apex of their influence in the 16th and 17th centuries and the city profited too, as they attempted to outdo each other in the grandeur of their palaces.

**Plaza de Vázquez de Molina Nowhere else is Úbeda's former greatness more manifest than on Plaza de Vázquez de Molina, the main square at the edge of the hill upon which the old town is built as it falls abruptly towards the Guadalquivir basin. The alcázar once stood over this precipice; today there is a wonderful view from here out over the groves of olive trees and the Sierra de Cazorla.

The eastern corner of the plaza is dominated by the ***Palacio de las Cadenas** (Palace of Chains) and is nowadays the site of the town hall

Úbeda

INFORMATION
Oficina de Turismo
Palacio Marqués de Contadero
Baja del Marqués, 4
E-23400 Úbeda
Tel. 953 77 92 04
www.ubeda.es

SHOPPING
The main shopping streets in the city
are Calle Mesones and Calle Otopo
Cobos, plus the streets between Plaza
de Andalucía and the Hospital de
Santiago.

EVENT
Semana Santa
Holy Week

Fiesta de San Miguel
Celebrated since 1234 at the end of
September with fireworks, bullfighting
and street festivals.

WHERE TO EAT
❷ *Parador Restaurante Nacional
del Condestable Dávalos*
Plaza de Vázquez de Molina
Tel. 953 75 03 45
The family-run restaurant has modern
furnishings and serves Andalusian dishes
with an innovative touch.

❶ *Zeitúm* €€€€
San Juan de la Cruz, 10
Tel. 953 75 58 00; www.zeitum.com
closed Mondays
Restaurant in a 17th century house with
three dining rooms, all of which are
decorated around the theme of olives.
Here as well Andalusian dishes are given
an innovative preparation with the best
regional olive oil.

❸ *El Seco* €
Corazón de Jesús, 8
Tel. 953 79 14 52
www.restauranteelseco.com
Whether albóndigas (meatballs), tortilla or
mushroom dishes, the small tavern offers
inexpensive and good home-cooking.

WHERE TO STAY
❹ *Parador de Úbeda* €€€€
Plaza Vázquez de Molina, s / n
Tel. 953 75 03 45
www.parador.es, 31 rooms
Unbeatable location right in the historic
centre in the Renaissance palace of
Conde de Dávalos with a fantastic patio.

❸ *Palacio de la Rambla* €€
Plaza del Marqués, 1   **Insider
Tip**
Tel. 953 75 01 96
www.palaciodelarambla.com, 8 rooms
One of Spain's most beautiful inns. The
16th-century palace is laid out around a
Renaissance patio; the rooms are outfitted
with wicker furniture and local an Portu-
guise pottery. The aristocratic owners live
under the same roof.

❷ *María de Molina* €€
Plaza del Ayuntamiento, s/n
Tel. 953 79 53 56
www.hotel-maria-de-molina.com
The hotel is in a 16th-century palace
on the town hall plaza with a patio and
restaurant/bar.

❶ *Husa Rosaleda de Don Pedro* €
Obispo Toral, 2
Tel. 953 79 61 11; www.husa.es
Beautiful rooms with wooden furniture.
For the guests there is a terrace, a spa
and an outdoor pool. The restaurant
serves Andalusian and Spanish food.

and tourist information office. The noted architect Andrés de Vandelvira built it for Don Juan Vázquez de Molina and chose a different form of column for each of the three storeys – Corinthian at the bottom, Ionic in the middle and Caryatid at the top. Two lions holding a shield guard the entrance. The name of the palace is explained by the chains enclosing the forecourt. The church of **Santa María de los Reales Alcázares** across from the Palace of Chains was built on top of the main mosque and instead of a bell tower has two slender bell supports. Inside there are magnificent Gothic chapels and Renaissance choir screens by Bartolomé de Jaén to admire. The cloister, once part of the mosque, has an atmosphere all its own and was remodelled into the Gothic style.

Next door to the Santa Maria on the left stands the **Cárcel del Obispo**, the former bishop's prison, now the courthouse. To the left is where the Marqués de Mancera, the viceroy of Peru, had his city palace built in the 16th century.

The most outstanding building is the ***Sacra Capilla del Salvador** on the northern side, a masterpiece of Renaissance architecture that was designed by Diego de Siloé, Andrés de Vandelvira and Alfonso Ruiz and was built in the first half of the 16th century. It was financed by Francisco de los Cobos, a state secretary to Emperor Charles I, who is buried in the crypt. The main façade, adorned with reliefs, is flanked by two low, round towers. An allegorical depiction of faith and justice as well as the Los Cobos and Molina coats of arms can be seen on the arch over the entrance portal, above which is a towering image of Christ the Saviour framed by Saint Peter and Saint Paul. The retable, decorated solely with the figure of Christ, stands behind a splendid choir screen beneath the high dome of the Capilla Mayor. It is the last remaining figure of a group of statues called the *Transfiguration of Christ* by Alonso de Berruguete that was destroyed by fire in 1936 during the civil war. The sacristy, in which some church silver is stored, was marvellously fashioned by Vandelvira.

Next, to the right behind the church, is the **Hospital del Salvador**, an excellent example of the various forms of column design used in the Renaissance. The façade of Francisco de los Cobos' palace is still standing to the left behind the chapel. Also to the left of the church is the Parador Condestable Dávalos, a two-storey Renaissance palace with three beautiful patios named after Fernando Dávalos, a general of the Castilian king, Juan II.

Sacra Capilla: Mon – Sat 10am – 2pm, 4pm – 6.30pm, Sun 11.15am – 2pm, 4pm – 7pm; admission: €3

Casa de los Salvajes C. Horno Contado leads away to the left from in front of the Salvador to Plaza del Primero de Mayo. Here the Casa de los Salvajes can be seen on the left. Its name translates as the »House of Savages«, so named because above the beautifully-worked portal are two »savag-

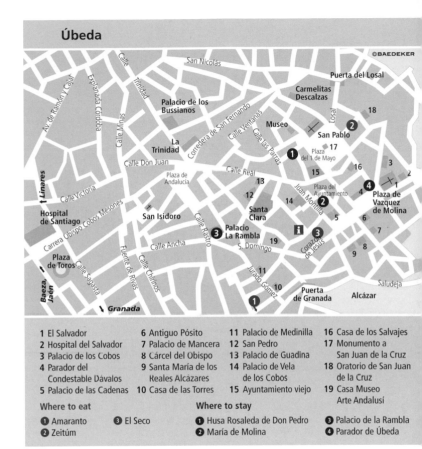

Úbeda

©BAEDEKER

Puerta del Losal

Carmelitas
Descalzas

Palacio de los
Bussianos

Museo

San Pablo

La
Trinidad

Plaza
del 1 de Mayo

Plaza de
Andalucia

Calle Real

Plaza del
Ayuntamiento

Plaza de
Vazquez
de Molina

Hospital
de Santiago

San Isidoro

Santa
Clara

Palacio
La Rambla

S. Domingo

Plaza
de Toros

Puerta
de Granada

Alcázar

Baeza,
Jaén

Granada

1 El Salvador	6 Antiguo Pósito	11 Palacio de Medinilla	16 Casa de los Salvajes
2 Hospital del Salvador	7 Palacio de Mancera	12 San Pedro	17 Monumento a
3 Palacio de los Cobos	8 Cárcel del Obispo	13 Palacio de Guadina	San Juan de la Cruz
4 Parador del	9 Santa María de los	14 Palacio de Vela	18 Oratorio de San Juan
Condestable Dàvalos	Reales Alcàzares	de los Cobós	de la Cruz
5 Palacio de las Cadenas	10 Casa de las Torres	15 Ayuntamiento viejo	19 Casa Museo
			Arte Andalusí

Where to eat

❶ Amaranto   ❸ El Seco

❷ Zeitúm

Where to stay

❶ Husa Rosaleda de Don Pedro   ❸ Palacio de la Rambla

❷ María de Molina   ❹ Parador de Úbeda

es« wearing skins and holding the coat of arms of the house's owner,
Francisco de Yago, the bishop's chamberlain.

The Plaza del Primero de Mayo that comes next on the tour was once
the market place, bull ring, and the place of execution for those convicted by the Inquisition. In its centre stands a memorial cross for
Juan de la Cruz, the mystic and companion of Saint Theresa of Ávila.
To the left is the town hall (Ayuntamiento viejo) built in the 16th
century.

**Plaza del
Primero de
Mayo**

*San Pablo church overlooks the northern side of the plaza, a building from the time of the Reconquista with an apse from 1380. After
the Capilla del Salvador, it is the most remarkable church building in

Palacio Condestable Dávalos now houses a parador

the city. A figure of the Apostle Paul is placed on the middle pillar of the Isabellian main portal from 1511, while above it angels float around the Virgin Mary. A fountain was set into the outside wall in 1559 and decrees were once proclaimed from a niche to the left of the portal. Worth taking a look at on the inside are the Plateresque Capilla del Camarero Vago by Vandelvira and the marvellous grille work.

Museo Arqueológico

The Casa Mudejar, Úbeda's archaeological museum, displays its treasures in C. Cervantes that leads away from the church portal.

Oratorio y Museo de San Juan de la Cruz

The mystic, Juan de la Cruz, died in 1591 in Úbeda. A chapel was erected in the 17th century over the house where he passed away, which is now a museum displaying relics and personal objects once belonging to the saint. The chapel is at the end of C. Juan de la Cruz that leads off from the northwest side of the plaza.

❶ Tue – Sun 11am – 1pm, 5pm – 7pm; admission: €2

Calle Real

The city's elegant shopping boulevard, C. Real, can be reached by taking C. Marqués de Molina from the southern corner of Plaza Primero del Mayo. Branching off from C. Real is C. Juan Montilla with another beautiful Renaissance palace, the **Palacio de Vela de los**

Cobos, which has a series of arcades on the upper storey that run around the corner. On the next street to the left is the **Monasterio de Santa Clara**. It was founded in 1290, but except for the Mudejar gate of the monastery chapel, its appearance is Baroque.

Next along C. Real is the Palacio de Guadiana and on the alley that branches off from there is the church of **San Pedro** which has Romanesque origins although it was faced with a Renaissance façade in the 17th century.

Finally, you come to **Plaza de Andalucía**, the traffic hub of the town. The Torre del Reloj (clock tower) stands here, built in the 16th century on top of the old town fortifications.

Hospital de Santiago

Somewhat outside the city centre, spread out along C. Otopo Cobos west of Plaza de Andalucía, is the Hospital de Santiago, a large, plain Renaissance structure with an arcade patio that Vandelvira began in 1565 and in which he died ten years later.

More Renaissance palaces

More Renaissance palaces can be found by heading south away from Plaza de Andalucía on C. Rastro. **Palacio de Rambla** is on Plaza del Marqués, and **Palacio de Medinilla** is on C. Jurado Gomez that branches off from the plaza; followed by Casa de las Torres, an exquisite urban palace with a Plateresque portal and a filigreed balustrade. This building was also once occupied by the Condestable Dávalos. Finally, winding up at **Plaza de San Lorenzo**, there is a church of the same name and Puerta de Granada, a well-preserved part of the fortification ring.

Casa Museo Arte Andalusí

In a 16th century townhouse Casa Museo Arte Andalusí exhibits Andalusian antiques, including furniture and Moorish architectural fragments from the 11th to the 16th century, which the owner of the museum collected over many decades.

❶ Calle Narváez, 11; Mon – Sat 11am – 2pm, 5pm – 8pm, admission: €1.50

Museo de la Alfarería Paco Tito

The Museo de la Alfarería Paco Tito, north-east of the old city and outside of the limits of the map on page 179, exhibits a cross-section of Spain's traditional pottery in its 12 rooms and naturally places the focus on local and Andalusian products (opening hours: Tue–Sun 10am–1pm, 4–7pm, Sat 10am–2pm).

❶ Calle Valencia, 2; Mon – Sat 8am – 2pm, 4pm – 8.30pm, Sun 10am – 2pm; free admission

AROUND BAEZA AND ÚBEDA

Puente del Obispo

How olive oil is produced, what can be made from it and the cultural history of the olive tree are all told in the **Museo de la Cultura del**

Olivo in the Hacienda de la Laguna. A pleasant hotel and a restaurant also belong to this 17th-century country estate in which, naturally, almost everything is prepared with olive oil.

To get there: A-316 toward Jaén, turn right after about 9km/5.5mi beyond Puente del Otopo and another 2km/1.5mi

Hours: Tue – Sun: summer 10.30am – 1.30pm, 5.30 – 8pm; spring and fall 10.30am – 1.30pm, 4.30pm – 7pm; winter 10.30am – 1.30pm, 4 – 6.30pm; admission: €3.60; www.museodelaculturadelolivo.com

Hotel: http://ehlaguna.com/hotel.

Vandelvira's buildings   Andrés de Vandelvira also left behind evidence of his architecture in the villages round about Úbeda. 10km/6mi west of Úbeda in the village of Canena is a Moorish castillo that he remodelled into a palace with a beautiful court. Sabiote, situated 9km/5.5mi to the northeast on the edge of a plateau, has a large Moorish castillo and a Carmelite convent as well as a church he designed. Finally, take the N-322 in a north-easterly direction past Torreperogil – a pretty village with picturesque streets – to Villacarillo, where he created the impressive church of **La Asunción**, one of the province's most important works of the Renaissance.

Iznatoraf   The mountain village of Iznatoraf can be reached by driving on past Villacarillo and taking a short mountain road to the left. Iznatoraf's parish church from 1602 is a beautiful example of country Renaissance architecture. There is a magnificent view of other villages and mountains from here. If the mood takes you, drive on to the pretty village of Villanueva del Arzotopo, where Juan de la Cruz used to live, and then on to Beas de Segura, which is dominated by a mighty castle. Saint Theresa of Ávila founded a convent for Discalced Carmelite nuns here.

✴ Cabo de Gata

 L 8

Province: Almería

Nowhere in Andalucía is the presence of Africa felt more strongly than in Cabo de Gata, jutting out into the sea southeast of ▸Almería. This has nothing to do with cultural heritage but rather with the prevailing climatic conditions that characterize the countryside. Here, in the extreme southeast of Spain, it rains scarcely 25 days a year.

Nature and bathing   The hot, dry climate leaves its impression on the landscape. The brown and occasionally rugged rocks punctuated by volcanic hills

Cabo de Gata is the south-easternmost point of Spain

only have a sparse covering of vegetation that includes esparto grass, gorse, agave, prickly pears, European fan palms and a grove of date palms here and there, sprinkled among whitewashed houses facing the azure of the sea – **echoes of North Africa**. Fan palms, seldom taller than half a metre/two feet, along with the Cretan date palm, are, by the way, the only palm species native to Europe. Esparto grass is used to produce wicker chairs, handbags and baskets – such as can be found on sale in Níjar and other places in large numbers. The local animals are mostly birds and reptiles; including among the more rare species, the trumpeter finch, Bonelli's eagle, thekla larks, flamingos, sandpipers, pied avocets, snub-nosed vipers and geckos. Scorpions also live here.

This unique and still relatively unspoiled countryside belongs in administrative terms to the district of Níjar near ▶Almería and is under conservation protection as the **Parque Natural Cabo de Gata-Níjar**. The tourist infrastructure is consequently somewhat undeveloped – no huge concrete hotels or tourist resorts, but rather isolated bungalow parks on the edge of villages and more modest hotels. Only San José has grown a little larger. Anyone spending their holidays here is probably looking to **experience nature**, mainly involving hiking and cycling, and will be able to bathe on beaches that are among the most beautiful in Andalucía, if only because they are not yet overcrowded.

Cabo de Gata

INFORMATION
Centro de Información
Avenida de San José - Nijar, 27
E-04118 San José, Tel. 950 38 02 99
www.cabodegata-nijar.com
daily 10am – 2pm, 5pm – 8pm
during winter Sun only 10am – 2pm

Centro de Visitantes las Amoladeras
between Almería and the cape before
the turn-off to Ruescas
Tel. 950 38 02 99

WHERE TO EAT AND WHERE TO STAY
Mikasa €€
In Agua Amarga
Crta. de Carboneras, s / n
Tel. 950 13 80 73, fax 950 13 81 29
www.mikasasuites.com, 16 rooms
Quiet, tastefully and lovingly designed
hotel with two restaurants, spa, whirlpool, sauna and tennis court. The rooms
have either a terrace or a balcony. The
interior has been an inspiration for
leading Spanish home-decorating
magazines.

Hotel Cala Chica €€
In Las Negras, C. Hélice, 1
Tel. 950 38 81 81
www.calachica.com, 26 rooms
Quite new, chic hotel 150m/500ft from
the beach. Restaurant, pool and roof
terrace, where parties occasionally are
held.

Cortijo del Aire €
Between Pozo de los Frailes and
Los Escullos
Tel. 950 38 94 01
www.cortijodelaire.com
8 rooms and 2 studios
open: Easter – Oct.
Very beautiful bed & breakfast in
the middle of the nature reserve,
800m/2600ft from the sea; Swiss
owner. Courses and workshops (music,
painting etc.) are also held here.

WHAT TO SEE IN THE CABO DE GATA REGION

West coast The cape can be reached from Almería by travelling on the well-sign-
posted secondary road that runs parallel to the west coast. It skirts
the fishing village of San Miguel de Cabo de Gata, behind which the
extensive **seawater salt flats** begin. They are still being worked. In
the neighbouring village, La Almadraba de Monteleva , mountains of
salt are piled up in the salt works near an abandoned fortified church
– simultaneously providing a habitat for large colonies of flamingoes
and stilts that can be observed from a hut (with a coin-operated
telescope) situated to the left of the road at about the halfway point.
To the right of the road, the long Playa de Cabo de Gata stretches
along the coast.

After La Almadraba the road winds up the mountainside until, beyond one tight bend, a fantastic view of the cape with the lighthouse
suddenly unfolds ahead. Although the name ***Cabo de Gata** liter-

ally means »Cape Cat«, it is actually a corruption of Cabo de Agata, which means »Agate Cape«. There is a breathtaking view from the platform beneath the lighthouse down to the volcanic rocks below, some of which bear names like »Las Sirenas«. A hiking trail leads from the cape along the top of the cliffs to San José.

Anyone wishing to travel by car to San José will have to retrace the route back from the lighthouse to the road that goes through Ruescas and El Pozo de los Frailes, where there is an old restored wooden watermill (»noria«) powered by a donkey. **San José** lies further south on the seashore. It is the largest holiday resort on the cape, a not unpleasant mixture of fishing port, yachting marina and holiday village.

East coast

If you fancy swimming, though, forget the beach to the left of the town and go 2km/1.5mi west along the bumpy road to the beautiful **Playa de los Genoveses** – over a kilometre (1,100 yards) in length, 50m/150ft wide, light-coloured sand, really shallow and yet with proper waves. Just as beautiful, but with black sand and only about 350m/400yd long is the **Playa del Monsúl**, 2km/1.5mi further on, which is adjacent to the Playa de Media Luna.
Back in El Pozo, take the turn-off to **Los Escullos**, which detours around the highest summit on the cape, the

> **!** *For a Fistful of Dollars* Insider Tip
>
> MARCO POLO TIP
>
> Something for Western film fans: Sergio Leone's *A Fistful of dollars* began the rise of the »spaghetti western« and the career of Clint Eastwood. The films were made in the village of Albaricoques ca. 10km/6mi east of Rodalquilar – today still as sun-burned and deserted that you almost expect to see Clint Eastwood walking around the corner.

493m/1,617ft-high Cerro del Fraile. Los Escullos is a holiday village with a lovely beach beneath a bizarre rock arch and a fort from the 18th century. It is followed by La Isleta del Moro, a tiny fishing harbour with a small holiday village and a pleasant bar. After that, the road climbs up to ***Mirador de la Amatista**, from where there is a stupendous view of the whole east coast.

The hilltop behind Mirador offers a view far into the valley of **Rodalquilar**. Things are rather quiet these days in the former mining village – the gold mine that can still be seen on the slopes was not abandoned until the 1960s. Its beach, El Playazo with the 18th century Batería de San Ramón, can be reached over a bumpy dirt road 3km/2mi to the east that goes by the remains of a former Nasrid castle called Castillo de la Batería. Within the same district is a farm called Cortijo del Fraile, where a family tragedy took place in July 1928 that Federico García Lorca used as the basis of his play **»Blood Wedding.«**

Once out of Rodalquilar and beyond the turn-off to the holiday resort of Las Negras, the road winds its way up between steep gorges

The bizarre coast of the Cabo de Gata
has wonderfully isolated beaches

then quickly drops down onto the plain of Almería where the view
gives way to the familiar sea of plastic cloches. Despite that, the route
is worth taking because it leads via Campohermoso and the A-7,
N-341 and AL-5106 to the very pleasant resort of **∗Agua Amarga** in
the north of the Cabo de Gata nature reserve. It has a well-tended,
sandy beach and nice bars right behind it and there are more beautiful bays to the south. The Playa de los Muertos joins it to the north
beyond Mesa de Roldán.

∗ Cádiz

∗ C 8

Province: Cádiz
Altitude: 4m/13ft
Population: 125,800

**The port of Cádiz is famous for its magnificent location spread
out on a shell limestone rock rising out of the sea at the end
of a promontory 9km/5.5mi long that projects out into the Bay
of Cádiz on the Atlantic Ocean. A fresh breeze constantly
wafts through the streets making a stay in midsummer pleasant and providing a shimmering, clear light in the city, which
earned it its nickname »una tazita de plata« (»little silver
cup«). Lord Byron even got carried away and claimed that
Cádiz is »the Siren of the Ocean«.**

»Una tazita
de plata«

Mighty walls up to 15m/50ft high protect the city from the waves.
The **tidal differential** here is almost 2m/6ft 6in (at spring tide it is as

high as 3m/10ft). The high, white flat-roofed houses with their characteristic glazed balconies (»miradores«) and the parks with planted gardens of palms endow the city with a charm all its own. The lack of space on the peninsula led to towering blocks of flats being erected in the new part of town, so that the long drive into the city through the residential and industrial areas gives a rather unpromising impression. The inner city, enclosed by a fortified wall, therefore appears all the more pleasant with its spacious plazas and narrow lanes, mostly laid out in the 18th century. Today, Cádiz is one of Spain's most important ports with large **wharves** and **refineries** in its outlying areas. Fishing and **fish canneries** are also of importance.

Cádiz is not only the oldest city on the Iberian peninsula, but also in Europe. The earliest archaeological finds, though, only date back to the 8th century BC. The Phoenicians founded Cádiz in around 1100 BC as a storage facility for tin and silver from Tartessos on the island that was not yet connected to the mainland in those days. They gave it the name Gadir (»fortress«) and built a temple to their god Melqart – later equated with the hero Hercules – on the island now called Sancti Petri. The Carthaginians occupied Gadir around 500 BC and from there pushed up into the south of Iberia. The city fell to the Romans during the Second Punic War and with its new name, Iulia Augusta Gaditana, the city flowered under Roman rule. Greek scholars studied the tides here, which were like nothing they had ever seen. Giditanian dancers, the »puellac gaditanae«, were coveted as slaves and even the cooking was famous. **Ancient mythology** assumed the **entrance to the underworld** to be nearby. Scholars like Plato and later Pliny believed this to be the site of the sunken **Atlantis**. After the Visigoths, the Moors captured the town, until the harbour, now called »Jezirat Kádis«, was attacked by the Normans in 844 after which sank into insignificance.

Resettlement only began after Alfonso X had taken the city in 1262. With the discovery of the New World – **Columbus** sailed from here on his second and fourth expeditions – Cádiz rose to become the most important port for the silver fleet after Seville. This attracted English competition, however. In 1587 **Sir Francis Drake** sank a fleet anchored in the roads and in 1596 the Earl of Essex destroyed over a third of the city. But Cádiz recovered and in 1717, after Seville had dropped out of contention due to silting of the Guadalquivir, it was granted the privilege of trading with the colonies.

In 1805, the Spanish-French fleet that was subsequently destroyed by **Admiral Nelson** at **Cape Trafalgar** set sail from here. The French were unable to take Cádiz during the Spanish War of Independence, which enabled the Cortes in the city to assemble in 1810 and in 1812 and proclaim a **liberal constitution**, »La Pepa«; although it was abolished two years later under Ferdinand VII. The patriots in Cádiz pro-

Europe's oldest city

claimed the constitution again eight years later, but this only lasted a short time because the French troops of the Holy Alliance crushed the patriots in the »Battle of Trocadero«.

WHAT TO SEE IN CÁDIZ

Plaza de España The train station and harbour lie behind Puerta de Tierra, which is where the ferries to the Canary Islands embark. The tour of the city begins here, on the Avda. Ramón de Carranza. To the left of where this palm-studded avenue begins is Plaza de San Juan de Dios with the stately city hall (**Ayuntamiento**), built in 1799 and remodelled in 1861. The broad Plaza de España at the end of the harbour boulevard provides the backdrop for a mighty monument in remembrance of the Cortes first convened in Cádiz between 1810 and 1812. The province government building stands on the north side of the plaza.

*Museo de Cádiz The most beautiful plaza in the inner city is **Plaza de Mina**, luxuriantly planted with palms and greenery. One of the buildings houses the Museo de Cádiz (Museo de Bellas Artes y Arquéológico) that has various collections on display. On the ground floor, the archaeological section provides information about the earliest settlements in the region of modern-day Cádiz, the Phoenician founders of the city and much more. Of particular interest are two anthropomorphically shaped sarcophagi depicting a man with a curly beard and a woman with very fine facial characteristics that were found in Punta de la Vaca and date from 400 BC. Other rooms cover the Roman town of Iulia Augusta Gaditana from various points of view, including burial techniques, sculpture (there is a large statue here of Emperor Trajan from Bolonia), trade (model of a boat), everyday life, religion, domestic arrangements and work. The collection of paintings on the first floor is the most important in Andalucía after the Museo de Bellas Artes in ►Seville. The centrepiece of the museum is a collection of 18 works by Zurbarán in room 2, including The Ecstasy of St Bruno, The Vision of St Francis of Assisi, Whitsun Festival, Angel with Incense and a series of portrayals of Carthusian monks from the Carthusian monastery in ►Jerez de la Frontera. Among the other important artists represented are Murillo (The Stigmatization of St Francis, Ecce Homo) and **Rubens** The Holy Family); in addition, there are Classic and Romantic works, portraits, painting of the 16th century (Luis Morales; Pedro de Campaña), historicism and paintings by artists from Cádiz. Finally, the top floor is dedicated to Andalusian ***puppet theatre**, which is cultivated particularly in Cádiz.

Insider Tip

❶ Tue 2.30pm – 8.30pm, Wed – Sat 9am – 8.30pm, Sun 9am – 2.30pm; admission €1,50, free for EU citizens

Across Plaza San Francisco and past the Iglesia de Rosario (with sculptures of San Servando and San Germán, the patron saints of the city,) is the church of Santa Cueva, which was built in 1783. It was designed as an oval structure with two chapels, arranged one on top of the other. Three of the five lunette window bays in the upper rooms were decorated in 1795 by **Francisco de Goya** with wall paintings (including *Wedding Feast at Cana*, *Miracle of the Loaves and Fishes*, *The Last Supper*), rare examples of religious themes by the master.

Santa Cueva

ⓘ summer: Mon – Fri 10am – 1pm, 4.30pm – 8pm; winter: Tue – Fri 10am – 1pm, 4.30pm – 7.30pm, Sat, Sun 10am – 1pm; admission €3

Cádiz

1 Museo de Cádiz	4 Nuestra Señora del Carmen	9 Santa Catalina	15 »La Pepa 2012«
2 Diputación Provincial (provincial government)	5 Casa Mora	10 Catedral Nueva	16 Centro Cultural Reina Sofía
3 El Rosario and Santa Cueva	6 San Felipe Neri	11 Santa Cruz	
	7 Museo de las Cortes	12 Teatro Romano	
	8 Torre Tavira	13 Ayuntamiento	
		14 Cárcel Real	

Where to eat
❶ Achuri
❷ Balandro
❸ El Aljibe
❹ El Faro
❺ El Sardinero

Where to stay
❶ Argantonio
❷ Hostal Bahía
❸ Pasador Hotel Atlántico
❹ Playa Victoria
❺ Regio

Cádiz

GETTING THERE
There are two ways to get to Cádiz. The more interesting is via Puerto Real on the N-IV bridge over the Bay of Cádiz with the city visible from afar. The other route goes around the bay by way of San Fernando. Both routes lead onto the access road that passes through the new town as far as Plaza de la Constitución, where it ends in front of the Puerta de Tierra that was built in 1755. The best way to explore the old town is on foot.

INFORMATION
Oficina de Turismo
Ayuntamiento, Paseo de Canalejos s/n
E-11006 Cádiz
9am – 6.30pm (Sat/Sun until 5pm)
Tel. 956 24 10 01
Avda. José León de Carranza / Avda. de La Coruña (south of the old city)
Tel. 956 28 56 01
www.cadiz.es; http://laciudad.cadiz.es

Hoch zu Ross geht es zur Feria

PARKING
Do not try to drive in the inner city. There are car parks at the entrance to the old town, at the train station, in the Cuesta de las Calesas and along the promenade.

ENTERTAINMENT
In the old city the meeting place before midnight is C. Zorilla at Plaza de la Mina, with bars and pubs around it. In the winter this meetingplace shifts a bit to the east to Plaza San Francisco/C. Rosario. Young people go out on the peninsula Punta San Felipe north of Plaza España until the early hours on weekends. In the summer after midnight the party rocks around Plaza Glorieta – on Paseo Marítimo there are also enough bars and discos; C. General Muñoz Arenilla is also busy during the winter.

SHOPPING
The shopping zone spreads out between Plaza de las Flores and Calle San Francisco and on Calle Columela along with its side streets. In addition, there is a covered market with a wide choice of merchandise.

Hecho en Cádiz
Plaza Candelaria
Culinary items and handicrafts produced in the province of Cádiz.

Mercado Central
Calle Libertad
Masses of succulent delicacies.

EVENTS **Insider**
Carnival **Tip**
Throughout Spain only the Canary island

of Tenerife celebrates its carnival more exuberantly than Cádiz. If you want to experience it at first hand, then it is best to book accommodation well in advance or, better yet, settle for an outlying area. For ten days – from the last Thursday before Lent to the first Sunday after Ash Wednesday – a state of chaos exists with the streets full of parading »murgas«, groups of costumed people singing satirical songs and performing sketches. There is a huge parade on the Sunday before Lent (www.carnavalcadiz.com).

Semana Santa
Holy Week

Ciudad de Cadiz
Folk festival in the Parque Genovés at the beginning of July.

WHERE TO EAT
❹ *El Faro* €€€€
San Félix, 15
Tel. 956 21 10 68
www.elfarodecadiz.com
One of the best restaurants in Andalucía, especially when it comes to fish and seafood. Enjoy the tapas here too.

❶ *Achuri* €€€€
Plocia, 15
Tel. 956 25 36 13
Achuri is a restaurant steeped in tradition. Basque and Andalusian cooking are combined here to perfection; e.g., in the stockfish recipe »Bacalao al andaluz« The portions are generous, too..

❷ *Balandro* €€€€
Alameda de Apodaca, 22
Tel. 956 22 09 92
www.restaurantebalandro.com
Closed Sunday evening and Monday

The whole, rich diversity of fish and shellfish is proffered. The specialities include fresh salads with Galician sea octopus (pulpo) and seabream.

❸ *El Aljibe* €€€€
Plocia, 25
Tel. 956 26 66 56
Under the direction of Pablo Grosso everything is available here: from simple tapas to sophisticated fish cuisine. Tapas in the ground floor, delicious meals in the 1st floor. Lamb and sea bass dishes are popular.

❺ *El Sardinero* €
Plaza San Juan de Dios, 4
Tel. 956 26 59 26
Typical homecooking from Cádiz. Specialty: bacalao. On the city's main plaza in the old city across from the city hall. The fried fish is the favourite.

WHERE TO STAY
❸ *Parador*
Hotel Atlántico €€€
Avda. Duque de Nájera, 9
Tel. 902 547 979
www.parador.es
Modern parador in a four-storey new building that replaces the previous one on the edge of the old town and that has a fabulous view of the ocean.

❹ *Playa Victoria* €€€
Glorieta Ingeniero La Cierva, 4
Tel. 956 27 54 11
www.palafoxhoteles.com; 188 rooms
Modern and comfortable hotel located south of the old town centre on the main road. All of the rooms have a terrace and a sea view. For the guests there is a restaurant, an outdoor pool and beach access.

❶ Hotel Argantonio €€
Argantonio, 3; tel. 956 21 16 40
www.hotelargantonio.es; 15 Zi.
Quiet, charming and stylishly furnished
hotel in a 19th-century house. All rooms
have relatively large bathrooms and a
balcony. Excellent breakfast buffet and
pleasnt service.

❷ Hostal Bahía €
C. Plocia, 5
Tel. 956 25 90 61

www.hostalbahiacadiz.com
No frills, cheap and large rooms. There
are rooms with and without bathrooms.

❺ Regio €€
Avda. Ana de Viya, 11
Tel. 956 27 93 31
www.hotelregiocadiz.com, 45 rooms
Not in the old town but in the newer
agglomeration on the busy access road,
but it is cheap, practical and only
200m/700ft from Victoria Beach.

*Casa Mora   Beyond Santa Cueva, the shopping street, C. Columela, turns off to
the right. House no. 28 in the pedestrian zone C. Ancha represents a
wonderful example of civic architecture of the 19th century. Among
the things worth seeing at the Casa Mora urban palace, aside from its
impressive façade, are an exquisite inner courtyard and a museum
with three floors displaying interior decoration from the period.

**Centro de
Interpre-
tación »La
Pepa 2012«**
A few steps further is the Centro de Interpretación »La Pepa 2012«,
which uses many interactive screens to explain the liberal constitution of 1812.
❶ Ancha, 19; Tue – Fri 10am – 2pm, 5pm – 8pm, Sat 11am – 2pm, 5pm –
8pm; free admission

***Plaza
Topete**

**Insider
Tip**
The C. Columela leads to the bustling Plaza Topete, also called Plaza
de las Flores because of its many flower stalls. Take a break here in
either one of the street cafés, the La Marina or the Andalucía, before
taking a stroll through the big redeveloped Mercado Central (market
hall), adjacent to the plaza at the southern end.

Torre Tavira   C. Londres and C. Nicaragua lead to the Torre Tavira, which was built
in 1704 as a watch tower and, at 34m/112ft, it is the highest in Cádiz.
A **camera obscura** installed on the top floor projects panoramas of
Cádiz every half hour. There were once as many as 160 of these towers in the city during the 18th century, allowing merchants to watch
over their ships in the harbour (opening hours: mid-June– mid-Sept
daily 10am–8pm, mid-Sept–mid-June until 6pm).
❶ May – Sept daily 10am – 8pm, Oct – April until 6pm; admission €4

**Oratorio de
San Felipe
Neri**
C. Santa Inés can be reached by way of C. Nicaragua, where the Ora-
torio de San Felipe Neri, an oval building from 1671, is located. This
is where the Cortes convened in 1812. Decorating the high altar is

Murillo's painting »The Immaculate Conception« as well as a »Head of John the Baptist« by **Pedro Roldán** (irregular opening times). Adjoining the chapel to the south is the **Museo de las Cortes de Cádiz**. Along with numerous documents from the time of the war for independence, there is also a very large model of the city fashioned out of ivory and mahogany that was made in the 18th century.

❶ Tue – Fri 9am – 6pm, Sat, Sun 9am – 1pm, free admission

The only painting by **El Greco** in Cádiz, the »Ecstasy of St Francis« is in the chapel inside the Baroque Hospital de Mujeres, along with various other works (Murillo's »Virgen del Carmen«).

❶ Mon – Fri 8am – 2pm, 5.30pm – 8.30pm, Sat 10am – 1.30pm

Hospital de Mujeres

Barrio de la Viña is just made for a stroll without the pressure of sightseeing. It is in the southwestern part of the city centre, where mainly fishermen and dock-workers lived in the 18th century. In the summer, stalls with tastily prepared fish titbits are lined up one after the other on the Tío de la Tiza plaza. Its name comes from the nickname of **Antonio Rodríguez Martiñez**, who defined the basic rules for the carnival in Cádiz.

Barrio de la Viña

The promenades on the Atlantic beachfront begin at Plaza de Mina with the Alameda de Apodaca and the adjoining Alameda Marqués de Comillas. At the end of the Alameda stands **Nuestra Señora del Carmen** (1737–1764), a Baroque church built in colonial style. Across from it is the Baluarte de Candelaría bastion. which was built in the 17th and strengthened in the 19th century.
If citizens of Cádiz feel the urge to take a walk, they go to the ***Parque Genovés** on the northwestern side of the rock. On the other side of the Castillo de Santa Catalina fortress, they can go swimming in the Bay of **La Caleta** at the city's edge where the nostalgic Balneario de la Palma (1925) is situated.

Beachfront promenades

Opposite the church Nuestra Señora del Carmen in the former building of the military goverment of Cádiz, a neo-classical house from 1759, is the Centro Cultural Reina Sofía, which was named after the Spanish queen. It exhibits 160 works by **Juan Luis Vasallo** (1908 – 1986), one of the most important spanish sculptors of the 20th century. A quay wall stretches from the southern side of the bay far out into the sea towards the Castillo de San Sebastián and the lighthouse.

❶ Paseo Carlos III, 9; Mon – Sat 9am – 9pm, Sun 9am – 3pm; free admission

Centro Cultural Reina Sofía

Campo del Sur leads away from the southern quay wall. On its left-hand side stands the former Capuchin monastery, now a psychiatric clinic. **Bartolomé Esteban Murillo** did the last picture he ever paint-

Campo del Sur

ed, »The Engagement of St Catherine«, for the high altar in the church he began in 1639, **Santa Catalina** (entrance through the courtyard). He fell from the scaffolding while working and died of his injuries on 3 April 1682 in Seville. There are other works of his to be seen in the church.

*Catedral Nueva
From the Campo del Sur, there is a view of the choir side of the cathedral with its great yellow dome. Its main entrance faces the city on Plaza de Pio XII. It was begun in 1722 by Vicente de Acero and completed by members of the Cayón family at the end of the 19th century. Its fairly plain main façade, completed in 1789 by Manuel Machucas, is flanked by two large, octagonal domed towers. In the interior of the church (85m/280ft long, 60m/200ft wide) are an impressive, massive pillar and a magnificent 52m/170ft-high dome over the crossing and the high altar that dates from 1862. The mahogany choir stalls by Pedro Duque Cornejo from 1702 were originally planned for the Carthusian monastery on Guadalquivir island in Seville. Among the side chapels, the Capilla de San Sebastián with a figure of St Bruno is worth seeing. The crypt is below sea level and contains, along with the graves of bishops, the tomb of the composer **Manuel de Falla**, who came from Cádiz but died in Argentina (▶Famous People). The Torre de Poniente, the highest tower in Cádiz, offers a wonderful view of the city.

Right next door, in the *** Museo Catedralicio**, three monstrances are particularly worth a look. One 17th-century **silver monstrance** made by Antonio de Suárez is almost 5m/16ft high, and the »Custodia del Millón« from 1721 is supposedly set with **one million precious stones**. The oldest monstrance has an amethyst cross at the top and was created by Enrique de Arfe, who came from Cologne to Spain in 1506. The museum has some other works by him and by his son Juan. Among the paintings there is a »Crucifixion« by Alonso Cano and an »Immaculate Conception« by Murillo.

❶ Tue – Fri 10am – 6.30pm, Sun 2pm – 6.30; admission €5

> **!**
> *Fish & Chips* **Insider Tip**
>
> **MARCO ⊕ POLO TIP**
>
> It's a fact: not the English but the fishermen of Cádiz invented battered fish. Try mackerel, for example, in all manner of »freidurías« or in the really quite inexpensive fish restaurants, perhaps on Plaza de las Flores, Plaza de San Juan de Dios or maybe on Plaza Tío de la Tiza.

Santa Cruz (Catedral Vieja)
Adjoining the cathedral is the archaeological grounds Casa del Obispo, where there are remains from the Phoenician-Punic times to the 18th century. Then comes the church of Santa Cruz, the »old cathedral« that originally dates back to the 13th century and, after its destruction by the English in 1596, was rebuilt in Renaissance style in 1602. The interior is decorated with paintings and a high altar

richly adorned with figures by Saavedra (about 1650). Excavations right behind Santa Cruz have uncovered the **remains of a Roman theatre**.

❶ daily 10am – 2.30pm, free admission

The former royal prison at the end of the Campo del Sur was built by Torcuato Benjumeda at the end of the 18th century as a Classicistic complex clustered around several inner courtyards. Today it is a courthouse.

Cárcel Real

Besides the city's beach, other beaches that are good for bathing include the long Playa de Santa María, Playa de la Victoria and Playa de Cortadura that lie parallel to the major access road behind the tower blocks. Playa de la Victoria is supposed to have the finest sand on the Costa de la Luz.

Beaches

AROUND CÁDIZ

The port of San Fernando on the southern shore of the Bay of Cádiz was built as Isla de León in the 18th century on the salt marshes where the Romans had once extracted salt and is nowadays a nature conservation area. San Fernando, which was the last refuge of the Cortes during the Spanish War of Independence, was and is an important **naval base**. Other sights worth a visit are the **museum of city history**, the observatory built in 1753 that the Spanish navy uses as a base to determine their position, and the Panteón de los Marinos Ilustres, where 52 statues of famous seafarers are on display. San Fernando is the hometown of the great flamenco singer **Camarón de la Isla** (▶Famous People).

San Fernando

Museum: Mon – Fri 9.30am – 1.30pm

The Puente Zuazo, a bridge probably of Roman origin, spans the Salinen des Caño de la Carraca and connects San Fernando with Chiclana de la Frontera. The town is well-known for its wine, particularly for its muscatel, and its **puppet factories**, one of which, Marín, also maintains a museum displaying the products (opening hours: Mon–Sat 9am–1pm). The Iglesia de Jesús Nazareno is also worth a visit. Chiclana lives, however, first and foremost from **beach holidays** because it is only a couple of miles to beaches like the 7km/4mi long Playa de la Barrosa that are among the most beautiful on the Costa de la Luz.

Chiclana dela Frontera

New urban housing estates owe their existence to them, such as La Barrosa or the community of quality homes, **Novo Sancti Petri**, laid out precisely by a draughtsman's pen and built in the 1990s around a golf course designed by the golfing legend Severiano Ballesteros.

Many Gaditanos wind down on the Playa de la Caleta after work

Most of the holidaymakers here are Germans. **Sancti Petri** took its name from the island lying off the coast, upon which a famous temple to Hercules/Melqart is said to have stood in ancient times. A now abandoned housing estate for fish factory workers built in the 1940s was also named after it.

✳ Carmona

 D 7

Province: Seville
Altitude: 248m/813ft
Population: 28,500

The little town of Carmona sits enthroned on an exposed ridge of a hill in the middle of the Vega de Corbones, one of Andalucía's most fertile strips of land. Its centre is among the most beautiful of the smaller towns of Andalucía – only ▶Baeza and Úbeda are prettier. With its vast fields of Roman graves, Carmona possesses a cultural monument of the first order.

The Romans encircled the hill that had already been inhabited in pre-historic times with a wall and gave the settlement the name Carmo. It became an important station on the road from Córdoba (Colonia Patricia) to Seville (Colonia Iulia Romula) and ►Itálica. The main street that crosses through the upper town follows this arterial route. Ferdinand III took the town away from the Moors, who called it Karmuna, and Carmona developed into one of the residences favoured by the rulers; among those who especially liked to come here were Pedro the Cruel and Isabella the Catholic. A great number of aristocratic residences testify to this period.

Small country town steeped in history

WHAT TO SEE IN CARMONA

The upper part of the town can be entered from the west through Puerta de Sevilla, which is within the fortress wall extended by the Moors. The gate with one horseshoe and three round arches is part of the alcázar de abajo, the lower castle with the Torre del Homenaje and the Torre del Oro. Today, the **tourist information** is housed here, which also means the building can be toured.

Puerta de Sevilla

To reach the Plaza de San Fernando, the town's main plaza, go a little up the hill from the gate on C. Prim and past the church of San Bartolomé (15th century) on the right. Some of the town houses in Mudejar and Renaissance style around the plaza are worth seeing. Take a look at the courtyard in the Baroque town hall; a Roman mosaic covers its floor.

Plaza de San Fernando

Close by is Santa María church, which was erected on top of an Almohad mosque in the 15th century. The Patio de los Naranjos, the Patio of Oranges, with its horseshoe arch is a reminder of the mosque. Evidence remains of the existence of an even earlier Christian house of worship predating the mosque: a Visigoth column from the 6th century with an engraved ***calendar** showing the name days of the local saints, the oldest of its kind in Spain. A prominent feature inside is the Plateresque high altar, completed in 1559 with Passion scenes by Ortega and Vázquez el Viej. Take a look at the altar in the Capilla del Cristo de los Martirios in the left aisle, recognizable by its magnificent choir screen; it is thought to be Flemish. Capilla de San José y San Bartolomé in the right aisle holds three retables; the one on the right is said to be by Pedro de Campaña.

Santa María

<table>
<tr><td colspan="2">!   *Solo with a view* ^{**Insider Tip**}</td></tr>
<tr><td>MARCO ⊕ POLO TIP</td><td>The terrace at the parador high above the Bétis Valley, originally a 14th century Moorish fortress, offers a panoramic view over the Vega de Corbones – a great place for a café solo.</td></tr>
</table>

Carmona

INFORMATION
Oficina de Turismo
Alcázar de la Puerta de Seville, s/n,
E-41410 Carmona
Tel. 95 419 09 55
www.turismo.carmona.org
Mon – Sat 10am – 6pm
Sun 10am – 3pm; July - Aug. Mon – Fri
10am – 3pm, 4.30pm – 6pm
Sat/Sun 10am – 3pm

EVENTS
Romería de la Virgen de Grácia
A pilgrimage on horseback and wagons
on the first Sunday in September.
Vibrant and colourful.

WHERE TO EAT
Molino de la Romera €€€
Sor Angela de la Cruz, 8
Tel. 954 14 20 00
www.molinodelaromera.com
open only on weekends
Regional dishes – incl. game – served
in the historical ambience of a 15th
century oil-mill near the alcázar.

La Almazara de Carmona €€€€
Calle Santa Ana, 33
Tel. 954 19 00 76
Very good traditional meat and fish
dishes at a reasonable price. Prety location and nice service. You can order
tapas at the bar.

WHERE TO STAY
Parador Alcázar del Rey
Don Pedro €€€
Tel. 954 14 10 10
www.parador.es, 63 rooms
A dream of a hotel with architecture in-
spired by the palace of Pedro the Cruel.
At the edge of the old town above the
Bétis valley.

Alcázar de la Reina €€
C. Hermana Concepción Orellana, 2
Tel. 954 19 62 00
www.alcazar-reina.es, 68 Zi.
Stylish accommodation in an historic
setting, quiet on ther northern edge
of town. Large pool in the patio,
restaurant, tapas bar, Irish pub.

Pension Comercio €
Torre del Oro, 56
Tel. 954 14 00 18, 13 rooms
Directly at the Puerta de Sevilla with a
pretty patio and a good and inexpensive
restaurant.

Across the Patio de los Naranjos is the entrance to an exhibition of
the most beautiful of the church treasures.

Noble palaces There are three noble palaces from the 17th and the 18th centuries in
the immediate vicinity of the church. To the right on the plaza is the
Palacio de los Rueda, across the street on the corner is the reddish-
brown painted Palacio de los Aguilar (formerly the town hall), and
behind the church to the left on C. San José is the Palacio del Marqués

de las Torres (completed in 1755, with beautiful doors and an iron balcony), today the **town museum** with exhibits on the town's history.

❶ Sept – mid-June Tue – Sun 11am – 7pm, Mon 11am – 2pm; mid-June to Aug. Mon – Fri 10am – 2pm, 6.30pm – 8pm, Sat, Sun 9.30am – 2pm; admission: €3

Along the main street past the Convento de las Descalzas is the Convento de Santa Clara on the right-hand side. It was founded in 1460. The church has a series of portraits of saints from the Zurbarán School, some probably by the master himself. The painting on the high altar is by Valdés Leal.

Convento de Santa Clara

Puerta de Córdobahe marks the eastern end of the town. This gate also dates back to Roman times but was remodelled in classical style in the 17th century, when the powerful octagonal towers on the flanks were set on Roman ashlar blocks.

Puerta de Córdoba

The upper castle, or alcázar de arriba, was on the highest point of the town, on the cliff edge of the town hill. It is also called Alcázar del Rey Don Pedro because **Pedro the Cruel** chose the Almohad castle for his favourite seat. Today, there is not much remaining of the castle, but a very nice parador has been built on the grounds.

Parador

The first thing that stands out in the lower part of town, west of Puerta de Seville, is San Pedro church (15th–17th centuries), whose tall Baroque tower is reminiscent of the Giralda of Seville. In the exuberantly furnished Baroque interior are several remarkable green ceramic baptismal fonts (around 1500) and the Capilla del Sagrario (1760), whose splendour even exceeds that of the rest of the interior. It is the work of the Sevillian artist Ambrosio Figueroa, who revived here the Moorish tradition of horseshoe arches.

San Pedro

The **Roman cemetery** (necrópolis romana), in the lower part of town across from the amphitheatre (C/Jorge Bonsor; follow the signs), has first place on the list of things to see in Carmonas. The cemetery contains close to 1,000 graves from the 2nd century BC up to the 4th century AD. About 250 of them have been excavated. Many are family tombs, recognizable by wall niches for urns, atriums and triclinia (benches) for the funeral meals. In many cases the remains of wall paintings and plasterwork can still be seen. The dead were usually cremated in crematory chambers that were part of the tombs, but interment tombs have also been found. A **museum** provides information about Roman methods of burial and displays burial objects (pottery, glass, jewellery, and bronze articles), gravestones, altars and sculptures.

**Necrópolis romana

Carmona Necrópolis romana

1 Mausoleo Circular
2 Tumba del Elefante
3 Columbario triclino
4 T. del las Guirnaldas

5 T. del los Cuatro Departamentos
6 Tumba del Ryton de Crystal
7 Tumba del Póstumo
8 Tumba del las Tres Puertas

9 Tumba del Servilia
10 T. del las Cuatro Columnas
11 Mausoleo Cuadrangular
12 Mausoleo Circular

The large **Tumba del Elefante** is the most remarkable of the tombs. Its name is taken from a well-preserved statue of an elephant, which might symbolize long life, but whose meaning remains a mystery in the end. The tomb consists of several chambers with triclinia (benches) and a stone cistern.

The best-preserved wall paintings in the cemetery are to be seen in the **Tumba de Servilia**, including a picture of a lady with a harp. The size of the two-storey tomb indicates that an important family must be buried here. This is corroborated by the large number of burial objects and the life-size statue of one of the dead found here with the name »Servilia« chiselled into the plinth.

The **Tumba del Póstumo** is an example of an interment tomb – though only for the master, because niches for the urns of his slaves are recognizable on both sides of the tomb.

ⓘ mid-June – mid-Sept Tue – Fri 8.30am – 2pm, Sat 10am – 2pm; mid-Sept – mid-June Tue – Fri 9am – 6pm, Sat, Sun 10am – 2pm, free admission

AROUND CARMONA

In the little country village of Marchena, situated 27km/17mi south-east of Carmona, the remains of the medieval town fortification can still be seen. The high altar in the Gothic-Mudejar church ***San Juan Bautista** is of particular interest. In the 16th century Alejo Fernández and his workshop created the panel paintings and sculptures that impressively depict the life of Christ and John the Baptist. Also of great artistic value are the 18th-century choir stalls and the late Gothic side altar with a picture of the Last Supper. The church museum is the proud owner of **nine paintings by Zurbarán**.

Marchena

This town, 23km/14mi east of Carmona, possesses a series of notable buildings, primarily Baroque. The ramparts and four towers of a Moorish castle are still standing on the main plaza. The most important church is Santa María de las Nieves, which has double aisles and was built from the 16th up into the 18th century. Its Capilla de la Virgen de Lurdes is lined with 16th-century azulejos. The altar of San José church (18th century) has two sculptures made for it by Juan de Mesa: Christ and Saint Joseph with Child.

Fuentes de Andalucía

Villanueva del Río y Minas, located past Lora del Río, 25km/16mi north of Carmona on the Guadalquivir at the foot of the Sierra Morena, developed out of the Roman »Flavium Munigense«, where mining has been going on since ancient times. The impressive **Castillo de Mulva** can today be seen on the site of the Roman fort. The well-preserved remains of a 4th-century Roman settlement lie outside the town.

Villanueva del Río y Minas

Ceuta

⊹ E 10

Spanish sovereign territory in Africa	**Altitude:** Sea level
	Population: 80,500
Status: autonomous city	

Ceuta (Arabic: Sebta) is one big bazaar. Passengers arriving by ferry are besieged by peddlers offering every kind of ware imaginable. The African port lying closest to Europe at the eastern entrance to the Straits of Gibraltar is a 19.4 sq km/7.5 sq mi Spanish enclave (Plaza de Soberanía) on the Moroccan coast. the El Hacho peninsula is also under Spanish sovereignty. It projects out into the Mediterranean 8km/5mi to the northeast, where the old town of Ceuta occupies an isthmus barely 350m/400yd wide.

North African enclave

The city and the peninsula is isolated from Morocco by a formidable metal fence. This is an attempt to prevent incidents like the one in 2005 when thousands of illegal immigrants tried to cross the border illegally. Ceuta has hardly any North African character – about 85% of its inhabitants are Spanish citizens; only 8% are Muslims. The city is divided into the walled old town and the new town, which was laid out in 1912 when the north of Morocco was a Spanish protectorate and Ceuta experienced an enormous economic upswing. The decline set in following Morocco's independence in 1956, but Ceuta remains an important centre for fishing, a ferry port and a free trade zone that attracts tourists. Ceuta also has military significance – last put to the test in the somewhat grotesque dispute over the bare Parsley Island west of town when Spanish troops drove out some Moroccan soldiers. Ceuta is also a **drug trafficking hub for hashish,** which is offered for sale at many places in the city. Do not under any circumstances purchase any! Ceuta, which used to belong the administrative district of the province of Cádiz, has been like ▶Melilla an **autonomous city** (Ciudad Autónoma) in Spain since 1995. This status gives the two Spanish enclaves in the North African coast some of the special privileges of the 17 Spanish autonomous areas (Andalucía is one of them). The two cities on the North African coast also have tax benefits, which are meant to strengthen their economies; these include not being part of the European Union customs region. The autonomy statute is being reconsidered in Spain since 2005. That means that Ceuta and Melilla could soon be autonomous areas.

History

It is thought that Ceuta was an important Phoenician settlement, but the Roman settlement of Septem Fratres, from which both the Arab and the Spanish names were derived, is the earliest of which there is evidence. It denotes the seven hills of Djebel Moussa, on whose slopes the city was built. After it was taken by the Vandals in 429 AD, it was not until 534 that Emperor Justinian I (527–565) managed to retake it. In 711 the Arabs seized Ceuta, which experienced its golden age in the 13th and 14th centuries as a customs zone, and Morocco's largest place of trade and most important port. In 1415, John I of Portugal succeeded in removing it from Arab control. When Spain and Portugal united in 1580, Ceuta became Spanish. Several attempts by the Arabs to retake it failed, the last in 1860 when it had already become very disreputable as a Spanish penal colony. It was here that Franco prepared the crossing of his troops to Spain in 1936. Morocco still maintains its claim to the disputed territory.

WHAT TO SEE IN CEUTA

Plaza de África

In the centre of Ceuta on Plaza de África stands the church of Nuestra Señora de África. It was built on top of a mosque between 1704

Ceuta

ARRIVAL
Four fast ferries of various boat companies sail hourly. ▶Algeciras (about
45 min.). The Spanish enclave can also
be reached by helicopter – from Algeciras in 7 min., from Málaga in 35 min.
www.ceuta.es, www.conoceceuta.com..

INFORMATION
Oficina de Turismo
Calle Edrissis, s/n, E-51001 Ceuta
Tel. 856 20 05 60
www.destinoceuta.com

WHERE TO EAT
El Refectorio € € € €
Poblado Marinero, 37
Tel. 956 51 38 84; www.elrefectorio.es
Restaurant with a rustic dining room,
run by two brothers. Fish, seafood, meat
dishes can be enjoyed on the terrace on
warm days with a wonderful view of
the sea.

WHERE TO STAY
Parador de Ceuta € €
Plaza Ntra. Sra. de África, 15
Tel. 956 51 49 40
www.parador.es; 106 rooms
Modern hotel facility in the centre of
town along the old royal city wall with
a wonderful view of the old city and the
sea. The rooms have views of the palm
garden with swimming pool. Terrace,
restaurant.

Ulises €
Camoens, 5
Tel. / fax 956 51 45 40
www.hotelceuta.com, 124 rooms
Most reasonably priced of the city's
upmarket hotels.

and 1726 and is consecrated to the city's patron saint. The high altar
with a statue of the Virgin (16th century) – presumed to be Portuguese – and the church treasures are both worth a look. The cathedral
with its two towers rises at the southern end of the plaza. It was built
with a neo-classical facade and a black marble portal in 1729 on the
remains of the former grand mosque that had served as a church
since 1432.

The massive walls divided by a deep moat just a stone's throw from   **Murallas**
Plaza de África are the remains of the fortress of El Canderlo, built by
the Portuguese in 1530. They recall Ceuta's past as a fiercely fought-
over garrison town. The new Museum **Revellín de San Ignacio** displays art from antiquity to modern times and architecture there.

The **city museum** (Paseo del Revellín 30) displays objects from all   **Museums**
eras of the history of Ceuta. Beneath the museum begin 2.5km/1.5mi-
long underground passages from the 16th and 17th centuries that
were meant to secure the city's water supplies and perimeters.
The **Museo de la Legión** south of the city museum on Paseo de
Colón is dedicated to the history of the Spanish Legion, the former

Spanish foreign legion and still an elite unit in the Spanish military, which maintains a garrison in Ceuta.

The **Museo de la Basílica Tardorromana** (Calle Queipo de LLano) exhibits include a Roman sarcophagus and ceramics from various periods; the most important sight is the AD 4th century basilica.

Parque Marítimo del Mediterráneo
This park on the north side of the old town with waterfalls, sculptures and a fake castle was designed by the artist **César Manrique** (1920–1992), who came from the Canary Island of Lanzarote.

*Monte Hacho
It is worth taking the 4km/2.5mi trip to the 203m/666ft-high Monte Hacho. It is probably the legendary Mount Abila, which was held to be **one of the Pillars of Hercules** in antiquity. Its counterpart on the European mainland is the Rock of Gibraltar. Drive up the mountain past the lighthouse on the cape – with a fantastic view of Gibraltar and the Rif mountains – to the fortress of Desnarigado where there is a **museum** describing the history of the garrison of Ceuta. The Ermita de San Antonio, founded in 1593, is also up there.

✶✶ Córdoba

 ✦ F 6

Province: Córdoba
Altitude: 123m/403ft
Population: 328,500

The most important city in Andalucía after ▶Seville lies on a plain gently sloping down to the Guadalquivir at the foot of the Sierra de Córdoba, outliers of the Sierra Morena. Narrow, winding alleyways, small plazas and white-washed houses, usually with their typical pretty patio – Córdoba possesses one of the largest old quarters of all Spanish provincial cities and, in addition, the fantastic Mezquita.

Capital of the caliphate
The Moorish character of Córdoba is still tangible, though less so in the Judería – once the Jewish quarter, now taken over by souvenir shops – than in the streets round about. But it is primarily the famous former mosque, today the Mezquita Catedral, that makes the one-time capital of the caliphate a »western Mecca« and the first place to visit in Andalucía. Córdoba is famous for its **silver and leather handwork** that is still produced in many workshops in the old town. Surrounding the city, metal working plants and the electrical goods and food industries have been established in the newer districts. Together with the tourist industry, they are the economic base of the city.

Highlights in and around Córdoba

▶ **Mezquita-Catedral**
Next to the Alhambra the largest Moorish structure in Europe, containing a world-famous, fascinating Muslim prayer room and an impressive forest of columns, as well as the magnificently decorated prayer niche (mihrâb).
▶page 207

▶ **Alcázar gardens**
Park with waterworks and fountains laid out for the Catholic Monarchs in the 15th century
▶page 217

▶ **Judería**
The heart of Córdoba with winding lanes full of souvenir and craft shops and antiques dealers.
▶page 218

▶ **Medina Azahara**
Ten kilometres (6 miles) to the west lies the old caliphate town legendary for its former splendour, where archaeological excavations have been under way since 1910.
▶page 335

Moses Maimónides

There was already a settlement here on the bend in the Bétis (Guadalquivir) in ancient Iberian times. It provided the Carthaginian General Hannibal with mercenaries for his military expedition over the Alps. Under the Romans, the village named Colonia Patricia in 152 BC rose to become the **capital of the province of Hispania Ulterior**. After being ravaged in the Roman civil war in 45 BC, it alternated with Hispalis (Seville) and ▶Itálica as the capital of the province of Baetica during the time of imperial Rome. In the 4th century AD, it was made the episcopal seat and eventually came under Byzantine domination, which was ended by the rampaging Vandals. When the Visigoth king, Leowigild, entered in AD 572, he found a town without any great significance.

The Umayyad **Abd ar-Rahman I**, who was driven from Damascus in 750 and in 756 became the first Emir of Córdoba, laid the cornerstone for the development of the town into **Europe's most outstanding city and its intellectual centre**. He introduced new cultivated plants and sophisticated methods of irrigation, started an extensive building program and promoted the sciences. The city was at its peak under Abd ar-Rahman III, who elevated himself to »Caliph of the West« in 929. At this time, the population of Córdoba was

History

Córdoba

1 Palacio de los Marqueses de Viana
2 Casa de Fernández de Córdoba
3 Casa de los Villalones
4 Museo Provincial Arqueológico

5 Arco del Portillo
6 Casa de los Marqueses del Carpio
7 Posada del Potro
8 Fuente del Potro

9 Museo de Bellas Artes
10 Museo Julio Romero de Tor
11 Museo Taurino
12 San Bartolomé

Where to eat
❶ Almudaina
❷ Casa Pepe de la Judería
❸ Casa Salinas
❹ El Blasón
❺ El Caballo Rojo
❻ Taberna Salinas
❼ Taberna de San Miguel »El Pisto«

Where to stay
❶ Albucasis
❷ Amistad Córdoba
❸ Conquistador
❹ Lola
❺ Casa de los Naranjos
❻ Mezquita Ho
❼ Parador de C.
❽ Riviera
❾ Séneca

probably about 300,000. There were almost 500 mosques, 600 public bathhouses, a number of magnificent palaces, a large Jewish community, 17 schools for higher education, abundant libraries and innumerable schools where a vigorous exchange between Christian, Muslim and Jewish scholars took place. Moorish Córdoba had paved and illuminated streets and provided work for a multitude of artisans. It radiated a brilliance that was unequalled in the rest of Europe. Only Byzantine Constantinople and Baghdad, the metropolis of the eastern caliphate, were comparable. But the Caliphate of Córdoba was torn apart by inner conflict and split into several small kingdoms, the »taifas«, in 1031. In succession, the city came under the rule of Seville (1078), the Almoravids (1091) and the Almohads (1148). In spite of that, during this period, two of the greatest scholars of the high Middle Ages, **Averroes** (Ibn Rushd) and **Moses Maimónides** lived within its walls. After being taken by Ferdinand III in 1236, Córdoba **slowly faded into obscurity** – thanks to this the old town still has a cohesive appearance, even though many buildings became dilapidated and the fertile campiña turned into a barren steppe. Trade and industry also came to a standstill and it was not until three centuries after the return of the Christians that the resumption of the production of leather wallcoverings revived trade.

> ! MARCO POLO TIP
>
> *Festival de los Patios*
>
> Normally, many flower-covered patios remain unseen by the public. Not so during the Festival de los Patios Córdobéses during the first week in May, which is all about picking the most beautiful patio.
> www.patiosdecordoba.net
> www.amigosdelospatioscord beses.es

Many famous people (▶Famous People) were born in Córdoba, including the rhetorician Marcus Annaeus Seneca (54 BC – AD 39), the Stoic Lucius Annaeus Seneca (4 BC – AD 65), the poet Marcus Annaeus Lucanus (AD 39–65); in addition, Averroes (Ibn Rushd, 1126–1198), commentator on Aristotle, Rabbi Moses Maimónides (1135–1204), the poet Luis de Góngora (1561–1627) and Manuel Rodríguez Sánchez (1917–1947), called »Manolete«, the most famous torero of his time (▶Linares).

Famous people

** MEZQUITA CATEDRAL

The mosque-cathedral of Córdoba can readily compete in beauty and size with the grand mosques of Mecca and Damascus, with the El-Azhar mosque in Cairo and the Blue Mosque in Istanbul. When they arrived here, the Moors found a Visigoth church consecrated to Saint Vincent built on the remains of a Roman temple of Janus. They used

Córdoba

Insider Tip

INFORMATION
Oficina de Turismo
Turismo de Córdoba Campo Santo de los Mártires (opposite Alcázar de los Reyes) E-14003 Córdoba
Tel. 902 20 17 74
www.ayuncordoba.es
www.turismodecordoba.org
daily 9am – 2pm, 5pm – 7.30
other information kiosk
Plaza de las Tendillas, Calle Rey Heredia, 4, and at the railway station

ENTERTAINMENT
The English newspaper »Córdoba in ...« has information on what's going on.
In the new city the streets C. Cruz Conde north of Plaza de las Tendillas as well as Avenida Tejares and Avenida Gran Capitán are usually the busiest at night.

Tablao Cardenal
C. Torrijos, 10
Tel. 957 48 31 12
The Tablao opposite the Mezquita has classical flamenco under the starry night sky after 10.30pm.

SHOPPING
Córdoba is known for its pottery and handicraft products from goatskin, sheepskin and silver. A good place to shop for fashion in the barrio is between Plaza de las Tendillas and Avenida del Gran Capitán and in the street that connects the two, Conde de Gondomar.

El Zoco
Calle Judíos
There is a quite wide range of silver and leather in this artisans' market in the Judíos at the Bullfighting Museum.

In his small workshop, Rafael Varo produces wallcoverings and pictures made of leather in the traditional Cordoban technique (Corregidor Luis de la Cerda, 52; east of the Mezquita).
A few paces further is Del Olivo, where it is possible to choose from amongst the finest regional olive oils (San Ferdinand 124 b).
Turronarte has typical sweets like pasteles cordobéses, manoletes and suspiros (Medina y Corella 2; east of the Mezquita). .

Espaliu
Céspedes, 12
Exquisite silver jewellery with oriental patterns.

Manuel Reyes Maldonado
Armas, 4
Musicians of note buy their guitars from Manuel Reyes.

Meryan, Lopez Obrero e Hijos
Callejón de los Flores, 2
Leather goods and pottery decorated with Moorish abstract designs.

Turronarte
Medina y Corella, 2; east of the Mezquita.
Typical sweets like pasteles cordobeses, manoletes or suspiros

PLAZA DE TOROS
Av. de Gran Vía Parque
Tel. 957 23 25 07
The most important fights are in May.

EVENTS
Semana Santa

Cruces de Mayo
Holy Crosses of May festival on the first weekend in May.

Festival de los Patios
In the week following Cruces de Mayo, the most beautiful flower covered patio is chosen.

Feria de Mayo
The major fiesta of the city is held on the last weekend in May on the opposite bank of the river Guadal-quivir.

Guitar Festival
1 June with flamenco, jazz and rock; guitar greats play at night in the garden of the Alcázar (www.guitarracordoba. com) – an unforgettable experience!

WHERE TO EAT
❶ Almudaina €€€€
Campo Santos de los Mártires, 1
Tel. 957 47 43 42
www.restaurantealmudaina.com
One of the best addresses in Córdoba, in an historic building with seven rooms and a lovely patio across from the alcázar. Guests dine under the glass-covered inner courtyard.

❹ El Blasón €€€
José Zorilla, 11
Tel. 957 48 06 25
It's hard to leave the tapas on the pation to go into the fine restaurant. Salmon with orange sauce are one of the house specialities.

❺ El Caballo Rojo €€€
Cardenal Herrero, 28
Tel. 957 47 53 75
www.elcaballorojo.com

Here too it's tempting to stay with the tapas – the lamb kidneys give a good idea of the treats in the restaurant. The cooking here has a Mozarabic touch.

❷ Casa Pepe »De la Judería« €€
Romero, 1
Tel. 957 20 07 44
www.casapepedelajuderia.com
The bar serves tapas of a somewhat more refined sort; in the restaurant fine Cordoban cuisine. The roof terrace has a nice view.

❸ Taberna Casas Salinas €€€€
Puerto de Almodóvar
Tel. 957 29 08 46
Good quality fare served to the sounds of flamenco. The tapas are very popular here

❻ Taberna Salinas €€ €
Tundidores, 3
Tel. 957 48 01 35
www.tabernasalinas.com
closed Sundays
Everything that Spaniards like. Rustic, very popular among the locals, in existence since 1879. Down-to-earth dishes as well as grilled calamares, pork chops and mushroom omelettes on the menu.

❼ Taberna de San Miguel »El Pisto« €
Plaza San Miguel, 1
Tel. 957 47 01 66
Very cosy, old-established tapas bar (1880). The manos de cerdo and rabo de toro are especially good. Moriles wine served in pitchers.

WHERE TO STAY

❸ *Conquistador* €€€
Mag. González Francés, 15–17
Tel. 957 48 11 02
www.hotel-conquistador.com
128 rooms
Luxurious and central near the Mezquita, which can be seen from many of the rooms and the dining room. Relatively large rooms. Much more expensive during Holy Week.

❷ *Amistad Córdoba* €€
Plaza Maimónides, 3
Tel. 957 42 03 35
www.nh-hoteles.com, 84 rooms
Luxurious hotel on the city wall in the Judería. The 17th century city palace also has a garage.

❼ *Parador de Córdoba* €€
Avda. de la Arruzafa, 37
Tel. 957 27 59 00
www.parador.es, 84 rooms
Soberly modern, but very quiet on the edge of town with a very beautiful garden and pool.

Abetos del Maestre Escuela €
Avda. San José de Calasanz, km 2.8
Tel. 957 76 70 63
www.hotelabetos.com, 36 rooms
House in colonial style somewhat outside town with a beautiful garden and view. There are two outdoor pools, a sun terrace and a restaurant.

❶ *Albucasis* €
Buen Pastor, 11
Tel. 957 47 86 25,
www.hotelalbucasis.com, 15 rooms
Typical house in the Judería, full of unexpected nooks and crannies, with a pretty patio and beautiful inner courtyard. There is a garage nearby.

❹ *Lola* €€
Romero, 3
Tel. 957 20 03 05
Fwww.hotellola.es; 8 rooms
Small, charming hotel in the Judería. Each room is named after an Arab princess and some are furnished with cast-iron bed frames and heavy red draperies.

❺ *Casa de los Naranjos* €
Isabel Losa, 8
Tel. 957 47 05 87
www.casadelosnaranjos.com, 20 rooms
Well-tended house with two pretty patios and shady walks; avoid the rooms on the main floor because of the street noise.

❻ *Mezquita Hotel* €
Plaza Santa Catalina, 1
Tel. 957 47 55 86
www.hotelmezquita.com; 21 rooms
A 16th-century house across from the Mezquita with flair, a pretty patio and well-furnished rooms.

❽ *Riviera* €€
Pl. de Aladreros, 5
Tel. 957 47 30 00
www.hotelrivieracordoba.es
Small, centrally located and still quiet. Large rooms. TV and internet access.

❾ *Séneca* €
Conde y Luque, 7
Tel. 957 47 32 34, 12 rooms
Really low-priced, near the picturesque Plaza del Potro, nice patio. The rooms are clean, but earplugs will help.

it as a mosque but let the Christians continue to use part of it. Abd ar-Rahman I acquired it and had it torn down in order to use the materials to begin building a mosque in 785. Eleven aisles were constructed opening to the Courtyard of the Orange Trees and the mihrâb, the prayer niche directed toward Mecca at the end of the somewhat larger central aisle. Hisham I had a first minaret put up at the main entrance that no longer exists today. Al-Hakam I surrounded the courtyard with arcades. The aisles were extended to the south under Abd ar-Rahman II from about 830 to 850. Abd ar-Rahman III had the minaret built in 931 that exists today in an altered form and Al Hakam II enlarged the mosque further to its current length of 179m/587ft. The unique »new mihrâb« and the maksûra, the caliph's prayer room, were also built during this expansion. Finally, it was Almansur who extended the mosque to its present width of 134m/439ft by adding eight additional aisles along the whole length of the building to the east so that the prayer space today has 19 aisles and the asymmetrically positioned prayer niche.

The Christians hardly touched the mosque for a long time; only King Alfonso X had the Capilla Villaviciosa built as the main Christian chapel on the site of the mihrâb from the second building phase. After five aisles had already made way for the first cathedral at the end of the 14th century, there followed one of the most radical changes. In 1523, Bishop Alonso Manrique decided to construct a large cathedral right in the middle of the Islamic prayer space. The town council recognized the danger and threatened with a death sentence anyone who sought to destroy the Moorish structure; but construction began with the consent of the young Charles V under the direction of the architect Hernán Ruiz. A few years later, when the emperor viewed the progress of the construction, he supposedly said to the canons, »If I had known, gentlemen, what you were planning, I would have never allowed it, because what you are building here you'll find everywhere, but what you have destroyed is to be found nowhere on earth.« The construction of the cathedral was essentially completed in 1599. Around this time, the remodelling of the minaret into a bell tower (campanario) also began.

Outside gates

The main entrance on the north side is Puerta del Perdón (pardoner's gate) beneath the campanario. The ticket counter is also here. The Courtyard of the Orange Trees can also be entered by Puerta de los Deanes, Puerta del Virgen de los Faroles, Puerta del Caño Gordo and Puerta de Santa Catalina, a Renaissance gate with a depiction of the old minaret. Of the remaining gates, those that most retain their original Moorish form are Puerta de San Esteban from 855 and Puerta de San Miguel. The caliph entered the mosque through Puerta del Palacio, but it was remodelled in Gothic style in the 15th century. Milk was distributed to orphans at Postigo de la Leche.

MARCO ⊕ POLO INSIGHT

** *Mosque and Cathedral*

The former main mosque of western Islam – one of the world's largest mosques – and today's cathedral (Mezquita-Catedral) is the most important Moorish religious work of architectural art in Spain.

❶ Mon – Sat 10am – 7pm (Nov – March until 6pm), Sun 8.30am – 11.30am, 3pm – 7pm (Nov – March until 6pm); admission: €8
www.catedraldecordoba.es

❶ Maqsûra
Originally the caliph's prayer room

❷ Cathedral
Bishop Alonso Manrique decided in 1523 to construct a large cathedral in the middle of the Islamic prayer room. Its mixture of Gothic and Renaissance styles made it seem like an architectural foreign body.

❸ Campanario (bell tower)
After the cathedral was built around 1599 it was decided to begin remodelling the minaret into a bell tower. The tower has a statue of the archangel Raphael on top, the city's patron saint.

❹ Crenelated walls
The structure is surrounded by a 9 – 20 m (30 – 66 ft) high wall with tower-like buttresses and the classical decorative elements of Islam – red-white horseshoe arches, floral and geometric patterns and Kufic writing.

❺ Water basins
The large water basins, not all of which have been preserved, ritual washings were carried out before entering the prayer hall, which used to be open facing the courtyard.

❻ Muslim prayer room
793 columns support the arches with alternating red and white wedge-shaped limestone or brick stones. In the Mezquita there were no markings for paths or direction. For Muslims every place at which he carries out his prayers is equally close to Allah. In the past daylight entered through the currently walled-up doorways and thousands of burning oil lamps also illuminated the room.

❼ Mihrâb Nuevo (New Mihrâb)
The prayer niche of the prayer leader, which shows the direction to Mecca – it is the most sacred place in the mosque. The dome was carved out of one single block of marble and symbolizes the globe of the world. It overflows with floral and geometric patterns, Koran verses and mosaics created by Byzantine artists.

❽ Capilla del Cardenal
The church treasure is kept here: the most valuable pieces are a silver monstrance (1510 – 1516) and a processional cross by Enrique de Arfe, nine statues of saints, an ivory crucifix by Alonso Cano as well as manuscripts in Arabic (9./10. cent.)

❾ Arcades
Students and teachers met under the arcades on the north side in order to debate. To the west of the bell tower doctors gave medical advice, to the east the qadis gave legal decisions.

Mezqui
,000 sq
ompare
Al-Hara
56,000 r
,200,00
kh Zayi
n for 40
an II me
n for 25

Campanario The campanario (Torre de Alminar), rising above Puerta del Perdón and built on the first storey of the old minaret, was given its form based on Herrera style in 1593 by Hernán Ruiz when he encased the minaret.

*Patio de los Naranjos Patio de los Naranjos (Courtyard of the Orange Trees), covered with orange trees and palms, opens out in front of the prayer areas. Puerta de las Palmas, today in the Renaissance style of 1531, is the entrance to the oldest part of the mosque.

Muslim prayer area Time and again the attempt has been made to describe the world-famous Mezquita – but the manner in which the **seemingly endless forest of 793 columns in semi-darkness reveals a different perspective with each step has to be experienced at first hand.

The columns of the first section are of jasper, marble and porphyry from Roman and Visigoth buildings in Andalucía and North Africa and were set on bases when necessary to compensate for their varying heights. The character of this part is defined by the four-cornered half-columns topped by round arches on the lower row of horseshoe arches in order to achieve the total height of 11.5m/37ft, resulting in rows of double arches. The beautifully coloured, richly carved timberwork of the old mosque has been revealed at Puerta de las Palmas and between the mihrâbs (prayer niches) orientated to Mecca. The columns in the second phase of building are the first to bear Corinthian capitals.

The third phase is recognizable by the fanciful clover-leaf cusped forms in the arrangement of the arches. The section built under Almansur is distinguished by its spaciousness, which allows the rows of arches to appear to their best advantage.

A grille on the southwest wall separates the ****Mihrâb Nuevo** from its anteroom – the Maksûra. Even the anteroom has the richest of decoration; particularly the multitude of arch forms, mosaics and ribbons of Kufic script give proof of the masterly skill of the craftsmen, which reached its apex in the **blossom-shaped dome**. The Mihrâb Nuevo (New Mihrâb) is incomparable and unsurpassed. It opens behind a horseshoe arch flanked by two pairs of columns from Abd ar-Rahman II's old mihrâb. A mosaic arch stretches over it with floral ornamentation bordered by an alfiz with bands of Kufic script recounting all the names of Allah.

Cathedral and chapels In the 18th century, Francisco Hurtado Izquierdo built the **Capilla del Cardenal** in which the church treasures are stored next to the mihrâb on the left.

The ***Capilla Villaviciosa** across from the Mihrâb Nuevo is the former mihrâb of Abd ar-Rahmans II's mosque. It was converted into the first Christian chapel in the mosque, but its Moorish col-

Mezquita - Catedral de Córdoba

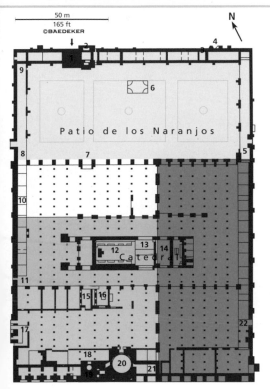

50 m
165 ft
©BAEDEKER

N

☐ First mosque under Abd ar-Rahman I (785)

▨ First extension under Abd ar-Rahman II (c. 850)

▨ Second extension under Al Hakam II (c. 960)

▨ Third extension under Almansur (c. 990)

1 Campanario (Torre de Alminar)
2 Puerta del Perdón
3 Puerta del Caño Gordo
4 Virgen de los Faroles
5 Puerta de Santa Catalina
6 Pool of Almansur
7 Puerta de las Palmas
8 Puerta de los Deanes
9 Postigo de la Leche
10 Puerta de San Esteban
11 Puerta de San Miguel
12 Coro
13 Crucero
14 Capilla Mayor
15 Capilla Villaviciosa
16 Capilla Real
17 Postigo del Palacio
18 Maksûra
19 Mihrâb Nuevo
20 Capilla del Cardenal
21 Capilla del Santo Cristo del Punto
22 Postigo del Sagrario

umn decoration and the daring construction of the dome are still captivating.

Next to it is the **Capilla Real** (14th century), beautifully worked in Mudejar style with faience and plaster facing. It was conceived as a mausoleum for the Castilian kings, Ferdinand IV and Alfonso XI, whose remains were transferred to the church of San Hipólito in 1706, however.

The Gothic **transept** serving as choir in the heart of the mosque and the **Capilla Mayor** form a church in its own right. The *Cathedral was built for the most part by Hernán Ruiz, his son and his grandson at the behest of Bishop Alonso Manrique following the demolition of 63 columns. The choir was built between 1523 and 1539, and the chancel between 1547 and 1599. The richly-carved

Byzantine artisans created the mosaics of the Mihrâb Nuevo

Baroque stalls (18th century) in the choir were created by Pedro Cornejo. There are five paintings by Palomino on the high altar (1618) by Alonso Matías. The two pulpits of mahogony and marble as well as the tomb of Bishop Leopold of Austria are also worthy of note.

AROUND THE MEZQUITA

Museo Diocesano

Across from the southwest corner of the Mezquita stands the epis-copal palace, built in the 15th century on the ruins of the old pal-ace of the caliph and remodelled in 1745. Today it houses the Museo Diocesano, which displays archaeological finds, paintings and religious sculptures from the 13th to the 18th centuries.

San Jacinto church and the Hospital San Sebastián, which con-tains the congress palace and the **tourist office**, are next to the episcopal palace.

❶ tgl. 9.00am – 14.00pm and 16.30pm – 19:30pm, admission: €2

The bank of the Guadalquivir is south of the palace. There on the terrace stands the Triunfo de San Rafael column from 1765 bearing a statue of the archangel Raphael. Puerta del Puente can be seen beneath the terrace standing below street level. It is a Doric triumphal arch, built in the 16th century to honour Philip II, that once served as a bridge gate. On the river bank, also below the terrace, is a restored **Moorish waterwheel** that Abd ar-Rahman II had built in the 10th century.

On the Guadalquivir

To the west lies the Alcázar de los Reyes Cristianos with the Campo de los Mártires in front of its main building, supposedly the place where Christians maryters were executed. The imposing ramparts and towers of the castle in part date back to Moorish times, Alfonso XI, however, started expanding most of it into a military installation with a rectangular groundplan in 1328. It was the royal residence of the Catholic Monarchs during their military expeditions against Moorish Granada. Once a giant Moorish waterwheel turned in front of the alcázar walls, but its creaking disturbed Isabella's sleep and so it was torn down. The castle was the seat of the Inquisition until 1821, and then a prison. The surviving towers include Torre de los Leones with **very beautiful Mudejar work**, Torre del Río and Torre del Homenaje, both furnished with remarkable ribbed vaults.

*Alcázar de los Reyes Cristianos

Insider Tip

Archaeological finds are on display in a **museum** in the alcázar Among the best pieces are a Roman sarcophagus from the 3rd century AD with fine reliefs and Roman mosaics.

Adjoining the main building within the walls are magnificent gardens with fountains, bounded to the west by the remains of the Moorish city wall with the Puerta de Seville. A monument to the great philosopher Averroes was erected outside the walls.

Insider Tip

Museum: Mid-Sept. – mid-June Tue – Fri 8.30am – 7.30pm, Sat 9.30am – 4.30pm, Sun 9.30am – 2.30pm; mid-June – mid-Sept Tue – Sat 8.30am – 2.30pm, Sun 9.30am – 2.30pm; admission: €4,50
Gardens: hours same as Museum, July/Aug also 9pm – midnight.

The six-arched Puente Romano over the Guadalquivir was built in about 48 BC after Caesar's victory over Pompey in the Roman civil war. The Moors later erected the present 223m/244yd-long bridge on the foundations. A dilapidated mill dating from Moorish times in the shallow waters of the Guadalquivir presents a picturesque view from the bridge.

*Puente Romano

The southern end of the bridge is marked by the imposing fortified tower Torre de la Calahorra, erected in 1369 under Enrique II. The museum inside it, ***Museo Vivo de Al-Andalus**, brings Moorish Andalucía to life in an impressive way. Each visitor is given a wireless headset that receives music and the text (also English) appropriate to

Torre de la Calahorra

The gardens of the Alcázar refresh the senses
with lush flowers and water fountains

each room entered. Great philosophers of the time are presented, including **Averroes, Maimónides, Ibn al-Arabi** and **Alfonso X, the Wise**. Another room is dedicated to medicine, astronomy and geography; the irrigation techniques of the Moors are explained using excellent models and dioramas. Islamic music is explained, and two models of the Alhambra of Granada as well as the mosque of Córdoba as it was in 1236 are shown in further rooms. A **multimedia show** in English presents the history and culture of Córdoba in understandable terms. There is a tremendous view of the old town from the roof of the tower.

❶ May – Sept daily 10am – 2pm, 4.30pm – 8.30pm, Oct – April daily 10am – 6pm; admission: €4.50; www.torrecalahorra.com

✳ JUDERÍA

The Judería, the **old Jewish quarter**, begins north of the Mezquita. Narrow lanes, white-washed houses with inner courtyards full of plants and secluded spots create their own distinct atmosphere that can best be experienced away from the streets directly around the Mezquita where the souvenir shops are lined up one next to the other. The main street, C/Judíos, runs alongside the wall.

Calleja de las Flores, »Flower Alley« decorated with blooms, can be reached by heading away from the northeast corner of the Mezquita on C. Velásquez Bosco and then turning right. | **Calleja de las Flores**

Plaza Maimónides can be reached from the northwest corner of the Mezquita, and further on there is a modern monument in memory of the great Jewish scholar **Moses Maimónides** (1135 – 1204) on Plaza de Tiberiades. | **Maimónides monument**

Everything about bullfighting has been gathered in the Museo Municipal Taurino in the Casa de las Bulas on Plaza Maimónides; posters, swords, costumes, the stuffed heads of famous bulls and, above all, tributes to bullfighters from Córdoba like Lagartijo, Machaco, Guerrito, Manuel Benítez (»El Córdobes«) and, first and foremost, Manolete, whose study and sepulchral sculpture are on display. Directly next to the museum is El Zoco, a covered handicraft market. | **Museo Taurino**

❶ Tue – Fri 8.30am – 20.45pm, Sat 8.30am – 16.30pm, Sun 8.30am – 14.30pm; admission: €4

> **MARCO POLO TIP**
>
> **❗ Bodega Guzmán** — Insider Tip
>
> The best place to take a tapas break in the Judería is Bodega Guzmán across from the synagogue (Judíaos, 9). The house drink is the (bitter) »amargoso montilla«. Locals, especially ones from the neighbourhood, also like to stop here. One room is totally dedicated to bullfighting.

The **synagogue** directly opposite is one of Spain's three remaining Jewish places of worship **from the high Middle Ages** (the other two are in Toledo). It shows typical Mudejar decorative elements. Hebrew inscriptions repeat Biblical psalms; one of them on a niche for the Torah scrolls in the east wall names 5075 as the founding date, which corresponds to the year 1315 of the Gregorian calendar. On the south wall steps lead to the women's gallery. | ***Sinagoga**

❶ Tue – Sat 9.30am – 2pm, 3.30pm – 5.30pm, Sun 9.30am – 1.30pm; free admission for citizens of the EU

How homes were furnished in Moorish Córdoba and how paper was produced is shown in the 12th-century Casa Andalusí next to the synagogue. | **Casa Andalusí**

❶ daily 10.30am–7pm; admission €2.50

The well-preserved Puerta de Almodóvar at the north end of C/ Judíos marks the entrance to the former ghetto. Beyond it stands the statue of **Lucius Annaeus Seneca** (▶Famous People), the poet, philosopher and tutor of Emperor Nero, who was born in Roman Córdoba. On the way from the gate into town is the 15th-century Casa del Indiano, which has a splendid Mudejar portal. | **Puerta de Almodóvar**

REST OF THE OLD TOWN

The rest of the old town north and west of the Mezquita is a maze of alleyways that developed in the course of the centuries. It imparts a much more authentic feeling of old Córdoba than the tourist-oriented Judería.

*Museo Arqueológico The archaeological museum in Casa Paéz, a Renaissance palace on Plaza Don Jerónimo Paéz, is among the finest in Andalucía. Prehistoric finds, Iberian artefacts like a hunting scene from Almodóvar del Río and a figure of a lion, Roman pieces (busts of Germanicus and Commodus, a Mithras altar, mosaics) and early Christian finds including a sarcophagus with almost three-dimensional scenes from the Bible, as well as gold crosses and jewellery from the Treasure of Torredonjimeno are displayed on the lower floor. The Moorish section on the upper floor is the centrepiece of the collection. The valuable objects displayed here are primarily from ►Medina Azahara, the caliphs' residence, including a 10th-century bronze stag with niello inlays.

The foal gave his name to the Plaza del Potro

❶ Tue – 2.30pm – 8.30pm, Wed – Sat 9am – 8.30pm, Sun 9am – 2.30pm

Plaza del Potro, east of the Mezquita near the riverbank, was the centre of the city and its market place in the 16th century. It takes its name from a small bronze sculpture of a colt from the 16th century. Cervantes once stayed in the old Posada del Potro inn; today it informs on the origins and history of the flamenco. The monastery church on the plaza, San Francisco, is richly decorated with paintings by Valdés Leal, Palomino and de Castillo, among others.

The **Hospital de la Caridad** opposite, which was founded by the Catholic Monarchs in the 16th century, today houses two museums. The Museo Provincial de Bellas Artes (museum of fine arts) definitely took a loss after giving up three Goyas and several Riberas, and now the best work it possesses is Valdés Leal's Virgin of the Silversmiths and Bartolomé Esteban Murillo's Immaculate Conception. In addition many **Cordoban artists** are on display.

❶ Tue 2.30pm – 8.30pm, Wed – Sat 9am – 8.30pm, Sun 9am – 2.30pm

Across and past the courtyard is the entrance to the museum of Spanish painter **Julio Romero de Torres** (1874–1930). He was the son of the director of the art museum and made a name for himself painting dark, beautiful women that many dismiss as kitsch, but are none the less extremely popular in Córdoba.

Museo Julio Romero de Torres

❶ Tue – Fri 8.30am – 20.45pm, Sat 8.30am – 16.30pm, Sun 8.30am – 14.30pm; admission: €4,50

The Moorish apses and two portals still survive in San Pedro (13th century), east of Plaza del Potro, the church in which Cordoban christians gathered to pray during the time of the caliphs. In 1542, Hernán Ruiz added the Renaissance facade.

San Pedro

Past Plaza del Potro to the north is Plaza de la Corredera, which was laid out in 1683 and is completely encircled by arcade houses. It was also the site of executions and bullfights. The bulls were penned up ready for their entrance in the Calleja del Torril on the east side. After a long period of neglect, the plaza was renovated and is once again the site of a daily market for clothing and handicrafts.

*Plaza de la Corredera

To the north is the town hall, to the left of which the remains of a 1st-century Roman temple have been uncovered.

Templo Romano

San Pablo church looms opposite the town hall. It was built in 1241 using material from the palace-city of Medina Azahara. Its nave and aisles have Mudejar artesonado ceilings and its walls are lined with azulejos. The **Capilla del Rosario** originated in Gothic style in 1409 and contains the tomb of the grand master of the Order of Calatrava, **Martín López**, while the chancel is decorated in Baroque style. The vault of the sacristy, on the other hand, is Moorish. A work of art worth seeing here is the figure group Virgen de las Angustias by **Juan de Mesa**.

*San Pablo

Close to the church lies Casa de los Villalones, built in 1560, which betrays Italian influence with its **triple loggia** in the upper storey.

Casa de los Villalones

The museum east of Plaza de la Corredera in the jewellers' quarter exhibits traditional and modern **Cordoban artisan jewellery**.

Museo Regina de Joyería

❶ Summer daily 9.30am – 2pm, 5.30pm – 9pm; winter 10am – 3pm, 5pm – 8pm; admission: €3

The favourite place of many Córdobans: Plaza de los Dolores

NORTHERN CITY QUARTERS

Plaza de las Tendillas combines the historical with the bustling side of Córdoba. The equestrian statue of Gran Capitán Gonzalo Fernández de Córdoba, the fountains and the bars are popular meeting points after shopping in the stores round about.

C/Conde de Gondomar runs west from the plaza to **Bulvar del Gran Capitán**, the elegant city boulevard. About in the middle is the church of **San Hipólito**, to which the remains of Ferdinand IV and Alfonso XI were brought in 1706 from the Capilla Real in the Mezquita. South of it, the remains of a smaller mosque can be seen. The bell tower of **San Juan** was once its minaret. It still has gemel windows with horseshoe arches. From the church square in front of San Miguel, north of Plaza de las Tendillas, head along Conde de Torres past the house where the torero Manolete was born and turn right at the corner at the Capucine convent into **Plaza de los Dolores**. Here stands one of **the symbols of Córdoba**, a stone cross with Christ crucified surrounded by eight wrought-iron street lamps, the Cristo de los Faroles, which presents a romantic sight, especially at night. The church holds the most popular Madonna figure of the city, the Virgen de los Dolores, heaped with gold and brocade.

Torre de la Malmuerta Further to the north on the northeast side of Plaza Colón towers the eight-cornered, crenellated Torre de la Malmuerta from the 15th century.

Santa Marina de Aguas Santas East of Plaza de Colón lies the fortress-like church of Santa Marina de Aguas Santas. It was begun shortly after the conquest of Córdoba and stands out because of its massive buttresses. On the church square there is a statue commemorating the bullfighter Manolete, who was born in this quarter.

*Palacio de los Marqueses de Viana On the way back to the old town is the Palacio de los Marqueses de Viana, the pompous former city palace of the Viana family with a **garden, twelve patios and 181 rooms** that are filled to overflowing with leatherwork, silver, porcelain, azulejos, furniture and paintings.
  ❶ Tue – Fri 10am – 7pm, Sun 10am – 3pm; admission: €6

AROUND CÓRDOBA

►p. 335

In early Christian times, Christians found refuge in the heights of the Sierra de Córdoba. The oldest of today's 13 hermitages was built in the 15th century. They are worth a visit primarily for the beautiful surroundings and the view of the Guadalquivir plains and Córdoba. To reach them drive north out of Córdoba at first in the direction of the parador and then take the road leading to the Arruzafa Nature Park. The hermitages can also be reached from ►**Medina Azahara**. Once there, take a walk along the very beautiful avenue lined with cypresses and palms to the chapel founded in 1732. A cemetery and a hermit's cottage can be seen in front of it. Below the wayside lies the lookout point with a statue of Christ.

Medina Azahara *Las Ermitas

❶ Tue – Sun 10am – 1.30pm; July, Aug. 5pm – 7.45pm, other months 4.30pm – 7.30pm or sunset; admission: €1.50

Nobody would travel 25km/16mi west of Córdoba into the hot Guadalquivir basin to Almodóvar del Río just to see the village. However, the **castillo** is visible for a great distance towering over the village. With its battlements and mighty towers, it is the perfect **picture-postcard medieval castle**. The Moors erected the castle in the 8th century to control traffic on the navigable Guadalquivir River. It became known as the »plague of the Christians« because it caused the Castilians and Aragonians so much trouble. **Ferdinando the Saint** captured it in 1240, and it gained its present appearance in the 14th century under Pedro the Cruel who used it to hold his treasures. A ring of ramparts, actually a double ring in the northwest and northeast, encloses the courtyard with its two fountains and café. From here there is a beautiful view of the surrounding countryside.

Almodóvar del Río

> **!** *La Taberna* **Insider Tip**
>
> MARCO ⊕ POLO TIP
>
> If you get hungry in Almodóvar del Río in the hot basin of the river Guadalquivir, try the »Taberna« (C. Antonio Machado, 20), which serves fine but authentic regional cooking – with local olive oil and wine.

❶ Mon – Sat 11am – 2.30pm, 4pm – 8pm, Sun 11am – 8pm, winter 1 hour less; admission €5

Though a bit out of the way, Montoro, the Roman Epora , can be found by taking the N-IV eastwards through 35km/22mi of cotton fields and olive groves to where it is picturesquely nestled above the left bank of Guadalquivir. It was an important fortress in Moorish times and is **typical for small towns in Andalucía** with its churches, nobles' houses and streets of houses. It is worth taking a stroll

Montoro

through this pretty place, especially around the Plaza de España with its 15th-century church, San Bartolomé, and 16th-century town hall. Take time to look inside the archaeological museum in the former church, Santa María de la Mota. Montoro is also suitable as a starting point for trips into the Parque Natural de la Sierra de Cardeña y Montoro to the north in the Sierra Morena where wolves and lynxes still live.

Costa de Almería

►Almería, ►Cabo de Gata, ►Mojácar

** Costa de la Luz

✦ A–C 7–9

Province: Huelva, Cádiz

The Spanish southern Atlantic coast between the Río Guadiana estuary at the Portuguese border and the headland of Tarifa on the Straits of Gibraltar bears the name Costa de la Luz (»Coast of Light«), because it is almost always bathed in blazing sunlight.

»Coast of Light« | Despite that, the summers here are not so unbearably hot as in the interior because a **wind, the »Poniente«**, constantly blows in from the sea providing a refreshing breeze, at least from Matalascañas up to the Portuguese border. The remaining section of the coast down to Tarifa, on the other hand, is swept the whole year, often with considerable force, by the dry **east wind, the »Levante«** – hardly bearable for »normal« tourists and locals, but for experienced **surfers**, in contrast, a dream. For them, the surfing off Tarifa is among the world's best.

Insider Tip

Almost all villages on the Costa de la Luz live at least in part from fishing, but tourism is an increasingly important source of income. Even though new resorts like Matalascañas or Novo Sancti Petri have been built from scratch, conditions are still a long way away from those on the Costa del Sol; so the Costa de la Luz remains a destination for all those who want to enjoy sun, sand and sea without being hustled by activity directors. Fantastic beaches (a total of 265km/165mi) with the finest sand, bordered inland by eucalyptus trees and pines, are inviting places for a swim in the Atlantic: Matalascañas between Sanlúcar de Barrameda and Rota, for example, or Chiclana de la Frontera, Barbate or Tarifa.

Sun on a fine sandy beach, surfing in a fresh sea breeze and swimming in the Atlantic – the »Coast of Light« is fun!

Nature lovers enjoy the unique Coto de Doñana National Park which, by the way, divides the coast in two; it takes a long drive around it to get from the north to the south. Tourists seeking culture will get their money's worth inland in cities like Jerez de la Frontera, the »pueblos blancos« and in Seville. The hinterland is the domain of the big landowners, who cultivate wine (sherry, Manzanilla) and olives and breed fighting bulls.

The Costa de la Luz also has great historical significance. Cádiz is the oldest city on the Iberian peninsula and goes back to the Phoenicians. Here on the border **between the Christian and Moorish spheres of power** decisive battles were fought, which is why many places bear the additive »de la Frontera« (»on the border«). It was from the ports on this coast that Christoph Columbus started on his expeditions.

Borderland

▶Cádiz, ▶Coto de Doñana, ▶El Rocío, ▶Huelva • Ruta Colombina, ▶Jerez de la Frontera, ▶El Puerto de Santa María, ▶Sanlúcar de Barrameda, ▶Tarifa, ▶Vejer de la Frontera

Destinations on the Costa de la Luz

✳ Costa del Sol

✦ D–L 8–9

Province: Cádiz, Málaga

For a long time the »Sun Coast« was defined as the whole Andalusian Mediterranean coastline from Tarifa (Cádiz province) to Cabo de Gata (Almería province). As a marketing strategy, the coastline around ▶Almuñecar (province of Granada) and around ▶Almería were split off and named the Costa Tropical, leaving the strip from Tarifa to the eastern border with the province of Málaga as the Costa del Sol.

»Sun Coast« The heart of the tourist area, the coastline from Málaga to Estepona, is considered to be **the largest continuous resort area in Europe**. Up until the 1950s, hardly a traveller strayed this way, but then organized mass tourism discovered the coast where the sun shines 320 days a year. The boom years began that transformed sleepy fishing villages into hotel cities for tens of thousands and, as tastes changed, holiday clubs and apartment complexes were added – about 300,000 non-Spanish nationals now live here. The price paid was the disfiguring of

The sun shines everywhere on the Costa del Sol, but few beaches are as undeveloped as this one near Nerja

the coastal landscape with piles of concrete and the four-lane N-340 (now A-7) cutting right through villages. The effects of this have been somewhat mitigated by the construction of the Autopista del Sol (AP-7) toll road, part of a programme begun in the 1990s to correct previous excesses, including the construction of sewage treatment plants and the redesigning of whole beach promenades. This has made the Costa del Sol indisputably more attractive. Despite that, visitors seeking peace and quiet will not be happy here because the **night life** is just as important as the **beach life**, so that there is no dearth of discos, nightclubs, restaurants, bars, fiestas and all manner of beach entertainment imaginable. Finally, the Costa del Sol is also a **paradise for golfers** – nowhere in Europe are more golf courses concentrated in such a limited space, which the world's best golfers acknowledged by staging the Ryder Cup in Sotogrande, the first time it was held in Europe outside Great Britain.

The **mountainous hinterland** is completely different from the coast. There it is possible to escape the hustle and bustle. With its white-washed houses, its agaves and cacti, its slopes covered by pines and olive trees, country estates and cheerful villages, this countryside is a **true image of Andalucía**.

►Algeciras, ►Estepona, ►Fuengirola, ►Gibraltar, ►Málaga, ►Marbella, ►Nerja, ►Torremolinos

Sights on the Costa del Sol

Costa Tropical

►Almuñecar

✶✶ Coto de Doñana

— ✳ C 7/8

Province: Huelva, Seville

Numerous migrating birds spend the winter here or take a break on their way to Africa and consort with their fellow birds living here, making the park a unique bird paradise and one of Europe's most beautiful nature reserves.

The **Parque Nacional Coto de Doñana** lies in the delta of the Río Guadalquivir, bordering it to the east. In the south it extends to the mouth of the river opposite ►Sanlúcar de Barrameda, in the west to the Atlantic and in the north to the A-483 between Matalascañas and ►El Rocío.

History

Coto de Doñana

PARK ACCESS
Access to the park is tightly regulated and not allowed without the accompaniment of game keepers.

Tours in off-road vehicles (about 4 hours) from the El Acebuche Information Centre
Departure: May – mid-Sept daily 8.30am and 5.30pm, Mitte Sept. – Apr. 8.30 and 15.00pm; Tel. 959 43 04 32, www.donanavisitas.es.

Boat trip (4 hours) on the »Real Fernando« from Sanlúcar de Barrameda with stop-overs in Entorno de Doñana on the border of the park, at the Monte Algaida salt-works and a reconstructed marsh village.
Departure: daily 10am, June – Sept also 5pm, March, April, May, Oct also 4pm; order tickets in advance at the Fábrica de Hielo Information Centre in Sanlúcar de Barrameda (Tel. 956 36 38 13).

Horse ride: Doñana Caballo, El Rocío, Tel. 674 21 95 68 www.donanaacaballo.es

INFORMATION CENTRES
http://reddeparquesnacionales.mma.es
www.donana.es.

El Acebuche Information Centre
4km/2.5mi from Matalascañas and 1.5km/1mi from the A-483
Tel. 959 43 96 29
Summer: daily 8am – 9pm, winter until 7pm
Exhibits, audio-visual show, caféteria, souvenir shop, two paths 1.5km/1mi and 3.5km/2mi in length with observation stations.

La Rocina
1km/0.6mi before El Rocío
Tel. 959 43 95 69
Audio-visual show, exhibition about Romería del Rocío, path 3.5km/2mi

El Acebrón
7km/4.5mi from La Rocina
Tel. 959 50 61 62
Opening times like above
Exhibit about charcoal burners, pine-cone collectors and fishermen in the Marisma, path 1.5km/0.9mi

José Antonio Valverde
In the middle of the marshlands west of Isla Mayor, accessible only on unpaved roads
Tel. 671 56 41 45
Summer: daily 8am – 8pm, winter until 6pm
Exhibit on ecosystem, walking path

Fábrica de Hielo
Fábrica de Hielo, Sanlúcar de Barrameda, Avenida de Bajo de Guía
Tel. 956 38 65 77
Summer daily 9am – 8pm, winter until 7pm
Permanent exhibition and observation point.

WHERE TO STAY
Parador de Mazagón €€€
Insider Tip
Mazagón, Playa de Mazagón
Tel. 959 53 63 00
www.parador.es, 53 rooms
Modern hotel in a fantastic location facing the sea, with fabulous beaches, behind it the national park.

Gran Hotel del Coto €
In Matalascañas, Sector D, 2. Fase
Tel. 959 44 00 17
www.granhoteldelcoto.com, 466 rooms
The largest and most expensive hotel in town. Matalascañas is a not particularly nice-looking new development with its hotel complexes but offers every kind of seaside recreation.

Hostal Rocio €
Matalascañas, Sector Inglesillo 60

Tel. 959 43 01 41
http://hostal-rocio-matalascanas.com
Bed & breakfast with double rooms and bath. Furnished very simply, family-run and clean

Los Tamarindos €
Almonte, Avda. Adelfas, 31
Tel. 959 43 01 19
17 rooms
Small but classy – well furnished pension.

This countryside was never much settled – the marshland (marismas) climate was too hostile, with malaria rampant until the middle of the 20th century. The area was of interest almost exclusively as **hunting grounds** (Spanish: coto), which is why it has remained unspoiled. Alfonso X, the Wise, was in the habit of hunting here in the 13th century and the dukes of Medina Sidonia, who came into possession of the land, followed his example. The 7th duke, Alfonso Pérez de Guzmán, commander of the Spanish Armada that was destroyed in 1588, erected a **palace** for his wife, Doña Ana, in 1595 in the middle of the present park. Today, it is a research centre. In the course of time, the name »Coto de Doña Ana« became »Coto de Doñana«. The dukes sold the area in 1897 to the sherry baron, William Garvey. Around this time, two British citizens, Abel Chapman and Walter Buck, called attention for the first time to the wealth of nature in Coto, but it was not until the 1960s that conservationists achieved the creation of that national park that opened in 1969 as »Parque Nacional de Doñana« with an area of 37,000 ha/90,000 acres. There followed an expansion in 1978 to 50,000 ha/125,000 acres with additional protected areas amounting to 26,500 ha/65,000 acres close by but not directly part of the park. The park has been a **UNESCO biosphere reserve** since 1994.

The national park is endangered. The immense rice and fruit plantations surrounding it use up a lot of land and water and toxic substances from the liberal application of fertilizer also reaches the marismas. The greatest catastrophe hit the park in 1998 when 5 million tons of acidic water and mud contaminated with heavy metals flowed into the Río Guadimar and reached right up to the park. Finally, tourism in the form of the Matalascañas holiday resort and its enormous water consumption is a threat to the park. A project planned near Matalascañas with 32,000 beds was stopped. On the

Endangered

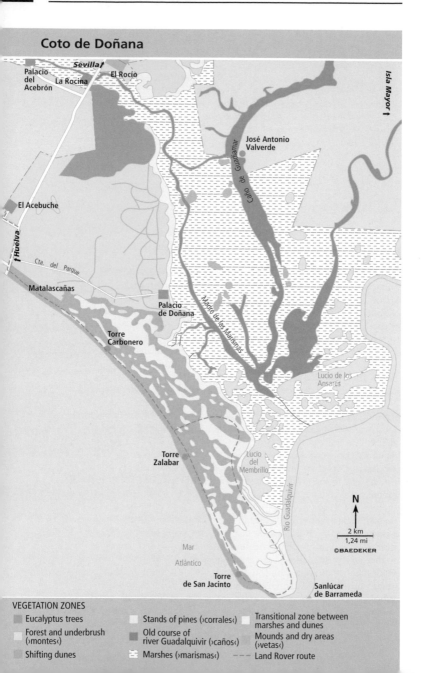

Coto de Doñana

Sevilla↗
Palacio del Acebrón
La Rocina
El Rocío
Isla Mayor ↑
José Antonio Valverde
El Acebuche
↑ Huelva
Caño de Guadiamar
Cta. del Parque
Matalascañas
Palacio de Doñana
Madre de las Marismas
Torre Carbonero
Lúcio de los Ansares
Torre Zalabar
Lúcio del Membrillo
Río Guadalquivir
N
2 km
1,24 mi
©BAEDEKER
Mar Atlántico
Torre de San Jacinto
Sanlúcar de Barrameda

VEGETATION ZONES

- Eucalyptus trees
- Forest and underbrush (›montes‹)
- Shifting dunes
- Stands of pines (›corrales‹)
- Old course of river Guadalquivir (›caños‹)
- Marshes (›marismas‹)
- Transitional zone between marshes and dunes
- Mounds and dry areas (›vetas‹)
- --- Land Rover route

other hand, the municipality of Sanlúcar de Barrameda and the Department of Environment approved a luxury holiday centre with golf courses north of the estuary.

Three eco-systems can be distinguished; the **wetlands** (Doñana húmeda: Marisma in the estuary and lagoons), the **arid region** (Doñana seca – forest and underbrush) and the **bands of shifting sand dunes** on the coast. The areas flooded for the most part of the year (almajales) are the backwaters of the Guadalquivir (caños), springs (ojos) and the long, flat lagoons (lucios). In between are small mounds (paciles) and higher dry areas (vetas).

Flora and fauna

The **marismas** (marshlands) are influenced by the subterranean water-level. During the dry season (July–September, lowest point in August), they lie dry and abandoned. The first **migratory birds** arrive end of September. Seaside bulrush, marsh rush and broad-leaved cattails are some of the plants that grow here. Ducks (European widgeons, northern pintails, teals, spoonbills, pochards) find best conditions here. Coots, great crested grebes, dabchicks, purple herons, gull-billed terns, whiskered terns and black terns nest in spring. They are joined by many mud-flat dwellers and marsh harriers.

The larger **lagoons** lie parallel to the coastline (Laguna de Santa Olalla, Laguna Dulce, Laguna del Taraje), the smaller further inland (Laguna del Moral, de Navazo del Toro, del Sapo, del Brezo and others). They are lined with cork oak, pine and tree heath; gorse and ferns provide greenery on the banks. The most important **aquatic inhabitants** are

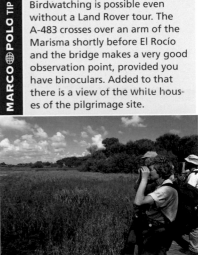

marsh frogs, European pond turtles and Caspian terrapins. The endangered red-knobbed coot has its last European refuge here. Fallow deer and red deer, as well as wild boar visit the banks; coypu live next to the water.

Cork oak woods have become rare. One strip of it divides the »marismas« from Monte de Doñana. These cork oaks are a habitat for **whole breeding colonies** of grey herons, little egrets, cattle egrets, spoonbills and some white storks. Uninvited guests in the nesting trees are birds of prey like the common buzzard (Buteo buteo), red

---

MARCO POLO TIP

Take binoculars! **Insider Tip**

Birdwatching is possible even without a Land Rover tour. The A-483 crosses over an arm of the Marisma shortly before El Rocío and the bridge makes a very good observation point, provided you have binoculars. Added to that there is a view of the white houses of the pilgrimage site.

Coto de Doñana nursery: whole colonies of storks brood here

kite, kestrels and jackdaws. The poisonous snub-nosed viper lives on the ground.

»Monte« is not the name of a mountain but rather a copse or thicket. **Monte de Doñana** consists of Mediterranean scrub sprinkled with cork oak. Among others, the philaria (common lime), rosemary, juniper, lavender and white thyme blossom here.

The **reptiles** include the Greek tortoise, the ladder snake, the Montpellier snake and, again, the snub-nosed viper. Along with the birds of prey mentioned above, there are magpies, great grey shrikes, nightjars and numerous red hens. The most common mammals are red and fallow deer and wild boar; in addition, weasels, polecats, wildcats und foxes. The small-spotted genet is less common; on the other hand, badgers are numerous and there are many wild rabbits. Pine trees thrive in the park, particularly in the southern part, and the undergrowth between them is made up of tree heath, rockrose, gorse and pistachio. The **pine forests** are the biosphere for woodpigeons, turtle-doves, blackbirds, mistle thrushes, common buzzards, red kites and kestrels; the short-toed eagle and the hobby return each year. The **azure-winged magpie** is very rare and is **almost only to be found here**.

The **sand dunes** that stretch along the coastline surround pine forests when they advance inland so that these forests stand like islands (corrales) in the sand until they are eventually smothered. The vegetation is very sparse, mainly consisting of beach grass and a scrub called camarina, whose sweet fruit is eaten by birds. The common spiny-footed lizard, the snub-nosed viper and the Montpellier snake are welcome prey for the short-toed eagle and the screech owl.

The **Spanish lynx** (about 25 pairs), smaller than the European lynx and spotted, as well as the snake-eating ichneumon or mongoose, the only representative of this species of viverrid that mostly goose-steps around in family groups, are only to be found in Coto de Doñana. The **imperial eagle** (about 18 pairs), purple moorhen (the only European breeding colony), white-eyed pochard as well as the **ruddy shelduck** and the white-headed duck that spend the winters here are all also very rare.

Indigenous species

✶ Écija

✶ E 6

Province: Seville
Altitude: 110m/361ft
Population: 40,500

Three things make Écija, located on the left bank of the Río Genil, well known. Its eleven church towers lined with azulejo tiles have given it the nickname »city of towers«. The Andalusian and Arab horses that breed here enjoy a nation-wide reputation; and, finally, it is the hottest city in Spain, which justifies its second nickname, »the frying-pan of Andalucía«.

Roman Astigi, which originated in an Iberian settlement, developed into a very important trading hub thanks to its location on the river. The Moors fortified the town and erected a number of mosques until Ferdinand III drove them out in 1240. The earthquake of 1755 that destroyed Lisbon also toppled many of the church towers that had been made from the minarets. As a result, they were rebuilt in the style of the time – today Écija's tourist asset.

History

WHAT TO SEE IN ÉCIJA

Before the dredgers moved in for an underground car park, **Plaza de España** with a fountain and date palms and flowers scattered about, was certainly one of Andalucía's most beautiful squares. During the

Écija

INFORMATION
Oficina de Turismo
Palacio de Benamejí C. Cánovas del Castillo, 4 E-41400 Écija
Tel. 955 90 29 33
www.turismoecija.com
daily 10am – 2pm

WHERE TO EAT
❶ Bodegón del Gallego €€€€
C. A. Aparicio, 3
Tel. 954 83 26 18
The fish and meat dishes at the »Gallician's« are not the cheapest, but the quality is worth it. Whether sea octopus, tuna in pastry or vegetable soups, what is served here is normally served in faraway Galicia in north-western Spain. Including the delicious white wines. The service is also excellent.

❷ Pasareli €€
Pasaje Virgen del Rocío, 2
Tel. 955 90 43 83; www.pasareli.com

Closed Sunday evening and Monday
Traditional old restaurant with good fish, meat and tortilla dishes right in the heart of town.

WHERE TO STAY
❶ Platería €
Platería, 4-A
Tel. 955 90 27 54
www.hotelplateria.net, 18 rooms
Orderly, very centrally located city hotel with a pretty inner courtyard and a restaurant that serves inexpensive home-cooking. The rooms have air conditioning.

❷ Sol Pirula
C. Miguel de Cervantes, 50
Tel. 954 83 03 00
www.hotelpirula.com; 33 rooms
Somewhat south of the centre with comfortably furnished rooms and a parking lot. The recommendable restaurant serves mainly Andalusian food.

excavation, however, **archaeological remains** were discovered, so that the plaza has long since been walled up as an excavation site. A Roman bath and two Roman mosaics as well as an extensive Muslim cemetery were found. In the city hall on the west side of the plaza a Roman mosaic from the 3rd century AD is worth seeing. In the municipal museum (►below) there are more mosaics to admire.

Santa María The cloister of the 18th-century church of Santa María, to the left behind the city hall, holds a sculpture collection with an outstanding marble head of Germanicus.

*Palacio de A little south of the church lies the unusually decorated 18th-century
Benameji Palacio de Benameji with the city museum inside **Museo Histórico Municipal**. The museum's oustanding xhibit is a 2.11m/7ft tal sculpture of an Amazon, a find from Roman times.
❶ Tue – Fri 10am – 1.30pm, 4.30pm – 6.30pm, Sat, 10am – 2pm, 5.30pm – 8pm, Sun 10am – 3pm; free admission

On Plaza de Santiago stands Santiago el Mayor, a church that was begun in the 15th century and remodelled after the earthquake, during which some Mudejar elements were restored. A scallop, the symbol of the pilgrims following the Way of St James, is recognizable above the portal. Among the paintings inside are pictures by Alejo Fernández and Pedro de Campaña, as well as a crucifixion scene by Roldán. The Mudejar palace standing behind the town hall dates back to the 14th century and is home to a Carmelite convent, the **Convento de las Teresas**.

Past the **Iglesia de la Concepción** to the right – it has a splendid artesonado ceiling –is the **Iglesia de los Descalzos**, whose Baroque interior is one of the most beautiful in Écija.

To the north of Plaza de España in Santa Cruz church, which was built on the site of a mosque, it is worth taking a look at the 13th-century portrait of Nuestra Señora del Valle and a 4th-century stone Visigoth sarcophagus decorated with reliefs that is used as an altar. In the attached **Museo de Arte Sacro** church treasures can be admired; worth mentioning is a collection of Baroque goldsmith work.

❶ Mon – Sat 9am – 1pm, 5pm – 8.30pm, Sun 10pm – 1pm, 6pm – 8.30pm; free admission

San Juan

Soaring above the maze of alleyways east of the plaza, the tower of the church of San Juan is undoubtedly the most beautiful in the city and reminiscent of the Giralda in Seville. The bell tower was built in 1745 and is now the city's landmark

Palacio de Valhermoso

Behind the church is the Palacio de Valhermoso (16th century); its Plateresque facade is on the corner of the building.

Palacio de Peñaflor

Palacio de Peñaflor, across from the Palacio de Valhermoso, particularly stands out among Écija's noble houses. It possesses a stunning

---

Écija

©BAEDEKER

Santa Cruz

Convento marroquíes

Convento filipensas

San Pablo y Domingo

Descalzos

Convento de las Teresas

Plaza de Abastos

San Francisco

San Juan

Palacio de Alcántara

Ayuntamiento

Plaza de España

❶

Palacio de Valhermoso

❶

Santa María

Santa Bárbara

❷

Castelar

Palacio de Peñaflor

Palacio de Benamejí

i

Palacio de Almenara Alta

San Gil

Palacio de Santaella

Palacio de los Aguilar

Convento de la Merced

Santiago

❷

Sevilla, Carmona ↓

Córdoba

Where to eat
❶ Bodegón del Gallego
❷ Pasareli

Where to stay
❶ Platería
❷ Sol Pirola

MARCO POLO TIP

!

Bizcochos **Insider Tip**

The nuns of Convento Marroquíes opposite the Iglesia de los Descalzos are very adept at baking »bizcochos« (biscuits). The mysterious recipe is kept cloistered nuns since immemorial time. These biscuits contain flour, yeast, eggs and sugar.
Selling hours: 9.00am – 14.00pm and 17.00pm – 19.00pm

facade adorned with 18th-century frescoes and a magnificent portal with straight as well as serpentine columns of rose marble. The marvellous **wrought-iron balcony** that stretches across the whole front of the building on the upper storey is considered to be **the longest in all of Spain**. The exterior Baroque splendour of the palace continues on the inside in the amazing embellishment of the grand stairway and in the patio.

Estepona

✳ E 9

Province: Málaga
Altitude: 21m/69ft
Population: 66,700

Estepona, at the foot of the Sierra Bermeja, is the province of Málaga's most western holiday resort on the ▶Costa del Sol. The former fishing village grew considerably during the 1960s with the emerging mass tourism, but managed to maintain its pretty village centre along with a substantial fishing and yacht harbour.

History   Possibly founded by the Phoenicians, Estepona was inhabited by the Romans, as the baths near Río Guadalmanso testify. It was not until the 15th century that the then Moorish town (called Alexthebuna) fell to the Christians led by Enrique IV.

WHAT TO SEE IN AND AROUND ESTEPONA

Estepona   The remains of a **Moorish fortress** and a **medieval watchtower** have been preserved. Most of the activity in the old part of town is at Plaza de las Flores and Plaza Arce. The majority of the restaurants are in C. Terraza; there is one bar after the other in C. Real. Worth visiting is the market hall; early risers can watch the fish auction held every morning in the harbour. Estepona's **town museum** is placed on the edge of an **unusual, elliptic bullring** and has four departments – bullfighting, ancient history, archaeology and local history.
Museum: daily 10am – 2pm, 4pm – 6pm

Estepona

INFORMATION
Oficina de Turismo
Avda. San Lorenzo, 1 (old city office),
E-29680 Estepona
Tel. 952 80 20 02
www.estepona.es
Torre Almenara (port office)

EVENTS
Fiesta Mayor
The town's biggest fiesta takes place the first week in July with bullfighting and fireworks.

Fishermen's fiesta
Virgen del Carmen
The fiesta of the patron saints with processions on land and water is celebrated on 16 July.

WHERE TO EAT
La Casa de mi Abuela €€€€
C. Caridad, 54
Tel. 952 79 19 67
»My grandmother's house« is a small, quiet restaurant with international cooking. The house speciality are Argentinian steaks. Nice service.

Los Rosales €€
Damas, 12
Tel. 952 79 29 45
Deep-fried fish and seafood – simple, cheap, good.

Las Gitanillas €€
C. Caridad, 107
Tel. 952806847
www.paulagitanillas.com
Estepona classic place for tapas and small fish dishes. Not far from the coast road.

WHERE TO STAY
Kempinski Hotel Bahía €€€€
Ctra. de Cádiz, km 159
Playa El Padrón
Tel. 952 80 95 00
www.kempinski.com/estepona
Luxury hotel located on a main road with a wonderful park. Elegantly furnished rooms with a balcony or terrace. Three outdoor pools, a heated indoor pool.

El Paraíso €€€€
Ctra. Cádiz-Málaga, km 167
Tel. 952 88 30 00
www.hotelparaisocostadelsol.com
180 rooms
Japanese garden and countless sports activities; sauna, fitness, golf course designed by a U.S. golf pro, Chinese medical centre and the largest heated swimming pool on the Costa del Sol – which all comes at a price.

Club Marítimo €€€
In Sotogrande, Puerto de Sotogrande
Tel. 956 79 02 00
www.clubmaritimosotogrande.com
41 rooms
Noble abode on one of the most elegant and bustling yachting harbours on the Costa del Sol with an ocean view from every room.

La Malagueña €
C. Castillo 1
Tel. 952 80 00 11
www.hlmestepona.com
16 rooms
Recommendable accommodation in a central location on the main square with balconies facing the plaza.

MARCO ◉ POLO TIP

!

Slow is beautiful **Insider Tip**

Plan a lot of time for a visit to Genalguacil because, first of all, it takes some while on the winding road through the hills of Manilva, Gaucín and Algatocín just to get to the village in the Serranía de Ronda.
Secondly, leave time for a leisurely stroll through the lanes where the works of contemporary Spanish artists are hanging or standing.
Twice a year the village community invites artists to work here – and leave their works behind.

The beaches totalling 21km/13mi on municipal territory offer a variety of **sports activities**: a sailing club, sea fishing, waterskiing, several golf courses, a riding school and tennis courts.

Adventurous parents and their offspring should not miss **Selwo Aventura Nature Park**, east of Estepona at km 162.5 on the A-7 – not cheap but exciting. More than 2,000 animals live here in the wild, including lions, elephants, tigers and even rhinoceros.

❶ Mid-Feb – mid-Dec; admission: €24.50; www.selwo.es

*Sierra Bermeja   Far away from the busy coast, the hinterland of the Sierra Bermeja has serene places in a countryside marked by cork oak and pine. The white village of Casares is especially pretty in its fabulous location on a mountain ridge only 15km/9mi from the coast in the hinterland. Until now, they have been able to keep the bustle of the tourist sites at a distance.

Sotogrande   Sotogrande, 23km/14mi to the southwest, is a luxury holiday resort where some of the most beautiful golf courses on the Costa del Sol are to be found. Its yacht harbour has anchorage right in front of the door. Fish restaurants, bars and cafés are lined up around the harbour basin. The sandy beaches directly to the south are in their natural state. To the north lies Playa del Puerto – its bars are the »in« places with the beach crowd.

Fuengirola

✦ F 8

Province: Málaga
Altitude: 6m/20ft
Population: 71,800

The real mass tourism begins at Fuengirola, a mecca for beach holidays. Beginning there, one towering hotel follows the other almost without interruption all the way to the gates of Málaga.

WHAT TO SEE IN AND AROUND FUENGIROLA

Fuengirola developed from the Roman settlement of Suel, which the **Fuengirola**
Moors named Sujayl and built a castle there. It was conquered in
1485 by the Catholic Monarchs. It cannot be said that Fuengirola is
exactly worth seeing, with the exception of the ruins of a castle on the
western edge of the town that Abd ar-Rahman III erected in the 10th
century.

While the coastline from ▶Marbella to Fuengirola, which is located
halfway between ▶Marbella und ▶Málaga, is moderately developed,
for the most part with entirely decent-looking bungalow complexes,
in Fuengirola hotel high-rises stand next to no-less monotonous bars,

Fuengirola

INFORMATION
Oficina de Turismo
Avenida Jesús Santos Rein, 6
E-29640 Fuengirola
Tel. 952 46 74 57
www.visitafuengirola.com
Mon – Fri 9.30am – 2pm, 5pm – 7pm
Sat 9.30am – 1.30pm

EVENTS
Fiesta de la Virgen del Carmen
Mid-July with music, dance and a mari-
time procession.

ESSEN

La Salina €€€€
Avenida Salinas, 28
Tel. 952 47 18 06
One of the best restaurants in town. Ex-
cellent fish dishes, try the Boquerones
salineros (sardines). Nice service.

La Pérgola €€
Larga, 5
Tel. 952 47 20 15
http://restaurantepergola.u-city.org
Classic Fuengirola eatery. Pizzeria with
excellent pasta dishes. Friendly service

WHERE TO STAY
Angela Playa €€€
Jaén, 2
Tel. 952 47 52 00
www.hotel-angela.com, 261 rooms
Large-scale hotel right on the beach
promenade. Rooms with balcony and
sea view. House-own disco and heated
outdoor pool.

Las Pirámides €€€
Miquel Márquez, 43, tel. 952 47 06 00
www.hotellaspiramides.com
320 rooms
One of the best among the large hotels.
All rooms with balcony or terrace and
with a view of the ocean. Two restaurants and a large pool.

Florida Spa €€€
Dr. Gálvez Ginachero
Tel. 952 92 27 00
www.hotel-florida.es
184 rooms
Rooms with a sea view. Whirlpool,
sauna, Turkish bath and outdoor pool.
The spa area includes a large selection
of beauty treatments, from peeling to
foot massages.

restaurants, souvenir shops, nightclubs and discos. On the other hand, the visitors' entertainment needs are well looked after; 7km/4.5mi of beaches, fiestas and bullfighting when in season, recreational activities from golf courses, yacht harbour, Bioparc, a zoo to a history museum and roman excavations to a large range of courses are enough to keep boredom at bay.

Mijas 9km/5.5mi to the north lies the village of Mijas, praised in Fuengirola as a typical **»white village«**. Once there, it can be seen that the majority of its white-washed houses are bars, restaurants and souvenir shops run by British, French and German owners, and the »typical Andalusian« touch is hardly authentic. The »burro taxis« fit in with all this – with donkeys decked out with rear-view mirrors, taxi signs and registration numbers, all in accordance with regulations. At least there is a super view of the Mediterranean from the southern slopes of the **Sierra de Mijas**. The part of the village on the coast, Mijas Costa, has a large water park. Nevertheless, Mijas has a history its own. In the 9th and 10th centuries a Christian king, **Samuel I**, and his sons ruled the kingdom of Mijas, which was distinguished by religious tolerance, with its predominately Muslim population here in the middle of Muslim territory.

Hinterland Real, typical »white villages« can be seen by venturing out into the hinterland of Mija. Here it is possible to wander around and explore serene places like **Alozaina**, Casarabonela or Alhaurín el Grande. From Alhaurín, head on to **Coín**, which has four splendid Gothic churches, as well as a bishop's palace dating back to the 16th century. A few miles outside the village are remains of a Roman aqueduct.

★★ **Gibraltar**

E 9

British Crown Colony (dominion):
Area: 6.5 sq km/2.5 sq mi
Population: 28,750
Altitude: 0–426m/1,397

The »key to the Mediterranean«, the famous rock peninsula of Gibraltar, under British sovereignty since 1704, lies near the southern tip of the Iberian peninsula. The massive rock that rises straight up out of the ocean on the east side of the Bay of Algeciras was called Jabal Ṭāriq by the Arabs; the English call it simply »The Rock«. On its west slope lies the city, on the east slope the fishing village of Catalan Bay with the beach and Sandy Bay.

The Gibraltarians are a mix of people from all parts of the British Isles, Spain, Portugal and Morocco. The **jumble of languages** is accordingly colourful; along with English in all variations and Spanish, there is an English-Spanish mishmash called »Llanito«. The Rock is an attraction for being a curiosity, a real British colony in sizzling Spain – replete with pubs and helmeted policemen – along with duty-free shopping and a fantastic view across to Africa. Since the withdrawal of the major part of the British military and the accompanying loss of many jobs, Gibraltar has concentrated successfully on tourism, postage stamp sales, the harbour – the cheapest ergo most important »fueling station« for ships in the Mediterranean – and its reputation as a tax haven and financial site – until recently around 30,000 offshore companies from all over the world were registered here. Since this was a thorn in the flesh of the EU taxes have been imposed since 2011. The currency is the Gibraltar pound, whose exchange rate is tied to the British pound. Euros are also accepted. The airport, whose runway was built in the Bay of Algeciras and is crossed by the road leading to the Spanish border (**traffic lights!**), has connections to, among other places, London and Manchester. In contrast to Great Britain, they drive on the right-hand side in Gibraltar!

Key to the Mediterranean

> **MARCO POLO TIP**
>
> **!** *Hassle-free to Gibraltar* Insider Tip
>
> Do not take a car to Gibraltar! The Spanish police often enough subject cars to an extremely thorough inspection on the border, causing long traffic jams. It is much easier to park in one of the multi-storey car-parks directly at the border and take the bus or go on foot to Gibraltar. Passports or identity cards are needed for entry.

The Strait of Gibraltar, called Fretum Gaditanum or Fretum Herculeum in ancient times, is the vital geographical as well as strategic link between the Atlantic and the Mediterranean. For the classical world, the rock named Calpe together with Mount Abyla (Djebel Musa) on the African side near ▶Ceuta were the **»Pillars of Hercules«**, the gateway to the great ocean, which, according to legend, were created by Hercules' tremendous strength.

In AD 711, the Moors, led by **Tariq**, for whom Jabal Tariq (»Rock of Tariq«) was named, first set foot on European soil here. It was not until 1462 that the Spanish were able to wrest Gibraltar away from the Arabs again. During the War of the Spanish Succession, British troops under George of Hesse-Darmstadt took the fortress by surprise in 1704. Gibraltar was awarded to the British in the **Treaty of Utrecht in 1713** »for all time«. Since then it has been a **British crown colony** and as such, autonomous in domestic affairs. It is subject to the British crown in matters of foreign policy, defence and internal security. The governor heads the colony, supported by the

History and constitution

Gibraltar

INFORMATION
Gibraltar Information Centre
Duke of Kent House Cathedral Square ,
GB-Gibraltar
Tel. (0 03 50) 20 07 49 50
www.gibraltar.gi/tourism
www.gibraltar.gov.uk

SHOPPING
All the good things from the island are
in Main Street …

ACTIVITY
Dolphin Watching **Insider Tip**
Three different species of dolphin live in
the Bay of Gibraltar. Boat tours to the
dolphins start mostly at Marina Bay.

EVENTS
National holiday
The 10th of September is celebrated in
Gibraltar in bikinis and shorts.

WHERE TO EAT
❶ *Bianca´s €€*
6-7, Admiral´s Walk
Marina Bay
Tel. (0350) 20 07 33 79
www.biancas.gi
Meat, fish, pasta and pizza dishes.

Friendly service and good value for
money.

Inexpensive
Gibraltar is full of British pubs, where
the famous pubfood is served, but the
proximity to spain also has a positive
effect. Many outdoor restaurants are to
find at Casemates Square

WHERE TO STAY
❷ *Rock Hotel €€€€*
3, Europa Road
www.rockhotelgibraltar.com, 104 rooms
Tel. (0350) 20 07 30 00
www.rockhotelgibraltar.com
Flagship hotel of the crown colony built
directly into the rock. Built in 1932 and
decorated in colonial style. Wonderful
panoramic views from the rooms and
the restaurant.

❶ *Caleta Hotel €€*
Catalan Bay
Tel. (0350) 20 07 65 01
www.caletahotel.com; 158 rooms
Four star hotel with bright rooms and a
wonderful view of the Mediterranean
sea. Nuno´s Restaurant serves its guests
outstanding pasta and seafood.

parliament, which consists of a speaker and 17 members. All attempts by the Spanish to regain Gibraltar, who consider it to be a
colonial thorn in their side, both militarily and diplomatically, have
been unsuccessful. This has provoked continued harassment at the
border. At least it was agreed in April 2000 not to upgrade Gibraltar's
status within the EU. The Gibraltarians have no interest in becoming
Spanish – in a referendum in 1967, all of 44 voters out of 12,182 expressed a preference for Spain; in the referendum of 2002 187 of
17,900 voted for Spain. Nothing has changed in this majority situation since then – bad prospects for British-Spanish discussions over
a sharing of sovereignty.

WHAT TO SEE IN GIBRALTAR

Gibraltar's old town (**North Town**) begins beyond the airport with Casemates Square, dominated on the east by the remains of a **Moorish castle**, which was built in the 8th century and rebuilt by the Almohads in the 14th century. A stone's throw northwest of the castle lies the market and the **harbour**. It was established as early as 1309 and has been noticeably built up in recent years.

Old city

Main Street, which has the most hotels, businesses, pubs and public buildings, goes from Casemates Square past the post office and stock exchange with the town hall at the back, then on to the Roman Catholic cathedral, a former mosque that was remodelled in Gothic style in 1502.

The **Gibraltar Museum** is down Bomb House Lane, which branches off to the right, where, besides everything about the city history, a 30 sq m/320 sq ft model of the rock peninsula from 1865, and a well preserved Moorish bath are also on display.

On **Cathedral Square** there is an Anglican cathedral constructed in 1821 in Moorish style. To the right on the south end of Main Street is the governor's palace (The Convent). It was built in 1531 as a Franciscan convent,. The changing of the guard can be seen here several times a day.

Gibraltar Museum: Mon – Fri 10am – 6pm, Sat until 2pm; admission: £2; www.gibmuseum.gi

Southport Gates at the end of Main Street lead to the Alameda Gardens, Gibraltar's botanical gardens with Trafalgar Cemetery behind it. At the beginning of the gardens are the **cable cars** that go up to signal station (395m/1,296ft). The Upper Galleries and Apes' Rock are up there. The fortress, the **Upper Galleries**, was dug into the Rock during the Spanish-French siege from 1779 to 1783. It is still possible to marvel at the cannons in the **Great Siege Tunnels** and enjoy the fantastic view from the battlements; for some time now the tunnel systems that were dug in World War II near Princess Caroline's Battery have been accessible **(WW II Tunnels)**. The Military Heritage Centre also explains more about the history of the fortress. About 150 Barbary apes live on **Apes' Rock or Apes' Den** – the only type of ape to live in the wilds in Europe. Their ancestors were brought over from Africa by British soldiers as pets in the 18th century. Churchill is said to have ordered that the number may never fall below 24, because it is said that as soon as the last monkey leaves Gibraltar it will return to Spain. A corporal is detailed to feed these living symbols of Gibraltar. Be careful, as the apes like to bite. The steps along the way from Apes' Rock to **St Michael's Cave** lead up to the Rock's highest point, 426m/1,398ft. St Michael's Cave, the biggest of the 143 caves in Gibraltar has beautiful stalactites and stalagmites.

Cable cars

Gibraltar

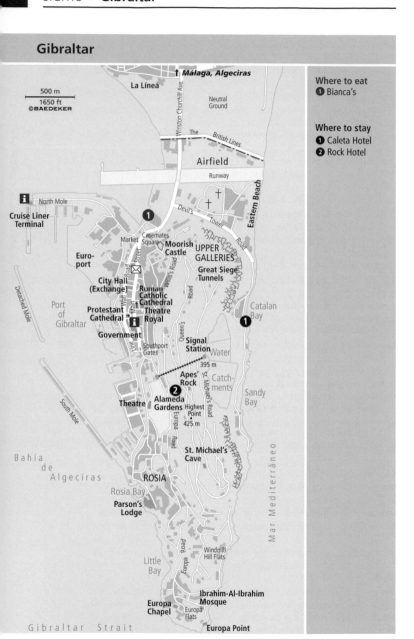

500 m
1650 ft
©BAEDEKER

↑ *Málaga, Algeciras*

La Línea

Neutral
Ground

Winston Churchill Ave.

The
British Lines

Airfield
Runway

Eastern Beach

North Mole

Cruise Liner
Terminal

Devil's
Tower
Road

Market Casemates
Square

Moorish
Castle

UPPER
GALLERIES

Euro-
port

Willis's Road

Great Siege
Tunnels

City Hall
(Exchange)

Roman
Catholic
Cathedral

Wall Road

Main Line

Protestant
Cathedral

Theatre
Royal

Catalan
Bay

Government

Southport
Gates

Queen's Road

Signal
Station Water

Port
of
Gibraltar

Detached Mole

395 m

Apes'
Rock

St. Michael's Road

Catch-
ments

Sandy
Bay

Theatre

Alameda
Gardens

Highest
Point
• 425 m

Europa Road

South Mole

St. Michael's
Cave

Bahía
de
Algeciras

ROSIA

Rosia Bay

Mar Mediterráneo

Parson's
Lodge

Little
Bay

Europa Road

Windmill
Hill Flats

Ibrahim-Al-Ibrahim
Mosque

Europa
Chapel

Europa
Flats

Gibraltar Strait

Europa Point

Where to eat
❶ Bianca's

Where to stay
❶ Caleta Hotel
❷ Rock Hotel

Concerts are also held here in the summer.

Cable Car: daily from 9.30am, last one upwards at 5.15pm, downwards at 5.45pm; tickets: €11.90

The Europa Road, a 5km/3mi-long, road on the heights with beautiful views, runs uphill from Alameda Gardens on the western slope of the Rock between the houses and gardens of the **South Town** and descends again past the fissured rocks of Europa Pass down to ****Europa Point** at the southern tip of the peninsula with its famous lighthouse. There is a stunning view here out onto the Bay of Algeciras, the African coast and Apes' Rock and, in good weather, all the way to the Moroccan Atlas Mountains.

North of Europa Point stands one of the largest mosques in a non-Islamic country: the Ibrahim al-Ibrahim mosque, which the Saudi Arabian king Fahd had built in 1997 for Moroccan guest workers in Gibraltar.

Living trademark: Gibraltar monkey

Parson's Lodge Parson's Lodge Battery on Rosia Bay, where the »HMS Victory« anchored in 1805 with the body of Admiral Nelson, who was killed at Trafalgar, was built in 1875. One of the two famous 100-ton cannons of Gibraltar still stands on the opposite side of the bay.

** Granada

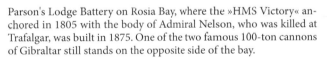

✦ H 7

Province: Granada
Altitude: 685m/2,247ft 5in
Population: 239,150

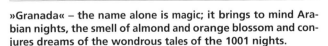

»Granada« – the name alone is magic; it brings to mind Arabian nights, the smell of almond and orange blossom and conjures dreams of the wondrous tales of the 1001 nights.

Moorish residence The former Moorish royal residence, today »just« the provincial capital, lies magnificently at the foot of the Sierra Nevada between two mountain spurs that drop sharply from the fertile Vega of the Río Genil. The northern ridge of the two, Albaicín, is at the same time the older part of Granada, divided by the gorge of the Río Darro, which goes underground in the inner city and empties into the Río Genil by the Alhambra. The wonderful Nasrid palace, the apex of and a unique testimony to Moorish-Arab architecture in Europe, sits enthroned on the Alhambra, shimmering in the red of the sunset. Visitors to Andalucía must see it and its city, as the Moorish poet Ibn Zamrak described in the 14th century:

»So come and see. The city is a lady, a mountain of a woman. A river shimmeringly encircles her body like a waist belt; flowerlike, jewels glisten at her throat.«

Visitors who approach the city today admittedly search in vain for Lady Granada at first, because they must first suffer the usual faceless concrete suburbs and then find their way through the hectic and noisy inner-city. But anyone who takes an evening stroll over Plaza Nueva or sits in front of a bar along the Río Darro with the majestically illuminated Alhambra as backdrop, or who delights in the panorama of the Moorish residence seen from Albaicín at sunset, will surely agree with Ibn Zamrak – Granada is a city of magical charm, a living university city with friendly people and the unforgettable climax of a trip to Andalucía. For it is said, »Quien no ha visto Granada, no ha visto nada – He who has not seen Granada, has seen nothing.«

History   Granada dates back to the Iberian settlement of Iliveri on the Albaicín, which the Romans rechristened Iliberis and enlarged with the two neighbouring settlements of Quastilla and Garnata. The first Christian council held on the Iberian peninsula was in Iliberis.

After the founding of the Emirate of Córdoba, a Berber tribe that settled in the Vega chose Iliberis as its chief town under the name of Elvira. When the Caliphate of Córdoba disintegrated in 1010, the governor, Zari ben Zirí, proclaimed an **independent Moorish kingdom**, a taifa, in 1013 and made Garnata its capital. It existed only until 1090 when the Berber Almoravids took over, but they in turn were forced to give way to the Almohads in 1149. Córdoba fell to the Christians in 1236. The surviving Moors retreated to Granada, where in the year 1238 Ibn al-Ahmar of the Beni Nasr tribe founded the Nasrid dynasty as Mohammed I. The Nasrids had to buy peace from Ferdinand III of Castile through tribute payments and military support. Subjugation and constant diplomatic manœuvring, however, were the prerequisites for the golden age of the kingdom that lasted 250 years. The 400,000 inhabitants of the 30,000 sq km/12,000 sq mi kingdom cultivated fruit, vegetables, grain and wine, sought-after goods which were shipped out of Málaga, Granada's harbour. By building the Alhambra in the 14th century, Yûsuf I and Mohammed V made the Nasrids immortal, at least as builders.

Granada

INFORMATION
www.granadatur.com

Oficina Municipal de Información Turística
Plaza del Carmen, 5; City Hall
E-18009 Granada; Tel. 902 40 50 45
Mon – Sat 10am – 7pm, Sun
10am – 2pm

Centro Municipal de Recepción Turística
C. Virgen Blanca, 9
(Parque Federico García Lorca)
E-18071 Granada
Tel. 902 40 50 45
Mon – Fri 10am – 2pm

Oficina de Información del Patronato Provincial de Turismo
Plaza Mariana Pineda, 10
E-18009 Granada
Tel. 958 24 71 28
www.turismodegranada.com

TOURIST PASS
»BONO TURÍSTICO«
For 5 days (€32.50) or 3 days (€27) free admission to the most important sights (incl. Alhambra, Cathedral), 9 or 5 free rides on the city bus lines and discounts. Available at Caja Granada (Pl. Isabel la Católica, 6) among other places, or in advance: www.cajagranada.es

ENTERTAINMENT
Nightowls go to the streets north of the cathedral, like Calle Granada. There are several discos and bars in Calle Pedro Antonio west of the city centre; on weekends the area west of Plaza Nueva comes to life.

El Camborio
Camino del Sacromonte, 47
The party starts after midnight in this in dance club with a garden terrace and a view of the Alhambra.

Zambra Gitana La Rocío *Insider Tip*
Camino del Sacromonte, 79
Tel. 958 22 71 29
In a whitewashed cave with family atmosphere a flamenco show is held every day from 9.30pm.

SHOPPING
Granada is famous for it guitar makers and intarsia artists. The main shopping boulevards are Calle Reyes Católicos and Gran Vía de Colón, and it is worth window-shopping in Cuesta de Gómerez (the street of the guitar makers), in Cuesta de Chapiz in the Albaicín, and in Calle Real de la Alhambra. The street for antique shops is Calle Elvira.

Cerámica Al-Yarrar
Joaquín Costa, 6
Pretty ceramics.

Taracea
C. Real de la Alhambra, 30
Intarsia woodwork – from tables and cabinets to small boxes and trays.

PLAZA DE TOROS
Av. Doctor Oloriz, 25
Tel. 958 22 22 72
The most important fights are in June.

EVENTS
Semana Santa
Especially on Maundy Thursday, when

»Cristo de los Gitanos« is honoured in a pilgrimage to Sacromonte.

Feast of Corpus Cristi
Granada's biggest fiesta with flamenco and corridas lasts a week.

International music and dance festival
Late June / early July – most important Spanish festival for classical and con-temporary music and ballet; perfor-mances in the Generalife open-air theatre (www.granadafestival.org).

Romería del Albaicín
End of September – pilgrimage goes directly through the Albaicín.

Festival de Jazz de Granada
The mood heats up in November at one of the major European jazz festivals (www.jazzgranada.net).

WHERE TO EAT
❹ Chikito €€€
Plaza del Campillo, 9
Tel. 958 22 33 64
Federico García Lorca was a guest in the former Alameda artists' café; Chikito is now one of the better restaurants in the city. Andalusian cuisine, but also tapas. Tables outside on warm days.

❶ Arrayanes €€€€
Cuesta Marañas, 4
Tel. 958 22 84 01
Since you are already in the city with the largest Islamic population in Spain, why not try some Moroccan food in an oriental atmosphere? Speciality: couscous dishes. No alcohol, but mint tea, juices.

❼ El Trillo del Reca €€€
Callejón del Aljibe de Trillo, 3
Tel. 958 22 51 82
Exquisite Basque-Andalusian cooking in a simply wonderful villa with garden in Albaicín.

❽ Mirador de Morayma €€€
Pianista García Carrillo, 2
Tel. 958 22 82 90
www.miradordemorayma.com
A pleasurable evening is guaranteed in this restaurant; enjoy deliciously prepared Granada cuisine in a typical carmen (villa with garden) in the Albaicín with a fabulous view of the Alhambra; flamenco Monday, Tuesday, Wednesday evenings.

❸ Castañeda € **Insider Tip**
C. Almíreceos, 1–3
(near Plaza Nueva)
Tel. 958 21 54 64
The Bodegas Castañeda are a real institution. The back one in Calle Almireceros is a lively, tastefully decorated bar with great tapas.

❷ Bodegas La Mancha €
Joaquín Costa, 10
Tel. 958 22 32 22
Tapas temple near Plaza Nueva. Large and tasty selection from albóndigas (meatballs) to calamares.

❻ Horno de Santiago €€€€
Plaza de los Campos, 8
Tel. 958 22 34 76
www.hornodesantiago.com;
closed Sundays
Andalusian food at the foot of the Alhambra hill.

WHERE TO STAY

❺ Parador Nacional San Francisco €€€€ *Insider Tip*
Real de la Alhambra, s/n
Tel. 958 22 14 40
www.parador.es
39 rooms
One of the finest, if not the finest parador; unique location in an old Franciscan monastery in the gardens of the Alhambra. Ask for a room with a view of the Alhambra.

❶ Alhambra Palace €€€
Plaza Arquitecto García de Paredes, 1
Tel. 958 22 14 68
www.h-alhambrapalace.es
126 rooms
Directly at the Alhambra. Comfortable establishment catering to the Alhambra tourism that started at the beginning of the 20th century, i.e. decorated in Moorish style; not particularly nice to look at, but a great view of the city and the Alhambra.

❹ Palacio de Santa Inés €
Cuesta de Santa Inés, 9
Tel. 958 22 23 62
www.palaciosantaines.com, 35 rooms
16th-century city palace at the foot of the Albaicín with a good view up at the Alhambra. Spacious rooms with different decors.

❼ Reina Cristina €€
Tablas, 4
Tel. 958 25 32 11
56 rooms
www.hotelreinacristina.com
Pleasant hotel near the cathedral. The Spanish poet Garcia Lorca spent the last days of his life here before being murdered at the beginning of the Spanish Civil War.

❸ Villa Oniria €€
San Antón, 28
Tel. 958 53 53 58
www.granadavillaoniria.com
31 rooms
Exemplary renovation of a city palace, glass-roofed inner courtyard. The rooms were decorated by the well-known interior designer Pascua Ortega.

❷ Casa »Los Naranjos« €
Barranco de los Naranjos, 10
Tel. 958 22 51 27
www.granadainfo.com/naranjos
Something different for a change; cave apartments in the Sacromonte quarter. Furnished for self-caterers.

❻ Pensión Rodri €
Laurel de las Tablas, 9
Tel. 958 28 80 43
Well-managed pension in the old part of town with ten small rooms.

Peace in the last Muslim stronghold in Europe came at an end with the marriage of Ferdinand of Aragón and Isabella of Castile. The Catholic Monarchs declared the **expulsion of the Moors** to be their primary goal. After the fall of Málaga in 1487, Granada stood alone against the Christian armies, weakened, into the bargain, by the year-long feud between King Muley Hassan and his mistress, Soraya, on the one side and his wife, Aisha, and their son and legitimate heir, Boabdil, on the other. After Muley Hassan's death in 1485, Boabdil ascended the throne as the last Moorish ruler of Granada. In 1491,

Highlights Granada

▶ **Alhambra**
World Cultural Heritage site and
Spain's most visited monument;
fabulously beautiful palace of the
Nasrids and enthralling view from
the Torre de la Vela.
▶page 250

▶ **Generalife**
Formerly the enchanting park of
the kings of Granada, today a shady
oasis with splashing water.
▶page 262

▶ **Cathedral**
The Catholic monarchs Ferdinand
and Isabella lie buried in the royal
chapel of the most important of
Andalucía's four great Renaissance
churches.
▶page 262

▶ **Albaicín**
Neighbourhood with a view of the
Alhambra, where the Moorish history
of Granada can best be sensed.
▶page 267

▶ **El Bañuelo**
Well-preserved 11-century Moorish
baths.
▶page 269

he abdicated and in the Treaty of Santa Fé ceded Granada to the
Catholic Monarchs, who entered the city on 2 January 1492 while
Boabdil left it and fled to the Alpujarras.
The downfall of the kingdom was followed by the bloody crushing of
the Morisco revolt from 1569 to 1571 and the final expulsion of the
Muslims in 1609 to 1614. The Alhambra fell into disrepair, and it was
the American writer Washington Irving who first called attention to
this unique cultural monument in 1830. In 1984, the UNESCO declared it to be a »cultural heritage of mankind«. Today, tourism is the
most import source of revenue in a city where many have again become aware of their Muslim heritage – Spain's largest Islamic community lives in Granada today. In the summer of 2003 the grand
mosque on Albaicín was opened.

** ALHAMBRA

Access   The main entrance with ticket counters and a large parking lot lies on
the extreme east of the hill. To get there, take bus no. 30 or 32 from
Plaza Nueva, or by car take Ronda del Sur. Be prepared for a long trek
on foot – from Plaza Nueva take Cuesta de Gomérez uphill and then
along Paseo Central staying below the Alhambra . Those who already
have a ticket can enter at Puerta de la Justicia and avoid the trek to
the main entrance.

Granada

↗ Jaén   ↑ Cartuja   ↗ Murcia

Estación RENFE
C. Ancha de Capuchinos
Jardines del Triunfo
Constitución
C. de Dios
Gran Vía
Hosp. San Juan de Dios
Jardines del Triunfo

San Ildefonso
Hospital Real
Cuesta de la Alhacaba
Plaza del Triunfo
Gobierno Civil
Sta. Isabel la Real
San Andrés
C. Sta. Isabel la Real
C. de Bocanegra

Camino de S. Antonio
Muralla
San Gregorio
Carretera   de   Murcia

San Luis

Árabe

San Miguel de Alto

Puerta de los Estandartes   El Salvador
ALBAICÍN
San Nicolás

San Juan

Casa del Chapiz

Internado Ave Maria

Río Darro

Universidad
C. de S. Jerónimo
C. de Colón
Elvira
Catedral
Capilla Real
Palacio Arzobispal
Corral del Carbón
Capitanía General
Ruerta Real
Ayunta-miento
Calle Recogidas
C. de San Antón
Acera del Darro

Mezquita Mayor del Albaicín
San José
Chancillería
Plaza Nueva
Madraza
C. de Gomérez
Torres Bermejas
Casa de los Tiros
San Matías
Santo Domingo
Santiago
Calle Molinos
San Cecilio
Hospital Militar

Carrera   del   Darro
Casa de Castril
Museo
San Pedro
Baños Árabes
Santa Ana

Cuesta del Chapiz

Generalife

Palacio Árabe
Alcazaba
Palacio de Carlos V
Puerta de las Granadas
LA ALHAMBRA
Paseo Central
Antequeruela   Alta
Antequeruela   Baja
Museo Falla

Parador Nacional ⑤
Alhambra

⑦   ④   ❶
⑥   ❷   ❸   ⑦   ❻   ⑥
❸   ④   ⑤   ❶

200 m
©BAEDEKER

Where to eat
❶ Arrayanes
❷ Bodegas La Mancha
❸ Castañeda
❹ Chikito
❺ Horno de Santiago
❻ El Trillo del Reca
❼ Mirador de Morayma

Where to stay
❶ Alhambra Palace
❷ Casa »Los Naranjos«
❸ Villa Oniria
❹ Palacio de Santa Inés
❺ Parador San Francisco
❻ Hostal Rodri
❼ Reina Cristina

Buy tickets two months in advance! The rush for tickets has become so great that now a **limited number of tickets** are made available. A total of a good 6,000 tickets (€14) are sold each day, of which only a small part are available for sale at the ticket counters. Only the really early birds have a chance at getting a ticket there. It makes sense, therefore, to get tickets in advance (with a surcharge). The simplest way: multi-lingual salespeople in the bookshop Tienda Librería de la Alhambra, C. Reyes Católicos, 40, will help you get the ticket with credit card at the ATM machine of ServiCaixa bank; telephone orders can also be done at ServiCaixa. Or online via www.alhambra-tickets.es. Tickets ordered in advance can be picked up at the Alhambra Pavillon (near the parking lot at the Generalife) at a counter (Taquilla de Reserva) by presenting a registration number and I.D. Tickets are available in advance for a time period from one day all the way up to one year. There is a limit of ten tickets per person. **There are tickets for the morning, afternoon and evening**. They set a half-hour time span within which the Nasrid palace must be entered (though the time for touring is not limited); there are no time limits for the rest of the Alhambra. The tickets are not valid for the museum in the palace of Charles V, however.

ServiCaixa: Tel. 00 34 / 902 88 80 01; www.alhambra-tickets.es

> **!** **MARCO ◉ POLO TIP**
>
> *Alhambra by moonlight* **Insider Tip**
>
> »Who can do justice to a moonlight night in such a climate and such a place?« wrote Washington Irving fittingly. To stroll in the evening through the illuminated chambers of the Nasrid palace and listen to the soft murmuring of the fountain is indeed an unforgettable experience.

*Alameda de la Alhambra Not far from Plaza Nueva is **Puerta de las Granadas**, built by Pedro Machuca in 1536 on the site of a Moorish gate and adorned with the coat of arms of Charles V, as well as the symbol for Granada, three pomegranates. Behind it are the Alameda de la Alhambra, the gardens laid out on the Moorish cemetery spreading up the slopes in a ravine between the Alhambra heights and Monte Mauror. Keeping watch on Monte Mauror is **Granada's oldest fortress** , the **Torres Bermejas**, which was erected in the 13th century upon an 8th-century fortress.

Museo Casa Manuel de Falla For a walk through the Alameda, take the path near the gate that forks off to the right and then another path branching off toward Antequeruela Alta through a beautiful villa quarter where the composer Manuel de Falla (1876–1946) owned a house. A little further on is the Convento Carmen de los Martíres founded in 1573. The stroll leads further to a hotel steeped in tradition, the »Washington Irving«, and from there eventually to the main entrance of the Alhambra.

❶ Tue – Sun 10am – 2pm

Alhambra and Generalife

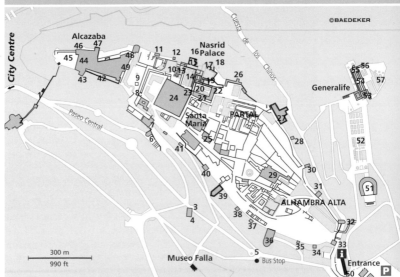

©BAEDEKER

300 m
990 ft

1 Puerta de las Granadas
   (Pomegranate Gate)
2 Torres Bermejas
   (Red Towers)
3 Fuente del Tomate
   (Tomato Fountain)
4 Monumento a Ganivet
   (monument to writer
   from Granada)
5 Fuente del Pimiento
   (Paprika Fountain)
6 Pilar de Carlos V
   (Column of Charles V)
7 Puerta de la Justicia
   (Gate of Justice)
8 Puerto del Vino
   (Wine Gate)
9 Plaza de los Aljibes
   (Cistern Court)
10 Patio de Machuca
11 Torre de las Gallinas
   (Hen Tower)
12 Torre de los Puñales
   (Tower of the Daggers)
13 Mexuar (former audience
   chamber)
14 Patio de los Arrayanes
   (Myrtle Court)
15 Salón de Embajadores
   (Ambassadors' Hall)
16 Torre de Comares
17 Habitaciones de Carlos V
   (apartments of Charles V)
18 Tocador de la Reina
   (dressing room)

19 Sala de las Dos Hermanas
   (Hall of Two Sisters)
20 Patio de los Leones
   (Lion Court)
21 Sala de los Abencerrajes
   (Hall of the Abencerrajes)
22 Sala de los Reyes
   (Hall of the Kings)
23 Crypt
24 Palacio de Carlos V
   (Palace of Charles V)
25 Baños (baths)
26 Torre de las Damas
27 Torre de los Picos
   (Crenellated Tower)
28 Torre del Cadi
29 Parador de San Francisco
30 Torre de la Cautiva
   (Prisoners' Tower)
31 Torre de las Infantas
   (Tower of the Infantas)
32 Torre del Cabo de la
   Carrera (Tower at the
   End of the Racetrack)
33 Torre del Agua
   (Water Tower)
34 Torre de Juan de Arce
35 Torre de Baltasar de la Cruz
36 Torre de Siete Suelos
   (Tower of Seven
   Storeys)
37 Torre del Capitán
   (Captain's Tower)
38 Torre de las Brujas
   (Witch Tower)

39 Torre de las Cabezas
   (Tower of the Heads)
40 Torre de Abencerrajes
   (Tower of the Abencerrajes)
41 Puerta de los Carros
   (Tower of the Wagons)
42 Jardines de los Adarves
   (Battlement Gardens)
43 Torre de la Pólvora
   (Gunpowder Tower)
44 Torre de la Vela
   (Watchtower)
45 Baluarte (barbican)
46 Torre de los Hidalgos
   (Tower of the Nobles)
47 Torre de las Armas
   (Weapon Tower)
48 Torre del Homenaje
   (Tower of Homage)
49 Torre Quebrada
   (Broken Tower)
50 Entrance to Alhambra
   and Generalife
51 Theatre
52 Jardines nuevos
   (New Gardens)
53 Pabellón Sur
   (South Pavilion)
54 Patio de la Acequia
   (Pool Court)
55 Pabellón Norte
   (North Pavilion)
56 Patio de la Sultana
   (Court of the Sultana)
57 Jardines altos (Upper Gardens)

The Alhambra glowing in the evening sun

★★ THE NASRID PALACE

Most beautiful palace grounds in Europe

Every visitor to the Alhambra is drawn to the Nasrid palace (Palacio Real or Palacio Árabe), the residence of the kings of Granada and a monument of Arab-Moorish architecture on European soil. The construction work began under Yûsuf I (1333–1354) with the Torre de Comares and the Myrtle Court and was completed for the most part under Mohammed V (1354–1391), who commissioned the Fountain of Lions. Like all Moorish secular buildings, the palace grounds appear unspectacular from the outside. Their artistic significance lies in the rich decorations of marble, fine hardwoods and azulejos, which represent the pinnacle of Moorish craftsmanship. Marble was one of the most important building materials in the palace grounds and was used in columns and floors. The ground plan is a **classic example of Islamic palace construction**, which is divided into three main sections; the Mexuar intended for holding public court and meetings, the royal palace (diwán or seraglio) and the women's chambers (harim or harem). All rooms open onto a courtyard, as had long been usual in Greek and Roman houses.

Mexuar

The low, azulejos-lined Mexuar, the former audience hall and courtroom, was converted into a chapel by Charles V. The Moorish decoration suffered in the process, hence Charles V's slogan, »Plus Ultra«, on the walls alongside ribbons of Kufic script. Next to the Mexuar, connecting it to the Myrtle Court, is the **Patio de Mexuar**.

The palace area begins with the Patio de los Arrayanes (Myrtle Court), the former seraglio, which remained undisturbed after the Christian conquest. The long sides of the 37m/122ft by 23m/76ft courtyard are whitewashed, but are pierced by artistically framed gates, gemel windows and niches. The southern front is closed off by a building with seven delicate arcades, over which a row of windows and in turn further arcades are arranged. These rooms are connected to the chapel in Charles V's palace. The **Torre de Comares** is on the north side. In front of it is the Sala de la Barca, where the ambassadors gathered for an audience, which was held in the **Sala de los Embajadores** (Ambassadors' Hall). It is one of the richest rooms in the Alhambra thanks to its fantastic cedarwood dome and the ornamentation of over 150 different floral and geometric patterns and verses from the Qur'an.

**Patio de los Arrayanes

Opening on to Myrtle Court is the Sala de los Mocárabes, which in turn opens to the Patio de los Leones (Lion Court), the centre of the royal winter residence built under Mohammed V with the harem joined to it. From the two pavilions that project at the ends, as well as from the long sides of the court, channels of water run to the Fountain of Lions. In its seemingly archaic simplicity, the Fountain of Lions presents a curious contrast to the exuberant design of the rest of the courtyard. The aura of oriental magic surrounding the Alhambra can be sensed most clearly here in the heart of the palace.

**Patio de los Leones

Nasrid Palace

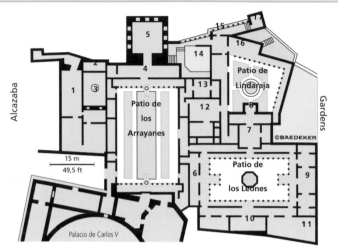

1 Mexuar
2 Cuarto Dorado
3 Patio Mexuar
4 Sala de la Barca
5 Torre de Comares /
   Salón de Embajadores
6 Sala de los Mocárabes

7 Sala de las dos Hermanas
8 Sala de los Ajimeces /
   Mirador de Lindaraja
9 Sala de los Reyes
10 Sala de los Abencerraje
11 Raudas

12 Baños reales
13 Sala de Camas
14 Patio de Cipréses
15 Galería del Peinador
16 Apartments of Charles V
17 Peinador de la Reina

The Sala de las dos Hermanas (Hall of the Two Sisters) on the north side of the Lion Court, together with the rooms lying behind it, was probably the winter residence of the women. The room with its decorations is the artistic zenith of the Alhambra. The vault, in the form of an eight-pointed star radiating 16 rays, is the **largest of all Arab stalactite vaults**. The room takes its name from the two large identical marble slabs set into the floor. Inscriptions with poems by Ibn Zamrak adorn the walls.

Adjoining the Hall of the Two Sisters is the **Sala de los Ajimeces**. Between the two arched windows (ajimeces) in the rear is the Mirador de Lindaraja, a charming projecting alcove with three windows that almost reach down to the floor and provide a view of the peaceful Patio de Lindaraja.

On the east end of the Lion Court lies the elongated ***Sala de los Reyes** (Hall of the Kings or Hall of Justice). The court scenes painted on leather and stretched on wooden domes are a great rarity, because Islam normally does not allow figurative art. The hall is divided into seven sections, and the side rooms are decorated with ceiling paintings from the late 15th century.

**Sala de los Abencerrajes can be entered from the southern side of the court. A twelve-sided marble fountain occupies the centre of the hall. The eight-pointed star of a stalactite dome arches above the fountain. It is said that the last Moorish ruler Boabdil had 36 members of the noble dynasty of the Abencerrajes decapitated.

OTHER PARTS OF THE ALHAMBRA

After leaving the Palace of the Nasrids, head down the steps to the left and again left to the former inner palace garden planted with cypresses and oranges, the atmospheric Patio de Lindaraja. It was laid out after the conquest by the Christian kings. The fountain used to stand in the court of the Mexuar.

Patio de Lindaraja

The small Court of the Cypresses adjoins the garden. Here there is a gallery leading to the **chambers of Charles V** that the emperor and his wife occupied when he lived in Granada. His son, Philip II, also lodged here. The writer Washington Irving, who is commemorated with a plaque, was a prominent guest here for four months in 1829. The same gallery, which is open toward the slope allowing a nice view of the Albaicín, leads to the **Tocador de la Reina** (»Queen's Dressing Room«) on the upper floor of the Torre del Peinador. At the south end of the courtyard are the baths, (**baños**), an extensive subterranean complex from the time of Yûsuf I.

Patio de Cipréses

After touring the palace, the **Gardens of the Partal** (Jardines del Partal) with their labyrinth-like paths, waterfalls, ponds and glorious greenery are an ideal place to relax. Rising on the north wall is the **Torre de las Damas**, to its right the Torre del Mihrâb with a discreet prayer room. In the upper gardens (Alhambra Alta) lies the Monastery of **San Francisco**, which has been converted today into Spain's most luxurious parador. It was founded in 1495 and held the graves of the Catholic Monarchs before they were moved into the cathedral.

*Jardínes del Partal

Insider Tip

Along the way to the Palace of Charles V is the church of Santa María, which was built on the site of the Alhambra mosque. After Granada was handed over, Holy Mass was read in the mosque. The stone columns to the right next to the main portal are a reminder the martyrdom of two Christian in 1397.

Santa María

Beginning construction in 1526, Charles V had a palace built on the east side of the Place of the Cisterns, directly on Myrtle Court, which he financed with a special tax levied on the Moors remaining

*Palace of Charles V

** *The Red Fortress*

The name Alhambra is derived from Arabic Kala al-Hamra, which means »red fortress«, because its walls and towers look red in the light of the setting sun. Alhambra refers not only to the Nasrid palace but also to the whole complex including Charles V palace, the Alcazaba and the garden palace Generalife.

❶ 15 March – 14 Oct daily 8.30am – 2pm/2pm – 8pm (evening visits Tue – Sat 10pm – 11:30pm), 15 Oct – 14 March 8.30am – 2pm/2pm – 6pm (evening Fri – Sat 8pm – 9:30pm), admission: €14 (evening €8)

❶ Mexuar

The Mexuar was used for public court of law and assemblies. Charles V converted it into a chapel.

❷ Diwan or Serail

The actual royal palace: The Patio de los Arrayanes (myrtle courtyard) with a water basin surrounded by myrtle is located here.

❸ Harem

The Patio de los Leones (lion court) with the lion fountain is in the centre.

❹ Patio de Mexuar

This court is marked by its marble and Azulejo tiling in warm colours, which show their qualities especially in the Cuarto Dorado (»golden room«).

❺ Torre de Comares and Sala de Embajadores

At 45m/148.5ft the Torre de Comares is the highest tower in the fortress. In the Sala de Embajadores (hall of the emissaries) audiences were held; thanks to the magnificent cedar vaulting and the ornamentation it is one of the most beautiful rooms in the Al-

hambra. The ruler's throne stood opposite the entrance.

❻ Sala de la Barca

Hall of seven arcades, whose name comes either from the boat-shaped Artesonado cediling or from Arabic »baraka« (blessing).

❼ Sala de los Reyes

Three court scenes painted on leather have shown themselves to be a great rarity since Islam forbids depicting people: they include a discussion between ten elaborately clothed men (hence the name »Hall of the Kings«).

❽ Tocador de la Reina

The »Queen's Dressing Room« is one of the most charming rooms in the palace: It was used by Isabella the Catholic and the wives of Charles V and Philipp II.

❾ Torre de las Damas

It is more decorative than defensive and one of the oldest parts of the Palace of the Nasrids, built under Mohammed III in the early 14th century.

❿ Palace of Charles V

Massive square shape with a two-storey circular structure. The Museo de la Alhambra is on the ground floor, the Museo Provincial de Bellas Artes is upstairs.

The Sala
jes
Aber
wh
numbe
to ha
here. Th
their wi

eight-
stalac
men
Sala de

Char
he had
most i

in Granada. It was designed by Pedro Machuca, whose son continued did not complete the work. However, the palace is one of the most significant works of **high Renaissance architecture** outside Italy. An eight-sided chapel was included with direct access to the Nasrid palace, but remained uncompleted.

The **Museo de la Alhambra** displays a large number of Moorish-Arab pieces, many of them from the Alhambra, on the ground floor. The exhibits include glass, pottery, decorative friezes, azulejos and metalwork. The prize pieces are the 1.30m/4ft 3in-high Alhambra Vase (1320), magnificently decorated with leaping antelopes and floral patterns in enamel painting, and a marble ablutions basin, thought to be from Córdoba, depicting lions chasing stags and an eagle, and bearing a later Kufic inscription praising Mohammed V.

The **Museo Provincial de Bellas Artes** on the upper floor mainly presents artists from the Granada school. The outstanding **sculptures** are the »Burial of Christ« by Jacopo Florentino, »San Juan de Dios« and »Virgin with Child« by Diego de Siloé, as well as a work on the same theme by Roberto Alemán; in addition, works by Pedro de Mena and, as showpiece, the »Triptych of the Gran Capitán«, a work in enamel by the master Léonard Pénicaud of Limoges. Among the **painters** represented are Fray Juan Sanchez Cotán (»Mary and the Sleeping Infant Jesus«) and Alonso Cano (»Virgin with Child, St Bernard of Siena, Head of Juan de la Cruz«). The Italian Fireplace Room« (16th century) is hung with tapestries procured for the palace from Genoa and Brussels.

Museo de la Alhambra: Tue – Sun 8.30am – 2.30pm, summer until 2pm; free admission

Museo Provincial de Bellas Artes: Mid-March – mid-Oct. Tue 2.30pm – 8pm, Wed – Sat 9am – 8pm, Sun 9am – 2.30pm; mid-Oct. – mid-March only until 6pm; free admission for EU citizens

Plaza de los Aljibes
To the west of the Palace of Charles V lies Plaza de los Aljibes, the Alhambra's main square. It was laid out at the end of the 15th century as a military training area. Beneath it are the cisterns that provide the Alhambra with its water.

Puerta de la Justicia
The way through Puerta del Vino, built under Mohammed V, leads down to the imposing Puerta de la Justicia, originally the entrance to the Alhambra. The gate built in 1348 under Yûsuf I, occasionally the site of executions, consists of one large and one small horseshoe arch. The keystone of the large arch displays a hand, the symbol of the **five basic principles (pillars) of Islam** – the profession that there is only one God, observance of prayer, charity through the giving of alms, abstinence through fasting, and the duty of a pilgrimage to Mecca. A key can be seen on the second arch, a symbol of the keys

Pure High Renaissance: palace of Charles V

to heaven bestowed upon the Prophet Mohammed by Allah. Set into the wall on the steps below the gate is a Renaissance fountain, **Pilar de Charles V**.

The wall of the Alcazaba, the oldest part of the Alhambra, runs along the west side of the Plaza de los Aljibes. **Mohammed I** began in the 13th century with the construction of the palace fortress around the original buildings from the time of the Zirids, of which only the double encircling wall with the powerful towers in the inner ring remain. The most impressive of them are in the entrance wall; the **Torre Quebrada** and next to it to the right the 25m/82ft-high **Torre del Homenaje**, in which the commandant lived. Towering up on the north wall is the **Torre de las Armas**, once the armoury, from which there is a good view of the Darro valley and the Albaicín, and next to it is the **Torre de los Hidalgos**. There is a view from the south wall, in which the **Torre de la Pólvora** is set, down to the **Jardines de los Adarves**, which were created in the 13th century between the outer and inner walls.

The best panoramic view, though, is from the 26m/85ft-high **Torre de la Vela** above the western outworks (Baluarte). In the 18th century, a belfry was placed on top of the tower, whose bells ring out annually on 2 January, the day the Catholic Monarchs, Ferdinand and Isabella, entered the city. There is a magnificent view of the city from the battlements to the massive cathedral; and in the opposite direction over the courtyard of the Alcazaba with the foundations of the munitions magazines, guards' quarters, baths and prison, behind

*Alcazaba

Insider Tip

them Charles V's palace, the towers of the palace complex and, in the distance, the Generalife.

Towers It is possible to take a closer look at some of the towers by walking through the **Alhambra Alta**, the upper gardens. Torre de las Damas, a fortress tower with an adjoining loggia, water basin and a small mosque, stands east of the palace. Beyond the Torre de los Picos (»Tower of the Points«) are Torre del Candil and the Torre de la Cautiva (»Prisoners' Tower«), which has a small patio and a magnificently decorated main hall. It is followed by the Torre de las Infantas with a richly decorated hall and a platform offering a wide vista. On the east end of the Alhambra hill stands the Torre del Agua with the reservoir for the Alhambra water system. The most interesting feature of the southern part is the tower **Puerta de los Siete Suelos** (Tower of the Seven Storeys).

✶✶ GENERALIFE

»Garden of the architect« The Generalife (Arabic: »Jannat al-'Arif«, the garden of the architect) lying to the east opposite the Alhambra on the slopes of the Cerro del Sol was the **summer residence of the Moorish kings** completed in 1319 under Ismail I. The charm of these grounds is to be found less in the rather unspectacular architecture when compared to the Nasrid palace than in the **harmony** between the buildings, the gardens

Insider Tip and the fountains. Many consider it to be one of the most beautiful gardens in the world. A cypress-lined avenue leads to the entrance building (16th century), followed by the Patio de la Acequia planted with laurel and myrtle as well as orange trees, and its fabulous row of fountains, which terminates in the simple residence of the rulers. There is a magnificent view of the Alhambra and the Darro valley from one of the side rooms. Above the building, the floral magnificence continues in more beguiling gardens, grottoes and water gardens, and among them a »water stairway« formed by a series of cascades. An exit here leads to Silla del Moro, an observation point outside the gardens.

AROUND THE CATHEDRAL

✶Catedral Santa María de la Encarnación The cathedral Santa María de la Encarnación, the **most important of Andalucía's four great Renaissance churches**, rises above the maze of houses in the city centre. Enrique de Egas began it in 1523 in Gothic style, Diego de Siloé carried on in Plateresque in 1525, and in 1561, still uncompleted, it was consecrated. In 1563, Juan de Orea renewed the work, which dragged on until 1703 and eventually

**Murmuring water fountains in the Generalife – the Moorish kings
enjoyed the present moment**

ceased without the two planned towers being built. Even the tower
that had been begun did not reach its planned height. The west facade (1667) is by Alonso Cano, the relief above the main portal by
José Risueño (1717). To the northwest lie the Puerta de San Jerónimo,
decorated with sculptures by Siloé, Maeda and others, as well as allegorical figures and the coat of arms of Castile, and the Puerta del
Perdón, also by Siloé, completed in 1537. Due to the fact that the
choir, formerly in the central aisle, was pulled down in 1929, the eye
can rove uninterrupted over the interior of the church. The nave and
four aisles, borne by massive clustered pillars, have a total extent of
116m/380ft in length and 67m/220ft in width.

The highest point in the interior is the 47m/154ft-high dome of the
*Capilla Mayor. Diego de Siloé designed it with two rows of balustrades arranged in a circle 22m/72ft in circumference resting on
round arches that open to the choir ambulatory. On the right between the arches stands the statue of St Paul by Alonso de Mena, left
the apostle Peter by Martín de Aranda. Paintings by Pedro Atanasio

Bocanegra and Juan de Seville can be seen in the first balustrade, and above are seven paintings by Alonso Canos with scenes from the life of the Virgin. The windows between and above hold Flemish stained glass from the 16th century. Statues of the Catholic Monarchs by Pedro de Mena are at the pillars of the entrance arch, above them the heads of Adam and Eve by Alonso Cano.

In the right aisle stands the closed ***portal of the Capilla Real**, a masterpiece of late Gothic stone masonry designed by Enrique de Egas. It bears the coats of arms of Castile and the Catholic Monarchs, and above are the Infant Jesus flanked by St James and St George the dragon slayer. Left of the portal is a large altar consecrated to the Spanish national patron saint Santiago (James), portrayed in his typical role as a slayer of Moors. A small painting of »Virgin of Grace«, a present of Pope Innocent III to Queen Isabella, is on top of it. To the right of the portal, the altar of Jesus of Nazareth, laden with gold, holds a few valuable paintings; on the right »St Augustine«, »Via Dolorosa«, and the »Holy Virgin« by Alonso Cano, as well as the »Martyrdom of St Lawrence« , »The Child Jesus Appearing to St Anthony« and, in addition, »Via Dolorosa« by Antonio Ribera, left »St Francis« by El Greco, »Magdalene« by Ribera and a portrayal of Christ by Cano.

The **sacristy**, accessible right of the choir ambulatory through a portal by Diego de Siloé, contains some fine works of art; once again, the works of Alonso Cano stand out. The church treasures can be viewed in the former chapter house in the tower.

❶ Mon – Sat 10.45am – 1.30pm, 4pm – 7pm, Sun 4pm – 7pm; admission: €3.50

Sagrario and Lonja

The Iglesia del Sagrario, which has a very fine Renaissance baptismal font, was added to the south side of the cathedral between 1705 and 1759. On its north side lies the Lonja, the former stock exchange with loggia, built between 1518 and 1522.

**Capilla Real

The Capilla Real can be reached by way of the loggia. It is the mausoleum of the Catholic Monarchs, erected on the south side of the cathedral under the direction of Enrique de Egas in late Gothic style from 1505 to 1521 upon earlier instructions of Isabella. First upon entering is the anteroom with a copy of a historical painting by Carbonero, the Surrender of Granada. An exquisitely beautiful gilded grille (Span.: »reja«) by Bartolomé de Jaén divides off the actual mausoleum. The grille bears the coat of arms of Castile supported by lions, next to it the symbols of the Catholic Monarchs, the yoke and arrows. A long series of biblical scenes, crowned by a depiction of the crucifixion, complete the work.

Next is the chamber with the ****tombs of the Catholic Monarchs**. To the right, the tomb of King **Ferdinand II** († 1516), with sword in

Catedral Santa María de la Encarnación

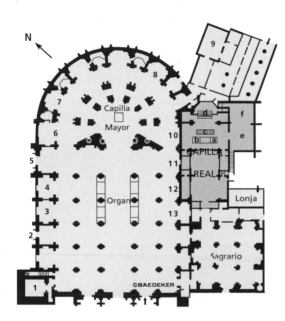

1 Tesoro
2 Puerta de San Jerónimo
3 Capilla de
   N. Sra. del Carmen
4 Capilla de
   N. Sra. de las Angustias
5 Puerta del Perdón
6 Capilla de la Antigua
7 Capilla de Santa Lucía
8 Capilla de Santa Ana
9 Sacristía
10 Altar de Santiago
11 Former entrance
   to Capilla Real
12 Altar de Jesús Nazareno
13 Capilla de la Trinidad

Capilla Real

a Tomb of the
   Catholic Monarchs
b Tomb of Philip the Handsome
   and Joanna the Mad
c Crypt (underground)
d High altar
e Museum
f Sacristy

hand, and **Isabella** († 1504), a lion and a lioness at her feet, worked in Carrara marble in 1522 by the Florentine Domenico Fancelli. To the left stand figures by Bartolomeo Ordóñez of **Philip the Handsome** († 1506) and **Joanna the Mad** († 1555), daughter of the Catholic Monarchs.

The large winged altar with carved biblical scenes by Felipe Vigarny is flanked by the statues of the Catholic Monarchs by Diego de Siloé. Richly decorated reliquary altars by Alonso de Mena (1623) have been placed in both transepts. The famous »Passion Triptych« by Dieric Bouts can be seen in the left transept next to the altar. The mortal remains of the Catholic Monarchs, as well as those of Joanna and Philip and Miguel, the royal couple's grandson and heir to the Portuguese throne, rest in simple lead coffins in the crypt.

In the sacristy of the Capilla Real is a ****museum** with personal items of the Catholic Monarchs including clothing, Ferdinand's sword, crown, and sceptre, and Isabella's reliquary and prayer books. Some outstanding paintings show that the queen was also an intelligent **art**

Insider
Tip

The Alcaicería – a little bit of a Souk

collector: »Christ on the Mount of Olives«, possibly by Botticelli, »Pietà« and »Virgin with Child« by Rogier van der Weyden, »Deposition from the Cross«, »Virgin with Child and Lamenting Women« by Hans Memling, another portrayal of the Virgin by Dieric Bouts, »Christ Suffering« by Perugino and »The Apostle John« by Pedro Berruguete. Two outstanding wooden sculptures of Ferdinand and Isabella praying by Felipe Vigarny are also displayed.

❶ Mon – Sat 10.15am – 1.30pm, 3.30pm – 6.30pm, Sun 11am – 1.30pm, 3.30pm – 6.30pm; admission: €3.50

Although the house opposite the Capilla and the Lonja has a Baroque facade and a Castilian coat of arms on it, it is considerably older. It is the **Arab university**, the Madraza, founded in 1349 by Yûsuf I. From 1500, the building was used as the city hall (Casa Cabildo). A prayer room with a mihrâb off the patio remains from the time of the Moors. Further on past the episcopal palace on Plaza de Alonso Cano is **Plaza de Bib-Rambla**. Enlivened by shops, florists, restaurants and bars and with the Fuente de los Gigantones splashing gaily between trees and kiosks, it is a wonderful place for a café solo.

Alcaicería   The Alcaicería extends between the plaza and the cathedral, the Moorish market and shopping quarter that mostly dealt in fabrics and burned down in 1843. Rebuilt, it today appears to be more of a collection of souvenir shops and boutiques; but for some, it radiates the atmosphere of an Arab souk.

Plaza Isabel   At the rear of the cathedral lies the Gran Vía de Colón. It meets Plaza
la Católica   Isabel la Católica, on which there is a monument from 1892 commemorating the moment Columbus presented his plans to the queen.

C. Reyes Católicos, the second most important shopping boulevard after Gran Via de Colón, goes east from the plaza.

A lane branches off to the left from C. Reyes Católicos not far from the plaza toward C. Mariana Piñeda. Here can be seen the horseshoe arch of Corral del Carbón, the only surviving caravanserai in Spain, a so-called funduq. The building, dating back to the early 14th century, has an anteroom with a stalactite dome and an inner courtyard with a gallery running around it. After the Moors had been driven out, it was used as a storehouse for charcoal dealers, then as a theatre on whose stage Lope de Rueda's dramas were presented and, finally, as a residence.

*Corral del Carbón

Casa de los Tiros in the C. de Pavaneras lies across from the military commandant's headquarters not far from Plaza Isabel la Católica. The very plain building was part of the city wall in the 16th century. Its only adornment consists of five figures representing Hercules, Theseus, Jason, Hector and Mercury.
In the building the **Museo de Artes y Costumbres Populares** displays, along with furniture, craftwork, old plans and pictures of Granada, a complete kitchen and two rooms commemorating Washington Irving and Eugenia de Montijo of Granada, who, as Eugénie, became the wife of Napoleon III. The most beautiful room is the ***Cuadra Dorada** with an artesonado ceiling and reliefs.

Casa de los Tiros

❶ Tue 2.30pm – 8.30pm, Wed – Sat 9am – 8.30pm, Sun 9am – 2.30pm; free admission for EU citizens, otherwise €1.50

** ALBAICÍN

The feeling of Moorish times is strongest on El Albaicín, the hill across from the Alhambra heights – not least because Muslims are moving into the neighbourhood and have transformed the Calderería Nueva, for example, into a bazaar street. Another visible sign was the opening of the Mezquita Mayor in 2003. It has less to do with spectacular sights than with the **atmosphere and magic** radiating from the narrow and steep alleyways, the angular, whitewashed houses, the patios and churches, but above all by the classic views of the Alhambra – enjoyed best in the afternoon. There are many ways to get up to it; one lane after the other leads up from Plaza Nueva, from Puerta Elvira in the university quarter and from Carrera del Darr. Do take a stroll in the evening along Carrera del Darro; this is where Granada lives far into the night – in crowds, loud and happy, partying in the bars and cafés directly beneath the extraordinary backdrop of the illuminated Alhambra.

Old Moorish quarter

*Plaza Nueva The »Plaza Nueva« is an elongated continuation of Calle Reyes Católicos below the Alhambra hill, with its fountains, bars and restaurants, one of the most popular places to meet in the evening in Granada. Even in earlier times a lot went on here – races, bullfighting, but also executions. The most imposing building on the plaza is the **Audiencia** (court house). Its design is attributed to Diego de Siloé and it was built between 1531 and 1587. The two-storeyed arcaded courtyard and a monumental stairway with a fine wood ceiling are impressive.

Río Darro The Río Darro divides the Alhambra hill from Albaicín. At the northeastern end of Plaza Nueva, where it flows below ground, stands Santa Ana, a Renaissance church erected from 1541 to 1548 to plans by Diego de Siloé with a Plateresque portal and minaret-like tower dating to 1563. This is the beginning of **Carrera del Darro**, one of Granada's oldest streets, as the second bridge over the river testifies – it is still Moorish. Before that, C. Santa Inés branches off to the 16th-century Palacio de Santa Inés, whose Renaissance inner

The Albaicín, the former Moorish quarter opposite the Alhambra

courtyard is decorated with frescoes by Alejandro Mayne, a student of Raphael. Further along on Carrera del Darro is the ****Bañuelo** (house no. 31), an 11th-century Moorish bath that still has the changing room and three bath rooms supported by Moorish arches with Visigoth capitals. Further on is the church of San Pedro y San Pablo on the right. Across on the left stands the **Casa de Castril**, a Renaissance building, whose Plateresque portal was probably designed by Diego de Siloé. The **Museo Arqueológico** presents there a collection of Moorish artefacts such as painted pottery, glass, jewellery and fabrics.

Bañuelo: Tue – Sat 10am – 2.30pm; free admission
Museo Arqueológico: Tue. 14.30pm – 20.30pm, Wed – Sat
9.30am – 20.30pm, Sun and holidays 9.30am – 14.00pm, free admission for
EU citizens, otherwise €1.50

At the end of Carrera del Darro is Cuesta del Chapiz, which plunges into the uphill maze of streets and alleyways of Albaicín. Right at the beginning, Casa del Chapiz presents a fine example of a well-to-do Morisco residence of the 16th century; it is now the seat of the Institute of Arab Studies.

Casa del Chapiz

Heading further on to the left is the Mudejar church of San Salvador, which stands on the site of the former grand mosque of Albaicín and was consecrated in 1499.

San Salvador

Straight ahead is Plaza Larga – an ideal place for a break. From here, a lane goes uphill to San Nicolás church, built in 1525, the heart of Albaicín. From the picturesque plaza in front of the church there is a spectacular and famous view of the Alhambra and the Sierra Nevada – an unforgettable experience, especially at sunset. The new mosque was opened nearby in July 2003.
The famaous Belgian painter **Max Moreau** (1902–1992) lived for 30 years in a house a little below San Nicolás. It is now the **Museo Max Moreau**.

San Nicolás

Insider Tip

Museo Max Moreau: Tue – Sat 10am – 1.30pm, 4pm – 6pm;
free admission

A well-preserved section of the Arab city wall (muralla árabe) runs from Plaza Larga down the hill along side Cuesta de la Alhacaba to Puerta Monaitia. A little further down on Plaza del Triunfo stands Granada's former main gate, the Puerta de Elvira, which dates back to the 9th century.

Muralla árabe

The lane facing the Alhambra that runs parallel to the wall leads downhill again past San Miguel Bajo church to Plaza Nueva, going past San José church, whose bell tower is the minaret of a 9th-centu-

San José

ry mosque and thus one of the oldest Moorish architectural monuments in Andalucía.

Mezquita Mayor del Albaicín

For the first time in 500 years, right next door to San José church and opposite the Alhambra, **there is again a mosque**. After fighting municipal bureaucracy and neighbours for 23 years, the mosque was built in Andalusian style with funds from Morocco and the United Arab Emirates and finally consecrated in July 2003.

The streets below the church have already been transformed in the last ten years into a bazaar full of Arab tea-rooms and restaurants. Around 20,000 Muslims again live among the 240,000 citizens of Granada; about half of them are labour immigrants, the other half students. A group of Spanish Muslims has grown up among the foreign Muslims, about 3,000 converts who have turned their backs on the Catholic church.

Sacromonte

A way leads from Cuesta del Chapiz up the mountain slope and past the former cave dwellings, in which Gitanos have been proven to have lived since 1532, to the former Benedictine monastery Sacromonte (12th century). The remains of the three saints Cecilo, Hiscio and Tesifonte were supposedly found here, which explains the name Sacromonte (holy mountain). Other paths, some of them steep through deeply-cut ravines full of boulders, ascend to the Ermita San Miguel de Alto, high up with a fabulous view all the way to the Sierra Nevada. Sacromonte is considered to be the home of the Gitano culture, where it is said flamenco can be enjoyed in its pure state, though closer inspection reveals that a lot of it is just to dupe tourists.

Tapas bar in Calle Navas (►Tip p.271)

On the hillside Barranco de los Negros is the **Museo de Cuevas del Sacromonte** or Centro de Interpretación del Sacromonte. The cave museum with an educational nature trail, informs on how people used to live in the caves on the Sacromonte. Various caves can be visted here: residential, kitchen, stable, but also caves with workshops for weavers, smiths and potterymakers.

❶ Barranco de los Negros, daily 10am – 2pm, 5pm - 8.30pm, winter 4pm – 7pm; admission: €5, www.sacromontegranada.com

> **MARCO ⊕ POLO TIP**
>
> ! *Pub Lane* **Insider Tip**
>
> The Navas is the best-known street for tapas bars and restaurants. But a few hundred metres further, around Calle Alhamar, everything from designer bars to neighbourhood pubs can be had – and much less oriented to tourists.

UNIVERSITY QUARTER LA CARTUJA

The university quarter in the northwest of the inner city is grouped around the Baroque former Jesuit college in C. San Jerónimo that was taken over in 1759.

University

Not far away in Calle del Gran Capitán is the Convento de San Jerónimo, founded in 1496. The church, which has 18th-century wall paintings, was built between 1496 and 1547 by Jacopo Florentino and Diego de Siloé as a burial church for the commander of the Catholic Monarchs' armies, Gran Capitán Gonzalo Fernández de Córdoba and his wife. Both kneeling figures flank the high altar with a retablo by Juan de Aragón and Lázaro de Velasco. Sculptures by Diego de Siloé stand in the choir. He also designed the magnificent gate of the patio, which was done completely in Gothic style. The second courtyard appears as a mixture of Gothic, Mudejar and Renaissance styles.

*Convento de San Jerónimo

One of Granada's most beautiful Baroque edifices, the double-towered church of the Hospital San Juan de Dios, lies a little south. west above San Jerónimo. The saint after whom it is named holds watch above the entrance portal. St Juan de Dios is buried in the decorated interior behind the retablo by Guerrero. He was the father of the Order of the Brothers Hospitaller and founder of the hospital in 1552.

*San Juan de Dios

The **Carthusian monastery** La Cartuja lies a little over half a mile away in a northerly direction from C. San Juan de Dios (bus lines U and C). The monastery was founded in 1506 on the orders of the Gran Capitán, but only completed after 250 years. The cloister, refectory, church and sacristy remain. The extremely lavish decora-

*La Cartuja

tion of the interior rooms represents a pinnacle of **Churriguerism**. The refectory and the adjacent rooms leading off from the cloister hold a collection of paintings by Juan Sanchez Cotán and Vicente Carducho.

The interior of the church was decorated in **effusive Baroque style**. The central choir is divided by a splendid grille into areas for the monks and for the lay brothers. The ceiling painting is by Pedro Atanasio Bocanegra. Above the sculpture of the Virgin by José de Mora is a seemingly light baldachin (canopy). Next to the chancel is the Sagrario, a work by Francisco Hurtado Izquierdo, arched over by an imposing dome with trompe-l'œil painting and furnished with paintings by Palomino and Cotán, as well as sculptures by Risueño and Duque Cornejo.

The highlight of the tour is the ****sacristy** by Luis de Arévalo with lavish plaster ornaments.

❶ daily 10am–1pm, 4pm–6pm; admission: €3.50

SOUTHWEST GRANADA

Huerta de San Vicente

The family of the young **Federico García Lorca** (▶Famous People) spent the summer in the Huerta de San Vicente country house. When his father acquired the house, it was surrounded by fruit trees, which have given way to the typical suburb development. Now a rose garden surrounds the house, which is used as a **museum**. Part of it still has the original furnishings.

ℹ Bus no. 4 from Gran Via de Colón; July/Aug. Tue–Sun 10am–2.30pm, April – June, Sept daily 10am–12.30pm, 5pm – 7.30pm, or Oct–March 4pm – 6.30pm; admission: €3

Parque de las Ciencias

The **Science Park** in Avenida Mediterráneo has nothing to do with Granada's past. It is an **interactive museum** offering hands-on natural science. The pavilions on the extensive grounds are dedicated to various topics; one pavilion offers a »journey through the human body«, in another pavilion means and methods of risk prevention at work and in everyday life are shown. There is also a planetarium to visit.

❶ Avda. de la Ciencia s/n; Tue–Sat 10am – 7pm, Sun until 3pm; admission: museum €6.50, planetarium €2.50; www.parqueciencias.com

Memoria de Andalucía

In the adjacent museum »Memoria de Andalucía«, which was built by the bank **CajaGranada** in 2009, audiovisual and interactive media in four rooms inform on Andalucía – its landscapes, towns, art, history, culture and the ways of life of its residents.

❶ Tue – Sat 10am–2pm, 4pm –7pm (summer 5pm–8pm), Sun 11am – 3pm; admission: €5; www.memoriadeandalucia.com

AROUND GRANADA

Federico Garcia Lorca was shot in 1936 by Falangists in the village of Viznar northeast of Granada. Today there is a memorial here to Lorca and all of the victims of the civil war.

Viznar

The **memorial** is in the Parque Federico García Lorca im Barranco de Viznar, which was dedicated in 1986. The memorial stone is located between bridges and hinking trails right next to the olive tree at which Lorca was probably shot in the back on the 18th of August 1936. His remains were never found. Fragments of his poems were carved into the wall that surrounds the memorial.

Parque Federico García Lorca

A few miles west of Granada on the A-92 lies **Santa Fé**, which was built in the **form of a Roman camp** on the orders of Queen Isabella the Catholic in 1491 to serve as headquarters during the siege of Granada. Three of the original four gates in the rampart have survived. The surrender of Granada was signed here in 1491 and it was here on 17 April 1492 that the queen signed the contract with Columbus for voyages that were to lead to the discovery of the New World. **Federico García Lorca** was born in **Fuente Vaqueros** to the northwest of Santa Fé. The **house he was born in** is now a museum; a statue in his honour has also been erected there.

Vega de Granada

❶ Mon–Sat 10am–1pm, afternoons vary, admission €1.80

Next stop is old **Loja**, where the towering ruins of a castle from Moorish times remain. The most interesting evidence of the Christian era is the church of San Gabriel (16th century) with a portal and dome by Diego de Siloé.

Loja

Shortly before Loja, a small side road branches off 26km/16mi to the south to a **charming spa** Alhama de Granada (»hot springs«). When the Moors, who enthusiastically took advantage of its healing waters, lost their baths to the Christians in 1482, they lamented bitterly with the cry »Ay de mi Alhama!«, which is a customary cry still used to this day. The springs bubbling out of the earth at a temperature of 45°C/113°F in a Moorish cistern resting on Roman foundations can be viewed in **Hotel Balenario** (about 1km/0.5mi outside the village). Some secular buildings worth noting are the Casa de la Inquisición with an Isabelline-style facade, the 17th-century former prison on Plaza de los Presos and a granary dating back to the 16th century.

Alhama de Granada

! *Fresh trout* **Insider Tip**

MARCO POLO TIP

If freshly prepared trout served in an idyllic, straw-covered patio sounds irresistible, then don't fail to make a short detour to the Venta Riofrío country inn in the village of Dorf Riofrío a bit south of Loja (tel. 958 32 10 66). There is nothing like a stroll along the inviting river afterwards.

✳ **Guadix**

✤ I 7

Province: Granada
Altitude: 949m/3113ft
Population: 20,400

Off the beaten track of major tourism, yet well within reach of ▶Granada on a day trip, the small town of Guadix lies on the Hoya de Guadix plateau. The route is enjoyable, leading as it does through bleak archaic-seeming tuff landscape to one of the largest settlements of cave dwellings in Andalucía. Pottery is a popular souvenir.

City of cave dwellings
Findings from the megalithic culture show that the region was inhabited early. The Romans built Julia Gemelli Acci on an Iberian settlement. Renamed Wadi Ash, from which its present-day name is derived, the city experienced a new peak following the invasion of the Moors. Only in 1489 did the Catholic Monarchs succeed in wresting Guadix back from the Moors again. Famous sons of the city are **Pedro de Mendoza** (1499–1537), the **founder of Buenos Aires**, and the poet Pedro Antonio de Alárcon (1833–1891).

WHAT TO SEE IN GUADIX

*Catedral
Begun in 1594 in place of a mosque, the towering cathedral cannot be missed when driving into Guadix. Diego de Siloé designed its apse and the chapel of San Torcuato. The tower was completed in the 17th century; Baroque and classical elements were added to the originally purely Plateresque main façade in the 18th century. Striking Churrigueresque choir stalls can be found inside the church; the museum possesses relics of San Torcuato, goldsmith work, manuscripts, and paintings.

Buildings to see
Built in the 16th century in the Mudéjar style, the **Convento de Santiago** is reached through a narrow alley to the right of the Plaza Mayor, bordered by arcades. The crest of Charles I can be identified above the Plateresque portal.
Yet probably the most beautiful secular building of Guadix is the 17th-century **Palacio de Peñaflor**.

Alcazaba
Built of red brick in the architecture typical of the 11th century, the Moorish castle ruin alcazaba lies enthroned above the old town. Some remains of its 9th-century predecessor are still preserved in the vicinity.

Guadix

INFORMATION
Oficina de Turismo
Avda. Mariana Pineda, s/n
E-18500 Guadix
Tel. 958 69 95 74
www.guadix.es

WHERE TO EAT AND
WHERE TO STAY
Comercio €
C. Mira de Amezcua, 3
Tel. 958 66 05 00
www.hotelcomercio.com; 44 rooms

Well-kept hotel in a house from 1905 in the town centre. Along with Spanish dishes international cooking is also served in the restaurant.

Cuevas Pedro Antonio de Alarcón € **Insider Tip**
Barriada San Torcuato
Tel. 958 66 49 86
www.cuevaspedroantonio.es, 19 rooms
Anyone who has always wanted to spend the night in a cave dwelling can try it out in Guadix.

However, the most interesting sight of the town is the **district of cave dwellings** Barriada de las Cuevas. The people in this bizarre »housing area« live in caves dug from the soft loess. Only the white-washed chimneys and porches are seen, and these do not hint at the often large and well-furnished rooms in the hill. The caves are an almost ideal form of living for the large fluctuations in the climate of this region. Pleasantly cool in summer, they store warmth in winter. The **museum cave** shows what such a cave dwelling looks like. It is at the end of C. San Miguel, at the Ermita Nueva.

Barriada de las Cuevas

❶ Mon – Fri 10am – 2pm, 5 – 7pm, winter 4pm – 6pm, Sat 10am – 2pm, admission €2.50

AROUND GUADIX

Lying 6km/3.5mi to the west in a tuffstone landscape, Purullena is made up almost entirely of cave dwellings. A row of souvenir shops, restaurants, and bars lines the A-92, yet just a few steps behind it the interesting side of Purullena can be seen.

Purullena

A hill with a castle constructed in the 16th century looms above La Calahorra, amidst a barren-looking landscape south of Guadix (17km/11mi) to the right away from the A-92. The fortress, never used as such, has an Renaissance patio that contrasts with its rugged exterior and the four round towers. The trip can be continued from La Calahorra driving south to ►Alpujarras, or southwest to►Almería.

Castillo de La Calahorra

❶ Wed 10am – 1pm, 4pm – 6pm, viewing also possible with advance booking, tel. 958 67 70 98

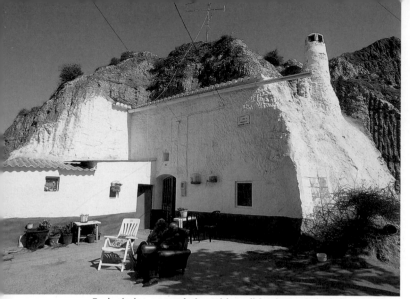

Ecological accommodation with tradition in Barriada de las Cuevas

Baza, near Guadix
It is a journey of 45km/28mi northeast from Guadix to Baza, which would have remained rather insignificant, had an exceptional **Iberian sculpture of a woman, the »Dama de Baza«**, not been discovered here in 1971. It may now be admired at the national museum of archaeology in Madrid. The sights of the town include a visit to the abbey church Santa María (16th–18th century) with its impressive octagonal tower, the alcazaba, and the sparse remains of Moorish baths. Ramblers find a large area for walking in the Parque Natural Sierra de Baza.

Continuation of the journey to the town of **Galera**, another 42km/26mi northeast, is recommended for those interested in archaeology. It was here that the **Iberian necropolis Tutúgi** with around 150 tombs dating from the 5th to 3rd centuries BC was discovered.

Huelva · Ruta Colombina
✳ B 7

Province: Huelva
Altitude: 56m/184ft
Population: 149,300

Situated on a peninsula bordered on either side by the Río Odiel and the Río Tinto, Huelva is characterized by industrial activity.

Huelva · Ruta Colombina

INFORMATION
Oficina de Turismo
Plaza de las Monjas s/n
E-21001 Huelva
Tel. 959 25 74 67
www.turismohuelva.org

ENTERTAINMENT
In the summer people gather at the
Punta Umbría. Bars can be found along
C. Concepción, C. Berdigón and Avda.
Pablo Rada north of Plaza de los Monjas.
Things also get lively around Plaza de
la Merced and Plaza Dos de Mayos.

SHOPPING
Shop after shop lines the pedestrian
zone from C. Concepción to C. Berdigón. A department store of the chain
El Corte Inglés is on the Plaza de España.

EVENT
Fiestas Colombinas
At the end of July/beginning of August,
sailing regattas and bullfights are held to
commemorate Christopher Columbus,
who embarked on his expedition from
Palos in 1492.

WHERE TO EAT   Insider Tip
❶ Las Candelas €€
in Aljaraque, Avda. de Huelva
Tel. 959 31 83 01
Huelva's best-known restaurant is
located 7km/4mi outside of town.
It serves excellent fish and seafood
dishes. In the winter there is always
a fire in the fireplace in the dining
room.

❷ Las Meigas €€€€
Avda. de Guatemala, 44

Tel. 959 27 19 58; www.lasmeigas.es
Superb restaurant with fish specialties –
prepared in the Basque, Galician and
Andalusian styles.

❸ Taberna El Condado €
Sór Angela de la Cruz, 3
Tel. 959 26 11 23
Rustic tapas bar with atmosphere
and the best ham in the area.

Casa Rufino €€€€
In Isla Cristina, Avda. de la Playa
Tel. 959 33 08 10
A good 40 years ago, Rufino Zaiño
pre-empted nouvelle cuisine with his
»Menú Tonteo«. Today his son runs
the restaurant, which is one of the
best in the region.

WHERE TO STAY
❶ Luz Huelva €
Alameda Sundheim, 26
Tel. 959 25 00 11
www.nh hoteles.es, 107 rooms
Reliable, centrally situated lodgings.
Bright, modern rooms with balconies,
restaurant, cafeteria, cocktail bar.

Parador de Ayamonte €€   Insider Tip
In Ayamonte
Avda. de la Constitución, s/n
Tel. 959 32 07 00, www.parador.es
Some of the 48 rooms have a view of
the mouth of the Río Guadiana. Garden
with terrace and pool as well as a res-
taurant that serves regional specialities.

Hotel Oasis Islantilla €€
In Isla Cristina, Avda. de Islatilla
Tel. 959 48 64 20
www.hotelesoasis.com, 479 rooms

Huge luxury hotel at the beach, indoor and outdoor pools, restaurants and a tapas bar. Pretty gardens..

El Paraíso-Playa €€
In Isla Cristina, Avda. de la Playa, s/n
Tel. 959 33 02 35
www.hotelparaisoplaya.com, 34 rooms
Well looked-after, friendly beach hotel in a nice location. The house also has a small pool, a cafeteria, a restaurant and terraces.

Pato Amarillo €€€
In Punta Umbria
Calle Esteros,3, Urb. Everluz
Tel. 959 31 12 50
www.hotelespato.com
Large beach hotel in the middle of a garden with buffet and grill restaurant andf two outdoor pools. All 136 rooms have a balcony

Seaport and industrial city Measured by its goods turnover, the **commercial port** is one of Spain's largest, primarily due to the loading of ores from Río Tinto and Tharsis, and due to the **petrochemical industry**, which also makes for a correspondingly dramatic environmental situation. Fishing for tuna and sardines, and the fish-canning industry are of further significance. In turn, the province Huelva is one of the **largest European areas for cultivating strawberries**, which are grown here under similar conditions to those of the vegetables from ▶Almería. All this does not necessarily indicate that Huelva is attractive – yet visitors to the surrounding area can follow in the footsteps of Christopher Columbus.

History Huelva was of great importance for the expeditions of the Genoese Christopher Columbus, who recruited a large part of his crew here. The beginnings of the city most likely lie in a Phoenician settlement, which the Romans took over as Onuba. Some researchers speculate that the legendary Tartessos (Tharsis) of ancient times lies here. Alfonso X wrested the city from the Moors in 1257; Pedro the Cruel gave it as a present to his mistress, María de Padilla, before it came to the dukes of Medina Sidonia in the mid-15th century. The earthquake which destroyed Lisbon on 1 November 1755 also had devastating ramifications for Huelva – it destroyed large parts of the city, so that today there is little to see in terms of impressive sights.

WHAT TO SEE IN HUELVA

Churches Churches of note are San Pedro (16th century), built over the ruins of a mosque and restored after the earthquake, and La Concepción (16th century), which possesses two small paintings by Zurbarán. The cathedral, which belonged to the La Merced convent (now a hos-

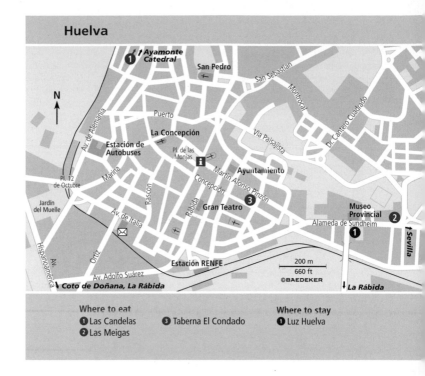

Huelva

Where to eat
1 Las Candelas   3 Taberna El Condado
2 Las Meigas

Where to stay
1 Luz Huelva

pital) and as such exhibits a somewhat uniform Baroque style, was only consecrated in 1953. The Nuestra Señora de la Cinta (Madonna of the Belt), located 3km/2mi north of the centre was originally built in the Gothic-Mudéjar style. The interior has a Mudéjar coffered ceiling and a figure of the town's patron saint, probably by Montañes; according to tradition she is supposed to have healed a cobbler of his pain by giving him a belt to wear.

To the east of the provincial museum the Reina Victoria quarter, built entirely **in the style of Victorian working class neighbourhoods** by the English Rio Tinto Mining Company in 1917, is an architectural gem. The Museo Provincial shows mainly archaeological finds but there is also a section with modern art.

Barrio Reina Victoria

At the south end of the city, a martial, 34m/111ft-high monument to Columbus guards the bridge crossing the Rio Tinto at the Punta del Sebo. The sculpture, a work of the American sculptress Gertrude Whitney, was a present from the USA to Huelva in 1929.

Monument to Columbus

AROUND HUELVA

Marismas del Odiel

Insider Tip

South of Huelva, the delta of the rivers Odiel and Tinto forms an extensive alluvial plain and protected habitat for many bird species, and can be reached by heading in the direction of Punte Umbría. More than 2000 flamingos winter here in **Paraje Natural Marismas** del Odiel, despite the close proximity to industry, as do wading birds, ducks and spoonbills. Except during winter, the Centro de Visitantes Calatilla organizes tours on foot, by canoe, and by boat.
❶ Tue – Sun 10am – 2pm, 4pm – 6pm

Along the Costa de la Luz

The part of the ►Costa de la Luz that lies to the north of the mouth of the Guadalquivir is easily reached from Huleva. Once the tanks, cranes, warehouses and factories in the south of the city have been left behind, the coast road passes miles of sandy beaches, behind which camping sites lie in pine forests. Although many private properties and military prohibited areas block the way to the water, there is access to the sea at two beach resorts: **Mazagón**, which boasts eight miles of beach and the **most sunshine hours on this coast**, and Matalascañas, at the national park ►Coto de Doñana.

Walk for hours along the beach near
Isla Cristina and enjoy the view of the ocean

On the headland west of the delta, Punta Umbría acts as Huelva's local beach, with beach bars and clubbing till late at night. Boats also come here from Huelva.

Punta Umbria

The N-431, leading to the Portuguese border, curves via Gibraleón, and provides several approaches to the beaches of the northwestern Costa de la Luz: El Rompido, La Antilla and Isla Cristina. After 60km/37mi it reaches the Spanish border town Ayamonte, a fishing port of Phoenician origin at the mouth of the Río Guadiana. Apart from mansions, there are also some noteworthy churches, including Nuestra Señora de las Angustias with its beautiful façade, and a Capilla Mayor with a Mudéjar roof. With the opening of the suspension bridge above the wide Río Guadiana delta in September 1991, a road connection between Spain and Portugal was created here for the first time.

Ayamonte

An excursion on the A-495 leads from Gibraleón northwest to Alosno, home to fandango. The **mining area of Tharsis** begins here. The name preserves the biblical **Tarshish**, which the Greeks called **Tartessos**. Tharsis is the centre of a mining area in which the Iberians and Romans already mined pyrite and barite. Spain sold the mining rights to the Rio Tinto Mining Company in the 19th century.

Tharsis

RUTA COLOMBINA

At the end of the 15th century, the estuary area of Río Tinto was the scene of events of world history: here **Christopher Columbus** planned and began the undertaking that resulted in the discovery of the New World. The most important historic sites can be discovered along the Ruta Colombina, which leads from Huelva to Moguer via the monastery La Rábida, and Palos de la Frontera.

Where world history was made

Events began at the monastery of La Rábida, the walls of which gleam from a hill 8km/5mi south of Huelva across the bridge over the Río Tinto. Franciscan monks founded it next to an older church in the 15th century. In 1485, after Christopher Columbus had tried in vain to convince John II of Portugal of his plans, he wanted to try his luck in Spain. On the way there he and his son found a welcome at the monastery and advocates in Father Juan Pérez and Father Antonio de Marchena, the confessor of Queen Isabella. Following long negotiations, Isabella was persuaded to conclude a contract that promised Columbus the means for his expedition, and made him viceroy of the countries yet to be discovered. The monastery offers little in terms of art, yet is still worth seeing as a **memorial to the sojourn of Christopher Columbus**, who is commemorated by a cast-iron cross

*Monasterio de La Rábida

Monasterio de Santa María de la Rábida

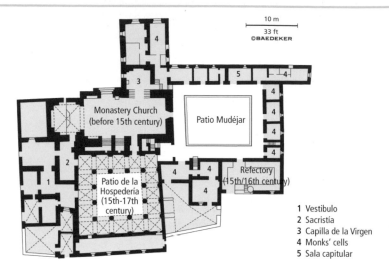

10 m
33 ft
©BAEDEKER

4

5 4

3

Monastery Church
(before 15th century)

Patio Mudéjar

4

4

4

4

2

1

Patio de la
Hospedería
(15th–17th
century)

4 4

4

Refectory
(15th/16th century)

1 Vestibulo
2 Sacristía
3 Capilla de la Virgen
4 Monks' cells
5 Sala capitular

mounted at the entrance in 1892. Busts of Columbus's two patrons frame the forecourt. The tall column at the exit was erected in 1892 for the 400th anniversary of the discovery of America. The Patio de la Hospedería (18th century) leads into the minster, the oldest part of the complex (14th century). It was rebuilt in the 18th century following the earthquake of Lisbon, and holds its most valuable treasure in the Capilla de la Virgen: the alabaster sculpture of Santa María de la Rábida, created around 1400, to which Columbus and his companions prayed for assistance before departure, and after which the flag ship Santa María is named. A cloister in the Mudéjar style is joined to the church, its gallery serving as a museum, with model ships, genuine artefacts from the age of discovery, and portraits. Tables, chairs and other items can be seen in the chapter house, at which Columbus held council with the brothers Pinzón – the captains of the other two caravels– and the two monks. Portraits of personages from the age of discovery decorate the walls; a medallion showing the head of Christopher Columbus, a copy of the original by Guido Mazzoni, is delicate work. The flags of all Latin American countries hang in the Sala de las Banderas, and earth from these countries is kept in the caskets underneath. Near the Foro Ibero-Americano below, at the ***Muelle de las Carabellas** lie replicas of Columbus's three ships, which can be visited. These, plus a medieval market and an Indian

Insider
Tip

village bring the age of discovery to life. Plants from Spain and Latin America thrive in the botanical garden José Celestino Mutis.

Monasterio: Summer: Tue – Sun 10am – 1pm, 4pm – 7pm (Aug. 4.45pm until 8pm); winter: 10am – 1pm, 4pm – 6.15pm; admission: €3; www.monasteriodelarabida.com

5km/3mi further east lies Palos de la Frontera, once one of the most important ports for ships travelling to the New World, and the centre of strawberry growing today. On 3 August 1492 Columbus put out to sea from here with the Santa María, the Pinta, and the Niña; this is where he also returned to on 15 March 1493. Hernán Cortés also disembarked in Palos after his trek through Mexico. The brothers Alonso Martín and Vicente Yañéz Pinzón, captains of the Pinta and Niña respectively came from Palos.

Palos de la Frontera

A monument near the town hall commemorates Martín; his birthplace, **Casa Museo Pinzón**, can be visited. The church **San Jorge**, constructed over a mosque, possesses a beautifully wrought pulpit and azulejo adornment. Columbus and the brothers Pinzón proceeded down to the anchorage, of which nothing can now be seen, through the Puerta de los Novios (Gate of the Betrothed). Somewhat below the choir stands the pump house La Fontanilla, which supplied the ships with water.

Casa Museo Pinzón: Mon – Fri 10am – 2pm; free admission

Lying 7km/4.5mi northeast of Palos, Moguer is the last stop on the Ruta Colombina, and of course also has its connection with Columbus, yet its people almost take more pride in the fact that the 1956 **winner of the Nobel prize for literature, Juan Ramón Jiménez** (1881–1958), was born here and raised a monument to his home town with the novel Platero y Yo (Platero and I). Ceramic plaques with quotes taken from this novel are everywhere in Moguer, and of course a monument honours the author on the square at the town hall. Both his birthplace and the house in which he lived with his life partner, Zenobia Camprubi, can be visited. A well belonging to the house is adorned with a figure of the donkey Platero, the »hero« of the novel. Moguer was one of the main places where Columbus recruited his crew. On returning from his journey, the discoverer spent his first night on European soil in Moguer at the ***Convento de Santa Clara**, and caused mass to be said there. This convent was founded in 1348 and, with its blend of Gothic and Mudéjar elements, is one of the most significant religious structures of Huelva province, not least due to its décor: Mudéjar choir stalls on a plinth of azulejos, a sculpture of the Virgin attributed to Montañés, and an alabaster tomb in the Capilla Mayor with lifelike recumbent figures of the founding family Portocarrero dating from the 15th century. The very beautiful cloister is supported by Mudéjar columns.

Moguer

A Mistake Makes History

Christopher Columbus wanted to reach Asia by sailing west from Spain. We know today that he was not the first European in America as the Vikings were there 500 years before him. He believed until his death that he had discovered an unknown part of India. America was only recognized a year later by the Italian Amerigo Vespucci and named after him. But Columbus' journeys are still of historical significance: the Spanish conquered the »New World« after him. Their home base was Andalucia.

CUBA

PUERTO RICO

HISPANIOLA · WESTINDIAN ISLANDS

TRINIDAD · Atlantic

Santa María

▶ **Columbus' fleet**
Columbus undertook his first voyage with three ships: the two caravels *Pinta* and *Niña* and the flagship *Santa María*, which ran aground off the coast of Haiti on the way back.

©BAEDEKER

23m/75ft

▶ **The conquerors of America**
The conquistadores penetrated the interior of the American continent and ruthlessly subjugated the peoples they found there.

A **Juan Ponce de León**
1460–1521
Ponce de León took part in Christopher Columbus' second trip and founded today's San Juan, the capital of Puerto Rico. He also discovered Florida in 1513, which he first took to be an island.

B **Hernán Cortés**
1485–1547
He conquered the kingdom of the Aztecs between 1519 and 1521 with the help of Indian allies. Afterwards he was the governor general of New Spain for nine years.

C **Francisco Pizarro**
1476–1541
Pizarro crossed the Andes Mountains from today's Ecuador into Peru and destroyed the kingdom of the Incas

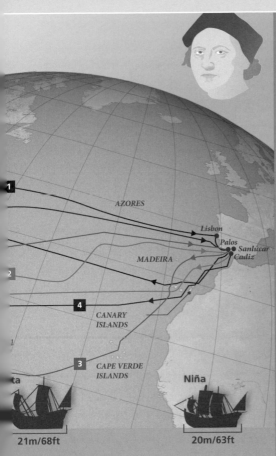

AZORES

Lisbon
Palos ● Sanlúcar
Cadiz

MADEIRA

1

2

4

CANARY
ISLANDS

3

CAPE VERDE
ISLANDS

Niña

21m/68ft   20m/63ft

D Pedro de Mendoza
1487 – 1537
He started an expedition of eleven
ships to America in 1535 and in 1536
he founded the colony of Buenos
Aires, the modern capital of
Argentina.

E Francisco Vásquez de Coronado
1510 – 1554
In 1539 – 1541 he crossed what
is now the southwestern USA in
search of the mythical seven
golden cities of Cibola.

▶ **Voyages of Columbus**

1 3. Aug. 1492 – 15. March 1493

His first voyage, during
which he made history,
began in Palos de la
Frontera. Columbus
discovered the Bahamas,
Cuba and Hispaniola and
sailed back to Lisbon.

2 25. Sept. 1493 – 11. June 1496

On his second voyage
he took 17 ships and
about 1,500 settlers; on
the way to Hispaniola he
discovered the Lesser
Antilles.

3 30. May 1498 – 25. Nov. 1500

On the third voyage he
discovered Trinidad and
Tobago and sighted the
mouth of the Orinoco.

4 9. May 1502 – 7. Nov. 1504

On his last big voyage he
explored the coast of
Central America and was
the first European to set
foot on the Central
American mainland.

The painted belfry of the church **Nuestra Señora de la Granada** (14th to 18th centuries) is reminiscent of the Giralda of ►Seville. A highlight inside is the painting Adoration of the Magi, ascribed to Murillo.

Juan Ramón Jiménez house: Tue – Sun 10.15am – 11.15am, 12.15pm – 1pm, 5.15pm until 7pm, Sun only mornings

✳ Itálica

 C 7

Province: Sevilla
Altitude: 20m/66ft

Just 10km/6mi north of ►Seville and west of the N-630 past Mérida near the village of Santiponce lie the well known ruins of the Roman city of Itálica. It was the very first Roman settlement on Iberian soil, and is unique among the Roman remains in present-day Spain in its size and seclusion – even though only the foundation walls have been preserved for the most part.

Ruined Roman city with magnificent mosaics
At nearby Ilipa (now Alcalá del Río) Publius Cornelius Scipio the Elder defeated a numerically superior Carthaginian army under the command of Mago and Hasdrubal Gisco, thereby ousting the Carthaginians from Iberia in 206 BC. He ordered the wounded and veterans to found a settlement at the site of present-day Santiponce, the »vetus urbs« (old town). Thus Itálica became the **starting point for the Latinization of Iberia**. The Roman emperors Trajan and Hadrian were members of two of the original families, favouring their native city with embellishments and founding »nova urbs«, the new city. It was at its prime in the 2nd and 3rd centuries AD, when it flourished primarily from the wine and olive oil trade. Into the 7th century Itálica was seat of a bishopric, thereafter fading into obscurity. In the 17th century the inhabitants of Santiponce used the houses as raw material to rebuild their village, which had been destroyed by a flood. However, the lower strata remained intact in the process.

Itálica

INFORMATION
Oficina de Turismo
C. La Feria, s/n

E-41970 Santiponce
Tel. 955 99 80 28
www.santiponce.es

Itálica Roman Town

1 Casa de la
  Exedra
2 Casa del Mo-
  saico Neptuno
3 Casa de los
  Pajaros
4 Casa de Hylas
5 Casa del
  Emparrado
6 Casa de la
  Cañada Honda
7 Insula del Mo-
  saico de Venus
8 Foro
9 Casa del
  Planetario
10 Termas Mayores

The village of Santiponce stands on the remains of the first veteran **Santiponce** settlement. A **Roman theatre** that exhibits so-called tabulae lusoriae and carvings is preserved here. The names of horses that ran races in the arena are recorded on them. The fortress-like San Isidoro del Campo monastery, comprising two churches and several courtyards, lies on the southern edge of the village. In 1294 the older of the two churches was founded by Alonso Pérez de Guzmán, referred to as El Bueno, the heroic defender of ▶Tarifa. Sculptures of him and his wife kneeling by Montañés are placed on either side of the retable, also by Montañés. The second church was founded by Guzmán's son Juan Alonso Pérez, who lies buried with his wife.

The path leads from the entrance to the **amphitheatre** (anfiteatro), ***Ruined city** one of the largest-known constructions of its kind, with a 160m/175yd **of Itálica** longitudinal axis, a 137m/150yd lateral axis, and seating for 25,000 spectators. Excessive animal hunts and gladiatorial contests took place here, as is documented by a bronze plaque on which the emperor Marcus Aurelius commanded the curtailing of such spectacles (now in the national archaeological museum in Madrid). The cruciform foundations in the oval's centre served as an animal enclosure and magazine. The rows of seats rise in surrounding tiers, the first row being reserved for patricians, as can still be seen today by the names engraved; the populace sat above.

❶ April – Sept. Tue – Sat 8.30am – 9pm, Sun 9am – 3pm; Oct – March Tue – Sat 9am – 6.30pm, Sun 9am – 3pm

In Italica the Romans built their first settlement on Iberian ground

Precinct After leaving the theatre, the paved main road, the cardo maximus, leads to the right up the hill to »**nova urbs**«. Columns that bore covered walks flank the road. It may be disappointing that so little of the buildings still stands, yet as the base walls have been preserved or rebuilt, the floor plans of the houses can be seen very clearly. Above all, though, the magnificent **mosaic floors** have remained, the most valuable of which have been removed to the archaeological museum in ▶Seville. Bird motifs can be seen in the building to the left in front of the cemetery, Casa de los Pajáros. Casa de Hylas lies further to the right in this side street, possessing a geometrically patterned mosaic floor. At the end of this path and to the left is a small incline adorned with a copy of Praxiteles' Aphrodite of Knidos. A path leads back to the main road from here, past Casa del Mosaico de Neptuno, which possesses the most beautiful mosaic decorations: the sea-god Neptune surrounded by dolphins, fish, and mythical creatures; before it a mosaic depicting what is thought to be the labyrinth of Cretan Knossos. The baths of Itálica are situated a little distance outside, slightly down hill and to the right of the main road.

Museo Mosaics, lamps, glasses, coins and a sculpture of Emperor Hadrian as a naked athlete are displayed in the entrance of the museum.

* Jaén

✦ H 6

Province: Jaén
Altitude: 574m/1883ft
Population: 116,700

The fact that Jaén, the ancient seat of a bishopric at the foot of Sierra Jabalcuz and Sierra de la Pandera in the northeast of Andalucía, is Spain's olive capital can be seen and smelled: the entire province – the largest uninterrupted expanse of olive groves in the world – is covered with olive trees, and the air is filled with the fragrance of olive pomace.

Spain's olive capital

Certainly the city is much less spectacular for tourists than ►Granada or ►Córdoba, yet after a stroll through its alleyways beneath the truly commanding castle, the visitor can feel its slightly rough, quiet charm. It is worth taking a short trip into the world of olives. There are particularly beautiful impressions of the landscape in the mountainous area south of the city, and to the east, where the hills roll more gently and olive plantations increasingly give way to corn fields.

History

The Romans who conquered the town fortified by the Carthaginians in 207 BC had more interest in the surrounding silver mines than in olive oil, which is why they named the place Auringis; even today people speak of »silver Jaén«. Under the rule of the Moors, who took over in 712, the town was made capital of a taifa as Yayyan or Geen (»place at the crossing of caravan routes«), following the disintegration of the Cordovan caliphate, and gained its urban character. In 1246 Ferdinand III drove off Ibn al-Ahmar, the founder of the Nasrid dynasty, who withdrew to Granada.
From now on Jaén formed a continuously embattled outpost of the Reconquista, and received the honorary title »Most Noble, Famous and Loyal City of Jaen, Guardian and Defender of the Kings of Castile« in 1466. In 1491 the armies gathered here for the conquest of Granada.

AROUND THE CATHEDRAL

*Catedral

An expertly rendered example of the Spanish Renaissance style, the imposing cathedral stands in an elevated position in the old town on the site of the main Moorish mosque. Its construction was begun around 1500, but the work only progressed more speedily under Andrés de Vandelvira from the mid-16th century, and the final completion was prolonged until the late 18th century. The wealth of statues (17th century) on the façade flanked by two towers are primarily by Pedro and Julián Roldán. Ferdinand III the Saint is in the middle of the balustrade, and to his side are the four evangelists and the four church fathers. The artists portrayed the Blessed Virgin in the tympanum. The north portal by Juan de Aranda also shows the Virgin, this time in prayer. Vandelvira created the south portal.

The **cathedral interior** is divided into a nave and two aisles of equal height, with a masterly dome by Juan de Aranda over the crossing. The magnificently carved early 16th-century ***choir stalls** are outstanding, with scenes from the Old and New Testament. Master Bartolomé executed the high altar of the Capilla Mayor with a depiction of the Virgin. Three chapels adjoin the east wall behind it. In a shrine of Cordovan goldsmith work, the middle one holds a renowned relic: the **veil of St Veronica**, called Santo Rostro, shown each Friday after mass. Admittedly this cloth, with which the saint wiped the face of Jesus on his way to Calvary, whereby the image of Christ's face was impressed upon the cloth, is one of three in existence (the other two are in Rome and Genoa). Above the shrine stands the Gothic sculpture of Nuestra Señora de la Antigua, which is said to have accompanied Ferdinand III on his crusades; the paintings are by Cellini and Titian, among others. An almost gaudy-looking Christ bearing the cross, carried at proces-

Catedral de Jaén

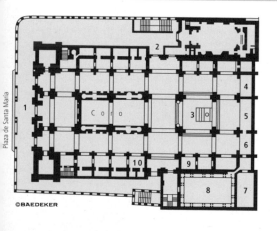

1 Puerta Mayor

2 Puerta del Norte

3 Capilla Mayor

4 Capilla de San Fernando

5 Capilla del Santo Rostro

6 Capilla de Santiago

7 Sala capitular

8 Sacristía

9 Capilla de la Virgen
  de las Angustias

10 Capilla de la Virgen
  de los Dolores

©BAEDEKER

sions, stands to the left in the Capilla de San Fernando; in the side chapels Capilla de la Virgen de las Angustias and Capilla de la Virgen de los Dolores visitors can see a retable by José de Mora and a depiction of the Mother of Sorrows by Pancorbo, respectively. To the right of the Capilla del Santo Rostro, in the chapter house, a retable is displayed with a painting by Pedro Machuca. Vandelvira completed the vestry with a coffered barrel vault. Beneath the vestry the **cathedral museum** displays paintings (by Ribera and others) and religious artefacts, including the large silver Custodia El Vandalino by Juan Ruiz, and a fifteen-armed candlestick by the master Bartolomé de Jaén.

❶ Mon – Fri 10am – 2pm, 4pm   7pm, Sat 10am – 2pm, 4pm – 6pm, Sun 10am – 12 noon, 4pm – 6pm; admission: €5

The cathedral of Jaén before the endless sea of olive orchards

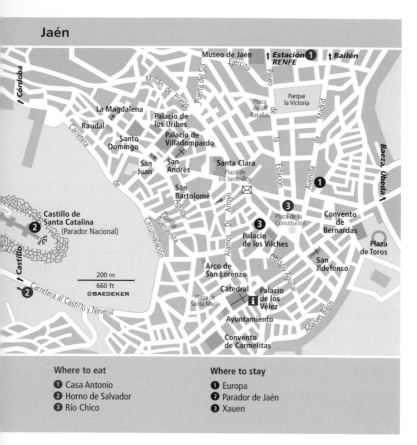

Jaén

Where to eat
1. Casa Antonio
2. Horno de Salvador
3. Río Chico

Where to stay
1. Europa
2. Parador de Jaén
3. Xauen

Convento de Carmelitas A little south of the cathedral the original manuscript of Cántico Espiritual by the mystic Juan de la Cruz (St John of the Cross) is kept in the Convento de Carmelitas (Monasterio de Santa Teresa) founded in 1615. Consecrated to St Teresa of Ávila, the convent was the first retreat of Carmelite nuns.

Houses of nobility The Palacio de los Vélez on the east side of the cathedral, and the Palacio de los Vilches somewhat further away, are two beautiful Renaissance palaces, of which there are several examples in the neighbourhood of the church and in the rest of Jaén's old town.

San Bartolomé North of the cathedral toward the Moorish old town lies the church of San Bartolomé, constructed in the 15th century, showing a Gothic ceramic baptismal font and a masterly Christ on the Cross by Martínez Montañés.

Adjacent to the church is the Monasterio de Santa Clara (13th century), the city's oldest monastery, possessing a beautiful cloister and a valuable sculpture of Christ, Cristo del Bambú.

Monasterio de Santa Clara

✳ LA MAGDALENA

Continue from the convent parallel to the castle to enter the old town with its Moorish character , named La Magdalena after its main church. From here narrow alleyways climb steeply up the castle hill.

Situated at the edge of the old town, this chapel was founded in 1515 by the treasurer to popes Leo X and Clement VII, Gutiérrez González Doncel. Originally it was probably a synagogue. A Madonna of the Andalusian school and a panel of the Virgen del Pópulo can be seen in its Capilla la Purísima; far more impressive, however, is the magnificent choir screen by Bartolomé de Jaén from the 18th century, which depicts which depicts plants and animals.

Capilla de San Andrés

A little further is the Palacio de los Villardompardo, beneath which the ****Baños Àrabes**, 11th-century baths, the most extensive of the Moorish era in Spain, were discovered in 1913. According to legend, the ruler of Jaén, King Alí, was murdered here by his rival. The baths consist of several rooms with an average width of 3–4m/10–13ft, which are lit and ventilated by shafts formed like eight-pronged stars. The building materials are marble and brick. The changing room was a 14m/45ft-long antechamber. Channels of hot water heated the floor of the steam-bath (al-bayt al Sajun), which is nearly 16m/50ft long. This room merges with a relaxation room (al-bayt al Wastani) of pleasant temperature, measuring about 11 sq m/120 sq ft, at the centre of which a pool is set as if beneath a canopy of horseshoe arches. The last stage of the bath took place in the 11.4m/37ft-long shower room (al-bayt al barid), in which bathers were doused with cold water from earthenware pitchers. The palace also houses a **museum of ethnology and a naive art museum**.

Palacio de los Villardompardo

❶ Tue – Sat 9am – 9.30pm, Sun 9.15am – 2.30pm, open for shorter periods in winter; free admission

Go past the Convento de Santo Domingo, which stands on the site of the palace of the Arab rulers and is connected with the baths by a subterranean corridor, to La Magdalena church, erected over an Arab mosque and probably the oldest church of the city. It has a late Gothic portal and a valuable retable, and above all a very impressive patio,

Iglesia de la Magdalena

Jaén

INFORMATION
Oficina de Turismo
C. Ramón y Cajal, 1
E-23001 Jaén
Tel. 953 19 04 55
Mon – Fri 9am – 7.30pm,
Sat/Sun 9.30am – 3pm
www.turjaen.org

ENTERTAINMENT
A few beautiful old bars with flair can
be found north-west of the cathedral
on C. Cerón and the streets Arco del
Consuelo and Bernardo López. Tapas
bars attract in C. Nueva. Nightlife as
such with live music takes place more
around the railway station and the
university.

SHOPPING
C. Roldán y Marín, Paseo de la Estación,
and C. de San Clemente are the main
shopping streets.

EVENTS
Semana Santa
Holy week

Feria de San Lucas
Mid-October: the city festival is celeb
rated for a week – with an end to the
season for Spain's best bullfighters,
who wish to recommend themselves
for engagement in Central and South
America.

WHERE TO EAT
❶ *Casa Antonio* €€€€
Fermín Palma, 3
Tel. 953 20 02 62
www.casantonio.es
closed Sunday evening, Monday

Restaurant with modern furnishings
and innovative cooking, which does
not forget its Andalusian roots. Best
restaurant in the city.

❷ *Horno de Salvador* €€€€
Carretera del Castillo
Tel. 953 23 05 28
closed Sunday evening, Monday
Classic dining room with very good
Andalusian food. In the summer the
terrace is also open. Good service.

❸ *Río Chico* €€€€
C. Nueva, 12
Tel. 953 24 08 02
closed Sunday evening, Monday
Andalusian cooking. Bacalao (cod)
is one of the house specialities.

WHERE TO STAY
❶ *Europe* €
Plaza de Belén, 1
Tel. 953 22 27 00
www.hoteleuropajaen.es
37 rooms
Central and quiet. Friendly service,
clean rooms, good breakfast. Sun
terrace

❸ *Xauen* €
Plaza de Deán Mazas, 3
Tel. 953 24 07 89
www.hotelxauenjaen.com, 35 rooms
Traditional old, central, well-priced accommodation with a view of the cathedral, the city and the mountains from
the terrace.

❷ *Parador de Jaén* €€ **Insider Tip**
Tel. 953 23 00 00
www.parador.es; 45 rooms

Among all the paradors the one in the castle of Jaén remains exceptional: high above the city the guest can feel like a knight, even though the rooms are not in the 14th century castle, but in an extension in the same style. The balconies offer an enjoyable and unsurpassed view over the hills of olive. Very good restaurant serving mainly Andalusian food in the knights' hall.

which still contains the basin for ritual ablutions before entering the mosque. At the church opposite is the Raudal de la Magdalena, a fountain going back to Roman times.

NEW TOWN

San Ildefonso

Heading east, it is not far from the Plaza de la Constitución down to the city's second largest church, San Ildefonso, completed in the 15th century. A patron saint of the city, the Virgen de la Descenso, is venerated here. Here, too, is the tomb of Andrés de Vandelvira, who made one of the three Renaissance-style portals. The Baroque altar by the brothers Roldán and the Capilla de la Virgen stands out from the décor.

Museo de Jaén

Passing the Plaza de las Batallas where a monument commemorates two great battles fought at Jaén (the battle of Navas de Tolosa against the Moors in 1212, and the battle of Bailén against the French in 1808), the Paseo de la Constitución leads northwards to the Museo de Jaén.

The museum consists of a collection of paintings and sculptures on the second floor (Alonso Cano: Madonna and Child; Pedro Berruguete: Flagellation of Christ), and an archaeological department on the ground floor. The most interesting pieces are a Roman mosaic, an early Christian sarcophagus from Martos, and Iberian sculptures such as the Bull Fighters of Porcuna.

The building also incorporates the 16th century entry to the former corn storehouse, and the façade of the former church of San Miguel (St. Michael).

● Tue 2.30pm – 8.30pm, Wed – Sat 9am – 8.30pm, Sun 9am – 2.30pm; free admission for EU citizens

Land of Olives

For most people Andalucía means Costa del Sol, Alhambra, Mezquita, flamenco and Carmen. But anyone who drives north from Granada winds up in the middle of España Incognita: the province of Jaén. And one thing especially will stand out there: the great variety around Andalusian oil.

Isabel Rojas Montes is a real seño-ra. She carries herself upright, wears a little rouge, greets her employees with a firm handshake and is surrounded by an aire of old Spanish rural nobility. She is the daughter of a respected psychologist and owns the Hacienda Madroño, an olive farm near Martos in the middle of the remote Andalusian province of Jaén. There are many pictures of her father in her living room: at work in Munich during the 1930s, with the family and meeting local dignitaries. Everywhere there are vases, icons and valuable furniture – and one thing is definitely not lacking here: oil. Isabel stands next to one of her trees and picks an olive. One single tree, she says, produces 80 kg of them every two years, unquestionably aceitunas are the economic backbone of her farm and the whole province.

Mystic

Olive trees are surrounded by something mystical, life-giving; a tree can live for several hundred years and still bear fruit like in younger years. Many people dream of planting an olive tree themselves and the Phonicians had this very idea more than 2500 years ago. The Romans especially were the ones who cultivated the oil

and improved production methods. Traders saw to it that they were distributed through the whole Roman Empire and sent the best oils to Rome. At that time the olive tree had a special reputation and images of the gods were carved from its wood. Olive groves were holy places and carrying an olive branch was supposed to protect the bearer from harm. Olive oil served in antiquity as an important source of nourishment but also medicine, cosmetics and illumination for oil lamps were used long before there were candles.

Trees, Trees, Trees

Today olive trees line up in rows on the shallow rolling hills of Jaén province, in exact order as if someone would be inspecting the troops at any moment. The only variety between Jaén and Úbeda is the transmission towers and it quickly becomes clear that Jaén is the largest producer of olives in Spain and in the whole world, pure monoculture and yet quite efficient. because of the EU subsidies aerial photographs were made of the province in order to calculate the exact number of trees: the results are mythical, more than 60 million! Olives are processed in minute detail according to various quality levels, and *Aceite de Oliva*

Andalucía's green gold grows here: the province of Jaén is the world's largest producer of olives

Virgen Extra is the star among oils. Harvest time is between October and March. But unlike the grape harvest only trained harvesters can work in it. The trees are cleared with jogging machines and staffs and the *Aceitunas* are brought to the oil factories as quickly as possible, where twigs and leaves are removed and the fruit presses run. Native olive oil is a pure, precious natural product and unlike other edible oils nothing is added to it. The harvested olives are first pressed into a paste, as they always have been, whereby the temperature may never rise above 30°C/86°F (hence the term »cold pressed«). In this way all of the heat-sensitive vitamins as well as the aromas and flavours are preserved completely. In the factories the pure oil is extracted from the paste by centrifu-ging or pressing. Then it is filtered. In this way harvest of between 700,000 and 900,000 tons are produced annually in all of Spain whereby Andalucía produced four fifths of the total amount. Almost half of the annual harvest is exported, but hardly anyone in the export regions knows where the majority of the olives comes from. Namely from the province of Jaén. The care and harvest is elaborate there and there is hardly any room for dreaming, even if the age-old trees

Olive harvest: a real test of strength

near Martos are called »Romeo and Julia« because the silver shimmering branches above the ochre-coloured ground cling to each other so beautifully.

Olive Ice Cream

During harvest time Martos, a town south-west of the provincial capital of Jaén, is a special place. Every year in December a festival is held in honour of the olive, something that, unlike the Sanfermines in Pamplona or the fire festival in Fallas de Valencia, no one from northern Europe knows about. In this fiesta in the shadows of a medieval fortification visitors from the neighbouring towns receive joyos, a roll with stockfish and oil. Meanwhile workers are using an old oil press to make oil the way it's been

made for almost 2000 years. No beauty or wine queen is chosen in Jaén province, rather an annual olive oil princess. The fruits are processed in modern factories to Virgen Extra and plain Aceite de Oliva, the crushed pits are used as heating fuel in many a wellness centre and the »region's gold« is alos used in the cosmetics industry, in trades and in cooking. It is even used to make ice cream, but this is more a matter of taste. The Piscual variety from Jaén province has especially made a name for itself and the popular, spicy oil is of course an obligatory part of local cooking, be it marinated partridge, grilled pork loin, roasted lamb, stockfish or the garlicky soup ajoatao. Ecven Spain's premiered cooks like Ferran Adrià or Juan Mari Arzak from far-away

Catalonia or the Basque region swear by this oil.

Tasting the Oil – an Experience!

But an experience of another kind in Jaén province is an oil tasting. In a Catas de Aceite visitors may smell and taste oils like the pros do, and even express an opinion. If the colour, taste and aroma are first class, the oil gets the highest grade: Aceite Virgen Extra!

Testing and grading olive oil is an experience not to be missed. The visitor is given several oils to taste, then he can try to guess which grade of quality they have. Between the different kinds of oil pieces of apple are eaten to neutralize the taste.

WHERE TO BUY OIL
Hacienda Madroño
Ctra. Santiago de Calatrava, km. 9
Martos, Jaén,
Tel 953 12 98 79
www.cortijoelmadrono.com
Isabels Rojas Monte's hacienda recently opened a small museum with traditional olive farming implements, but it is first of all a real old finca, which can be visited upon request.

Aceites La Laguna
Aceites La Laguna S.A.
Camino de la Laguna s/n
Puente del Obispo, Baeza
Tel. 953 76 51 00
www.aceiteslaguna.com
This Jaén olive oil is considered by experts to be especially good; its aroma is reminiscent of tomatoes, artichokes and cut grass. It is very pleasant and balanced and has the slightly bitter and spicy nuances typical of this region that fit so well with lamb and fish. It is cold pressed from the Piscual, Arbequina and Manzanilla varieties. The small shop attached also sells unfiltered oil, which tastes just as good but is not exported because of its cloudy appearance. You eat with your eyes first.

Piel de Oliva – oil for the skin
Piel de Oliva, S.L.L.
Ctra. de la Yedra, s/n; Baeza
www.pieldeoliva.es
Piel de Oliva produces cosmetic oil for the skin based on Aceite de Oliva Virgen Extra. Body lotions, soaps and shampoo for her and for him are available.

PLEASANT ACCOMMODATION
Hotel Sierra de Cazorla & Spa Óleo Salud
Carretera Sierra Cazorla Km 2
23476 Cazorla; Tel 954 15 51 44
www.hotelsierradecazorla.com
What is special about this country hotel is its unusual spa. The heating system for the pool and sauna is fueled all year round by thousands upon thousands of olive pits (cheaper than wood).

Hotel Torres I
Avda. Valencia, 126
23330 Villanueva del Arzobispo
Tel. 953 45 10 42; www.htorres.com
Well-situated hotel for excursions into the interior of Parque de Cazorla, Segura y Las Villas and the surrouding area, like the pretty mountain village Iznatoraf. Moreover, the restaurant is dedicated to everything about olive oil and the owners organize visits to nearby cooperatives where olive oil products can be tried.

Versatile Fruit

Most of the olives consumed worldwide come from Spain, where Andalusia is the main producer, especially in the province of Jaén with 60 million olive trees as the world's largest continuous growing area. Olives are not just used to make oil, but they are also used to produce soap and other cosmetics. And of course it is the classic tapa to a glass of sherry fino …

▶ **Oil and oil are not the same**
Quality grades of Spanish olive oil:

1 **Aceite de Oliva Virgen Extra:**
pure oil of the best quality,
free acidity of max. 0,8 %

2 **Aceite de Oliva Virgen:**
intense taste,
free acidity max. 2 %

3 **Aceite de Oliva:**
mixture of native and
refined oil, neutral taste
and inexpensive price

4 **Aceite de Orujo:**
raw rest oil mixed
with native oil

The olive
In Spain there are about 200
varieties of olives. About 50% of
the olives grown are of the variety
»Picual«; more than 90% of
the olives grown in Jaén are
of this variety.

▶ **Growing areas in Andalucía**

- Campiñas de Jaén
- Montoro-Adamuz
- Sierra Mágina
- Sierra de Cazorla
- Sierra de Segura
- Montes de Granada
- Poniente de Granada
- Antequera
- Sierra de Cádiz
- Priego de Córdoba
- Estepa
- Baena

©BAEDEKER

▶ **Olive harvest**
Most of the olives harvested in the large olive groves from October until March are still picked by hand. In some regions machines are used to shake the trees.

Vareador
long wooden pole used
to shake and beat the trees

Olive tee
10 to 20 m tall; green-gray,
smooth bark; can be more
than 100 years old; first
harvest after seven years,
largest harvests after 20 years

Olive farmers
do most of their hard
work by hand

Net or cloth for collecting
Olives are caught up in this way. Then the olives are
collected and packed into crates.

Regions with the largest harvests
About 282,696,000 olives are harvested every year in Spain, where Andalucía is the largest producer. The number of olives from each region is shown below.

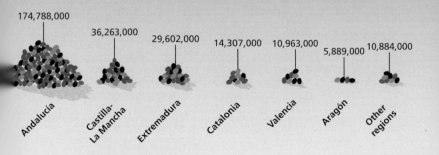

174,788,000

36,263,000

29,602,000

14,307,000

10,963,000

5,889,000 10,884,000

Andalucía

Castilla-
La Mancha

Extremadura

Catalonia

Valencia

Aragón

Other
regions

** CASTILLO DE SANTA CATALINA

West of the city centre looms a mountain ridge with one of the **most beautiful and impressive fortifications of Andalucía**, Castillo de Santa Catalina, which Ferdinand III conquered in 1246. The best way to get there is by car on the 5km/3mi-long stretch marked Parador Nacional. The Carthaginians built a tower on the hill, but the present-day castle dates back to an Arab fortress which Ibn al-Ahmar expanded to its present imposing size. As Ferdinand captured it on St Catherine's Day it bears her name. Parts of the old fortification walls are visible when coming from the old town.

The castle consists of a large forecourt and the mighty Torre del Homenaje, which is connected by battlements to other towers; an exhibit and film informs on its history. A vantage point (only for those unafraid of heights) marked by a large cross and jutting out like a ship's bows offers a stunning view over the city and the olive plantations.

Insider Tip

❶ Tue – Sun 10am – 2pm, 5 – 7pm; admission €3.50

AROUND JAÉN

La Guardia de Jaén

The remains of Roman buildings point to the origin of the small town La Guardia de Jaén (11km/7mi southeast); additionally the ruins of an ancient castle are located here, as well as a lovely parish church and cloistered courtyard created by Vandelvira, all that remains of a Dominican monastery founded in the 16th century.

*Martos

Dominated by two castles, Martos, 20km/12mi west of Jaén, **is the olive capital of Spain** – nowhere else in the kingdom do so many olive trees grow within the communal boundaries. Having developed from the Iberian settlement of Tucci, Martos was wrested from the Moors by Ferdinand III in 1222, and was a vital outpost in the reconquest of Córdoba. The overall impression of the town alone makes a visit to Martos worthwhile: the castle hill rises at its centre, square white houses huddling on it along narrow alleys; the ruins of the Castillo de la Peña de los Carvajales are visible on the rugged rock. The brothers Carvajal were thrown from it to their deaths, despite their innocence, after they had been accused of murdering a favourite of Ferdinand IV. Inside the walls of the second fortress, the citadel, stands the church Santa María de la Villa, built in the 13th century and modified in Gothic style in the 15th century. Its greatest treasures are a Baroque retable and an early Christian sarcophagus dating from the 4th century. The town hall of 1577 and the Renaissance fountain Fuente Nueva (1580) are also worth seeing.

Alcaudete, 22km/13mi southwest of Martos, saw many battles, **Alcaudete** changed hands often and was finally conquered by Ferdinand III in 1245. He gave it to the Order of Calatrava, its remains still dominate the village. Below the fortress are the 15th-century Gothic church Santa María and the grand palace Casa del Almirante.

✶✶ Jerez de la Frontera

✦ C 8

Province: Cádiz
Altitude: 56m/183ft
Population: 208,800

Not far inland from ▶Cádiz lies Jerez de la Frontera, world famous as the place of origin of Jerez wine, better known as sherry. Of equal importance is the breeding of thoroughbreds, the epitome of fiery Andalusian horses, at the national stud farm; the Royal Andalusian Riding School is also located here. Lastly, Jerez de la Frontera is a centre of flamenco and the cante jondo ▶p.62.

Sherry, horses, and flamenco are combined in three large annual festivals: the **Festival de Jerez** (flamenco), the **Feria del Caballo**, and the **Fiestas del Otoño** following the grape harvest. It becomes particularly clear on such occasions that Jerez de la Frontera is a town of aristocratic character, where the sherry barons call the shots. Their sweeping bodegas, surrounded by high walls, set themselves apart conspicuously from the rest of the townscape. Grand domiciles in well-tended parks, noble horses and fighting bulls that they breed on their huge estates are shown with great pride, and there is hardly a trace of social responsibility towards the thousands of day labourers who live on the fringes of town, and for whom the grape harvest is the most important source of income. Lastly, Jerez has also made itself a name in motor sports. 10km/6mi outside the town towards ▶Arcos de la Frontera lies the Circuito de Jerez, at which races of the World Motorcycle Championship are held.

Sherry, horses and flamenco

> **? Why »Sherry«?**
>
> **MARCO POLO INSIGHT**
>
> The Moors made Jerez a fortified city, and renamed it Saris, Sharis, Seris or Sherish – thus the rumour that the English invented the name »sherry« for wine from Andalucía because they were unable to pronounce »Jerez« is refuted. Following the reconquest by King Alfonso X in 1264, the city developed into a centre for the wine trade, and from the corruption of the Moorish town name the product name »sherry« emerged.

Jerez de la Frontera

INFORMATION
Oficina de Turismo
C. / Larga, 39
E-11403 Jerez de la Frontera
Tel. 956 33 88 74 or 956 34 17 11
www.turismojerez.com
Mon – Fri 9am – 3pm, 4.30pm – 6.30pm
(summer 5pm – 7pm), Sat/Sun
9.30am – 2.30pm (Aug. 8am – 4pm)

ENTERTAINMENT
Nice weekend nights happen in Jerez
near the bullfighting arena, along the
streets Pastora and Cádiz and around
Canterbury Plaza.

Tablao Lagá de Tio Parilla
Plaza Becerra, 5

Tel. 956 33 83 34
The Tablao offers good flamenco shows
from 10.30pm – there's no admission
charge but the price of the first drink
after the show starts makes up for it!

BODEGAS
In Jerez, the city of sherry, do not fail to
book a tour of a bodega. Many are conducted in English, and they always ending
with a tasting. You can find out the times
for tours on the websites or by telephone
and also make reservations (▶MARCO
POLO Insight, p.306–311).

SHOPPING
All around C. Larga fashion, crafts (speciality: riding equipment, wickerwork),

You find one of the oldest market halls in Spain in Jerez

ceramics, leather-wear and jewellery are on sale. Don't miss the market hall at Plaza Estévez.

Casa del Jerez
C. Divina Pastora, 1, Local 3, opposite the riding school
Sherry of all brands and a large variety of handicrafts.

EVENTS
Festival del Jerez
In February / March
www.festivaldejerez.es.

Semana Santa

Feria del Caballo
Gymkhana and horse fair in May.

Fiestas del Otoño
This includes several festivals from September to October, such as the grape harvest festival and a large horse parade.

WHERE TO EAT
Bodega La Andana €€€€
C. Moscatel, 4
Urbanización Parque Serrana BL. 5
Tel. 956 30 73 85, closed Sundays
High-class cuisine somewhat outside of the centre, known for its fine tapas.

❷ Gaitán €€€€
Gaitán, 3
Tel. 956 16 80 21
www.restaurantegaitan.com
closed Sundays; one of the most popular restaurants in Jerez. Highly praised cooking (Andalusian and Basque). Antlers and pictures of past guests on the walls.

❸ La Mesa Redonda €€€€
Manuel de la Quintana, 3

Tel. 956 34 00 69; closed Sundays
Indisputably the best traditional cuisine to accompany sherry in Jerez de la Frontera – be trusting and let the menu entice you.

❶ Bar Juanito €€€€   *Insider Tip*
Pescadería Vieja, 8–10
Tel. 956 33 48 38
This place has the best tapas in the city, a huge selection. The assortment of finos is almost equally large.

WHERE TO STAY
❸ Jerez & Spa €
Avda. Alcalde Alvaro Domecq, 35
Tel. 956 30 06 00
www.jerezhotel.com, 121 rooms
With its five stars the best hotel in town, amidst beautiful gardens, yet close to the centre. Restaurant with traditional cooking, pool and sauna.

❶ Doña Blanca €
Bodega, 11
Tel. 956 34 87 61
www.hoteldonablanca.com, 30 rooms
Good, located centrally with spacious rooms. Breakfast buffet, cafeteria, own parking lot.

❷ El Coloso €
Pedro Alonso, 13
Tel. 956 34 90 00
www.elcolosohotel.com, 28 rooms
Central and low-priced, own parking garage.

❹ Nuevo €
Caballeros, 23
Tel. 956 34 7 61
www.nuevohotel.com
Friendly and modest accommodation in a 19th century house. Roof over patio.

The Secret of Sherry

Sherry is not a vintage wine (and definitely not distilled!), but rather a mixture of wines of different vintages but of the same character. It is produced in a complicated process of ripening and production, which takes years, called the solera process.

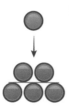

▶ **After picking**

After the grapes are picked in September the grapes are spread out to dry for a few days. Then the »stormy fermentation« takes place (3 – 7 days), in which 90% of the sugar is transformed into alcohol and carbon dioxide. The second phase (»quiet fermentation«) lasts until late November. Then the young wine is fortified with brandy until it has 15 – 18% alcohol and filled into solera barrels according to the desired type of sherry.

▶ **Solera system**

Solera comes from the Spanish word suelo for floor. The oldest sherry is always in the barrels that are stored on the bottom,, so that it can be bottled for sale. The amount removed has to be replaced by the same amount of sherry from the criadera (layer) above it. The top row is filled up with fresh vintage wine.

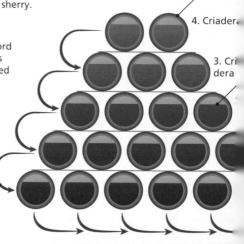

4. Criader

3. Cri dera

Moved down every 3 – 4 months

©BAEDEKER

▶ **Bodegas in Jerez**

Visiting a bodega, with wine-tasting of course, is a must in Jerez de la Frontera.

Bodegas Tio Pepe/ González Byass
Manuel María Gonzalez, 12
tel. 956 35 70 16
www.tiendatiopepe.com

Harveys
Pintor Muñoz Cebrián, s/n
Tel. 956 15 15 00
www.bodegaharveys.com

Very British with stylish antique cars in the entry area

Bodegas Domecq
San Ildefonso, 3
tel. 956 15 15 00
www.domecqbodegas.con

Famous large producer

Williams & Humbert
Ctra. N-IV, Km 641,75
tel. 956 38 31 00
www.bodegas-williams-humbert.com

With stables and garden

Only three kinds of green grapes can be used for making sherry, palomino (for the best finos), Pedro Ximénez and Muscatel (for sweet sherry).

Pedro Ximénez

Botas (solera barrels)
Oak barrels holding about 600 litres (160 gallons) are piled up lying in 3 to 5 layers.

────── The barrels are only maximally 4/5 full so that the flor can develop, a layer of yeast fungus that protects against oxidation.

...dera

...riadera

Solera

The wine has to age at least 3 years in the solera.

▶ **The most important sherry types**

Fino (15 – 18 Vol.%)
Light, straw yellow, dry

Manzanilla (15 – 19 Vol.%)
Very dry fino from Sanlúcar de Barrameda

Amontillado (17 – 22 Vol.%)
Amber coloured, soft

Oloroso (17 – 22 Vol.%)
Amber to mahogany coloured, with a typical strong walnut aroma

Palo Cortado (17 – 22 Vol.%)
Originally a fino, in which the flor has died, which makes the wine oxidize more; amber to mahogany coloured, rarely found.

Cream (15,5 – 22 Vol.%)
Sweet mixture of a basic wine (pale cream: fino; medium cream: Amontillado; cream: Oloroso) with other wines or ciders.

Pedro Ximénez (15 – 22 Vol.%)
Very sweet, oily; brown-black sherry from this kind of grape

...deman
...rro, 10
...956 31 29 95
...w.sandeman.eu

...estro Sierra
...a de Silos, 3
...956 34 24 33
...w.maestrosierra.com

...io Lustau
...s, 53
...956 34 77 89
...v.emilio-lustau.com

▶ **www.sherry.org**
Website of
Consejo
Regulador

▶ **Consejo Regulador**
The official control council monitors the quality and certifies the wine. Highest certificates are:

V.O.S.
(vinum optimum signatum / very old sherry)
aged 20 – 30 years

V.O.R.S.
(optimum rare signatum / very old rare sherry)
aged more than 30 years

Wine in Andalucía

You see them in every bar and eventually, overcome by curiosity, you too order a »copita«, the small glass that narrows at the top allowing the incomparable bouquet of sherry to unfold fully. But be careful not to order »sherry«, because there are many kinds, e.g., a »fino« or an »amontillado« …

The best known of all Andalusian wines owes its international fame to the British, whose naval hero **Sir Francis Drake** took home a considerable amount of »wine from Jerez«, among other things, from a raid on Cádiz in 1587. The importers soon bought the vineyards in order to produce the sherry themselves, so that today some of the most famous bodegas like **Williams and Humbert** or **Harveys** are still in British ownership. Probably the most famous sherry baron, however, was from France: **Pedro Domecq**, who came to Jerez in 1730.

The Sherry triangle

Sherry is cultivated exclusively in the province of Cádiz in a 23,000-hectare (57,000-acres) coastal region formed by the triangle of towns **Jerez de la Frontera, Sanlúcar de Barrameda** and **El Puerto de Santa Maria**. It is only here that the interplay of the chalky soil (»albarizas«) and the mild Atlantic climate fundamental for the quality of sherry works out right. The types of grape grown are **Palomino** for the best finos, and **Pedro Ximénez** and muscatel, used for sweeter wines.

Taste it!

No trip to Andalucía is complete without a tasting in a bodega (in this case a sherry bar and not a sherry producer's storehouse)! Finos and amontillados are served ice cold. Only the sweeter wines are drunk at room temperature. Most people who have tried sherry soon realize that a small glass of fino can be enjoyed on any occasion and not only as an aperitif, especially when there is a small tapa to go with it.

Types of Sherry …

Fino is a light yellow, very dry, slightly acidic and lively wine with an alcohol content of 15% to 17%. It is the most typical of all sherries and is drunk the most. **Amontillado**, the name given to wine from Montilla, is aged a bit longer than fino, amber coloured, softer, but still has the characteristic bouquet and an alcohol content of 16-18%. An **Oloroso** has a dark golden colour. It is still dry to lightly sweet and gives off a decidedly nutty aroma with an alcohol content of 18% to 20%.

Raya, of a slightly lesser quality, and the seldom obtainable **Palo Cortado**, are varieties of this. Finally, **cream sherries** are the sweetest and heaviest of sherries, produced from a blend of oloroso and a sweet wine (often muscatel). They have an alcohol content of around 20%.

Cathedral of Sherry: the bodega of Pedro Domecq in Jerez

... and Where They Come From

Everything worth knowing about sherry can be found out on the internet on the website www.sherry.org. But that is no substitute for the real thing – a tour of the bodega of a sherry producer is **a must** when visiting Jerez de la Frontera. As a matter of rule they can be visited in the morning as part of a tour (with **wine tasting**). Do register in advance. Bodegas are not cellars but partially huge halls in which one solera row is stacked on the other (addresses ►p.306/307).

Little Brothers

Two other wine-growing regions produce wines very similar to sherry. In the direct vicinity of Sanlúcar de Barrameda grapes are grown for **manzanilla**, a very light, bone-dry fino, which many prefer to the fino from Jerez. Its slightly salty flavour comes from the sea winds blowing through the bodegas; moreover, it is not fortified. In the 18,500ha/46,000-acre wine-growing region of **Montilla-Moriles** in the sweltering south of the province of Córdoba – and this is the **first great difference to sherry** – the grapes grown are primarily the Pedro Ximénez variety. The

Wine growing regions in Andalucía

second difference is in the storage during the maturing process; it is blended according to the solera process not in oak casks but in large earthenware jugs, the »tijanas«. Montilla-Moriles produces the same varieties as Jerez and in addition Pedro Ximénez, which is produced this grape alone; it is very dark and has an alcohol content of 28%.

Cousins

Málaga, a classic dessert wine, comes from the Costa del Sol. The grapes – muscatel and Pedro Ximénez – are grown around Estepona and to the east and north of Málaga on an area of 2,500ha/6,000 acres, but have to be brought to Málaga for processing. This wine is also produced using the **solera system**, but concentrated grape juice is added to make it sweeter. The best known Málaga is **Dulce Color**; of a dark amber-like colour, it has an alcohol content of 15% to 23%. The fruity **muscatel** is also dark with 15% to 20% alcohol. The light reddish **Pedro Ximénez** is produced only from the grape variety of the same name (16% to 20%). The lightest in colour and most rare Málaga is **blanco seco**; dry and usually with less alcohol than the rest. The golden-coloured **Lágrima** is very expensive. Its grapes are not pressed; the must is squeezed out by the pressure of the grapes' own weight. Finally, 16,000ha/40,000 acres of vineyards are cultivated around Huelva. The same type is produced in the D.O. region of **Condado de Huelva** as in the sherry regions, though without achieving the same quality. For this reason the area has moved more into the production of house wines, and produces quite good, fresh white wines.

Spirits

Last but not least the sherry triangle also produces spirits. Although the distillates for the **brandies** produced here mostly come from Mancha in central Spain, only what has been aged in Jerez, Sanlúcar or El Puerto de Santa Maria – also using the solera system – may be called »Brandy de Jerez«. The difference can be tasted and it also has its price – top brandies like **Gran Duque de Alba Oro** from Williams & Humbert or **Hidalgo 200 Solera Gran Reserva** cannot be had for under €50 per bottle.

Sherry is poured in a high arc into a glass using a long glass pipette

Bodegas

JEREZ DE LA FRONTERA
►MARCO POLO Insight, p. 306

EL PUERTO DE SANTA MARÍA
Bodega Terry
Toneleros, 1
Mon – Fri 10.30am, 12.30pm;
Sat 12 noon
Admission: €8
Probably the most beautiful bodega, where not only wine and brandy can be tasted, but noble Andalusian horses and magnificent coaches can also be admired.

Osborne
Los Moros, 7
Tel. 956 86 91 00

Mon – Fri 10.30am, 11am, 12 noon
Sat 11am, 12 noon
Admission: €7.50
The best-known bodega of El Puerto de Santa María. In the cellars in the town centre sherry is produced, outside of town on the A-4 brandy is produced.

Gutiérrez Colosia **Insider Tip**
Avda. Bajamar, 40
Mon – Fri 1pm
Sat 12.30pm, 1.30pm
Admission: €4
Small but fine family-run business right on the Río Guadalete. Sometimes the owner reveals the secrets of sherry production.

History
The area between Jerez and the Cabo de Trafalgar was the site of the final battle between the Visigoths under Roderic and the Moors under Tariq in 711. The Muslim victors named the place Seris and upgraded it to a fortress. In 1264 Alfonso X reconquered the city, yet only in 1340 did a further battle at the Río Saladom, from which the Christians emerged victorious, forestall the last invasion from North Africa. Jerez has shared the byname de la Frontera (on the border) with other western Spanish-Moorish frontier towns since 1379.

OLD TOWN

Plaza de la Asunción
From Alameda Cristina via C. Tomería go to Plaza de la Asunción with the Plateresque Cabildo Municipal, the former town hall, built by Andrés de Ribera in 1575. The Torre de la Vela, which once served as a signal tower, and the church San Dionisio, built in the Mudéjar style in 1430, also stand on the square. The church has a noteworthy 20m/65ft-high Baroque retable.

San Miguel
Begun in 1482, conspicuous for its blue-tiled tower and its three-storey 17th-century west façade, the church San Miguel is reached by going southeast across the Plaza del Arenal; its high altar carries a retable with reliefs by Martínez Montañés and José de Arce (1625) – amongst the paintings of the Zurbarán school a Divine Countenance is the outstanding work.

*Alcázar
A little to the west of San Miguel, an elevated plateau directly at the Bodegas Gonzáles Byass is the site of the alcázar, an impressive Almohad building that has undergone renovations in the recent years. Enter via Puerta de la Ciudad, to discover behind its walls a well-preserved domed mosque with a restored mihrâb and 14th-century baths. Reconstructed in the Renaissance style, the Palacio de Villavicencio has a **camera obscura** in its tower that produces unusual views of the town.
❶ Mid-July – mid-Sept. Mon – Fri 9.30am – 8pm, Sat, Sun 9.30am – 3pm, otherwise daily 9.30am – 6pm (Nov – Jan only until 3pm; admission: €3)

*Catedral
From the alcázar the back of the cathedral Colegiata de San Salvador is visible. It was constructed in 1695 to replace a 13th-century church that in turn was built on the foundations of a mosque. The free-standing belfry, the flying buttresses protecting against earthquake damage, the dome surrounded by sculptures, and the beautiful Baroque perron in front of the main façade are remarkable. A valuable baropque crucifix by Juan de Mesa is remains in the vestry; above all, take a look at the **Zurbarán painting** *La Virgen Niña*, a rare depiction of the Virgin as a sleeping child. In September, on the square in

Jerez de la Frontera

Where to eat
① Bar Juanito
② Gaitán
③ Mesa Redonda

Where to stay
① Doña Blanca
② El Coloso
③ Jerez
④ Nuevo

▪ Bodegas

Map labels: Palacio del Tiempo, Parque Zoológico, Sandeman, Real Escuela, Museo Taurino, Sevilla ③, ③, Santiago, Ponce, Ancha, Merced, Cristal, Ayuntamiento, Palacio Domecq, Fundación Andaluza de Flamenco, Porvera, Francos, San Marcos, Santo Domingo, San Juan, Cristina, Alameda, Arcos de la Frontera, San Mateo, San Lucas, Museo Arqueológico, Carmen, Torneria, Circuito, Pedro Domecq, San Dionisio, Larga, Honda, Arcos, Pedro Domecq, Diez, Cabildo, Medina, Catedral, Pza. del Arenal, ①, Mercado, Puerta del Arroyo, Pza. de las Angustias, Chapara, Sanlúcar, Calzada del Arroyo, Gonzales Byass, Alcázar, Puerto de Armas, Maestro Sierra, San Miguel, ④, ②, 200 m, 660 ft, Torresoto, Ronda Muleros, ©BAEDEKER

front of the cathedral, the annual grape harvest festival begins on the Plaza Encarnación, where the grapes are still pressed in the traditional manner: barefoot.

NORTHERN AND WESTERN QUARTERS

It is not far from the cathedral – cutting along the Bodegas Domecq – to the northwestern neighbourhood and the church San Mateo, which was begun in the 14th century and has a Mudéjar-style chapel.

San Mateo

Near the church the archaeological museum displays as its greatest treasure a Greek helmet from the 7th century BC, evidence of early colonization of the region by the Greeks. Furthermore, Iberian, Roman, Visigothic and Moorish findings are exhibited. The cafeteria on the top floor is a nice place to take a break.

Museo Arqueológico

❶ Tue – Fri 10am – 2pm and 4pm – 7pm, Sat and Sun 9am – 2.30pm, admission €5

Majestic Andalusians in the Real Escuela Andaluza del Arte Ecuestre

*Centro Andaluz de Flamenco

Insider Tip

Past the church San Lucas (14th century) is the Palacio Pemartín on Plaza de San Juan. The 18th-century palace houses the Centro Andaluz de Flamenco. Here, exhibitions, films, performances, and the library teach all you need to know about flamenco; even dancing and guitar courses are offered (www.centroandaluzdeflamenco.es). The San Juan de los Caballeros church (15th century) opposite catches the eye with its nine-part apse.

❶ Mon – Fri 9am – 2pm; www.centroandaluzdeflamenco.es

*Parque Zoológico

Embedded in a botanical garden, the recipient of several awards, the zoological garden of Jerez is the largest in Andalucía, and one of Spain's finest. A chimpanzee house and a white tiger are the attractions (opening hours: summer Tue–Sun 10am–8pm, winter to 6pm).

❶ Summer Tue – Sun 10am – 7pm, winter until 6pm

Palacio del Tiempo

The former **clock museum** La Atalaya was completely re-designed, and now operates as Palacio del Tiempo. However, it continues to show over 300 antique clocks from all over Europe, some of which are extremely valuable. The **Misterio de Jerez**, an audiovisual show about the wine that made the city so famous, has been added.

❶ tours only; tel. 956 18 21 00; www.elmisteriodejerez.org

To the north of the city, the rambling premises of the **Royal School of Andalusian Equestrian Art** stretch along the Avda. Duque de Abrantes. Charles Garnier, architect of the Paris opera house, built the administrative building in the 19th century. 60 of the noblest Andalusian horses are kept in the adjacent stables, and have been used to refine both English thoroughbreds and Lipizzaners. They are bred at the national stud farm nearby. Visitors can tour the stables and the showroom, and can watch the training. The show Cómo bailan los Caballos Andaluces (»how Andalusian horses dance«) in the great hall is the highlight.

❶ Performances: Tue, Thu 12 noon, in Aug also Fri 12 noon, Nov–Jan only Thu 12 noon; www.realescuela.org

*Real Escuela Andaluza del Arte Ecuestre

AROUND JEREZ DE LA FRONTERA

A few miles southeast ▶Medina Sidonia lies the former Carthusian monastery La Cartuja, founded in 1463, where the cross-breeding of German, Italian, and Andalusian horses resulted in **the Carthusian thoroughbreds race**. The building has a superb free-standing Renaissance gate (1571) and a Gothic church, to which an opulent façade was added in 1667. Sculptures of Carthusian monks stand in its niches, St Bruno uppermost. The famous depictions of Carthusians painted by Zurbarán for the church altar are now in the possession of the department of art of the museum of ▶Cádiz.

*La Cartuja

Another tip for fans of Carthusian horses: on the Finca Fuente del Suero, also towards Medina Sidonia, located 6.5km/4mi outside of Jerez, **the stud Yeguada de la Cartuja** has specialized in breeding the famous steeds, which can be admired on a guided tour.

❶ Tours Sat 11am; from €15.50 on

Lebrija, Roman Nebrissa, 30km/19mi north of Jerez de la Frontera, is the birthplace of Juan Díaz de Solís, the **discoverer of the Río de la Plata** in today's Argentina.

Lebrija

The elevated **Santa María de la Oliva**, founded in a mosque in 1249, and altered several times since, has a prominent place among the churches of the town. Its belfry is reminiscent of the Giralda of Seville; within is a high altar by Alonso Cano, with a sculpture of the saint after which it is named.

Further places worth seeing are the hermitage Nuestra Señora del Castillo, founded on the site of a Moorish fort in 1535, and provided with a beautiful coffer ceiling, as well as the Plaza Mayor, surrounded by houses of the nobility. There is a memorial to the **humanist Antonio de Nebrija** (1442–1522) who was born here. He was the author of the first Castilian Spanish grammar and chronicler to the Catholic Monarchs.

Linares

✴ **H 5**

Province: Jaén
Altitude: 418m/1371ft
Population: 61,300

The industrial and mining town of Linares lies in the north of Jaén province at the edge of the Sierra Morena, in the middle of a region of copper and lead ore that has been worked since ancient times. Today Linares lives from the motor industry – Suzuki and Land Rover produce here.

Linares originated as a suburb of ancient Iberian Cástulo, which was excavated 6km/3.5mi to the northeast. **Imilce, Hannibal's wife**, is said to have come from there. However, the town gained notoriety throughout Spain due to an incident in 1947: one of the country's most famous toreros, **Manolete**, lost his life during a corrida in the arena of Linares. His nemesis was the bull Islero. The bull had rammed a horn into Manolete's right thigh. The torero probably died of a blood transfusion of the wrong blood type or because of spoiled plasma in the transfusion.

Today Linares is also known in the world of chess: Since 1978 one of the best master tournaments has taken place here.

> **!** **MARCO POLO TIP**
>
> *Classical guitar* **Insider Tip**
>
> Naturally classical Spanish guitar music is played in the home town of Andrés Segovia. Information on concerts in the Fundación Andrés Segovia is obtainable under tel. 953 65 13 90 or www.segoviamuseo.org.

WHAT TO SEE IN AND AROUND LINARES

Palace buildings
Although less grand than in the neighbouring Renaissance towns ▶Baeza and ▶Úbeda, some remarkable palaces from this era have survived in Linares: the Palacio de los Zambrana, and the Antigua Casa de la Minicion, the mint of Charles III in the 18th century, later an ammunition factory. The main church dates back to the 13th century and exhibits a fine 16th-century retable; the tower of the former castle leans against the church.

Museo Arqueológico
In a 17th century palace (Calle General Echagüe, 2) the archaeological museum features early, Phoenician, Greek, Iberian, Roman and Moorish pieces, including findings from Cástulo.

Museo Segovia
The world-famous guitarist **Andrés Segovia** (1893–1987) was born in Linares; his birthplace is at once museum and tomb.

Linares

INFORMATION
Oficina de Turismo
Paseo de Linarejos, s/n
E-23700 Linares
Tel. 953 60 78 12
www.linares.net
www.turismolinares.es

WHERE TO EAT
Los Sentidos €€€€
Doctor, 13
Tel. 953 65 10 72
www.restaurantelossentidos.com
Old house with four modern rooms, one
of which leads out into the small inner
courtyard. Innovative cooking. Good
value for money.

WHERE TO SLEEP
Hotel RL Aníbal €
Cid Campeador, 11
Tel. 953 65 04 00
www.rlhoteles.com; 126 rooms
Hotel right in the centre of town with
a beautiful roof terrace and grill restaurant. Fitness centre, private parking
places at a fee. Elegant rooms with
dark wooden furniture.

Hotel Victoria €
Cervantes, 7; Tel. 953 69 25 00
www.hotelvictoria.org; 56 rooms
Hotel also in the town centre. Large
rooms, restaurant with traditional cooking. Private parking places at a fee.

❶ Cánovas del Castillo, 59; Sept – May Tue, Thu 10am – 2pm, 4pm – 7pm,
Sat 10am – 2pm; June until Aug Tue, Thu, Sat 10am – 2pm,
www.segoviamuseo.com

Bailén

Situated 13km/8mi to the west, Bailén offers no sights, yet is of great
historical significance. This is where Publius Cornelius Scipio the Elder defeated the Carthaginian Hasdrubal in 208 BC; about 2000 years
later, on 22 July 1808, Spanish troops under General Castaños van-
quished the French under Dupont, thus inflicting the first defeat
upon the Napoleonic armies – a victory of great symbolic value for
all of Europe. Castaños is interred at the church La Encarnación.

Along the A-4

The A-4 leads from Bailén through never-ending olive plantations to
the north into the Sierra Morena. Soon a cul-de-sac turns left to
Baños de la Encina at the edge of the Sierra de Andújar. Above its
picturesque lanes rises the Moorish castle Burgalimar, constructed
with its 14 towers and the mighty keep Torre de Homenaje in the
10th century.
Further north along the A-4 lies **La Carolina**, main location of the
mining settlements set up by **German and French colonists** whom
Charles III brought to the Sierra Morena between 1767 and 1769. The
once rich lead mines of the surrounding area have been abandoned;
the town itself has some grand houses, the classical church La Concepción, and a Carmelite monastery founded by Juan de la Cruz. In

Last performance Linares: Manolete

the immediate vicinity, 2.5km/1.5mi to the right of the A-4, lies **Navas de Tolosa**, likewise a former colonists' village, at which the united armies of the kings of Castile, Aragón and Navarre utterly defeated the Almohads on 16 July 1212, thereby giving the **signal for the final Reconquista**. The A-4 finally winds its way across the »ravine of the falling dogs« (**Desfiladero de Despeñaperros**), the historic crossing from Andalucía into Mancha; today, the wild countryside is a protected region.

✳ Málaga

✦ G 8

Province: Málaga
Altitude: 8m/26ft
Population: 588,500

Situated at the foot of Montes de Málaga, Málaga, the second-largest city in Andalucía and economical and cultural centre of the ▶Costa del Sol, enjoys sunshine on 300 days of the year.

Hub of the Costa del Sol

Most travellers visiting Andalucía see the city at best from a bird's eye view when landing and taking off, for it is the traffic hub of the sunshine coast, from which they are then transferred to the beach resorts. Just about 13 million tourists arrive at the airport every year. And yet Málaga certainly has its charms, even if it cannot compare to the classic destinations ▶Córdoba, ▶Granada and ▶Seville. Its parks, museums and its location on the mountainside sloping down to the Bahía de Málaga, in particular, make a day trip worthwhile and compensate for the faceless suburbs. The west of Málaga is the lush Vega or Hoya de Málaga, where oranges, figs, bananas, sugar cane and cotton thrive. The city is especially famous for its raisins (pasas) and its dessert wines, of which Pedro Ximénez and the moscatel wines Dulce and Lágrimas are particularly well known.

Pedro de Mena (1628–1688), the famous sculptor, lived and died in Málaga; another famous son of the city is the Jewish philosopher and poet Ibn Gabriol (11th century). Nowadays, however, the star of

Pablo Picasso shines brightest, even though he left the city of his birth when he was 15 (►Famous People).

The usually dry bed of the Río Guadalmedina divides Málaga into two large sections: the new town in the west, with rows of high-rises and criss-crossed with wide, busy roads; in the east below the alcazaba is the old town with the cathedral at its centre.

Málaga was founded by the Phoenicians, who had a trading centre for salted fish here, which probably explains the city's name: the Phoenician Malaka is derived from »malac«, meaning »to salt«. The Greeks followed the Phoenicians with their colony Mainake in the 8th century BC. The Carthaginians fortified the city, until the Romans conquered it and incorporated It into their empire under the name Malacitanum. After a Byzantine intermezzo came the Visigoths, who were supplanted by the Moors in 711. For a considerable time the city was a small kingdom that did not submit to the emirs of Córdoba. Málaga was at its zenith as the port of the kingdom under the rule of the Nasrids of Granada.

History

In 1487 the troops of the Catholic Monarchs reconquered Málaga. This period saw the construction of many churches, of which over 40 were set alight and destroyed following the proclamation of the republic in May 1931; the city also suffered heavily during the civil war. Málaga's comeback started with the emergence of tourism on the Costa del Sol.

> **MARCO ● POLO TIP**
>
> **!** *El Pimpi and Café Central* **Insider Tip**
>
> There is only one place for the true Malageño to have his afternoon coffee, a small glass of wine or a tapa: El Pimpi on Calle Granada, covering two floors. Mind you, this bar only opens at 5pm; if you want to visit a classic café before then, try Café Central at the Plaza de la Constitución.

HARBOUR DISTRICT

There are two particularly striking monuments on Paseo del Parque, Málaga's most beautiful square, adorned with exotic plants and bordered by avenues of palms and plane trees. They portray typical people of Málaga who have now vanished from the streets: the biznaguero, who sold fragrant flowers in spring, and the cenachero, who offered fresh fish. The Fuente de Cisne fountain, created in Genoa in 1560 and originally intended for the Alhambra in Granada, is situated opposite the town hall (1912–1919). The classical **Aduana**, the former customs office on the north side of the paseo, will soon be the home of the **Museo de Belles Artes**. Its works include ones by Alonso Cano (*John the Evangelist*), Ribera (*St Francis of Assisi*), Murillo (*St Francis of Paola*), Luis de Morales (*Ecce Homo, Mater Dolorosa*), and Zurbarán (*St Jerome*).

*Paseo del Parque

Málaga

INFORMATION
Oficina de Turismo
Plaza de la Marina, 11
E-29001 Málaga
Tel. 951 92 60 20
daily 9am – 8pm, in winter until 6pm
C / Granada, 70
E-29015 Málaga
Tel. 952 21 33 29
daily 10am – 2pm, 3pm – 6pm
www.malagaturismo.com

ENTERTAINMENT
stages for the lively nightlife are Plaza de
la Merced and north of the cathedral,
the streets C. Granada and C. Beatas as
well as the area around Plaza Uncibay
south of the bullfighting arena and in
Malagueta. In summer things get lively
along the coast the suburb of Pedregalejo and on its main street Juan Sebastián
Elcano.

SHOPPING
Magnificent fresh foods from sea and
land, as well as fashion items, are available on the morning market in C. Marqués de Larios. Naturally the 19th-centu-
ry market hall presents treasures from
the Hoya and from the sea, wine too.
Further shopping areas include the
streets around Plaza Flores, Plaza de Félix
Sáenz, C. Puerta del Mar, and C. Nueva.
The gigantic department store of the El
Corte Inglés chain is on the Avenida de
Andalucía.

PLAZA DE TOROS
Paseo Reding
Tel. 952 22 17 27
The most important fights are in
August.

EVENTS
Carnival
Carnival is celebrated wildly in Málaga.

Semana Santa
Holy Week is truly remarkable in Málaga, for here the largest and heaviest
processional altars of all of Spain are
carried through the streets – the biggest
weighs five tons and has to be shoul-
dered by 260 men! As if that weren't
enough, these tronos also get swayed
back and forth.
❶ Museo de las Cofradías de Semana
Santa, C. Muro de San Julián, 2

Feria
In the first half of August the largest
feria of Andalucía takes place with fireworks, music, and dancing; at night
celebrations continue on the festival
grounds Cortijo de Torres, 4km/2.5mi
southwest of the city centre.

WHERE TO EAT
❷ *Antonio Martín* €€€€
Paseo Marítimo, 4
Tel. 952 22 21 13 (closed Sun and in July)
In summer there are rows of fish restau-
rants by the seaside in Pedregalejo sub-
urb – Antonio Martín has top quality.

❸ *Café de París* €€€€
Plaza de la Capilla
Puerto de Málaga
Tel. 952 22 50 43
www.rcafedeparis.com
closed Sun and Monday evening
Gourmet restaurant – the young celeb-
rity chef José Carlos García Cortés cooks
here, supported by a team of young
cooks. Try the Menú Degustación.

Tapas, wine and ambience in the streets of Málaga

❺ *Montana* €€€€

Compás de la Victoria, 5
Tel. 952 65 12 44
www.restaurantemontana.com
closed sunday, Monday
Restaurant in an old palais with a pretty
inner courtyard. Fine mediterranean
cooking

❶ *Antigua Casa de Guardia* €€€

Alameda Principal, 18
Traditional bodega in the government
building; best address for Málaga wines
and seafood tapas.

❹ *El Chinitas* €€€

Moreno Monroy, 4 - 6

www.elchinitas.com
In several rooms, on three floors, mainly
fish and seafood are served. Very stylish
ambience. The service is quick and
attentive.

WHERE TO STAY
❹ *Parador de Málaga*
Gibralfaro €€€

Castillo de Gibralfaro
Tel. 952 22 19 02
www.parador.es
38 rooms
The renovated parador on the castle
hill commands unrivalled views. Roof
terrace with swimming pool and sun
terrace.

❺ *Parador de Málaga Golf* €€
Autovía A7 Málaga-Algeciras
Salida Coín km 231
Tel. 952 38 12 55
www.parador.es, 70 rooms
Málaga's second parador– in the regional style, right above the beach – is ideal
for golfers as it has its own superb golf
course beneath palms.

❶ *California* €
Paseo de Sancha, 17
Tel. 952 21 51 64

www.hotelcalifornianet.com
26 rooms
Town house with terraces and balconies,
not far from the La Malagueta beach.

❷ *Hostal Pedregalejo* €
Conde de las Naves, 9
Tel. 952 29 32 18
Fax 952 29 75 25
10 rooms
Lovely guesthouse in Pedregalejo
sub-urb, which is known for its
fish restaurants.

Mercado At Plaza de la Marina the paseo merges with Alameda Principal.
From there it is not far to the market hall via C. Atarazanas. Apart
from the delicacies on sale, the marble gate, **Puerta de Atarazanas**, is
also worth seeing. It is shaped as a 14m/45ft-high Moorish horseshoe
arch with Kufic characters and is all that remains of the gigantic ship-
yard of Málaga built under Abd ar-Rahman III.

Centro de On the eatsern banks of the Río Guadalmedina in a former market
Arte Con- hall from 1939 is the Centro de Arte Contemporáneo (CAC). Exhib-
temporáneo ist include works of art starting in the 1950s by Louise Bourgeois,
Olafur Eliasson, Thomas Hirschhorn, Damian Hirst, Julian Opie,
Thomas Ruff and Thomas Struth.

❶ C. Alemania; daily 10am – 8pm; www.cacmalaga.org

OLD TOWN

*Catedral La The massive limestone cathedral, one of the most important church-
Manquita es of the Renaissance in Andalucía next to those in ▶Cádiz, ▶Jaén
and ▶Granada, was begun in 1528 on the site of a mosque according
to plans by Pedro López and Diego de Siloé, and consecrated in
1588. Famous masters such as Enrique de Egas, Andrés de Vandelvira and Diego de Vergara had a part in the construction, which was
discontinued in 1783 due to lack of funds. Two towers were to flank
the main façade containing three portals, yet only the 86m/282ft-
high north tower has been completed. Of the south tower, only
stumps of pillars jut above the façade, which is why the cathedral is
also called La Manquita – »the one that's missing something«. The
115m/377ft-long and 52m/170ft-high **church interior** is remarkable
for its splendid proportions and mighty Corinthian clustered

Catedral de Málaga

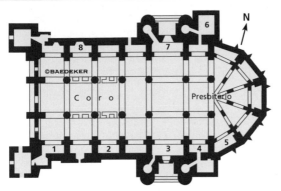

1 Capilla Nueva
2 Capilla del Rosario
3 Puerta del Sol
4 Capilla de
   N. Sra. de los Reyes
5 Capilla de San Francisco
6 Sacristía
7 Puerta de las Cadenas
8 Capilla del Cristo
   de la Buena Muerte

columns. The most prominent piece of church furnishings are the
*stalls (1647–1660) in the choir (1592–1631) with 103 carved statues, 40 of which were done by Pedro de Mena, who from 1658 continued the work of Luis Ortíz and José Micael, the originators of two
and ten statues of the apostles respectively. The modern altar in the
Capilla Mayor bears scenes of the Passion from 1580. Of the side and
ambulatory chapels the most interesting are the following: The first
chapel in the right aisle is the Capilla Nueva with the *Madre Dolorosa de Camponuevo* by Pedro de Mena. The Capilla del Rosario
contains a *Madonna of the Rosary* by Alonso Cano. The Puerta del
Sol follows with paintings by Palma Vecchio; next is the Capilla de
Nuestra Señora de los Reyes, containing the most significant works
of art in the cathedral: the kneeling statues of the Catholic Monarchs
by Pedro de Mena (1681), as well as the statuette of the Virgin which
the couple are said to have carried with them on their crusades. In
the left aisle the Capilla del Cristo de la Buena Muerte has sculptures
by Pedro de Mena. The cathedral museum exhibits religious objets
d'art in the chapter house.
❶ Mon – Fri 10am – 6pm, Sat until 5pm; admission: €5

Opposite the cathedral the 18th-century **Palacio Episcopal** (bishop's
palace) now serves as an exhibition hall.
❶ Tue – Sun 10am – 2pm, 6pm – 9pm

This small chapel on the north side of the cathedral catches the eye   **Sagrario**
with its very beautiful Isabelline portal. It was the episcopal church
until the consecration of the cathedral.

Málaga

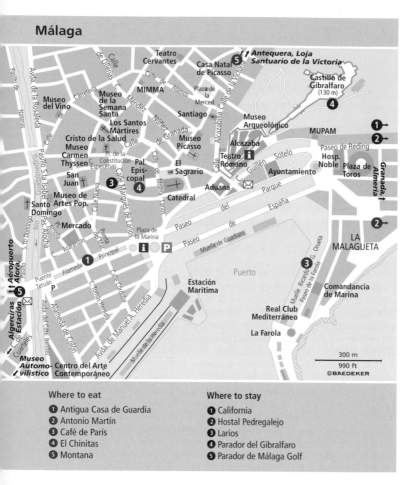

Where to eat
1. Antigua Casa de Guardia
2. Antonio Martín
3. Café de París
4. El Chinitas
5. Montana

Where to stay
1. California
2. Hostal Pedregalejo
3. Larios
4. Parador del Gibralfaro
5. Parador de Málaga Golf

*Museo Picasso North of the cathedral a new **attraction for all Picasso enthusiasts**: the Picasso Museum in the Renaissance palace Palacio de los Condes de Buenavista at C. San Agustín no. 8 (www.mpicassom.org). An endowment of 138 of Picasso's works by his daughter-in-law is the basis of the collection. Great works are lacking, as is a conceptual thread. Oil paintings, drawings, sculptures, and ceramics from all the artist's creative periods are exhibited, insofar as they are represented in the family collection. However, the museum affords an intimate look into **Picasso's personal and family environment**.

❶ Tue – Sun 10 – 8pm, Fri, Sat until 9pm; admission: €6

Further north on Plaza de la Merced lies the next famous Picasso site, house no. 15, where Pablo Picasso (▶Famous People, p. 79) was born in 1881.

Museo Casa Natal de Picasso

Both the study centre of the Fundación Picasso and – in the family's erstwhile residence – a museum displaying ceramics and graphics by the artist, are held here.

❶ daily 9.30am – 8pm; admission: €2

On the spot where the Catholic Monarchs made camp in 1487 the **Nuestra Señora de la Victoria** church was erected. Inside within a camarin it holds the Virgen de la Victoria (15th century), a statue of the city's patron saint, a gift to the Catholic Monarchs from Emperor Maximilian I. Two sculptures by Pedro de Mena and the crypt of the counts of Buenavista merit attention.

Museo Interactivo de la Música de Málaga (MIMMA) moved into the Calle de las Beatas no. 15 (south-west of Plaza de la Merced) in 2012. It exhibits more than 300 instruments from different epochs, countries and cultures. Some of the instruments may also be touched and visitors are taken into the world of music by means of the latest technology.

MIMMA

Further to the south-west in the Palacio Villalón is the Museo Carmen Thyssen-Bornemisza. Its collection of paintings consists of more than 350 works by Spanish and especially Andalusian artists of the 19th century.

Museo Carmen Thyssen-Bornemisza

❶ Calle Compañía, 10; daily 10am – 8pm, Fri, Sat until 9pm; admission: €6; www.carmenthyssenmalaga.org

To the north-west in an 18th century building the Museo del Vino de Málaga informs on winegrowing around Málaga or about the wines from the regions »Málaga« (sweet dessert wines) and »Sierras de Málaga« (white, rosé and red wines).

Museo del Vino de Málaga

❶ Plaza de los Viñeros, 1; Mon – Fri 12 noon – 2.30pm, 4.30pm – 7.30pm; admission: €5 (incl. 2 samples, every additional sample €1); www.museovinomalaga.com

The Museo de Arte y Tradiciones Populares is located in the 17th-century inn **Mesón de Victoria**, right in the west of the old city centre on the Río Guadalmedina. Amongst other things, coaches, wine presses, a bakery, furniture, and a collection of small figurines in

Museo de Arte y Tradiciones Populares

18th- and 19th-century garb can be seen here in a higgledy-piggledy arrangement.

❶ Mon – Fri 10am – 1pm, 4pm – 7pm (summer 5pm – 8pm), Sat 10am – 1pm; admission: €2

Museo Automovilístico de Málaga

In Málaga's former tobacco factory in the south-western part of the city, in the old tabacalera, the Museo Automovilístico de Málaga awaits visitors with more than 90 valuable vehicles from all epochs, including a Bugatti from 1936, a Mercedes from 1937 and a Porsche from 1956.

❶ Avenida Sor Teresa Prat, 15; Tue – Sun 10am – 7pm; admission: €6; www.museoautomovilmalaga.com

Art Natura Málaga

Insider Tip

The Tabacalera is supposed to house a museum complex covering that fields of nature and art, including the world's largest collection of gemstones, but there have been conflcits between the museum and the Málaga city government. Hopefully the museum will be opened, but at the time of this printing no agreement was in sight.

❶ Avenida Sor Teresa Prat, 15; www.art-natura.es

* ALCAZABA

Sightseers climb to the alcazaba, the castle of the Moorish rulers enthroned above the harbour and the old town, from the C. Alcazabilla, which proceeds below the western flank, via a steep stair passing through gardens. This route passes the remains of a Roman theatre situated on the slope, built in the time of Emperor Augustus and discovered in 1951.

Construction of the fortress began on Roman remains in the 11th century, with considerable enlargement to a size approaching that of the Alhambra of Granada under the Nasrids in the 14th century. After the downfall of the Moors the castle fell into disrepair, with earnest reconstruction only being undertaken from 1931 on, so that it is now possible once more to get an impression of its former glory. However, it is the **wonderful gardens** in the courtyards that constitute the alcazaba's charm. Two curtain walls circle the castle hill. The inner fortress is entered by the Arco de Cristo, opening onto the weapons court. To the right and behind another gate lies the Cuartos de Granada, which was modelled on a simplified form of the architecture of the Alhambra during reconstruction. Beyond that lie the reconstructed palace rooms of the Nasrids and the residences of the royal household, with patios, baths, and cisterns. At the highest point rises the massive Torre del Homenaje. The Moorish collections of the Museo Arqueológico are presented in the castle.

❶ Summer Tue – Sun 9.00am – 8pm, winter to 7pm, admission €2.10

View of Málaga and the bay from the mountain slopes

From the alcazaba there is a view across to Gibralfaro (from the Arabic Yabal-Faruk meaning »lighthouse hill«). The Phoenicians probably already built a lighthouse on this spot. In the 14th century Jûsuf I of Granada constructed a fortress with six towers, connecting it to the alcazaba via a covered wall walkway, but this is no longer walkable. Other than the curtain wall little is preserved; an exhibition in the restored powder magazine outlines the castle history since 1487. It is reached either on foot (a lengthy trek via Camino Nuevo northeast of the Plaza de la Merced), by car, or by bus no. 35 from Paseo del Parque. A magnificent view of the city, harbour and sea, as well as a break at the parador are the reward.

Castillo de Gibralfaro

❶ Summer daily 9am–8pm, winter to 7pm

South of the Castillo lies the Museo del Patrimonio Municipal (MU-PAM), which owns more than 4000 art objects (paintings, sculptures, furniture etc.). 94 of these works make up the permanent exhibit, including some by Pablo Picasso.

Museo del Patrimonio Municipal

❶ Paseo de Reding, 1; Tue – Sun 10am – 3pm, 5pm – 9pm; free admission

AROUND MÁLAGA

Sports and leisure

Málaga has a large yacht harbour; the beaches Baños del Carmen, El Palo, Acacias, Pedregalejo, El Chanquete, and San Andrés lie with the city limits. Golf (several courses), tennis, riding and aqua parks provide a wealth of recreational opportunities.

*Jardín Botánico La Concepción

Take the motorway towards Granada, then the exit to Finca de la Concepción to a lovely botanical garden about 10km/6mi north of Málaga that was **established by the Englishwoman Amalia Loring** in the 19th century and has belonged to the city of Málaga since 1990.

Insider Tip

A fabulous variety of exotic plants and trees from the earth's warm climate zones, more than 3,000 different species, can be discovered on five different nature trails. The garden also have Roman statues as well as springs and small waterfalls.

❶ Tue – Sun from 9.30am, times vary with the season

Rincón de la Victoria

Going east through sugar-cane plantations the coast road reaches Rincón de la Victoria after 10km/6mi, a beach resort popular among the inhabitants of Málaga. Above it is a **large cave** containing Neolithic paintings which was a hideaway for Christians and Moors. The name Cueva del Tesoro stems from the popular belief that the Moorish monarchs buried treasure here.

Montes de Málaga

Just 14km/8.5mi north of Málaga lies a national park 4762 ha/11,767 acres in size; take the A-45 towards Casabermeja to get there. It has Mediterranean vegetation and nesting places for birds of prey.

* Marbella

 ✦ F 8

Province: Málaga
Altitude: 14m/46ft
Population: 136,300

While Marbella was the glamorous centre of the ►Costa del Sol for decades the bloom is meanwhile off the rose. More than a hundred court cases against public officials and their instigators have made the city a symbol for the uninhibited building speculation coursing along the coast, which was fuelled by corruption.

Pleasant holiday venue

The sheikhs and nobility have left Marbella and were replaced by new money, which does not like to reveal the sources of its wealth. And yet: don't be unfair to Marbella. It was never a site for mass tourism

Marbella was once the hot spot of the jet set – now the expensive limousines belong to other people

and shows itself to be a cultivated, still expensive holiday resort. While it is a fairly welcome change from places such as ▶Fuengirola and ▶Torremolinos. But here as well new buildings with bars, restaurants and boutiques line the beach promenade and the traffic meanwhile needs several lanes to get through town. While there are large hotels here as well Marbella is above all a place of villa owners – correspondingly, the number of up-market and luxury restaurants, shops and hotels surpasses that of every other location on the sun coast.

Marbella also holds all manner of diversions for the less well-off: long beaches with a variety of water sports; in addition to 16 golf courses, a large number of tennis courts, stables, four yacht harbours, and sailing clubs. The Playa de Fontanilla and Playa Nagüeles are considered the best beaches with regards to quality and services, and are accordingly well frequented.

Sports and leisure

Marbella

INFORMATION
Oficina de Turismo
Glorieta de la Fontanilla, s/n
Paseo Marítimo
Tel. 952 77 14 42
Mon – Fri 9am – 9pm, Sat 10am – 2pm
Plaza de los Naranjos, 1
Tel. 952 82 35 50
Mon – Fri 9am – 8pm, Sat 10am – 2pm
www.marbellaexclusive.com

ENTERTAINMENT
In the centre nightlife collects around
Plaza Puente de Roda, C. Pantaleón and
Plaza Africa. Also in Avda. Ramon y Cajal and in the marina, Puerto Deportivo.
The no-longer-twenties meet around C.
Camilo José Cela. Discos tend to be
further away from the centre, mostly in
luxury hotels: About 10 km towards
Málaga in the summer the disco **Oh!
Marbella** attracts (CN 340, km 192).
The rich and beautiful meet in **La Notte**
on Camino de la Cruz between Marbella
and Puerto Banús. For the largest disco
on the Costa del Sol, **Dreamers**, take
the first exit in Puerto Banús. The jet set
hangs out in the millionaires harbour
Puerto Banús in the luxury-exclusive
bars. The tourist information offices
have the **Guía Marbella – Día y Noche**,
a Spanish/English event guide.

EVENT
Feria de San Bernabé
Around 7 June: the town's major
festival.

WHERE TO EAT
La Meridiana €€€€
Camino de la Cruz, s/n, 3.5km/2mi
towards Puerto Banús

Tel. 952 77 61 90
With its Mediterranean cuisine La
Meridiana numbers among the best
restaurants in Spain. Next door is the
classy nightclub La Notte.

Cuarto Hondo €€€€
In Benahavis, Plaza del Castillo, 1
Tel. 952 85 54 30
Fish and meat in a restaurant in the
Moorish castle.

Refugio de Juanar €€
Near Ojén, Sierra Blanca, s/n
Tel. 952 88 10 00
Situated in the middle of hunting
grounds, 10km/6mi outside Ojén.
Pleasant with rosemary is highly
recommended.

❶ *Altamirano* €
Plaza Altamirano
Tel. 952 82 49 32
Very good fish dishes and tapas in the
old town. Typical Spanish decor and
very loud, but pleasant.

❷ *Bodega La Venecia* €€€
Avda. de Miguel Cano, 15
Tel. 952 85 79 13
www.bodegaslavenencia.com
Tapas and lots of young people. There
are three more Venecian eateries in
town.

❸ *Restaurante*   **Insider
Santiago* €€€€   **Tip**
Avda. Duque de Ahumada, 5
Tel. 952 77 00 78
www.restaurantesantiago.com
On the sea promenade the Santiago
with its fish dishes and seafood is one

of the best. Large wine list. On warm days food is served outdoors.

WHERE TO STAY
❸ Marbella Club Hotel €€€€
Blvd. del Príncipe Alfonso de Hohenlohe
Tel. 952 82 22 11
www.marbellaclub.com
132 rooms
Small luxury bungalows for lots of money, spa and golf too.

❷ Fuerte Marbella €€€
Avda. El Fuerte
Tel. 952 86 15 00
www.fuertehoteles.com
263 rooms
This high-class house by the sea – and yet close to the old town centre – offers nice rooms, a spa and sports, surrounded by beautiful gardens and with two pools. Along with Fuerte Marbella there is also the Fuerte Miramar Spa on Plaza José Luque Manzano

❶ El Castillo €
Plaza de San Bernabé
Tel. 952 77 17 39
27 rooms
This very well-priced small hotel occupies an old building in the city centre. Not far from the Plaza de los Naranjos. Some rooms offer a balcony or a roof terrace.

The Phoenicians founded a settlement on the coast here called Salduba (salt town). In 1485, after the Catholic Monarchs had driven out the Moors, Queen Isabella, upon seeing the coast, is said to have cried out: »¡Qué mar bella!« – »What a beautiful sea!« – and the name of the city was born. Marbella's entry into the world of tourism occurred in 1953, when **Prince Alfonso of Hohenlohe** founded the Marbella Club, centre of high society for decades. This is where members of European nobility, industrialists, playboys, and all who wanted to be part of it met, and they turned the small fishing village into a place of incessant parties and luxury. Yet only at the beginning of the 1970s did the truly rich come: **Arab potentates**, the King of Saudi Arabia among them, selected Marbella for their summer retreats and had palaces built in which admittedly they led an existence relatively secluded from the rest of the hustle and bustle, yet spent a lot of money in Marbella's shops. When Costa del Sol tourism went through a deep crisis in the mid 1980s many investors withdrew. The sheikhs also stayed away during the Gulf War in 1991, the **scandalous figure of Jesús Gil y Gil**, an extremely rich contractor and president of the Atlético de Madrid football club, appointed himself saviour by gaining election as mayor – avowedly because his socialist predecessor did not approve his real estate speculation. Gil now permitted this to both his friends and himself, governed Marbella like a feudal lord, and brought in new money, not caring whether it came from Russian Mafiosi or shady arms dealers. The Arabians also returned. In 2002 however, Spain's supreme court deposed Gil from

History

Marbella

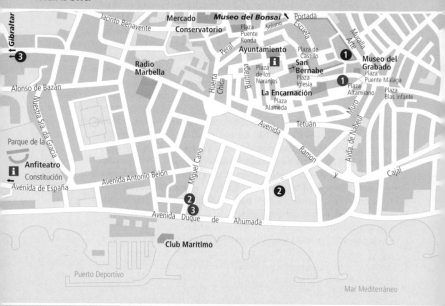

Where to eat
1 Altamirano
2 Bodega La Venecia
3 Restaurante Santiago

Where to stay
1 El Castillo
2 Fuerte Marbella
3 Marbella Club Hotel

office; shady doings at Atlético earned him a prison sentence at the beginning of 2003; he resigned as the club's president. After his death in 2004, a woman from his political party, Marisol Yagüe, became mayor and continued Gil's methods until the swamp of corruption was so big – the damages were estimated at more then 2 billion Euros – that the Spanish government dissolved the city council in April 2006. Yagüe and 22 of her cohorts were arrested.

WHAT TO SEE IN MARBELLA

*City centre Compared with the rest of Marbella the town centre is somewhat calmer with its white houses adorned with flowers, and the remains of the medieval wall. People meet at the Plaza de los Naran-

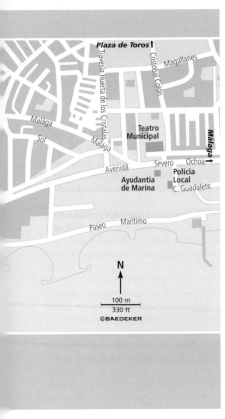

jos lined with orange trees, bars, and restaurants, by the fountain that has been flowing since 1704; the town hall is here, too, its upper storey painted with 16th-century frescoes. The **Museo del Grabado** explains the **art of engraving**, and displays pertinent works by Picasso, Miró, and Tapiés; take a look at the Baroque retable in the Nuestra Señora de la Encarnación church not far from there. Above the city the remnants of a Moorish fort, including walls, bailey, and keep, still stand.

Museum: Mon, Sat 9am – 2pm, Tue – Fri 9am – 9pm, (summer 9am – 2pm, 3pm – 9pm); admission: €3

An impressive collection of bonsai plants can be admired at the Parque de Arroyo de la Represa.

Museo Bonsai

❶ daily 10.30am – 1.30pm, 5pm – 8pm, winter 4pm – 6.30pm; admission: €4

On the western edge of town in the direction of San Pedro and to the left above the coast road shines the mosque of Marbella, which Prince Salman, governor of the Saudi Arabian capital Riad, caused to be built as **the first Muslim place of worship in Spain since the 15th century**. It has rooms for 800 pray-ers. Naturally stables and a helipad are included. Incidentally, King Fahd and family reside in a palace modelled on the White House, the residence of the president of the United States in Washington D.C.

Mezquita del Rey Abd-el Aziz

❶ summer Sat – Wed 7pm – 9pm, winter 5pm – 7pm

On the northwestern outskirts an oil mill in C. José Luis Morales y Marín was converted into an exhibition hall full of character, mainly showing **modern art**.

Cortijo de Miraflores

❶ Mon – Fri 9am – 2.30pm, 5pm – 9.30pm

AROUND MARBELLA

*Puerto Banús Amateur sailors with a deep enough pocket can anchor at the luxury yacht marina Puerto Banús, 6km/3.6mi west of Marbella. In Spain's probably most exclusive marina, built in neo-Moorish style, those without a boat may still marvel at **massive luxury yachts with a Rolls or Ferrari** to match, and watch celebrities , who like to dine at one of the luxury restaurants on the promenade before they go to party at a disco or casino.

Sierra Blanca In Marbella's backcountry, the Sierra Blanca, only a few miles distance from the hustle and bustle of high society, nature reigns serenely. There are worthwhile trips to **Ojén** with its 16th-century church, then on to Monda, where a lovely town centre encloses the Baroque Iglesia de Santiago, whereas the remnants of the Moorish castle have been integrated into a hotel – which in turn provides beautiful and not-too-expensive accommodation.

SAN PEDRO ALCÁNTARA

A new town The commune of Marbella includes San Pedro Alcántara adjoining it to the west. It is outshone by its sophisticated neighbour, particularly as it lies about half a mile inland. The advantage is that the central Plaza de la Iglesia is reasonably quiet, and the disadvantage is that it takes a little longer to reach the sea front. Nevertheless, tourism manifests itself in a multitude of holiday apartments and bungalows. Marqués del Duero founded San Pedro as a country settlement in 1860; the **sugar refinery El Trapiche de Gaudaiza** dates from this time. Additionally there are three noteworthy antiquities.

Basílica Vega del Mar A eucalyptus grove by the beach contains the preserved foundations of the early Christian basilica Vega del Mar. It was built in the 4th century, destroyed by a flood shortly after completion, and then rebuilt. Following a renewed collapse in 526, it served the Visigoths as a burial ground. Around 200 stone graves were found by archaeologists. **Two baptismal fonts** can be seen on the grounds, one forming a cross, as well as two apses, one facing west and one facing east.

Roman baths West of the basilica, at the mouth of the Río Guadalmina next to the watchtower Torre de las Bóvedas (16th century), lie the remains of a Roman bath from the 3rd century BC, consisting of a pool with seven rooms around it.

Roman ruins Going 4km/2.5mi back towards Marbella, remains of the AD 1st century Roman settlement Silniana were discovered near Río Verde: a rotunda with five arches, which served as a reservoir, and a villa with exquisite **mosaic floors** depicting ancient kitchen utensils scenes from the life of fishermen and the head of a Medusa.

** Medina Azahara

✦ F 6

Province: Córdoba
Altitude: 649m/2129ft

After Abd ar-Rahman III had established his position as caliph of Córdoba, he began construction of a residence outside the city in keeping with his status. For this he chose a slope of the Sierra de Córdoba above the plain of Guadalquivir, and named it Madinat al-Zahrá (the flower), presumably in honour of his favourite.

Even though most of the palace city is now destroyed, the remaining buildings, surrounded by cypresses, palms, holm oaks and orange trees, do give an overwhelming impression of the splendour that once was. Now called Medina Azahara, the place is best reached on the A-431 from ▶Córdoba, where an access road turns off to the right after 8km/5mi. The entrance to the area is at the highest point of the former city; a signposted circuit leads from here to the most important excavated structures.

Palace city of the caliphs of Córdoba

Construction began in November 936 under the direction of Abd ar-Rahman's son Al-Hakam and took almost 25 years. Over 10,000 workmen and craftsmen were engaged in building a city from lime-

History

The best preserved part of Medina Azahara is the hall of Abd ar-Rahman III

stone, bricks and most precious materials, including red, blue, and white marble, ebony, ivory and gold. At its peak, the city accommodated 30,000 people. It sprawled over an area of 1500 m by 750m (1640yd by 820yd) and except for its northern side, was surrounded by a double wall. Two gates provided admittance, the Mountain Gate in the north, and the Gate of the Three Domes (Bab al-Cubbá) in the south, which is crowned by the ancient sculpture of a woman believed by many to be an image of Zahrá. Medina Azahara was the setting for magnificent celebrations and receptions for ambassadors. Yet the glory did not even last 75 years – the internal strife that destroyed the Caliphate of Córdoba did not spare Medina Azahara, either. In 1010 the Berbers, who saw extravagance and sumptuousness as blasphemy, invaded the city and destroyed it. The Almohads and Almoravids used the debris as a quarry, and Medina Azahara sank into oblivion. Excavations only started at the beginning of the 20th century, and have not been completed to this day. On the edge of the excavation site the architects Nieto and Sobejano built a **new museum**, which opened in 2009: its shape unites Arab style with a modern structure and thus leaves the ambience of Medina Azahara untouched. The museum informs on the history of the palace and exhibits finds like ceramics, column capitals and glass.

Circuit The city was subdivided into three districts: the highest level was taken up by the palace district with the caliph's residence, the houses for the highest dignitaries, the hall of ambassadors, the military buildings and gardens. It was separated from the other parts of the city by a wall. Gardens and a menagerie were laid out in the second level; residential houses for the servants of the royal household, shops and workshops were located on the lowest level.

To the right of the entrance building lie the inaccessible remains of the caliphs' palace proper and the house of the grand vizier. The circuit leads to the left and downhill from the entrance to the northern gate, and then continues on ramps to the Dar al-Yûnd on the right, which, with several inner courtyards, served as **military quarters**. It then leads to the Dar al-Wuzara, the **house of the viziers**, where a spacious basilica forms its centre, in which the vizier held audience. Four massive arches are visible below and to the left of this building. They formed the gate to the **parade ground**, on which drills and parades took place. From the parade ground, there is a fine view of the **foundations of the mosque** below, which in 941 was the first building to be completed, including forecourt, a fountain for ritual ablutions, and a five-aisle prayer room. The orientation towards Mecca is clearly visible.

❶ Tue – Sun from 10am on, closure varies; admission free for EU citizens, otherwise €1.50€;
www.museosdeandalucia.es/cultura/museos/CAMA

In the middle of the complex lies the hall of Abd ar-Rahman III, also called **hall of ambassadors** , for the caliph received the ambassadors of foreign princes here. It is the best restored and most magnificent building of the ruins. At first an antechamber opens behind a front of five horseshoe arches resting on red and blue marble columns with ornate capitals. A three-aisle main room adjoins, likewise partitioned by horseshoe arches borne by red and blue columns. Beyond the two side aisles, partitioned off by walls, lay the bedrooms and relaxation rooms, so that the building altogether consists of five aisles. The diversity of forms of the walls carved with the most delicate stonework (ataurique) is stunning: floral themes such as the tree of life alternate with depictions of birds, and Kufic characters, which praise the caliph, give the names of the sculptors and the construction time of the palace (from 952 to 957).

**Hall of Abd ar-Rahman III

In the days of the caliph the gardens, filled with exotic plants and irrigated by an ingenious system of channels, extended below the ramp in front of the hall of ambassadors. Exactly opposite the hall the remains of the caliph's pavilion can be seen, surrounded by four water basins. The area beyond the gardens is inaccessible.

Gardens

AROUND MEDINA AZAHARA

Only a little further up from the palace city lie the ruins of San Jerónimo monastery. It was built in 1408 and frequently hosted Isabella the Catholic, who had the banners stored here that were captured during the conquest of Granada in 1492. The grounds are private property.

San Jerónimo

►Córdoba, surrounding area

Las Ermitas

►Córdoba, surrounding area

Almodóvar

Medina Sidonia

✛ D 9

Province: Cádiz
Altitude: 300m/984ft
Population: 11,700

Seat of the eponymous house of dukes, Medina Sidonia's white cubic houses gleam from a knoll in the middle of a region famed for breeding fighting bulls.

Old aristocratic estate The dukes are among to the wealthiest landowners of Andalucía – they have exchanged their political power for economic power that is no less great.

The beginnings of Medina Sidonia go back a long way: the name refers to the Phoenician Sidon, so it is presumed that Phoenician sailors founded a settlement here. In 1267 Alfonso X drove the Moors from the city; in 1296 Guzmán el Bueno got the place after he successfully defended Tarifa against the Moors. His family was elevated to the rank of duke in 1440 and became one of Spain's most powerful families. Alonso de Guzmán, Duke of Medina Sidonia, was commander of the Spanish Armada which sunk in the English Channel in 1588. He survived the fiasco, and was made Capitán General del Mar Oceanao in 1595. A later duchess and head of the house of Medina Sidonia, Luisa Isabel Álvarez de Toledo (1936 until 2008), was known as **La Duquesa Roja** (the red duchess), for she made herself conspicuous as a vehement opposer of Franco and fighter for social justice, and once went to prison for her convictions. She lived in ►Sanlúcar de Barrameda until her death.

> **!** MARCO POLO TIP
>
> *Temptations* **Insider Tip**
>
> The Moors brought confectionery with them to Andalucía. Medina Sidonia's confectioneries developed particular proficiency, and the city is a centre of this sweet craft even today. The **alfajores** made from almonds, hazelnuts, honey and cinnamon are famous – they are especially delicious at the confectionery Sobrina de las Trejas at Plaza de España no. 7. The barefoot Augustinuan nuns from Convento de Jesús, María y José convent at the Plaza de las Descalzas are also skilled at baking.

WHAT TO SEE IN MEDINA SIDONIA

Town gates Three medieval town gates are preserved: Arco de Belén, Arco del Sol, and, forming the gateway to the old town, Arco de la Pastora, constructed as a double horseshoe arch during the Moorish era.

Torre de Doña Blanca Narrow alleys leading uphill reach the fortress district. The most important remnant of the castle is the Torre de Doña Blanca, where in the 14th century **Pedro the Cruel** imprisoned his consort Blanca de Borbón who he had married for political reasons, preferring to amuse himself with María de Padilla. Queen Doña Blanca only reached the age of 22 here. It was soon said that she was poisoned on orders by her unfaithful husband, but the poor woman probably died of a disease like consumption, as scientists suppose today.

*Santa María la Coronada In the late 15th century the parish church Santa María la Coronada was built on the castle hill. The **Inquisition** had its seat here, as carv-

Medina Sidonia

INFORMATION
Oficina de Turismo
San Juan, s/n
E-11170 Medina Sidonia
Tel. 956 41 24 04
daily 10.30am – 2pm, 4.30pm – 6.30pm
www.medinasidonia.es

WHERE TO EAT
Cádiz €€€€
Plaza España, 13
Tel. 956 41 02 50
The locals too meet here at the main
square for regional cooking. By all
means try the excellent tapas.

Mesón Rústico Machín €€€€   **Insider Tip**
Plaza Iglesia, 9
Ctra. Medina-Chiclana, km 2,5
Tel. 956 42 03 52
House speciality is seafood and grilled
dishes. Excellent tapas here too. Terrace
with beautiful view.

WHERE TO STAY
Los Balcones €
C. La Loba, 26
Tel. 956 42 30 33
www.losbalcones.net; 7 rooms
Small and pretty town hotel in an
zolder townhouse (late 19th century).
Apartments furnished in various styles.
Roof terrace.

ings– sword, palm tree, Dominican cross – on a bench behind the
choir stalls show. A portrait by Ribera, and the giant retable of the
Virgin by Vazquez the older and Turín are also worth seeing.
❶ Summer 11am – 2pm, 5pm – 8pm; admission: €2.50

The excavated **sewer system** allows a spectacular look at everyday   **Roman**
Roman life. It dates from the 1st century BC and is a masterpiece of   **excavations**
Roman engineering, with sewers about 30m/33yd long and 2m/6ft 6
in high.
❶ C. Espíritu Santo 3; daily 10.30am – 2pm, 5.30pm – 7.30pm

The Ermita de los Santos Mártires on the edge of town dates from the   **Ermita de los**
first half of the 7th century. It is a **rare example of Visigothic archi-   Santos**
tecture in Andalucía. Very popular processions in honour of the   **Mártires**
Virgen de Loreto take place here each year in the last week of
September.

AROUND MEDINA SIDONIA

In Alcalá de los Gazules, another white village 23km/14mi to the east,   **Alcalá de los**
the remains of an Arab castle and two gates of the town wall can be   **Gazules**
seen. Alcalá is an ideal starting point for exploring the wildlife park
►Los Alcornocales.

Medina Sidonia at dusk

Cuevas del Go southeast of Medina Sidonia via Benalup de Sidonia to reach the
Tajo y de las caves of El Tajo and Las Figuras, in which prehistoric paintings, tools,
Figuras and arrowheads were discovered.

Melilla

Outlying

Spanish sovereign territory in Africa
Province: Málaga
Population: 76,000
Altitude: sea level

The seaport and garrison town of Melilla, termed Mlilya or Ras el Querk in Arabian (Berber: Tamlilt), a 12,3 sq km/4.7 sq mi Spanish enclave (so-called Plaza de Soberanía) and free trade area, lies on the Moroccan Mediterranean coast in a bay of the Beni Sicar peninsula, 25km/16mi south of Cabo Tres Forcas (Cap des Trois Fourches).

The majority of Melilla's citizens are of Spanish nationality. The An- **Enclave in**
dalusian character of the town, which stretches in a semicircle **North Africa**
around the harbour and the coast, corresponds to this. It has a
typically Spanish atmosphere with broad, straight streets crossing
at right-angles, spacious squares and parks. The old centre, encircled by battlements and situated 30m/100ft up on a small headland,
has remained almost unchanged since the 16th century. Although
Melilla had a purely Spanish character until recently, it is noticeable
that legal and illegal Moroccan immigrants are settling in the
periphery and suburbs. They now constitute about 10% of the
population.

Economically, the Spanish enclave is almost entirely dependent
upon the mother country. The harbour was established at the time
of the Spanish protectorate for the export of iron and lead ores from
the eastern foothills of the Rif mountains above Melilla. At present,
however, sardine fishing is more significant; a large part of the catch
is processed on the spot in canning plants. Besides Christians and
Muslims, an active Jewish community lives in Melilla, and there is
even a Hindu temple.

Melilla developed from the Phoenician Rusadir, the oldest Phoeni- **History**
cian settlement in Morocco other than Lixius. It suffered the same
fate as all Phoenician settlements, first becoming Carthaginian, then
Roman, Vandal, Byzantine, and finally Arab. The Arabs completely
destroyed it during their second campaign of conquest in 705, yet
rebuilt it in the 10th century, and from the 13th century made it one
of the most important ports of the North African coast under the
Merinids. The Spanish captured Melilla in 1497. Although it was
heavily fought over in the following period, the last time being
against Abd-el Krim in 1921, it remained in Spanish hands. Following its elevation to a duty-free area in 1887, Melilla finally reached its
second economical peak during the protectorate period between
1914 and 1956. Melilla's importance decreased again when the hinterland was lost due to Morocco's independence, and customers for
duty-free goods from Algeria stayed away after this country's independence in 1962. The decline in population from 100,000 to about
65,000 clearly shows this.

In 1995 Melilla, which until then had been part of the province of
Málaga as far as administration was concerned, became like ▶Ceuta
Ciudad Autónoma (autonomous city) and duty free zone. For the
500th anniversary of capture by the Spanish, celebrated in 1997, Melilla decked itself out and treated itself to a new marina. Like in Ceuta illegal immigrants tried in 2005 to cross the border in great masses into Mellila. It happened again in 2008, except this time the
African refugees did not try to storm the border fences, but rather to
overrun the military posts at the border crossings. Some of the

Melilla

GETTING THERE
Planes leave from Almería (once a day) and from Málaga (eight times a day); Trasmediterránea ferries go from Almeria and Malaga 6 times a week (journey time 8 – 9 hrs or 7 – 8 hrs respectively).

INFORMATION
Oficina de Turismo
Plaza de las Culturas, 2
E-52001 Melilla
Tel. 952 97 61 90
www.melillaturismo.com
Mon – Sat 10am – 2pm,
4.30pm – 8.30pm, Sun 10am – 2pm

SHOPPING
The city's shopping area are the streets of the so-called Golden Triangle (Triángulo de Oro) west of Plaza de España. Here Arab, Jewish and Indian shops sell artisanal products made of leather, ceramics and wool. The best jewellery shops in town are to be found in this area as well.

EXCURSIONS
Excursions into to Moroccan desert are organized by **Delfi Aventura**.
i Tel. 951 77 91 88
www.delfiaventura.com
www.melilla500.com

WHERE TO EAT
La Almoraima €€€€
Explanada San Lorenzo, s / n
Tel. 952 69 55 25
Refined restaurant in the four star Hotel Melilla Puerto next to the marina with Mediterranean cooking. Meat, fish, seafood. The central inner courtyard is very nice.

WHERE TO STAY
Parador de Melilla €€
Avda. Cándido Lobera, s / n
Tel. 952 68 49 40
www.parador.es; 40 rooms
Modern place above the city with a view of the ramparts and harbour. For hot days there is a swimming pool in the garden.

guards are supposed to have been injured by stone-throwers. Only a few refuges got into the city and thus into Spanish sovereign territory.

WHAT TO SEE IN MELILLA

Melilla Vieja (old town) The Plaza de España lends itself as a starting point for a stroll around the town. To its west lies the new town (Ciudad Moderna or Nueva) and to its northeast is the old town, situated on a small, somewhat elevated peninsula with precipitous rocks above the sea. It is also called Pueblo, and is surrounded by fortification walls and bastions from the 16th century; it is entered via the Tunel de San Fernando, which soon leads to the central square Plaza de Armas, where stands the Capilla de Santiago, **the only Gothic chapel in Africa**. The town wall commands a view of the city and the coast. In the eastern part

South of Melilla there are wide beaches

of the old town are the **Iglesia de la Concepción** (16th century), containing the Madonna Virgen de Victoria (17th century), the town's patron saint, and the spectacular and especially venerated statue of Christ, Cristo del Socorro, dating from the 16th century. North of the church lies **Museo Mililtar**, which exhibits weapons and military vehicles. In the south-western part of the old city are the Almacenes de las Peñuelas with the **Museo Etnográfico de las Culturas Amazigh y Sefardí** and the **Museo de Arqueología e Historia de Melilla**, which exhibit finds from the Neolithic period, pottery, coins, and iron items from Roman and Punic times, as well as weapons, flags, and plans from recent town history as well as historical exhibits from the life of the Jewish and Muslim population.

A sight one would hardly expect to see in Africa: **rows of art nouveau buildings**, e.g. the telegraph office (C. Cándido Lobera) or the Casa de los Cristales (C. General Prim). Developed from 1898 on, the new town was a **playground of Modernism**, for its planning was

Ciudad
Moderna
(new town)

determined by Gaudí's pupil Enrique Nieto for almost 50 years. Joining the Plaza de España from the northwest, Avenida de Rey Juan Carlos I is the new town's main shopping street; shopping is also possible in C. del Ejército Español / C. López Moreno running parallel and to the north, as well as in some side roads. Parque Hernández lies to the west of the Plaza de España.

At the town's southern exit Playa de San Lorenzo and Playa de los Cárabos are good beaches for swimming.

*Cabo Tres Forcas 25km/16mi north of Melilla at the end of the peninsula Cabo Tres Forcas, the Moroccan mainland plummets **400m/1300ft to the sea below**. The view from the lighthouse is magnificent. A short trip to the lovely sandy beach Playa Charranes on the northwest coast of the Beni Sicar (Gelaia) peninsula is recommendable. As the whole area belongs to Morocco, the border needs to be crossed on this tour (remember to take your passport!) – usually a very time-consuming affair, particularly as the road is difficult.

Mojácar

✦ M 7

Province: Almería
Altitude: 172m/564ft
Population: 7745

Forty years ago Mojácar, in the north of province Almería, dozed in peaceful solitude. Then it was discovered by foreign visitors, initially by artists and people looking to escape, and tourist development took its course.

Beach fun and spruced up village in a spectacular location A new district was constructed with the tourist development: Mojácar Playa, the discos, bars and hotels of which spread along the beach to both sides of the parador, whilst dispensing with ugly piles of concrete. This development has also left its mark on the old town seated about a mile inland, especially noticeable during the high season when the British in particular, but also many Germans, virtually occupy the place. Many have meanwhile settled down as permanent residents. Yet Mojácar's spectacular location on a ridge is still captivating, its gleaming white houses seemingly piled one on top of the other. The nearby beach is one of the most beautiful on this coast.

History Mojácar lies in an area settled since the second millennium before Christ. It owes its present-day characteristic appearance to the Moors, who called the town Murgisacra. Mojácar received its title as city under the the Catholic king Ferdinand II.

Mojácar

INFORMATION
Oficina de Turismo
Plaza del Frontón, s/n
E-04638 Mojácar
Tel. 950 61 50 25
www.mojacar.es

EVENT
Moros y Cristianos
In early June, Mojácar colourfully calls to memory the battles between Moors and Christians which once raged about the town.

WHERE TO EAT
L´Incanto €€€€
Paseo Mediterráneo, 14
Tel. 950 47 22 24
Italian restaurant with excellent pasta and delicious pizza. Terrace facing the sea. Friendly service.

L´Arlecchino €€
Plaza de las Flores

Tel. 950 47 80 37
Another Italian. Pasta dishes, but there is also grilled meat. The pretty terrace with a view is open in the summer.

WHERE TO STAY
Parador de Mojácar €€
Paseo del Mediterráneo, 339
Tel. 950 47 82 50
www.parador.es, 87 rooms
The modern parador is located down on the coast, several yards from the beach in a large park. The cuisine is generally acclaimed.

Mamabel's €
Embajadores, 5
Tel. 950 47 24 48
www.mamabels.com, 8 rooms
The pretty hotel high above the coast has an equally pretty restaurant. Some rooms with sea view. evenings on the terrace are quite pleasant. Specialities: paella and couscous.

WHAT TO SEE IN MOJÁCAR

Other than the 15th-century church Santa María and the Mirador del Castillo, the remains of the Moorish alcazaba, which provide a fantastic view of the coast and hinterland, Mojácar does not possess any noteworthy sights.   ****Views**

The platform at the Plaza Nueva offers nice views as well. Mojácar's charm lies in the clean and decked-out romance of its narrow lanes, which, with many flower arrangements, aim to convey to tourists the **atmosphere of a village of Moorish character** – with some success, provided one overlooks the host of bars, souvenir shops, restaurants and tourists taking a painting course.

Indalo, the town symbol modelled on a prehistoric cave painting found in the Cueva de los Letreros near► Vélez Blanco, is encountered everywhere, and has also become the tourist emblem of the Costa de Almería.

AROUND MOJÁCAR

Cuevas de Almanzora
Going 24km/15mi north of Mojácar via Garrucha – now a lido, yet also still a fishing village, and thus known for its fish restaurants – and the small country town of Vera, Cuevas de Almanzora is reached. It owes its name to prehistoric caves found outlying in a high escarpment (route is signposted). However, in town the fortress-like 16th-century Palacio del Marqués de los Velez, containing an archaeological museum, a museum for contemporary art, and an open air theatre, is perhaps more interesting.

Carboneras
South of Mojácar the road at first follows the coast, then turns off to Agua de Enmedio heading inland, circumnavigating the promontory in sharp curves. Many spectacular vistas open up on the way, until on the northern edge of the wildlife park ►Cabo de Gata the road reaches Carboneras, a relatively quiet and not too expensive beach resort – maybe because the huge power station behind the beach puts visitors off. 8km/5mi further is the much more lovely Agua Amarga in the ►Cabo de Gata wildlife park.

The nature reserve is also home to Spain's most famous **unfinished building**, the luxury hotel El Algarrobico, which has meanwhile also become a tourist attraction.

Montilla

 ✳ F 6

Province: Córdoba
Altitude: 379m/1243ft
Population: 23,900

South of ►Córdoba lies Montilla, which gave its name to the wine produced in the DO region Montilla-Moriles. The wines here resemble those from ►Jerez de la Frontera so closely that a whole brand of sherry is called Amontillado.

Home of Montilla wine
Montilla wine is nothing short of sherry; the main difference is the variety of grape (Montilla: Ximénez; Sherry: Palomino), which is harvested a little earlier – Montilla gives the **starting signal for the grape harvest throughout Spain**. The wine is filled into tinajas, pear-shaped earthenware jugs holding up to 5000 litres/1320 US gal. (►MARCO POLO Insight p.309).

Also known for its olive products, the region is one of the hottest in Spain with summer temperatures often exceeding 40°C/104°F. Not far from the present-day town the battle of Munda Baetica took place between the civil war factions of Pompey and Caesar in 45 BC. Gon-

Montilla

INFORMATION
Oficina de Turismo
C. Capt. Alonso de Vargas, 5
E-14550 Montilla
Tel. 957 65 23 54
www.montilla.es

EVENT
Fiesta de la Vendimia
Grape harvest festival in the beginning
of September.

WHERE TO EAT
Meson Las Camachas €€€€
Avda. Europa, 3

Tel. 957 65 00 04
Meat and fish – fried and grilled. The
restaurant with a garden terrace was
established in 1962 and is among the
best in the region.

WHERE TO STAY
Don Gonzalo €
Ctra. Nac. 331 Córdoba-Málaga, km 47
Tel. 957 65 06 58
www.hoteldongonzalo.com
40 rooms
3 star hotel 2km/1.2mi outside of
Montilla with a restaurant, cafeteria,
fitness area, garden, outdoor pool.

zalo Fernández de Córdoba, named El Gran Capitán, the famed general of the Catholic Monarchs, was born in Montilla.

WHAT TO SEE IN MONTILLA

Alvear

Alvear is the largest **bodega** on the square, and having been **established in 1729** is one of the oldest in Spain: 20,000 barrels and tinajas are stored between the pillars of the Solera hall.
ℹ María Auxiliadora, 1; Mon – Fri from 12.30pm

Casa Museo del Inca Garcilaso

Inside the palace now occupied by the municipality a small museum commemorates Garcilaso de la Vega, the Inca Garcilaso (1539–1616), son of a Spanish nobleman and a cousin of the last sovereign of the Incas, Atahualpa. He made a name for himself as chronicler of Andean empire with his work Comentares Reales de los Incas.

Castillo

The castle built by Moors on Roman foundations once possessed 30 towers, yet lies in ruin today – the Catholic Monarchs had it razed to punish its defiant lord Pedro Fernández de Córdoba.

Churches and convents

Of Montilla's sacred buildings, the Mudéjar convent Santa Clara, built in the 16th century by Hernán Ruiz el Viejo in late Gothic style and furnished with an artesonado ceiling, the Convento de Santa Ana with sculptures by Pedro Roldán on the high altar, and the Iglesia de Santiago are worth a visit.

Museo Histórico Local	In C. Beato Miguel Molina, 2, the Museo Histórico Local de Montilla exhibits items related to local history – from ancient history to the Siglo de Oro. ❶ Tue – Sun 11am – 2pm, Thu also 5pm – 7pm; free admission

ROUND TRIP THROUGH WINE AND OLIVE COUNTRY

Aguilar de la Frontera	Aguilar de la Frontera, a Visigothic seat of a bishop until conquered by the Moors, huddles on a hill 13km/8mi south of Montilla. It is a town characteristic of Andalucía, where visitors walking around its small lanes and streets discover beautiful mansions time and again. The classical ***Plaza de San José** has an extraordinary design: a three-storey row of houses completely encloses the octagonal square, onto which four gateways open. Two other buildings worth seeing are the Baroque Torre de Reloj, which soars among the ruins of the Moorish castle, and the Churrigueresque church interior of the convent of the barefoot Carmelite nuns, completed in the 18th century. Opulent Baroque ornamentation in side chapels and the apse are the features of Nuestra Señora del Soterrano, the town's main church.
Lucena	Lucena, another 19km/12mi southeast, is the economic centre of Montilla-Moriles. This is where the tinajas are manufactured. Only once in Spanish history did the town make the news: in 1483 the Count of Cabra kept the Moorish King of Granada, Boabdil, imprisoned here. He was only released once he had paid a ransom and had declared himself to be neutral. Only the tower of Castillo del Moral where King Boabdil was kept is still in good condition. Adjoining this is the Plaza Nueva with the church ***San Mateo**, constructed in the 15th and 16th centuries. Its Capilla del Sagrario is a **treasure of Andalusian Rococo art**. A retable by Rivas showing scenes from the life of Jesus is also striking. Cross Plaza del Coso to the convent Santo Domingo, the 19th-century façade of which conceals a Mannerist cloister; the abbey church dates from the first half of the 17th century. Visit the chapel in the whitewashed Hospital de San Juan de Dios with its flamboyant Churrigueresque altar. The magnificent Baroque portal contrasts with the stark exterior. Dating from the first half of the 16th century, the late Gothic Iglesia de Santiago, mixed with Mudéjar elements, possesses a monumental belfry and a painting by Pedro Roldán. A two-storey covered cloister adjoins the abbey church Madre de Dios, furnished by the local artist Francisco de Lucena in the 17th and 18th century. On a ridge a little to the south outside of Lucena, right amid a ruggedly romantic nature reserve, lies the hermitage **Nuestra Señora de Araceli**.

Zuheros thrones on a moutain peak like a huge white eagle's nest

Aniseed liqueur is distilled according to a traditional recipe at **Rute**, 21km/13mi to the southeast. Visitors can find out how it is made at the **aniseed museum**. A scenic route then continues from Rute to **Iznájar**, an attractive village on the edge of the reservoir of the same name, around which there are pleasant paths.

Cabra, 12km/7.5mi north of Lucena, is the next stop; called Igabrum **Cabra** by the Romans, and later Egabrum by the Visigoths, it became a bishop's seat as early as the 4th century. Outside the town centre a little way uphill the Iglesia de la Asunción dating from the 17th and 18th centuries rests on the foundations of a former mosque. Next to it stand the preserved remains of the Moorish alcazaba. A small road branches off the road to ►Priego de Córdoba, 6km beyond Cabra, leading to the 16th-century **Ermita de la Virgen de la Sierra**, where, in the middle of the beautiful Parque Natural de la Sierra Subbética, the patron saint of Cabra is venerated. At a height of over 1200m/3937ft there is a stunning view.

At Doña Mencia a small road branches off the scenic route that runs ***Zuheros** 25km/16mi northeast to Baena and leads to the charming village of Zuheros, where white houses hang above a vast canyon and cluster around the ruins of a Moorish castle. At the viewing platform the archaeological museum exhibits finds from the **Cueva de los Murciélagos**: this **bat cave** lies in the mountains 4km/2.5mi away from Zuheros (signposted). The one-hour tour reveals magnificent **dripstone formations and murals** dating from the Neolithic period.

*Baena   The countryside around Baena has changed: olive trees have taken the place of vines. Perched picturesquely on a hilltop, the small town of Baena, centre of this **DO olive region**, is known not only for its production of very high-quality olive oil, but also for its **tambourine players** who accompany the Easter processions during Holy Week in fantastic uniforms. The **upper town** (barrio alto), in which several Renaissance palaces are preserved, is still partially surrounded by a curtain wall. Santa María, the late Gothic main church of the town, features a remarkable Plateresque grille in front of its main chapel and displays its treasures, above all goldsmith work, in the vestry. The belfry developed from the minaret of the Moorish mosque. Inside the church of the convent Madre de Dios founded in 1510, the large statue of Mary (15th century), Virgen de la Antigua, catches the eye, as she is holding a pear in her hand. Over 60 paintings on the walls show scenes from the life of Jesus; the ceiling of the main chapel is lined with azulejos. The **lower town** is called El Llano. On the Plaza de España stands the pilgrimage church consecrated to the Madonna of Guadalupe, an oil painting painted directly onto the wall, and splendid artesonado ceilings can be admired inside.

The next section of the route is a return from olive country to wine country. The second half of the 19km/12mi-long journey from Baena to northwestern Castro del Río follows the Río Guadajoz, where many traces of settlement dating from the Neolithic, Iberian, Carthaginian, Roman and Moorish periods were found in the surrounding area. The town of Castro del Río itself grew around a Roman bridge crossing the river; the remnants of the town wall and the foundations of the Moorish castle also date from this period. The Plateresque portal of the church La Asunción, which dates back to the 13th century, is particularly worth seeing. The cell in the town hall that **Miguel de Cervantes** occupied for three months in 1592 is shown with pride. As tax collector he had committed the gross error of demanding taxes from a clergyman, even though the clergy enjoyed tax exemption. Legend has it that Cervantes began writing Don Quixote here.

Via the pretty wine-growing village **Espejo**, dominated by the castle of the dukes of Osuna, the route reaches the starting point at Montilla again.

Nerja

✦ H 8

Province: Málaga
Altitude: 21m/68ft
Population: 21,900

Nerja, situated where the Río Chillar flows into the Mediterranean, was known under the Moors as Narixa (abundant spring), and experienced its greatest prosperity during this period.

Today it is a well-frequented beach resort which, although new suburbs and amusement zones show that it has not been spared by the tourist boom, nevertheless is one of the quieter places on the Costa del Sol. Nerja has famous dripstone caves, in which the annual summer festival takes place with music and ballet between the second half of July and the first half of August.

Beach resort with famous caves

WHAT TO SEE IN AND AROUND NERJA

The dome of the Ermita de las Angustias in the old part of Nerja (16th century) was decorated with frescoes by Alonso Cano.

Nerja

Balcón de Europa: during the Moorish period a fortified tower, now an observation point with a tremendous panorama

Nerja

INFORMATION
Oficina de Turismo
C. Carmen, 1; E-29780 Nerja
Tel. 952 52 15 31
www.nerja.org/turismo
Mon – Sat 10am – 2pm, 5pm – 9pm
Sun 10am – 2pm

EVENT
Festival de las Cuevas
End of July/beginning of August: music
and ballet festival in the caves (tel.
952 52 95 20).

WHERE TO EAT
Casa Luque €€€€
Plaza Cavana, 2
Tel. 952 52 10 04; closed Wed

Bizarre: the dripstone caves of Nerja

Excellent innovative cooking, wonderful
tapas. Terrace with view of the ocean.
Service can be a little arrogant.

El Refugio €€€€
Diputación, 12
Tel. 952 52 41 39
Prime address for paella, fish, and sea-
food.

Bar-Restaurante El Pulguilla €€€
C. Almirante Ferrándiz, 26
Tel. 952 52 13 84; http://elpulguilla.com
Tapas bar and restaurant, specialises in
baked fish and seafood. Large dining
room and terrace. They also rent apartments.

WHERE TO STAY
Parador de Nerja €€€€
Almuñécar, 8
Tel. 952 52 00 50
www.parador.es, 73 rooms
Modern building with nice garden;
above the coast, with access to the
beach. Rooms with terrace or balcony
and sea view. Outdoor pool and tennis
courts as well as an elegant restaurant.

Paraíso del Mar €€
Prolongación Carabeo, 22
Tel. 952 52 16 21
www.hotelparaisodelmar.com, 10 rooms
Two Andalusian-style houses in a fantas-
tic location on a cliff above the sea.

Insider
Tip

Across from the town hall, where once a castle stood, the ***Balcón de
Europa** juts out over the sea. High above the waves this **viewing
platform** commands a magnificent view of the varied coast and hinterland mountains. Nerja's beaches extend on both sides of the balcony. The best of them are Playa de la Burriana right in the east, and
Playa de la Torrecilla right in the west.

Discovered by children in 1959, the Cuevas de Nerja are found a few miles northeast above the village of Maro. They form a system of **dripstone caves** over 4km/2.5mi long, of which a section about 1400m/1531yd long can be visited. The caves have bizarre stalactite and stalagmite formations – the gigantic dripstone in the Sala del Cataclismo is stunning – yet also wonderful effects produced by means of artificial lighting. People of the Mesolithic period left **rock paintings and artefacts**. Remains of skulls, pottery, tools, and other objects are on display in the small archaeological museum at the entrance.

**Cuevas de Nerja

❶ Daily 10am – 2pm, 4pm – 6.30pm, Jul – Aug daily 10am – 7.30pm, admission €8.50; www.cuevadenerja.es

The four-tiered aqueduct crossing the gorge of La Coladilla at Maro near the N-340 was built not by the Romans, but by the local architect Francisco Cantarero in the 19th century.

Acueducto del Águila

The part of the coast and hinterland of the Costa del Sol between Nerja and ▶Málaga is called La Axarquía. As it is protected from the cold north wind by the mountains of the Sierra Alhama, Sierra Tejeda, and Sierra Almijara, La Axarquía is known for its distinctly mild climate. The Moors made use of this, and grew vines and fruit, bred silkworms, and also withdrew here to the seclusion of the mountains following the fall of Granada. It is quiet in the villages of Axarquía even today.

La Axarquía

In ***Frigiliana**, 5km/3mi north of Nerja, Málaga wine is pressed. The village, awarded a prize for its improvement activities, is exceptionally lovely, its centre dating back to Moorish times, and offers a magnificent view of Nerja and the sea.

> **!** MARCO ⊕ POLO TIP
>
> *Delicacies from Frigiliana* **Insider Tip**
>
> Sweet Málaga wine is not the only thing to purchase in the narrow streets of Frigiliana. Many shops also sell olive oil from the village, and – a rarity – honey made from sugarcane (miel de caña).

Its lanes are too narrow for cars. Frigiliana was a Moriscan stronghold: ceramic plaques on the houses recount a – quelled – revolt of the Moriscos against the Christians in 1569, the Batalla del Peñon.

A short tour through Axarquía leads from Nerja to the west through the holiday resort Torrox-Costa, and from there to Torrox, which is charmingly located in the mountains 4km/2.5mi further north. The Moors founded it in the 12th century. After Torrox the trip continues on a winding and scenic route to Cómpeta, 15km/9mi distant, where whitewashed houses nestle amid a wine-growing region on the mountainside. Visitors to the **Museo del Vino** can sample the

Tour through Axarquía

dessert wine produced here from the Moscatel grape. The route then returns to the coast via Archez, Corumbela, and Vélez-Málaga, a pretty little town up high, its appearance characterized by white cubic houses and the Moorish alcazaba.

On the way back the route passes between Caleta de Vélez and Algarrobo, the **Necrópolis Fenicias de Trayamar**, where Punic and Phoenician tombs dating partly from the 8th century BC were discovered. The most significant finds are exhibited in the Alcazaba Museum in ▶Málaga. Return to Nerja via Caleta de Vélez, a fishing town right on the coast, and enjoy the beautiful drive along the Mediterranean.

* **Niebla**

B 7

Province: Huelva
Altitude: 39m/127ft
Population: 4200

The small town of Niebla in the wine-growing region Condado de Huelva is one of the few Spanish places that still has a medieval curtain wall completely surrounding its centre – an imposing sight when coming from the east.

Ancient walls and wine
The first sign of the town's long history is the bridge over the Río Tinto, built by the Romans. Their settlement of Ilipula was renamed Elebla and made a bishop's seat by the Visigoths. The Moors called the town Lebla and erected its massive town fortifications; belonging at first to the Caliphate of Córdoba, it became the capital of a petty Moorish kingdom, a taifa, after the collapse of the caliphate. Alfonso X was able to overcome the ramparts after half a year's siege in 1257.

Niebla

INFORMATION
Oficina de Turismo
Calle Campo del Castillo s/n
Castillo de los Guzmanes
E-21840 Niebla
Tel. 959 36 22 70
daily 10am–3pm, 5pm–9pm, July and
Aug Sat only 10am–3pm

WHERE TO EAT
La Gamba €€
Calle Cruz de los Mozos
Tel. 645 51 11 95
Delicacies from the sea. Excellent gambas but also meat dishes. Very friendly service.

Niebla is surrounded by a medieval city wall: because of the red tone the Moors called the city »The Red One«

WHAT TO SEE IN NIEBLA

3km/2mi of enormous battlements gird the small town. Iberians, Visigoths, Romans and particularly the Moors built the **walls and their total of 46 towers**. Five gates lead inside: Puerta del Agua to the south, both Puerta de Sevilla with Roman and Moorish traces and Puerta del Agujero to the north, Puerta de Socorro with a horseshoe arch to the northwest, and finally Puerta de Buey, on which the art of Moorish craftsmen is most notably visible, to the southeast.

*Murallas

Right next to Puerta de Sevilla is the **castle of Guzmanes**, constructed in the 15th century, and destroyed by the French in 1813, yet meanwhile restored. Some rooms such as the kitchen and the dungeon have been renovated or contain exhibitions, e.g. on falconry, as **hunting falcons from Niebla** were treasured in Europe and the Orient.

Castillo de los Guzmanes

● Daily 10am – 3pm, 5pm – 9pm, July / Aug Sat only 10am – 3pm; admission: €4.

San Martín Behind Puerta del Soccorro, the church San Martin is a **curiosity** beyond compare: in the 1920s, unused at the time, the nave had to make way for a road, yet both apse and belfry with the main portal remained standing either side of the road. The church can be traced back to a mosque that Alfonso X gave to Niebla's Jewish community as a synagogue, which was then converted to a Mudéjar, and later Gothic church in the 14th century.

Santa María de la Granada On the site of a Visigothic predecessor, the church Santa María de la Granada stands at the central square. Two of its portals date from the 10th and 11th centuries, when Christians were allowed to use it under Moorish rule. The conversion to a mosque did not occur until the 13th century; the horseshoe ambulatories at the entrance derive from this period. In the 15th century the building was made into a church, whereby the minaret was retained as a belfry. Inside the mihrâb and the bishop's throne are preserved.

Bollulos Par del Condado Bollulos Par del Condado, 15km/9mi east of Niebla where the A-49 and A-483 intersect, is called »city of wine«. Try the tangy white wines or the heavy dessert wines of the Condado de Huelva region here, preferably at one of the bodegóns, where there is food and the wines are for sale.

Dolmen de Soto The A-472 leads to the Dolmen de Soto, about 8km/5mi to the west. It is a Neolithic tomb with a passage leading 20m/21yd to a burial chamber containing rock drawings.

❶ Summer Mon – Fri 9am – 2pm

✳ **Osuna**

✦ E 7

Province: Sevilla
Altitude: 326m/1069ft
Population: 17,900

Right on the southern edge of the hot plain of the Guadalquivir the houses of Osuna climb a slope. The town was seat of the dukes of Osuna, who beautified the town with marvellous Baroque palaces and churches, which makes a walk through the old quarter an experience.

Baroque ducal town Under the Romans Osuna was called Urso, and supported Pompey against Julius Caesar for a long time, until Caesar overthrew it. The Moors, who called the town Oxuna, lost it to the Castilian king in 1239, who transferred it to the Order of Calatrava; the order ceded it

Osuna

INFORMATION
Oficina de Turismo
Carrera, 82 (Antiguo Hospital)
E-41640 Osuna
Tel. 954 81 57 32
www.turismosuna.es

WHERE TO EAT
Restaurante Doña **Insider**
Guadalupe €€€€ **Tip**
Plaza Guadalupe, 6
Tel. 954 81 05 58
Vegetables, meat, and fresh fish are also
served outside on a lovely small square.
The Doña Guadalupe rates as one of the
region's best restaurants.

Mesón del Duque €€€
Plaza de la Duquesa de Osuna, 2
Tel. 954 81 28 45
Traditional Andalusian dishes and tapas,
which can be enjoyed on the nice ter-
race on warm days.

Casa Curro €€
Plaza Salitre, 5
Tel. 955 82 07 58
The tastiest tapas in Osuna,
said to be more than 200.

WHERE TO STAY
Hospedería del
Monasterio €
Plaza de la Encarnación, 3
Tel. 955 82 13 80
www.hospederiadel
monasterio.com
10 rooms
Hotel with nicely furnished rooms.
Restaurant, terrace with pool

Hostal Caballo Blanco €
Granada, 1
Tel. 954 81 01 84
www.lacasadelduque.com
12 rooms
Friendly hostel in a 16th century house
in a quiet location. There is a restaurant.
Nice but rather small rooms.

to the lords of Girón. In 1548 Juan Téllez de Girón founded the university at which only students who professed the dogma of the Immaculate Conception might enrol. This college, praised by Miguel de
Cervantes, made Osuna into a spiritual centre of 16th- and 17-cen-
tury Spain. Philip II bestowed upon Pedro Téllez de Girón the title of
Duke of Osuna in 1562; in the 17th and 18th centuries this noble
family was one of Spain's most powerful.

WHAT TO SEE IN OSUNA

Four beautiful aristocratic palaces of Osuna dating primarily from
the 17th century are of note: in C. San Pedro the Palacio del Marqués
de la Gomera, with a grand Baroque façade dominated by a balcony
onto which an extravagant door framed by spiralled columns opens;
in the same street and no less beautiful is the **Palacio del Cabildo**

*Aristocratic
palaces

Colegial, which has a façade adorned with white decorative tiles and displays a replica of Giralda of Seville above the portal; lastly the Palacio de los Cepedas (now a court; C. de la Huerta) and the Palacio de Govantes y Herdara in C. Sevilla.

*La Colegiata   The abbey church, located higher up, was built with three Plateresque portals from 1535 to 1539. Four paintings by Ribera (*Saints Jerome, Peter, Sebastian, Bartholomew*) hang in the Capilla Mayor, and were brought to Osuna during the third Duke of Osuna's time as Viceroy of Naples, where Ribera worked primarily; another Ribera painting shows the crucified Christ. Further treasures include a Madonna by Alonso Cano, a retable by Sebastián Fernández, the *Catalan Madonna with the Pomegranate* and a Flemish triptych (both 16th century), and lastly Cristo de la Misericordia by Juan de Mesa, a sculpture from the church Santo Domingo. Enter by the Plateresque Patio del Capellán, surrounded by a two-storey arcade, to reach the mausoleum of the Dukes of Osuna (***Santo Sepulcro** or Panteón). Juan Téllez de Girón had it built in 1545; its magnificent stucco, paintings, sculptures, and the small but superb choir stalls gave it the **byname Escorial of Osuna**.

> **MARCO ⊕ POLO TIP**
>
> *In the casino*   **Insider Tip**
>
> An ideal place for relaxing with a cup of coffee and watching the goings-on on the Plaza Mayor is the terrace of the casino, built in the 1820s. The interior is decorated with magnificently tiled walls and ceilings in a mix of art nouveau and Mudéjar styles (a must!).

❶ May – Sept Tue – Sun 10am – 1.30pm and 4pm – 7pm, Oct – Apr Tue – Sun 10am – 1.30pm and 3.30pm – 6.30pm, July/Aug closed Sunday afternoon; admission: €2

Convento de la Encarnación   The Convento de la Encarnación across from the church was founded as a hospital in 1549. Take a look at the cloister lined with coloured azulejos and visit the Museo de Arte Sacro, with four rooms dedicated to sacred art (same opening hours as La Colegiata).

Antigua Universidad   Cervantes mentions the university opposite the eastern façade of the Colegiata in Don Quixote. The former university (until 1824) encloses a Plateresque inner courtyard with gallery.

Museo Arqueológico   Between La Colegiata and the Plaza Mayor stands the Torre del Agua, an Almohad tower dating from the 12th century and thus the oldest building of the town; it houses the archaeological museum. Copies of Roman bronze work are of note here.

❶ May – Sept Tue – Sun 10am – 1.30pm, 4 – 7pm; Oct – April Tue – Sun 10am – 1.30pm, 3.30 – 6.30pm, July/Aug closed Sunday afternoon; admission: €2.50

Palacio del Cabildo Colegial is decorated with a model of the Giralda of Sevilla

AROUND OSUNA

Estepa, situated 24km/15mi east of Osuna at the foot of the epony-   **Estepa**
mous Sierra, was Carthaginian Astapa, where in 207 BC the inhabitants burned themselves to death rather than surrender to Scipio Af-
ricanus. The mighty Torre del Homenaje is the most striking remnant
of the castillo; the terrace of the Gothic church Santa María de la
Asunción next to the castle features a beautiful panoramic view. The
parish church Iglesia del Carmen possesses an elaborately ornament-
ed main entrance with black azulejos. Thanks to the jasper-encrusted
✳**Camarín de la Vera Cruz**, created by Nicolás Bautista Morales in
1745, the church Nuestra Señora de los Remedios is among the most
significant Baroque churches of Andalucía.

* Priego de Córdoba

✦ **G 7**

Province: Córdoba
Altitude: 652m/2139
Population: 23,500

The small town of Priego de Córdoba lies at the edge of the Sierra Subbética wildlife park in marvellous mountain scenery. Moreover Priego still retains a town centre with characteristic Andalusian charm.

Baroque pearl of the province

Just like in the old days the small town is still a centre of textile manufacture and olive oil production, though less important than in the 17th and 18th centuries. During that time Priego de Córdoba experienced a period of prosperity from silk production, which enabled **sumptuous Baroque churches** to be constructed.

WHAT TO SEE IN PRIEGO DE CÓRDOBA

Castillo

A square, three-storey keep with twin windows juts out above the castle, which was built in the 13th and 14th centuries and towers virtually at the entrance to the Moorish quarter.

**Nuestra Señora de la Asunción

Nuestra Señora de la Asunción, a church begun opposite the castle in 1525, was rebuilt in Baroque style in the 18th century. Numerous altars decorate the aisles; the life of Christ and the Assumption of the Virgin are the themes of the high altar. The undisputed highlight, the Sagrario, is entered from the left aisle. This octagonal chapel, surrounded by balustrades, was adorned between 1772 and 1784 by Francisco Javier Pedrejas with biblical scenes rendered in exuberant stucco. Sculptures of the apostles are placed before the columns, the fathers of the church in the middle.
❶ Tue – Sun 10.30am – 1.30pm

*Barrio de la Villa

The layout of the old town quarter Barrio de la Villa behind Nuestra Señora de la Asunción is unmistakeably Moorish. Its lanes, flower-bedecked façades and tiny squares are a pleasant place for a walk. The viewing point ***El Adarve**, high above the valley, is reached by going this way. It commands a wonderful panorama of the surrounding area.

Iglesia de San Pedro

Inside the Iglesia de San Pedro at the eponymous plaza near the castle, adorned with spiral columns and gold leaf, the high altar displays the patron saint of the church. The chapel behind it holds

Priego de Córdoba

INFORMATION
Oficina de Turismo
Plaza de la Constitución, 3
E-14800 Priego de Córdoba
Tel. 957 70 06 25
www.turismodepriego.com

WHERE TO EAT
Balcón del Aldarve €€€
Paseo de Colombia, 36
Tel. 957 54 70 75
www.restaurante-elaljibe.com
Nice bar with lots of tapas downstairs,
restaurant with good meat and fish
dishes upstairs. Attentive service.

El Aljibe €€€
Abad Palomino, 7
Tel. 957 70 18 56
Restaurant opposite the Castillo.
The restaurant serves mainly meat
dishes. On the ground floor Moorish
baths can be seen through the glass
floor.

WHERE TO STAY
Casa Baños de la Villa €€
Real, 63
Tel. 957 54 72 74
www.casabanosdelavilla.com
9 rooms
Boutique hotel with individually
decorated rooms accesible via the
verandah around the inner courtyard. Make sure to visit the Arab
baths here, too.

Huerta de las Palomas €€
Ctra. Priego-Zagrilla, km 3
Tel. 957 72 03 05
www.zercahoteles.com
34 rooms
Hotel built in Andalusian style
and surrounded by olive orchards,
located 4km/2.4mi outside of Priego.
The rooms are furnished tastefully.
Restaurant, fitness area, swimming
pool.

Hostal Rafi €
Isabel la Católica, 4
Tel. 957 54 70 27
www.hostalrafi.es
26 rooms
Family-run guest house and restaurant
with mainly regional dishes.

Villa Turistica de Priego €
In Aldea Zagrilla
Tel. 957 70 35 03
52 villas
Holiday park in Andalusian country
style in natural surroundings, 7km/4.5mi
outside Priego de Córdoba. Beautiful
countryside, pretty decor and attentive
personnel.

an Immaculada, ascribed to the group of artists around Alonso
Cano.

Below Iglesia de San Pedro lies the former 16th-century abattoir and
the town market. A Mannerist portal opens onto the central patio
with columned arcades, corner towers, and a stone spiral staircase
that leads to the previous abattoir, which now contains an exhibition
room.

**Carnicerías
Reales**

Iglesia de las Angustias	Above the Placa de la Constitucion with the town hall, C. Río leads to the Iglesia de las Angustias, where the Rococo-style interior was completed in 1773 by Juan de Dios Santaella. The major works here are the Baroque Pietà on the high altar and statues by José Risueño portraying the Holy Family.
Casa Niceto Alcalá-Zamora	Follow the street downhill to reach the birthplace, furnished true to the original, of Niceto Alcalá-Zamora (1877–1949), who was **President of the Second Spanish Republic** from 1931 to 1939. The town's tourist office is located on the ground floor. ❶ Tue – Sun 10am – 1.30pm, 4.30pm – 7.30pm, Sun 10am – 1.30pm
*Fuente del Rey	C. Río runs past the Iglesia del Carmen to the monumental fountain Fuente del Rey, erected in the 19th century. Water pours into the main basin from **139 marble openings**, in its centre Neptune on a chariot slicing through the waves. The first fountain here was Fuente de Salud, erected a little higher up in the 16th century.
Further churches	In the eastern part of the town centre there are two more interesting churches: the 16th-century Iglesia de la Aurora, its glorious façade a typical example of this region's Baroque style, and not far from there the Iglesia de San Francisco, containing an enormous number of Baroque side altars, its high altar portraying Christ at the Column.
Museo Histórico	In Carrera de las Monjas in the western part of town the town museum mainly exhibits archaeological finds from the surrounding area. Here, too, are the **Museo de Paisaje** with contemporary landscape art and a museum commemorating the local painter **Adolfo Lozano Sidro**, who lived in this house for many years. ❶ Tue – Fri 10am – 1.30pm, 6pm – 8.30pm, Sa. 10.00 – 13.30, 5pm – 7.30pm, Sun 10am – 1.30pm

AROUND PRIEGO DE CÓRDOBA

Carcabeuy	7km/4.5mi west of Priego at the foot of a massive ruined castle amidst a beautiful landscape of mountains and hills lies the small village of Carcabeuy. The imposing Iglesia de la Asunción dating from the early 17th century is easy to find here.
Alcalá la Real	From afar the mighty castle of Alcalá la Real, located 24km/15mi to the east, is already visible. Built from the 13th to the 15th century, the Castillo de la Mota still betokens the strength of Moorish Al-Kalaat be Zayde, which gave protection to many refugees from those areas which remained Moorish after the Christian conquest. The tower of the castle chapel provides a panoramic view of the surrounding olive

**Montefrio, watched by Castillo de la Villa,
is located in a unique hilly landscape**

groves. In the town itself are remains of the town fortifications, the
church Santa María, in which the sculptor Martínez Montañés was
baptized, a Plateresque fountain, and the classical town hall at the
main square.

Montefrío is situated 44km/27mi southeast in spectacular scenery ***Montefrío**
between two mountain spurs each crowned by a church.
Whereas the Iglesia de la Villa, designed by Diego de Siloé, stands on
the ruins of the Moorish alcazaba, the Baroque Iglesia de San Antonio once belonged to a Franciscan monastery. In the town centre the
classical rotunda of Iglesia de la Encarnación, vaulted by a grand
dome, catches the eye.
8km/5mi further east towards Illora lies an extensive Neolithic site,
Peña de los Gitanos, where megalithic tombs and cave paintings were
discovered.

* El Puerto de Santa María

Province: Cádiz
Altitude: 6m/19ft
Population: 88,500

18km/11mi north of ►Cádiz, where the Río Guadalete empties into the Atlantic, wine from the traditional sherry triangle Jerez de la Frontera – Sanlúcar de Barrameda – El Puerto is shipped from the harbour of El Puerto de Santa María. Yet sherry, and especially brandy, is also produced in the town itself at such traditional bodegas as Osborne and Terry (►MARCO POLO Insight p. 306–311).

Andalucía's sherry harbour

The bodega Osborne has even given Spain a national symbol: the **oversized advertising bull**, standing conspicuously by main roads throughout the country. Thanks to the protests after some Madrid bureaucrats wanted to do away with the bull on the grounds that it was a blight on the countryside, it is now even protected as a national treasure. In summer Sevillians come to bathe at the beaches between here and ►Sanlúcar de Barrameda; for them El Puerto's old town with its 18th-century noble palaces and numerous tapas bars is just the right place for a change, which they also get at the casino.

History

El Puerto de Santa María was founded by the Greeks, and was called Portus Menesthei in the days when it was a Roman seaport. Alfonso X ousted the Moors in 1264. He arranged for the reconstruction of the port, which held great significance for the voyages to the new colonies. Columbus started on his second journey from here; men such as Juan de la Cosa, a helmsman of Columbus and first cartographer of the New World, and Amerigo Vespucci stayed here.

WHAT TO SEE IN EL PUERTO DE SANTA MARÍA

At the place where the ferry Adriano III moors, sailors were supplied with water from the 18th-century **Fuente de las Galeras**. Also called Vaporcito (»little steamship«, from a

El Puerto de Santa María

INFORMATION
Oficina de Turismo
Palacio de Aranibar, Plaza del Castillo
E-11500 El Puerto de Santa María
Tel. 956 48 37 15
Nov – Apr Mon – Sat 10am – 2pm,
5.30pm – 7.30pm; Sun 10am – 2pm,
May – Oct daily 10am – 2pm, 6pm – 8pm
www.turismoelpuerto.com

EVENTS
Virgen de los Milagros
Grape-harvest festival on 8 September

BODEGAS
▶MARCO POLO Insight, p.306–311)

WHERE TO EAT
Los Portales €€€
C / Ribera del Marisco, 7
Tel. 956 54 21 16
www.restaurantelosportales.com
The best restaurant on the »Ribera del
Marisco« offers excellent cuisine, fresh
seafood.

Mesón del Asador €€€
Misericordia, 2
Tel. 956 54 03 27
For everyone who doesn't feel like fish
and seafood: meat galore, which guests
can even grill at the table themselves.

WHERE TO STAY
Monasterio de San Miguel €€
Virgen de los Milagros, 27
Tel. 956 54 04 40
www.jale.com/monasterio, 175 rooms
Very beautiful hotel in a magnificent
Baroque monastery at the town centre.
The cloister and the Andalusian-style
closed inner courtyard of the monastery
still remain The pretty restaurant serves
regional cooking.

Los Cántaros €€
Curva, 6, Tel. 956 54 02 40
www.hotelloscantaros.com 39 rooms
A conversion done with loving care of
the former women's prison at Plaza del
Cárcel, one of El Puerto's nightlife hot-
spots – thus not always quiet.

time in the 1950s when steamships did indeed ply these waters), the
ship is a novel way to travel from Cádiz to El Puerto – the trip takes
45 minutes across the Bahía – and the return is even more impressive, for a panoramic view of Cádiz can be seen from the sea here.

A little to the north at the Plaza del Castillo stands the crenellated
Castillo de San Marcos, which the Moors built in the 13th century
and was later the seat of the dukes of Medinaceli. Christopher Columbus and Juan de la Cosa took quarters here. Six towers and the
curtain wall are still well preserved. The castle chapel was once part
of the mosque, as remnants of the mihrâb, Kufic characters, and
horseshoe arches attest. The shape of the former minaret is clearly
visible in the octagonal main tower.

***Castillo de
San Marcos**

❶ Thu, Sat 10.30am – 1.30pm, admission: €5; Tue 11.30am – 1.30pm,
free admission

The Osborne bodega, whose logo is the Osborne bull, produces fin brandy and sherry

Fundación Rafael Alberti C. Santo Domingo leads northwest away from the castle to the birthplace of the **poet Rafael Alberti** (1902–1999), which has now been converted into a small museum.
❶ Tue. – Sun 10.30am – 2.30pm; admission: €5

Iglesia Mayor Prioral It is not far from Alberti's birthplace to the Plaza de España, where the Gothic Iglesia Mayor Prioral Nuestra Señora de los Milagros stands. Its 13th-century façade has remained; the Plateresque south portal Puerta del Sol, which portrays the Virgin amongst saints between pairs of columns in a tympanum, is exceptionally beautiful. The church received its name from a Madonna dating from the 13th century that stands in the Capilla Mayor under a domed canopy. The Virgin Mary, the patron saint of the town, is said to have appeared to Alfonso X during the conquest.

Museo Municipal Opposite the church the town museum presents local history in the Casa Palacio Marquesa de la Candia.
❶ Tue – Fri 10am – 2pm, Sat, Sun 10.45am – 2pm, free admission

East of the Iglesia Mayor lies Plaza Isaac Peral. It is the city's official centre, for the old town hall, Palacio Imblusqueta, stands here. On the way there look out for Casa de los Leones, which contains an exhibition devoted to Baroque art in El Puerto.

Plaza Isaac Peral

● daily 10am – 2pm, 6pm – 8pm, free admission

Built in 1880 the bullring somewhat north of Osborne is **Spain's third-largest** after those in Madrid and Seville: it seats 15,000 aficionados. In the entry area the mounted heads of the most courageous bulls that lost their lives in the arena are on display.

*Plaza de Toros

In the early 1990s the yacht harbour Puerto Sherry was developed beyond the trading port. 790 berths make it one of the largest in Andalucía. The attractive town beach Playa Santa Catalina adjoins it.

Puerto Sherry

AROUND EL PUERTO DE SANTA MARÍA

Those wishing to get from El Puerto to Rota, only a few miles westwards, have a long drive nevertheless, for the road curves around the huge area of the US naval and air-force base. It is worth the effort, for Rota is a very pleasant, uncrowded resort with long beaches lined with pines to the north, a pretty promenade, and a small marina as well as pretty, white houses and medieval towers.

*Rota

Insider Tip

Advertising itself as a 21st-century holiday village, **Costa Ballena**, the »whale coast«, was constructed on the coast to the north around an 18-hole golf course with a 4km/2.4mi-long beach, where holiday comfort is supposed to be environmentally friendly.

El Rocío

✳ C 7

Province: Huelva
Altitude: 36m/118ft
Population: 1600

El Rocío on the northern edge of Coto de Doñana national park is Andalucía's most famous place of pilgrimage. The Romería del Rocío, during which the pilgrims wander through the Coto, attracts tens of thousands at Pentecost every year.

The Madonna venerated at the Romería del Rocío, carved out of wood in the 13th century, and decked with jewellery and a brocade cloak from the 18th century, is kept in the 1960s pilgrimage church. Brotherhood buildings surround the church; when a rider or horse

Andalucía's most famous place of pilgrimage

Three Days of Commotion and Devotion

On 362 days of the year, El Rocío is a dusty village of 800 souls with a curiously large plaza and a striking white church. But from Whit Saturday until Whit Monday, the most boisterous pilgrimage in Andalucía takes place here: the Romería del Rocío. It is so boisterous that even the Church observes the goings-on with a certain reserve.

Our Lady of the Morning Dew (Nuestra Señora del Rocío) is the object of veneration. She is also called La Paloma Blanca (White Dove) and Clavel de las Marismas (Carnation of Marismas). The morning dew is understood to be a **fertility symbol**. According to legend, a black Madonna figure was worshipped in this village in early Christian times. It had to be hidden after the invasion of the Moors and was forgotten over the centu-

ries. In the 13th century, a hunter claimed to have found her again in a hollow tree in a wood called La Rocina. **King Alfonso X the Wise** had a chapel erected in 1725 that thereafter became a destination for pilgrims from all over Andalucía. The cult gained followers in the rest of Spain and since the 17th century brotherhoods (cofradias or hermandades) have formed that make pilgrimages to the Madonna figure still to this day.

A Merry Atmosphere

On Whit Saturday, the pilgrims stream from all parts of the country to El Rocio in their hundreds of thousands. Most of them come by car, but the close to 80 traditionally-minded brotherhoods take several days to **march, ride or drive** there – with special permits – through the **Sanlúcar de Barrameda National Park**. The caballeros ride in their Sunday best, the señoras and señoritas in colourful **flamenco dresses** behind them on the horse's croup. They accompany the two-wheeled, festooned procession carts (carretas), pulled by donkeys or oxen. The pilgrims camp at night, partying and singing (and drinking) around the **campfire** on which they prepare their meals. Upon arrival, the brotherhood of Rocio greets its guests and a **three-day folk festival** begins, celebrated day and night with music, dance, sumptuous food and a lot of alcohol. Each brotherhood celebrates in a bar.

The climax on Whit Saturday consists of mass and the procession in which the figure of the Virgin is carried around in a **tumultuous parade** by the brotherhood of Almonte – and only by them – to the accompaniment of the racket of firecrackers and musical instruments. The following day the pilgrims leave – leaving behind a mountain of trash, particularly all along their path through the national park.

El Rocío

INFORMATION
Oficina de Turismo
Avda. de la Canaliega, s/n
E-21750 El Rocío
Tel. 959 44 21 66, www.rocio.com

EVENT
Romería del Rocío
Tens of thousands of pilgrims regularly turn the tiny village into Andalucía's festival centre at Pentecost.
❶ www.pastorayreina.com

WHERE TO STAY
Aires de Doñana €€€
Avenida Canaliega, 1; Tel. 959 44 22 89
www.airesdedonana.com
Situated on the edge of the national park, with a great view. Best address around.

WHERE TO STAY
Toruño €€€
Plaza del Acebuchal, 22
Tel. 959 44 23 23
www.hoteltoruno.com
30 rooms
Right on the edge of Coto de Doñana national park; some rooms are excellent for watching birds. Quiet rooms and restaurant with regional cuisine

Rocío Doñana €
Avenida del Canaliega, 1
Tel. 959 44 24 35
www.rociodonana.com
On the main road; large, elegant and in the middle of gardens, restaurant with traditional cooking, bar and terrace outdoors.

and cart come around a corner, the town almost seems to be a scene from a Western. At its eastern and southeastern edges El Rocío also offers excellent opportunities for birdwatching in Coto de Doñana (e.g. Observatorio del Madre de Rocío with an information centre); watchers can also go by car on the dirt road via Villamanrique de la Condesa to the observation point Cerrado Garrido (30km/20mi; the shorter route of 15km/9mi should be attempted with four wheel drive only!).

Matalascañas lies 16km/10mi southeast of El Rocío. The artificial village, containing large hotel complexes, offers every type of seaside recreational activity. The place is not attractive, but the beach is terrific.

Matalascañas

** Ronda

 E 8

Province: Málaga
Altitude: 723m/2372ft
Population: 36,900

Ronda is considered to be the cradle of modern bullfighting. It became a place of pilgrimage for bullfighting aficionados, amongst them celebrities such as Ernest Hemingway and Orson Welles. This in itself would not make Ronda an absolute must on a tour of Andalucía, but in addition the town has a fantastic setting.

The **Romero bullfighter dynasty** lived in Ronda. Francisco, José, Juan, and Pedro Romero were amongst the most renowned toreros of their time, and it was **Pedro Romero** (1754–1839), who developed the rules of the Ronda school, and who still entered the arena aged 80. The Ronda school teaches bullfighting using the Capa, Muleta, and Espada, with which the torero or matador confronts the bull on foot and not on horseback, while not showing the least fear, and fearing shame more than the bull's attacks. Ronda is also reflected in literature: the archetype of **Prosper Merimée's Carmen**, epitome of the fiery-eyed temptress and immortalized in **Bizet's opera**, is said to have turned men's heads in the smugglers' hideout Ronda.

Cradle of bullfighting in a breath-taking location

Even authors less interested in bullfighting tarried in the town: **James Joyce** completed *Ulysses* here; **the sojourn of Rainer Maria Rilke** in Ronda has become famous. The town perches breathtakingly on the brink of a rocky plateau that plunges down in rocky walls to the west, and is divided into two parts by the gorge of the Río Guadalevín (El Tajo), 40–90m/130–300ft wide and up to 160m/520ft deep. Ronda has spread over these two heights – the wonderful Moorish old town (La Ciudad) to the south, joined by three bridges with the new town (El Mercadillo) to the north.

Ronda is one of the oldest towns in Spain. Iberians founded a settlement on the seemingly impregnable heights. They were succeeded by the Carthaginians, who were expelled by the Romans, who then founded their colony of Arunda. The dominion of the Moors

History

Ronda

INFORMATION
Oficina de Turismo
Paseo de Blas Infante
E-29400 Ronda
Tel. 952 18 71 19
www.turismoderonda.es

EVENTS
Fiestas de Pedro Romero
The era of the Romero brothers comes to life annually around 12 September

Tragabuches was a bullfighter and a bandit

when Ronda celebrates the festival named for Pedro Romero, who invented bullfighting. Bullfighting isn't for everyone, but the grand parade, flamenco and the awarding of prizes for the carriages can be enjoyed by all.

WHERE TO EAT
❹ Tragabuches €€€€   **Insider Tip**
José Aparicio, 1
Tel. 952 19 02 91
www.tragabuches.com
The shooting star of the Ronda restaurant scene: imaginatively varied Andalusian cuisine.

❶ Don Miguel €€€€
Plaza de España, 3 y 5
Tel. 952 87 10 90
www.dmiguel.com
The tables here are on the terrace, below Puente Nuevo and directly over the gorge – Andalusian cuisine served with a breathtaking view into the abyss.

❸ Pedro Romero €€€€
Virgen de la Paz, 18
Tel. 952 87 11 10
www.rpedroromero.com
Delicious local cooking, for example »rabo de toro«, in a restaurant obviously decorated by a bullfighting aficionado.

❷ Albacara €€€€
Calle Tenorio, 8
Tel. 952 87 38 55
The restaurant is in the former stables of Montelirio Palace. Very creative dishes, and the view from the terrace is fantastic

WHERE TO STAY

❷ *En Frente Arte* €€

Real, 40
Tel. 952 87 43 12
www.enfrentearte.com
Rooms decorated with antiques; pool
and sauna. Terrace over the gorge.

Molino del Santo €€

Ronda Estación, Benaoján
Tel. 952 16 71 51
www.molinodelsanto.com
Small but fine country inn south-west
of Ronda near the railway station, with
down-to-earth but sophisticated cooking. Owners are English

❹ *Reina Victoria* €€

Insider Tip

Jerez, 25
Tel. 952 87 12 40
www. hotelreinavictoria.com; 89 rooms
Irresistible charm from the turn of the
last century flows out of every corner.
Rainer Maria Rilke spent the winter of
1912 / 1913 here in room 208 (today a

memorial room); wonderful terrace
right above the cliffs, grand views. You
don't have to stay in the Reina Victoria
right away. You can enjoy the same

view that Rainer Maria Rilke did from
the terrace of the restaurant and the
bar – unforgettable on a summer
evening.

❺ *Parador de Ronda* €€

Plaza de España, s / n
Tel. 952 87 75 00
www.parador.es, 78 rooms
Modern hotel behind a historic façade,
centrally located directly above the Tajo
gorge and in the vicinity of the bullring.

❻ *San Gabriel* €€

C. José M. Holgado, 19
Tel. 952 19 03 92
www.sangabriel.com
Nicely furnished hotel in a house built
in 1736, in the old part of town. There
is a small cinema with seat from the
Ronda Theatre.

❶ *La Alavero de los Baños* €€

C. San Miguel
Tel. 952 87 91 43
www.alaveradelosbanos.com
10 rooms
A new, cosy Andalusian country house
in an unusual place; not high up above
the gorge, but down below near the
Moorish baths, which also inspired the
interior decorating. Fantastic evenings
on the terrace are guaranteed. The
house restaurant is open twice a week,
which true to its location specializes
in Arab cooking.

❸ *Virgen de los Reyes* €

Lorenzo Borrego, 13
Tel. 952 87 11 40
52 rooms
Respectable, well-managed, reasonably
priced accommodations in the new
town large rooms.

Ronda

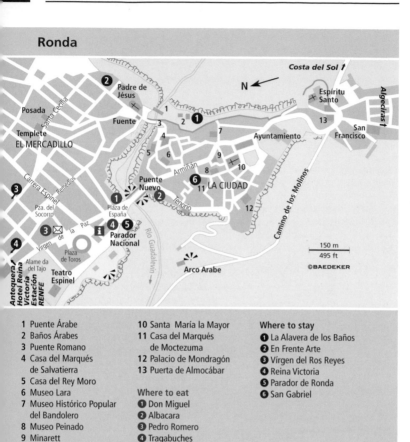

Costa del Sol

N

Espíritu Santo

Posada

Padre de Jésus

Fuente

Templete
EL MERCADILLO

San Francisco

Ayuntamiento

13

Carrera Espinel

Puente Nuevo

LA CIUDAD

Arminán

Pza. del Socorro

Plaza de España

Tenorio

Camino de los Molinos

Parador Nacional

Virgen de la Paz

Río Guadalevín

150 m
495 ft

©BAEDEKER

Plaza de Toros

Alame da del Tajo

Arco Arabe

Antequera / Hotel Reina Victoria Estación RENFE

Teatro Espinel

1 Puente Árabe
2 Baños Árabes
3 Puente Romano
4 Casa del Marqués
de Salvatierra
5 Casa del Rey Moro
6 Museo Lara
7 Museo Histórico Popular
del Bandolero
8 Museo Peinado
9 Minarett

10 Santa María la Mayor
11 Casa del Marqués
de Moctezuma
12 Palacio de Mondragón
13 Puerta de Almocábar

Where to eat
❶ Don Miguel
❷ Albacara
❸ Pedro Romero
❹ Tragabuches

Where to stay
❶ La Alavera de los Baños
❷ En Frente Arte
❸ Vírgen del Ros Reyes
❹ Reina Victoria
❺ Parador de Ronda
❻ San Gabriel

lasted over 770 years; in the 11th century the town was seat of a taifa emir and called Madinat Runda. Not until 1485, after a week-long siege, did Ronda fall through treachery to the Catholic Monarchs, who subsequently founded the new town. In 1808 Ronda suffered heavy destruction during Napoleon's campaign. In the years following it grew into a stronghold of smugglers and highwaymen, who controlled the greater part of the illegal goods flowing from Gibraltar to the north. The activities of these malefactors, who found plenty of backing among local people, became so rampant that **in 1844 the Guardia Civil was founded especially to combat them**.

✱✱ EL TAJO

The first thing every visitor to Ronda wants to do is have a look down into Río Guadalevír gorge. It was created by a tectonic fissure through which the river carves it course over several cascades. The name Tajo has nothing to do with the central Iberian river of the same name, it means to cut or slice or a drastic slash, and the gorge actually does seem to have been hacked out of the rock with an axe.

✱✱Puente Nuevo

Of the total of the three bridges, Puente Nuevo offers the most beautiful and impressive view. The bridge has three arches, is 70m/230ft long, and over 150m/490ft high and was built between 1751 und 1793 by José Martín de Aldehuela. It was said that he jumped to his death from this bridge. But actually he died a natural death at the age of 72 in Málaga. The view looking down from the bridge, with swallows and crows swooshing underneath it, is truly breathtaking. Above the middle arch, a door and a gallery can be seen that used to be the entrance to the **former prison**, which now houses an exhibition explaining the history of the structure.

❶ Mon – Fri 10am – 7pm (winter until 6pm), Sat, Sun 10am until 3pm

Down into the gorge

The daring construction can really only be appreciated from below, however. There are three ways down from the old town. The shortest leads from Plaza del Campanillo a little right of the Casa de Mondragón down the slope of the town's rock-face in steep bends and after some distance meets the main road, Camino de los Molinos. The longer version begins on the southern end of the old town to the right of Puerta de Almocóbar and leads to the dilapidated mills on the riverbank. A very steep path branches off to the right where both routes meet leading to the Moorish gate Arco árabe (Arco del Cristo), the remains of the city fortifications. Here are the best views of the waterfalls, the Puente Nuevo and the houses perched on the rock face. The descent to the **lower bridges** and the Arab baths is less strenuous. Turning left on the old town side eventually leads to Puerta de Felipe V, a city gate built in 1742, from which the well-preserved city wall is visible all the way to the Espíritu Santo church. Behind that, the Puente Viejo (Puente de la Mina; 1616) spans the river with a 30m/98ft-high horseshoe arch. From the bridge there is a view down onto Puente de San Miguel, which was quite possibly originally constructed by the Romans. Around 1300, the Moorish rulers had **✱✱Baños árabes**, a large bath built. It was divided into three rooms by horseshoe arches.

Insider Tip

❶ Opening times like Puente Nuevo

Ronda, the cradle of bullfighting, in a breath-taking location on the cliffs of El Tajo gorge

* LA CIUDAD (OLD TOWN)

Museo Lara Palacio de los Condes de las Islas Batanas is only a short way to the left from Puente Nuevo along C. Armiñan. Here the Museo Lara is housed, one of Spain's largest private collections. It offers a huge range of exhibits, including weapons, folk art, archaeological items and particularly beautiful clocks.

❶ Daily 11am – 8pm, in the winter until 7pm

*Museo del Bandolero Almost at the end of the street there are two museums, the Museo de Caza (hunting museum) and the much more interesting Museo del Bandolero, which very vividly portrays banditry in and around Ronda and the **careers of famous bandits** through weapons, wanted posters and dolls. One of the most famous was Diego Mateos, known as El Bandido Generoso, who was hanged and then quartered in 1781.

❶ Daily 11am – 8.30pm, in the winter 10.45 until 7pm

C. Armiñan leads into Plaza de la Duquesa de Parcent, where the church of **Santa María la Mayor** (16th century) stands. It was originally a mosque and still has four Moorish domes. The bell tower stands on the foundation walls of the former minaret. The three-storey portico is unusual. The interior holds Renaissance pews, as well as the remains of the Moorish mihrâb left in the entrance area. The very beautiful arcade of the town hall in which the Infante Juan lived after the conquest of Ronda occupies the east side of the plaza.

Plaza de la Duquesa de Parcent

A side-trip can be made from the plaza to the southernmost tip of Ronda, the barrio de San Francisco. Parts of the town's fortifications have survived the passing of time here, above all the Moorish Puerta de Almocábar, which for centuries was the main entrance to the town and was enlarged by an additional gate under Charles V. The remains of the wall of the Alcazaba destroyed in 1808 run from both gates. The Catholic Monarchs had the fortress-like church of Espíritu Santo built after they had taken Ronda.

Barrio de San Francisco

Back at Plaza de la Duquesa de Parcent, the alley left of Santa María leads around it to the 16th-century Palacio de Mondragón, which was built over the precipice. It has a beautiful Renaissance portal with a typical Moorish gemel window above, two very beautiful Mudéjar inner courts and a terrace from where a magnificent view can be enjoyed. The palace, in which among others the Catholic Monarchs resided, today houses the **Museo Municipal** for the region's history, folklore and natural history.

❶ Opening times like Puente Nuevo

***Palacio de Mondragón*

The way back to the main road leads past two more houses of the nobility. First, the Renaissance palace Casa del Marqués de Moctezuma, which, despite its name, has no connection with the Aztec ruler and is where Joseph Bonaparte had his quarters in 1810 – today it is a museum for the Ronda-born painter Joaquín Peinado (1898–1975); diagonally opposite is the **Casa del Gigante** dating from the 14th century, Ronda's most original Arab palace with all the appropriate decorative elements and a beautiful patio.

❶ Opening times like Puente Nuevo; admission to Peinado Museum: €4

Casa del Marqués de Moctezuma

On the main road back toward Puente Nuevo, Cuesta Santo Domingo branches off to the right before the bridge. Here stands Casa del Rey Moro, which has a terrace garden and an observation tower. Its name is deceptive because the present building was constructed in the 18th century. An Arab palace most likely stood here prior to that, however, and there remains a stone stairway dating back to that time with 365 steps leading from the river up to the house on which Christian slaves had to heave water upwards in bucket chains.

***Casa del Rey Moro*

*Palacio del Marqués de Salvatierra A little way down the alley, Palacio del Marqués de Salvatierra can easily be recognized by the unusual decoration on its balcony above the portal. The gable is supported by two naked Indian figures, a reminder of the Spanish conquests in Central and South America. The lower bridges are further on past the palace.

Templete Virgen de los Dolores The chapel of Templete Virgen de los Dolores from 1734 can be found in the east part of the old town. This was Ronda's place of execution, as shown by the mythical creature with a noose around its neck.

MERCADILLO (NEW TOWN)

Plaza de España opens up on the other side of Puente Nuevo, dominated by the parador – no historic building this, but a totally new structure. The new town is where everyone goes to shop or for a night out. The main shopping street is the pedestrian zoned Carrera de Espinel, which leads into the C. Virgen de la Paz.

Bullfighter Cayetano Ordoñez in front of the arena in Ronda

Across from the junction is the attraction for bullfighting enthusiasts, Plaza de Toros. Built in 1785, it is Spain's oldest bullfighting arena and the place where the Romeros performed. Even visitors who have no liking for this spectacle should tour the arena: it is architecturally interesting due to its two-storey spectator ring, 66m/217ft in diameter. The very worthwhile **bullfighting museum** set up in the rooms of the arena contains a lot of different memorabilia of famous bullfighters, above all the Romeros and the Ordoñez, as well as photos of prominent visitors like Hemingway and Orson Welles.

Plaza de Toros

❶ Summer daily 10am – 8pm; winter 6pm or 7pm; admission €6

The observation walkways enclosed by railings jutting out over the cliffs that run behind the arena offer a spectacular view of the river canyon carved out almost 200m/650ft deep below and beyond the Vega to the ▶Sierra de Grazalema mountain range. In Alameda del Tajo park there is a memorial to Pedro Romero.

**Observation walkways

AROUND RONDA

After driving 12km/7.5mi in the direction of ▶Arcos de la Frontera on the A-473 through attractive landscape, there is a turn-off to the left near La Quinta that leads past Montejaque to Benaoján (11km/7mi); from there it is another 4km/2.5mi on a small, narrow mountain road to Cueva de la Pileta, a limestone cave with stalactites and stalagmites. When this cave was discovered in 1911 it was found to contain, along with bones and tools, realistic Stone Age paintings of animals similar to those found in Altamira, Cantabria, but older. The oldest drawing, a depiction of a horse, is about 25,000 years old). Visitors should be prepared for waiting times, as only groups of up to 25 persons are allowed to enter. The tour through the cave, which has a constant temperature of 15°C/59°F and 100% humidity, is in an adventure. All visitors receive petroleum lamps in order to light their own way. Further caves in the vicinity are Cueva del Hundidero, where Río Guadiaro River disappears, and Cueva del Gato, where it reappears.

*Cueva de la Pileta

Insider Tip

❶ **Tours:** daily 10am – 1pm, 4pm – 6pm, Oct – March until 5pm; admission €8; www.cuevadelapileta.org

Ronda la Vieja (12km/7.5mi north-west of town) dates back to Roman Acinipo, from which remains of the theatre still exist.

Ronda la Vieja

Take time to look at Olvera when on the way to ▶Arcos de la Frontera. It is a White Village in a beautiful setting dominated by the 16th-century La Encarnación church and the castle rock with the 12th-century castillo as a counterpoint.

*Olvera

The Corrida – Last Bastion of Machismo

What is for many Europeans and meanwhile even for Spaniards nothing more than a bloody spectacle, is for aficionados, the bullfighting connoisseurs and enthusiasts, great art. They speak of »arte de lidiar«, the art of enchanting the bull, standing up to it in battle and not just physically defeating it.

Giving up bullfighting, however, would mean for the Spanish the loss of a part of a deeply rooted culture, yes, even a part of their own identity. For many, the corrida de toros is one of the last approximations to the **primordial battle** between man and beast. A battle in which there can be more than just one loser and in which the animal is accorded more dignity than in many other expressions of culture in our time. The **classic bullfighting region** is Andalucía, even though matadors face bulls in rings in all major cities in

Practicing the great pose

Spain, in some countries in Latin America and even in southern France. Madrid may have the largest **Plaza de Toros**, but Ronda in Andalucía has the oldest. So it is no wonder that the **most celebrated toreros of all time** were mostly Andalusians: Manolete, Lagartijo, Joselito, Paquirri and El Cordobés, some of whom lost their lives in the arena. The »**toros bravos**«, half wild beasts bursting with strength, have been raised for generations predominantly by Andalusian **dynasties of breeders**. Their great latifundia lie in the provinces of Seville, Huelva and Cádiz, and are still the absolute epitome of old señorito splendour.

Origins

The historical traces of the battle between man and bull are ancient, lost in prehistoric times in a variety of cultures. Until the **rules** valid today crystallized in the course of the 18th century, there were many forms of the fight. During and after the **Reconquista**, it was primarily the **upper class** that took on the bull at court fiestas and during shows of combat on **horseback**. During the course of the **18th century**, the Bourbons began to tolerate martial sports at court less and less – so it became the **servants** of the aristocrats who fought the bulls **on foot** before an audience, thus founding the present-day form of bullfighting. At the same time, the **systematic breeding** of »toros bravos« began in the vicinity of the village of Utrera, and today the pedigrees of some of the

Costume fitting

most famous animals reach back to that time.

Goya captured the historic moment in the 18th century when the equestrian bullfighters were pushed into the background and replaced by the *torero a pie*, the bullfighter on foot, in his cycle of etchings »Tauromaquia«.

Drama in Three Acts

Generally, bullfighting takes place during feria or other local fiestas. Then, from Easter until the end of autumn the aficionados gather in their thousands late in the afternoon in the circular Plaza de Toros. Those who can, avoid the almost unbearable heat of the »sol seats« situated on the sunny side and procure a much more expensive ticket for the shady »**sombra side**«. There are almost always **three toreros or matadors**, who have six animals to kill each afternoon with their cuadrilla, the assistants.

The ceremony begins with the vibrantly **colourful entrance** of all participants to the sounds of a stirring paso doble. The uniforms (socalled **suits of light**), embroidered all over with sequins and spangles, are a relic from the aristocratic era of bullfighting.

Before the bull can be killed, it must first be **goaded and weakened** by the cuadrilla. It is brought to a state of **excitement** by the flashy-coloured, wide capa so that its energy is shown to the public and the torero can assess its strengths and weaknesses. After this first contact between matador and toro, the picadors appear on horseback. While the bull attacks his protectively padded horse, the picador tries to weaken it by **jabbing it in the neck** with a lance. Next appear the **banderillas**. With quick, prancing steps, they run up to the animal head on and at the last moment stick in it a pair of banderillas, sharp barbed sticks decorated with tinsel. Only after three banderillas have been placed does the matador again appear and begin the **climax and end of the fight**.

The skill of the man must master the brute force of the 500 kilo/1,100 pound animal. The torero must **captivate the bull** with his scarlet cape, the muleta, and **lead it past his body**. In Andalucía it is said, »a bull can only be deceived once – the second time it seeks the body«. Each of the dancing movements (»paso«) has its own name in **bullfighting terminology**.

Only when the will of the bull has been broken and the torero dares to turn his back to the bull to receive acclaim from the audience may the **death-thrust** be dealt. The bull must sink its head so that the sword, called an estoque, can enter a certain area of its neck and **pierce the heart**. Matadors who miss this spot are mercilessly booed and ridiculed by the public.

Archaic Survival

In his book *Death in the Afternoon*, **Ernest Hemingway**, himself an aficionado, described like no other the torero's fear of and respect for the bull, the playful ease as well as the deep sadness of this ritual act of killing in the ring. **Courage, contempt of death and physical strength**, as well as **aesthetics** and, in some movements, **eroticism**, are combined in a single figure, the torero, in the hot afternoon hours of a corrida. He is the very personification of the proverbial Andalusian machismo, which, however, essentially already belongs to the past.

The Matadora

It makes no difference that even a woman – **Cristina Sánchez** – has succeeded in becoming a recog-

Just before the fatal thrust

nized *matadora*. But in the end, she fell **victim to machismo** because despite her performances in the most important rings in Spain, the male toreros no longer wanted to appear with her. After her last fight on 12 October 1999 in Las Ventas in Madrid, she withdrew at the age of 27.

Dymystification

Full arenas, loud cries from the spectators and a beaming winner – all of this is long past. Today the seats are often empty except for a few tourists resting their foot and who don't even know how important this spectacle once was. If the older people are to be believed it was a matter of honour, pride and fair play, but these ideals are long since passé and have had to give way to corruption and greed. The bullfighting critic Joaquín Vidal, who died in 2002, estimated that about 90 % of the bulls were manipulated. Spectators today wonder if the bull's horns were shortened in order to weaken his aim or if he is full of drugs; deliberately forcing the animal against the sides of the arena so that it injures its neck is cheating, but most often cannot be proved. Bullfighting has long since stopped being profitable, so it has to be subsidized with public funds.

Bloody Relict

Bullfighting continues to hold a firm position in the cultural identity of many Spaniards and especially Andalusians. But the signs are changing: more and more Spaniards are against the bloody spectacle, which developed in its present form in Andalusian Ronda in the 18th century.

▶ **»Torero«** iis a general expression for participants in a »corrida« (bullfight).

»Matador de toros« (bull killer)
Appears in phase 2 and 4. His sequin covered, gold embroidered suit (»traje de luces« = light clothing«) is a relict from the noble times of bullfighting.

»Toro de lidia« (fighting bull)
Weight: min. 460 kg
Age: 5–6 years

©BAEDEKER

▶ **Order of the »corrida« (bull fight)**

1 **»Paseíllo«**

Participants march into the arena

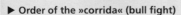

2 **»Suerte de varras«**

The matador provokes the bull with a cloth in order to test its character. The picador weakens the bull by stabbing it with lances in its neck.

Montera
head covering

Corbatín
similar to tie

Camisa (shirt)
always white,
decorated with lace

Capote de paseo
(cape) usually with
religious motifs

Taleguilla (pants)

Medias (stocking)
traditionally pink

Zapatillas (shoes)
specials soles to
prevent slipping

»Picador« (lancer)

Appears in phase 2. His pants
are made of leather and he
wears iron boots. The horse is
protected by thick padding. Its
eyes are bound to suppress the
natural instinct to flee.

»Banderillero«

Appears in pase 3. He plunges
the »banderillas« (3cm/1in
long hooked spears, decorated
with ribbons) into the bull's
neck. Wears clothing woven
with silver threads.

▶ **Protest movement**
SBullfights are very
controversial in Spain as
well. The lack of interest
and active protest are
growing more and
more. Animal protection
organizations have
been fighting to get
bullfighting banned
for a long time.

Ban on bullfighting
Canary Islands: since 1991
Catalonia: since 2012

Change of opinion
Spain 1980–2002

	opponents	proponents
'02	**69 %**	**31 %**
'99	68	32
'93	62	38
'92	68	32
'87	62	48
'85	51	49
'80	53	46

50 %

The trend against is
clearly stronger. The
difference between
men and women is
only very small.

3 **»Suerte de banderilleros«**

The banderillo stabs
three pairs of
banderillas into the
bull's neck muscles in
order to weakn it
further.

4 **»Suerte de matar«**

The matador fends
the bull off with a
red cloth. As soon as
the bull lowers its
head he places the
final stab into the
neck with his
dagger.

*Setenil It is 18km/10mi from Ronda to Setenil, a little town in a fantastic setting in a valley that has been carved out by a river. It is dominated by a Gothic church. Far more interesting, however, are the numerous homes built into the rocks.

*Serranía de Ronda The barren rocky mountains of the Serranía de Ronda stretch to the south-east of Ronda. Iberian ibex and royal eagles still live in Sierra de las Nieves, an area placed under nature conservation that is only accessible over a poor road. The Spanish fir tree, an ancient type of conifer, is native here. Take an excursion and discover picturesque villages like Yunquera or Tolox.

Insider Tip

Júzcar In 2011 a hamlet about 21km/13mi south of Ronda made the news: Júzcar – *el pueblo pitufo*, the Smurf village. Until then this little village of white-washed houses, situated in forest-covered mountains, was a

Júzcar – Smurf Village

quiet and peaceful place that hardly a tourist happened upon. But all of that changed overnight when the 221 residents along with their mayor gave in to the pressure of an advertising agency in Madrid and painted all of their 180 houses blue within two weeks in order to make publicity for the premiere of the Hollywood film »The Smurfs« in August 2011. In December 2011 the mayor had the village, which overnight had become a popular tourist attraction, vote on whether it should remain blue. The majority said yes – and still do.

Gaucín

Drive from Ronda towards Marbella, follow the A-369 just outside of town for an excursion deep into the Serranía. After just 30km/18mi comes the picturesque mountain village Gaucín, where many artists live who like to open their studios on weekends.

✱ Sanlúcar de Barrameda

✦ C 8

Province: Cádiz
Altitude : 0–30m/100ft
Population: 66,500

Sanlúcar is the home of the bone-dry Manzanilla wine that comes exclusively from the local bodegas and can hold its own against its much better-known rival from Jerez de la Frontera, sherry. But Sanlúcar is also famous nation-wide for its seafood specialties – which, in turn, go wonderfully with Manzanilla.

History

Taken from the Moors in 1246, Sanlúcar de Barrameda was the seat of the dukes of Medina Sidonia and the port for Seville. It is from here that **Christopher Columbus** embarked on his third voyage to America in May 1498. **Hernán Cortes** also sailed from here to the New World and finally, coming from Seville, **Fernão de Magalhães** (Magellan) set off in 1519 from Sanlúcar on the first circumnavigation of the globe.

WHAT TO SEE IN SANLÚCAR DE BARRAMEDA

Orientation

Sanlúcar consists of three parts. The Barrio Alto, the historic old town, lies on the heights, while the Bajo de Guía, the fishing and restaurant quarter, is below on the waterfront. The Barrio Bajo (lower town), with Calle Ancha and Calle de San Juan meeting at Plaza del Cabildo, forms a hinge between the two. This is where the tourists and locals flock to the bars in the evenings. There is a market every morning on the adjoining Plaza de San Roque.

Sanlúcar de Barrameda

INFORMATION
Oficina de Turismo
Calzada del Ejército, s/n,
E-11540 Sanlúcar de Barrameda
Tel. 956 36 61 10
www.aytosanlucar.org
Mon – Fri 8.30pm – 2.30pm

EVENTS
Feria de la Manzanilla
End of May

Romería del Rocío
At Whitsun, the pilgrims cross the Guadalquivir from here (►MARCO POLO Insight »Three Days of Commotion and Devotion« p.368).

Carreras de Caballo de Sanlúcar de Barrameda
This is a must-see – at least for anyone in Andalucía in August. These horse races held on the beaches of Sanlúcar are among the most spectacular events in Andalucía. The exact times are determined by the changing tides, so ask in the tourist office or check the internet at www.carrerasanlucar.com.

Exaltación al Río Guadalquivir
Boat procession in praise of the river.

WHERE TO EAT
Mirador de Doñana €€€€
Bajo de Guía
Tel. 956 36 42 05
One of the best addresses in the town. Fish and seafood are served on the terrace with a wonderful view of the Guadalquivir and the national park on the opposite bank.

Casa Balbino €€€€
Plaza del Cabildo, 11
Tel. 956 36 05 13
The fantastic selection of tapas here will win you over (the tortillas with crabs are delicious) and the many varieties of Manzanilla – a must in Sanlúcar.

Casa Juan €€€€ **Insider Tip**
Bajo de Guía
Tel. 956 36 26 95
Low-cost option among the restaurants that line the Guadalquivir with a terrace facing the sea. Good paella with seafood

WHERE TO STAY
Posada del Palacio €€
Caballeros, 9-11
Tel. 956 36 48 40
www.posadadelpalacio.com, 34 rooms
Posada means inn, but the name is deceptive; the hotel in the town centre is situated in a 17th century nobleman's palace.

Los Helechos €
Pl. Madre de Dios, 9
Tel. 956 36 13 49
www.hotelloshelechos.com, 56 rooms
Near the old city this hotel offers pleasant and tasteful accommodation. Two

Not found everywhere: turf on the beach at Sanlúcar

inner courtyards make for light and Andalusian atmosphere.

restaurant (meat, fish, hamburgers, pizza).

Tartaneros €

Tartaneros, 8
Tel. 956 38 53 78
Fax 956 38 59 94, 22 rooms
Charming Art Nouveau gem in the town centre. Delicious cocktails in the café and the hotel recently opened its own

La Española €

In Chipiona, Isaac Peral, 4
Tel. 956 37 37 71
www.hotellaespanola.com, 21 rooms
Pretty hotel in the centre of town. The restaurant serves good Andalusian cooking.

From Plaza de San Roque – passing on the left-hand side the small church of the Holy Trinity with its magnificent 15th-century artesonado ceiling – climb up C. Bretones to the old town hill, passing by the so-called **Covachas**, part of the late Gothic façade of the palace of the dukes of Medina Sidonia, consisting of ten arches adorned with mythical creatures.

On the top to the right of C. Caballeros is the Palacio de Orléans y Borbón, now the town hall, which was constructed in the middle of the 19th century for Antonio de Orléans and his wife. Heading left to

*Nuestra Señora de la O

the Church of Nuestra Señora de la O founded by Isabel de Cerda in 1360. It appears nondescript on the outside, except for its magnificent Mudéjar portal, but this is a hint of the richness of the decoration inside. The tile-covered interior is richly decorated with plaster work and has a splendid panelled Renaissance ceiling. The Capilla Mayor, in which the high altar by Esquivel (18th century) stands, is no less beautifully painted.

The **Capilla del Sagrario** to the left with its open-work dome also has magnificent paintings.

Palacio de los Duques de Medina Sidonia
The Palacio de los Duques de Medina Sidonia adjacent to the church is the residence of the Dukes of Medina Sidonia. It was begun in the 16th and extended in the 17th century.

❶ Tours: Sunday 11.30am, 12.30pm, admission €5, café on the patio

Castillo de Santiago
Go past Bodegas Antonio Barbadillo to Castillo de Santiago (13th–15th century), the castle of the dukes of Medina Sidonia that towers above the old town. The castle commands a marvellous view of the old town and the Coto de Doñana National Park on the opposite bank of the Guadalquivir.

Barrio Bajo
There are two further interesting churches in C. de Santo Domingo in Barrio Bajo: Santo Domingo with the tomb of Medina Sidonia (17th century) and San Francisco, whose façade was donated by the English king Henry VIII.

The lower town of Sanlúcar de Barrameda, called **Bajo de Guía**, stretches along the mouth of the river. There is a row of fish restaurants here. They procure their wares from the fish auction that is held workdays around 5pm 4km/2.5mi up the river at the port of Bonanza – well worth a visit. Columbus and Magellan both set sail from there.

Bajo de Guía is also a good place for an excursion by boat into ▶Coto de Doñana national park. First obtain information in the **Fábrica de Hielo** (with a large exhibition on nature and history, films, and an observation terrace), and then cruise along the opposite bank with the Real Fernando. This cruise lasts about four hours and includes two stops on land.

Tickets in the Fábrica de Hielo; departures: daily 10am, June – Sept also at 5pm; March, April, May, Oct. also at 4pm; www.visitasdonana.com.

Manzanilla wine tasting   **Insider Tip**

Manzanilla can be sampled at: Bodega Antonio Barbadillo with its Manzanilla museum near to the castle (Luís de Eguilaz, 11; www.barbadillo.com; tours in English Tue – Sat 11am) Bodega Delgado Zuleta, whose Manzanilla »La Goya« was served at the wedding of the crown prince and his bride (street towards Chipiona km 1.5; www.delgadozuleta.com).

A very nice bar in Barrio Bajo

AROUND SANLÚCAR DE BARRAMEDA

Wide and fine beaches for swimming stretch to the south-west all the way to the seaside resort of **Chipiona**, which is very popular with the Andalusians. Full of action on the weekends, rather tranquil during the week, Chipiona has been able to avoid the ugly concrete developments of the Costa del Sol until now, making do with lower blocks of flats, though they are constantly multiplying. Waves from the Atlantic roll in on the most beautiful beach, Playa de Regla, which stretches south of the lighthouse. Activities on the beach can be spoiled, however, by the constantly whistling wind and the fine sand. At the end of the beach, almost on the edge of the breakers, stands the church of Santuario Nuestra Señora de la Regla, which enshrines a miraculous image venerated by seamen.

Plaza de España with the tile-adorned church of Nuestra Señora de la O in the heart of Chipiona turns out to be a cosy little place. There is even a castle. The inhabitants of Chipiona are very proud of their lighthouse; built in 1867. With a height of 69m/226ft, it is **Spain's tallest lighthouse**.

** Sevilla (Seville)

✦ C/D 7

Province: Seville
Altitude: 8m/26ft
Population: 704,200

Seville is one of the hottest places on the European mainland. No wonder that the city wakes up only when elsewhere everybody is already in bed – the nights in Seville, making the rounds of the bars, one after the other, are an experience. Although there is by no means dancing and singing everywhere, as the cliché would have it, Seville is still undoubtedly the most Andalusian of all cities. This is still apparent in the old and traditional quarters.

Even if Seville cannot match the Moorish heritage of ▶Córdoba or ▶Granada, the synthesis of Muslim and Christian architecture was most convincing here, as can be seen and admired in the cathedrals and Alcázar built in Moorish style for the Christian king Pedro the Cruel. This wealth of superb artistic and cultural monuments from all eras of the city's lively history certainly justifies the old saying »Quien no ha visto Sevilla, no ha visto maravilla« – »He who has not seen Seville, has not seen a miracle«. Seville is the birthplace of the painters **Diego Velázquez** (1599–1660) and **Bartolomé Esteban Murillo** (1617– 1682). Plaques commemorate scenes from Cervantes' works. **Seville is well-known as a backdrop for operas:** Mozart's *Don Juan* and *The Marriage of Figaro* as well as Bizet's *Carmen* were set here, and several streets vie for recognition as the site of the shop in Rossini's *The Barber of Seville*. Here is where the Río Guadalquivir reaches the Andalusian lowlands and flows through this, the capital of Andalucía and Spain's fourth-largest city. Although almost 100km/60mi from the sea, the tide is still noticeable here, allowing large sea-going vessels to enter the harbour outside the city.

For Seville has another side: an industrial city that produces foodstuffs, textiles and metal products. Yet another aspect is that of a city with over a million people surrounded by a belt of, to some extent,

Capital of Andalucía

> ! **Not too late!** **Insider Tip**
>
> MARCO ⬤ POLO TIP
>
> Anyone who wants to be in Seville for the Semana Santa or the Feria de Abril should book well in advance. And don't be surprised at the hefty holiday surcharges.

The semi-circular Plaza de España in Sevilla is one of the highlights of Spanish urban design

An institution: El Rinconcillo

lished in 1939 is fish and seafood.
Attentive service

❼ *El Rinconcillo* €€ Insider Tip
Gerona, 40 and Alhóndiga, 2
Tel. 954 22 31 83
www.elrinconcillo.es
Bar with a long tradition: since 1670 –
meet here at the bar and chat under
a ceiling of smoked hams.

❷ *Sol y Sombra* €€
Castilla, 151; tel. 954 33 39 35
www.tabernasolysombra.com
The tapas bar in a house from 1861 is
one of the best in the city. They also
serve many kinds of omelettes.

WHERE TO STAY
❶ *Alfonso XIII* €€€€
San Fernando, 2
Tel. 954 91 70 00
www.hotel-alfonsoxiii-sevilla.com
146 rooms
Grand hotel of the luxury class, built
for the World's Fair of 1929, flagship
of the Andalusian hotel industry and
very expensive. This is where the Spanish
king and queen stay when they visit
Seville; other crowned heads are also
among the guests.

❻ *Las Casas de la Judería* €€€€
Cp. Santa María la Blanca, 5
Tel. 954 41 51 50

www.casasypalacios.com; 118 rooms
Almost a district in its own right in the
Barrio de Santa Cruz; this enchanting
city hotel has stylish rooms and fountain
courtyards. It is comprised of several of
the Duque de Béjar's houses, connected
to each other by patios and arcaded
walkways.

❼ Patio de la Cartuja €€€€
Lumbreras, 8 – 10
Tel. 954 90 02 00
www.patiosdesevilla.com
56 apartments.
A small pearl away from all the grand
luxury at the north end of Alameda de
Hércules; classy, comfortably and simply
furnished, spacious apartments grouped
around a central patio.

❺ Un Patio en Santa Cruz €€
Doncellas, 15; Tel. 954 53 94 13
www.patiosantacruz.com; 13 rooms
Small, but tastefully furnished rooms in
Barrio de Santa Cruz. Wonderful view
from the roof terrace of the cathedral.
Request a room facing the street since

the ones facing the courtyard only
have small windows.

❷ Simón €€
García de Vinuesa, 19
Tel. 954 22 66 60
www.hotelsimonsevilla.com, 29 rooms
Traditional, house with a family atmo-
sphere not far from the cathedral.
Charming inner courtyard, individually
furnished rooms.

❹ Los Seises €€
Segovias, 6
Tel. 954 22 94 95
www.hotellosseises.com, 42 rooms
Architectural gem from the 16th century
with tasteful interior in close vicinity to
the cathedral. The Giralda can be seen
from the roof terrace.

❸ Europa €
Jimios, 5, Tel. 954 21 43 05
www.hoteleuropasevilla.com 16 rooms
Stylish 18th-century house between
Plaza Nueva and the cathedral with
a pretty patio.

** CATEDRAL DE SANTA MARÍA DE LA SEDE

The cathedral was built between 1402 and 1506 on the site of the
main Moorish mosque. The Visigoths had already built a church here
on top of a Roman temple that the Moors left untouched for a long
time. It was not until 1172 that the Almohads began building the
grand mosque in its place. The Giralda and the Court of the Oranges
are all that remain of it today. At first, the Christians only slightly remodelled the mosque, but when it became unsafe after an earthquake, it was decided to build a new church. It is not known who
originally drew up the plans for the cathedral. The first known master
builder was the Fleming Isambret, and among his successors were
Pedro de Toledo, Simón and Alfonso Rodriguez, Jean Norman and
Simon of Cologne. After the dome collapsed in 1511, Enrique de
Egas and Gil de Hontañon constructed a new one. On 18 March
1995, Elena María Isabel Dominica of Silos Bourbon and Greece –

Sevilla

ISLA DE
LA CARTUJA

Río Guadalquivir

26

Convento de
San Clemento

C. de Becquer

Hospital Regional
Muralla

Calatrava

Convento de
Santa Clara

7

San Lorenzo

C. de Juan Rabadan

Baños
Parlamento
de Andalucia

San Vicente

Alameda
de
Hercules

Relator

Mercado

San Luis

LA MACARENA

Castellar

9

Ronda de Capuchinos

3

4

5

7

6

8

CENTRO

Metropol
Parasol

Casa de la
Condesa de
Lebrija

10

Estación
de Autobuses

Huelva, Itálica

Marqués

Canalejas

Católicos

Reyes

Zaragoza

Imagen

11

12

13

7

Pl. Ponce
de León

Córdoba

Estación Santa Justa

15

1

14

Plaza
Nueva

Pl. S.
Francisco

3

3

4

16

17

18

19

20

4

21

Sta. Cruz

5

SANTA
CRUZ

6

TRIANA

Santa Ana

Pagés

Puente de Isabel II

Río Guadalquivir

Plaza
de Cuba

Plaza
de Toros

2

Avenida de Constitución

Dos de Mayo

27

28

Catedral

5

Pl.
Triunfo

24

25

Alcázar

Jardines
del Alcázar

Demetrio de los Ríos

6

Estación
de Cádiz

Granada, Málaga

29

EL ARENAL

Puerta de
Jerez

1

Universidad
(Fábrica de
Tábacos)

6

Pl. de
D. Juan
de Austria

31

Puente
San Telmo

Juan Sebastián Elcano

30

Palos
de la
Frontera

Glorieta
S. Diego

Av. de Carlos V

200 m

©BAEDEKER

LOS
REMEDIOS

Av. de la República Argentina

Asunción

Museo Arqueológico
Jerez

Paseo de las Delicias

Av. de María Luisa

32

Av. de Isabel
la Católica

Capitania
General
Museo de Artes
y Costumbres
Ponulares

Av. de Portugal

Plaza de
España

Dr. Pedro
de Castro

1 Puerto Macarena	9 Casa de las Dueñas	18 Casa de Pilatos	25 Archivo de Indias
2 Basílica de la Macarena	10 Museo de Bellas Artes	19 Museo del Baile Flamenco	26 Museo de Arte Contemporáneo
3 Omnium Sanctorum	11 Universidad Vieja	20 Monolitos Romanos	27 Teatro La Maestranza
4 Santa Marina	12 San Pedro	21 Santa María La Blanca	28 Hospital de la Caridad
5 San Julián	13 Santa Catalina	22 Acueducto	29 Torre del Oro (Museo Marítimo)
6 Convento de Santa Paula	14 Ayuntamiento	23 Palacio Arzobispal	30 Palacio San Telmo
7 Santa Isabel	15 San Salvador	24 Hospital de los Venerables	31 Estación de Autobuses
8 San Marcos	16 Convento de San Leandro		32 Teatro Lope de Vega
	17 San Illdefonso		

Where to eat

❶ Bodega Góngora
❷ Sol y Sombra
❸ Taberna de Alabardero
❹ Casa Robles
❺ Bar Giralda
❻ Egaña Oriza
❼ El Rinconcillo

Where to stay

❶ Alfonso XIII
❷ Simón
❸ Europa
❹ Los Seises
❺ Un Patio en Santa Cruz
❻ Las Casas de la Judería
❼ Patio de la Cartuja

the eldest child of the Spanish royal couple – married the aristocratic financier Jaime de Marichalar in the cathedral of Seville.

Among the richly decorated doorways **Puerta del Bautismo** (portal of baptism) and **Puerta del Nacimiento** (portal of birth) to the left and right of **Puerta Mayor** on the west façade are especially worthy of note. The figures in its tympanums by Lorenzo Mercadante and Pedro Millán represent the birth and baptism of Jesus and Sevillian patron saints in vestments. **Puerta del Perdón** with its horseshoe arch is to the left on the north side. On the east side are **Puerta de Oriente, Puerta de los Palos**, a the relief of the adoration of the Magi by Perrin, as well as **Puerta de las Campanillas**, with the procession into Jerusalem by the same artist. P**uerta de San Cristóbal**, dating from the 19th century, also called **Puerta de la Lonja**, opens into the southern transept.

Exterior view (portals)

Between Puerta de los Palos and Puerta de Oriente on the north side of the cathedral the Giralda, built 1184–1196 as a **minaret of the grand mosque**, reaches for the sky. It is the **symbol** of Seville. The architects Ahmed ibn-Basso and Ali al-Gomara set their towering brick structure on a Roman base. It is covered by sebka, a rhombus pattern, and punctuated by gemel windows with columned capitals taken from the palace of ►Medina Azahara. In Moorish times, the tower was capped by four gilded copper globes until the belfry was

The belfry was only added to the Giralda in 1568

set on it in 1568. This consisted of a casement with 24 bells and the »Matrarca«, a wooden pendant with clappers used during Holy Week instead of bells. A 4m/13ft-high weathervane »Giraldillo«, a female figure by Bartolomé Morel personifying faith holding Constantine's banner, crowns the tip of the 97m/318ft-high Giralda (the word means literally »it turns«, a reference to the weathervane). A gently rising ramp, 2.50m/8ft wide so that two horse-riders can ascend side-by-side, leads up to the gallery at a height of 70m/230ft where there is a splendid view of the rooftops of Seville.

The Puerta del Perdón and Puerta de Oriente lead to the **Patio de los Naranjos** (Court of the Oranges). The cathedral chapter library, founded in the 13th century, is in the east wing. The **Sagrario** forms the west end of the Court of Oranges. Parts of the earlier Visigothic church have been uncovered in the Capilla de la Granada in the south-east corner of the court. In the same corner is the horseshoe arch opening of the Puerta de Lagarta (Lizard Gate), so named because of the wooden crocodile mounted above it. Here is the entrance to the interior of the cathedral.

Interior of the cathedral   The interior is Spain's most impressive Gothic church. The clarity of its proportions and the beauty of its lines stand out particularly. Lighting and mirrors allow an exact study of the vault construction and its decoration. Among the 75 **stained glass windows** dating from the 16th to the 19th centuries the most notable are those by Enrique Alemán (1478–1483) in the Capilla de San José, by the Flemish Arnao de Vergara (1525–1538; *Virgin of Mercy*); and by his country-

Catedral de Sevilla

12 Capilla Real
13 Sacristy
14 Puerta de las Campanillas
   (Gate of the Little Bells)
15 Contaduría Mayor
16 Sala Capitular
17 Antecabildo
18 Sacristía Mayor
19 Sacristía de los Cálices
   (Sacristy of the Chalices)
20 Puerta de San Cristóbal
   (Puerta de la Lonja)
21 Dependencias de la Hermandad
   Sacramental
22 Capilla de Santa Ana
23 Capilla de San Laureano
24 Puerta del Nacimiento
25 Gravestone of Fernando
   Colón
26 Coro
27 Capilla Mayor
28 Sacristía Alta
29 Capilla de San Antonio
30 Capilla de Escalas
31 Capilla de Santiago
32 Capilla Sacramental
33 Capilla de San Francisco
34 Capilla de las Doncellas
35 Capilla de los Evangelistas
36 Capilla del Pilar
37 Capilla de San Pedro
38 Capilla de la Concepcíon Grande
39 Capilla del Mariscal
40 Antesala (vestíbule)
41 Capilla de San Andrés
42 Capilla de Dolores
43 Funerary monument to Columbus
44 Capilla de la Antigua
45 Capilla de San Hermenegildo
46 Capilla de San José

1 Puerta Mayor
2 Puerta del Bautismo
2a Giraldillo
3 Sagrario
4 Puerta del Perdón
5 Biblioteca Colombina
6 Puerta de Oriente
7 Capilla de la Granada
   (Pomegranate Chapel)
8 Puerta del Lagarto
   (Lizard Gate)
9 Giralda
10 Puerta de los Palos
11 Sala Capitular

man Arnao de Flandes (1525–1557; in the Capilla de los Evangelistas). Go diagonally right from the Lizard Gate to the **choir**. The **Capilla Mayor** adjoining beyond the crossing is enclosed on three sides by magnificent ironwork by Fray Francisco de Salamanca, Sancho Muñoz and Bartolomé de Jaén. Here the mighty **retable** towers above everything.

The **Capilla Real** in the axis with the Capilla Mayor terminates the nave. The 38m/125ft-long Renaissance building was built from 1551 to 1575 on the site of the old royal sepulchral chapel by Martín Gainza, Hernán Ruiz and Juan de Madea and completed in 1773 with latticework upon which Ferdinand is depicted being presented with the keys to Seville. The decorative pieces include paintings by Cano and

** *Largest Gothic Cathedral*

At the wish of the cathedral chapter it was supposed to be so big that
»they call us (the capitulars) mad«. It worked: at 115m/380ft in length,
74m/244ft in width and a height of 40m/132ft where the aisles cross it
became the largest gothic church in the world.

❶ Mon – Sat 11am – 5pm, July / Aug
9.30am – 4pm; Sun 2.30pm – 6pm;
admission: €8

❶ Giralda
It was built as a minaret for the main
mosque of 1184 – 1196.

❷ Gallery
The observation deck is at 70m/230ft.

❸ Well
The octagonal well is the remains of
a Muslim midhâ, a well used for religious washing rituals.

❹ Library
The collection of the library of the cathedral chapter, which was founded in
the 13th century, includes manuscripts
by Columbus and the Bible of Alfonso
the Wise.

❺ Sagrario
The Sagrario (1618–1662), a Baroque
building, houses a retable with a *De-*
scent from the Cross by Pedro Roldán.

❻ Church aisle
Théophile Gautier describes the five-
aisled sanctuary like this: »Notre Dame
of Paris could walk with its head held
high down the centre aisle.«

❼ Choir
The choir is closed off by a screen
(1519) ; the Gothic choir stalls are from
1475 – 1479. The Capilla de la Concepción Chica on the south wall has the

La Cieguecita (The Blind Woman), a
wooden sculpture of the Virgin Mary.

❽ Capilla Mayor
Here the retable dominates; with
a height of 23m/80ft and width of
20m/66ft it is the largest altar picture
in the world.

❾ Capilla Real
In front of the retable with the picture
Virgen de los Reyes (13th cent.) in a sil-
ver shrine made in 1729 are the bones
of Ferdinand III the Holy, to the left is
Ferdinand's son Alfonso X the Wise, to
the right is Ferdinand's wife Beatrice of
Swabia.

❿ Sacristía Mayor
It holds most valauable art objects,
including the keys to Seville (1248),
a reliquary of Alfonso X shaped like a
triptych (Tablas Alfonsinas), a cross relic belonging to St Helena, the bronze
candelabra Tenebrario by Bartolomé
Morel and the painting Descent from
the Cross by Pedro de Campana.

⓫ Capilla de San Antonio
Here are the paintings *Baptism of*
Christ and *The Christ Child Appears*
to St Anthony of Padua by Murillo,
among others.

⓬ Capilla de Santiago
In this chapel art works including a picture of St James by Juan de Roelas and
a picture by Valdés Leal (*St Lawrence*)
can be seen.

The Pa
was onc

Murillo, among others, as well as flags, swords and even a finger of St Ferdinand. The crypt can be reached from the Capilla Real, where Pedro the Cruel, his mistress María de Padilla, and several Infante are buried. The statuette of the Virgen de las Batallas (14th century) can also be seen here. It is supposed to have led St. Ferdinand into battle. The Capilla de San Pedro left next to the Capilla Real holds a retable by Zurbarán with nine scenes from the life of St Peter. To the right of the Capilla Real is the entrance to the oval **Sala Capitular** (1530–1592), which is completely dominated by Murillo's painting of the Immaculate Conception.

The ***Sacristía Mayor** is a magnificent 16th-century structure by Diego de Riaño and Diego de Siloé with a beautiful domed ceiling. Next to the Sacristía Mayor in the **Sacristía de los Cálices**, built in 1529, there are numerous paintings of particular interest, including Goya's St Justa and Rufina, Morales' Pietà, Valdés Leal's The Three Kings and Murillo's Holy Family. The famous crucifix by Martínez Montañés is also a demonstration of great skill.

Whether or not the famous explorer's remains are actually in the **tomb of Christopher Columbus** was questioned for a long time because the body was taken on a veritable odyssey. After his death in 1506, he was first buried near Seville; then, however, the body was taken to Santo Domingo on Haïti in 1596, and after Spain lost Haïti it was transferred to Havanna on Cuba, where in 1892 the tomb created by Arturo Mélida was erected in the cathedral. But when Cuba was also lost in the Spanish-American war of 1898, the tomb was brought to its present location. Recently carried out DNA tests of the bones show that these really are the remains of Columbus.

Particularly noteworthy among the **side chapels** are the Capilla de la Virgen de la Antigua (to the right of Columbus' tomb) on the site of the former mihrâb of the mosque with the fresco of the Virgin and the Renaissance tomb of Archbishop Diego Hurtado de Mendoza, a work of the Italian Domenico Fancelli from 1509; followed by the Capilla de San Hermenegild with the Gothic tomb of Archbishop Juan de Cervantes of Lorenzo Mercadante and a Zurbarán painting. Further sights are the Altar del Ángel de la Guarda at the left pillar of Puerta Mayor, named after the famous painting of the guardian angel Raphael by Murillo (1666); then, set in the floor opposite Puerta Mayor, the gravestone of Fernán Colón, Christopher Columbus' illegitimate son.

Of the chapels on the north wall, the first next to the Giraldillo, Capilla de San Antonio, is interesting; followed by the Capilla de Santiago, and then the picture of the *Virgen de Belén* by Alonso Cano at the Puerta de los Naranjos. Finally, beyond the gate, is the Capilla de los Evangelistas.

❶ Mon – Sat 11am – 5pm, Juliy/ Aug 9.30am – 4pm; Sun 2.30pm – 6pm; admission: €8

BETWEEN THE CATHEDRAL AND ALCÁZAR

The Giralda side of the cathedral gives onto Plaza de la Virgen de los Reyes, the north side of which is taken up by the Baroque Palacio Arzobispal (archbishop's palace).

Palacio Arzobispal

The conspicuous building to the right in front of the Alcázar on Plaza del Triunfo is the severely rectangular Casa Lonja, built from 1583 to 1598 and designed by Juan de Herrera in high Renaissance style to house the stock market that was held prior to that in the Court of Oranges. Since 1781 the first floor has been home to the ***Archivo General de Indias,** which preserves **close to 40,000 Spanish documents about the discovery and conquest of the Americas and the Philippines**. Among them are documents in the hands of Magellan, Pizarro and Cortés, Columbus' diary and the street plans of places founded by Spanish conquerors in the New World – a treasure trove not only for researchers, as the most valuable pieces are on display in cabinets or shown in videos.

*Casa Lonja

❶ Mon – Sat 9.30am – 4.45pm, Sun 10am – 1.45pm; free admission; guided tours 12 noon and 1pm

** **REAL ALCÁZAR

The Alcázar located directly opposite the cathedral was originally one of the castles of the Moorish rulers, who worked on it continuously from the 9th century. After Ferdinand III took Seville, the Christian kings moved in. Pedro the Cruel (1350–1369) then decided to have royal accommodation built for his mistress, María de Padilla. He brought Moorish architects and craftsmen come from allied Granada and Toledo, who created the most splendid example of Mudéjar architecture in Spain, the palace section today named after him. The Catholic Monarchs remodelled some rooms and an extension was added under Charles V.

❶ April – Sept daily 9.30am – 7pm; Oct – March daily 9.30am – 5pm, royal rooms: daily 10am – 1.30pm; admission: €9.50

The Puerta del León on Plaza del Triunfo is an entrance through the high walls surrounding the Alcázar leading into the Patio del León. The patio is planted with oranges and flowers and its wall foundations in part date back to Almohad times.

Patio del León

To the left are the Salón de Justicia, built under Alfonso XI in 1330 and, behind it, the Patio de Yeso, »Plaster Patio«, which owes its name to the plaster ornamentation and building elements of the gallery and its seven arches, which in part were taken from the Medina Azahara.

Patio de Yeso

Alcázar of Sevilla

©BAEDEKER

Jardínes del Alcázar

Patio de las Doncellas

Patio de
Crucero

Patio de
la Montería

Patio de las
Banderas

Patio
del
León

N

Palace of Pedro
the Cruel

1 Puerta del León
2 Salón de Justicia
3 Patio de Yeso
4 Cuarto del Almirante
5 Stair to the royal
  chambers on the
  upper floor
6 Pasillo
7 Dormitorio de los Reyes moros

8 Patio de las Muñecas
9 Sala de los Príncipes
10 Apartments of the
   Catholic Monarchs
11 Bedchamber of Philip II
12 Salón de Embajadores
13 Comedor
14 Apartments of
   María de Padilla

15 Salón Carlos V
16 Capilla
17 Salón de Tapices
18 Salón del Emperador
19 Baños de María de Padilla
20 Galería de los Grotescos
21 Puerta de Marchena
22 Coach house

Straight ahead is the Patio del León on the spacious Patio de la Montería, once the forecourt to the private chambers of the Almohads and gathering place for hunting parties and used under the Christians as a parade ground. World history was made in both of the lower rooms of the right wing. Here, in the so-called **Cuarto del Almirante**, Isabella the Catholic negotiated the contract with Columbus that made his voyage of discovery possible, and it was here that she received him after his second voyage. The Casa de Contratación, the chamber solely responsible for the trade with – to be more exact the exploitation of – the New World, had its seat here from 1503. Decorated with tapestries, portraits of mariners and a beautiful coffered ceiling, the rooms are used today for official occasions. Alejo Fernández' painting of the Virgen de los Navigantes, the patron saint of seamen, hangs in the back room. Left, next to the door to the admiralty rooms, is a magnificent stairway – usually blocked – that leads up to chambers of the Catholic Monarchs.

Patio de la Montería

The stunning façade of the palace of Pedro the Cruel completes the enclosure of the courtyard. The entrance is between two multi-foiled cusped arches. Above it, after a row of sebeka pattern, two gemel windows and a triplet window, followed by a Latin inscription in praise of Pedro, a blue ceramic ribbon with Kufic script proclaims »There is no conqueror but Allah« – the Christian king apparently could not read Arabic.

**Palace of Pedro the Cruel

Turn left in the anteroom, the Pasillo, and go down a narrow passage into ****Patio de las Doncellas** (Patio of the Maidens), the enchanting centre of the palace. Built from 1369 to 1379, it features fantastic cusped arches and open-work upper walls supported by 52 marble columns, plus azulejo tiling and plaster ornaments. The fanciful décor and forms are reminiscent of the Alhambra in Granada. In the 16th century, Renaissance-style round arches were put up in the gallery. When facing the west wall, the Salón de Carlos V can be seen to the left, furnished with a magnificent coffered ceiling; to the right is the wonderfully tiled Dormitorio de los Reyes moros, where, despite the name, the Moorish kings did not sleep.

Straight ahead is the entrance to the ****Salón de los Embajadores** (the Ambassadors' Room). This, the oldest and most beautiful room in the Alcázar, is laid out over two floors and covered by a stunning stalactite dome of cedar wood from 1420. A row of frescoes under the dome displays portraits of Spanish kings from the times of the Visigoths to Philip II, but what makes the room unique is the sheer exuberance of the Arabic script and the geometric patterns of larch wood and plaster on the azulejos radiating in the warm, yellow-gold light. The room was witness to the marriage of Charles V with the Portuguese heiress to the throne, Isabella, in the year 1526. Consummately executed horseshoe arches open the room on three sides to the

Arabic writing and azulejos with geometric patterns decorate the Salón de los Embajadores most beautifully

adjoining rooms that almost match the splendour of the Salón de los Embajadores. Straight ahead runs the elongated Comedor, Philip II's dining room, with a carved ceiling by Juan de Simancas. To the right and through Philip II's bedchambers is the idyllic little **Patio de las Muñecas** (Patio of Dolls), which takes its name from the doll-like faces in the spandrels between the arcade arches. It was the centre of the private royal chambers. Many of the building elements here are also from Medina Azahara. It leads directly into the Sala de los Príncipes where Juan, the only son of the Catholic Monarchs, was born. Left of the Patio of Dolls are the bedchambers of the Catholic Monarchs with their very beautiful artesonado ceilings. The chambers are in turn connected to the Comedor. To the left of the Salón de los Embajadores, Pedro the Cruel had two chambers furnished for his favourite, María de Padilla. She was the reason he held his lawful wife, Doña Blanca de Borbón, prisoner in ►Medina Sidonia.

Palacio de Carlos V

Left of the Patio de la Montería and through the Patio del Crucero is Charles I's (or Charles V's, ►Famous People) palace, whose great halls effuse the coolness of Renaissance style. The twelve impressive

*Brussels tapestries that hang there depict the siege of Tunis by imperial and royal Spanish troops in 1535. They were made by Willem Pannemaker in 1554 to designs by Jan Vermeyen, who was an eyewitness to the campaign. The private chapel is richly decorated with tiles.

The Alcázar gardens unite in a remarkable way Islamic and Renaissance horticulture – on the one hand the play of forms and colours of the plants, water courses and grottoes, on the other, the rigour manifested in the geometry of the layout. A stroll through the flowers leads to the old baths, to the Galería de los Grotescos at the large decorative pool with a bronze Mercury in the middle and, next to it, the Plateresque Puerta de Marchena from one of the palaces of the dukes of Arcos. In the middle of the spacious grounds stands the Pabellón de Carlos V, erected by Juan Hernández in 1543.

**Gardens of the Alcázar

The royal stables, in which several coaches are on display, leads to the exit from the Alcázar and a square enclosed by white walls and shaded by orange trees, the Patio de las Banderas. The Patio of Flags originally was also a part of the Alcázar and served as an armoury courtyard.

Patio de las Banderas

*** BARRIO DE SANTA CRUZ**

Bordering directly to the east of the Alcázar is the Barrio de Santa Cruz, the Jewish quarter (Judería) in the times of the Moors and a perfect place to stroll about – even if some aspects of it seem too prettied-up. Meander through flower-covered squares, look in on shady patios, wander down C.jón del Agua, where the Roman aqueduct ran, or C. de Pimienta, where a pepper merchant once lived. In the evening, the quarter is one of the liveliest places in Seville.

The chapel in the 17th-century clerical hospice Hospital de los Venerables Sacerdotes has some notable works of art, including frescoes and paintings by Valdés Leal, an ivory figure of Christ by Alonso Cano, as well as sculptures and paintings by Roelas, Rubens and Sassoferrato.

Hospital de los Venerables Sacerdotes

❶ Daily 10am – 2pm, 4pm – 8pm, admission €4.75

C. Santa Teresa branches off to the right in front of the Iglesia de Santa Cruz, the largest church in the barrio. House no. 8 is thought to have been the home of the painter Bartolomé Esteban Murillo. Today it has been converted into a museum. Although it contains not a single painting, it presents **the painter's life**. The Convento de las Descalzas opposite was founded by Saint Teresa of Ávila.

Casa Murillo

❶ Tue – Sat 10am – 2pm

No one stays long in a bar – there are more to discover and the nights in Seville are long

Plaza de Santa Cruz
It is only a couple of steps from Murillo's house to the luxuriantly planted Plaza de Santa Cruz decorated in the centre by the La Criteria wrought-iron cross from 1692. Finally, at the eastern end of the barrio is the church of Santa María la Blanca, a synagogue until 1391; It has paintings on the underside of the dome and a Last Supper scene by Murillo.

BETWEEN THE CATHEDRAL AND PLAZA LA CAMPANA

*Ayunta-miento
Executions, tournaments and bullfights were held on Plaza de San Francisco north of the cathedral. The Ayuntamiento (city hall) rises on its west side, a stately Renaissance structure (1527–1564) by Diego de Riaño. The richly decorated façade is considered one of the most delightful creations in the Plateresque style. West of the city hall

lies Plaza Nueva with a sculpture of St Fernando on horseback, created by Joaquín Bilbao. Here the façade of the Ayuntamiento is in neo-classical style.

East of the city hall there is a new star in the heavens of flamenco: The **Museo del Baile Flamenco** uses the most modern technology to make flamenco, its origins and variations, and of course all the accessories like costumes and instruments audible and visible. The 18th cent. building is used for art exhibits and there is a flamenco shop.

❶ Rojas Marcos, 3; April–Oct. daily 9am until 7pm; admission: €10

C. Sierpes (snake street), the city's main shopping street, begins on the north side of the Plaza. It is vaunted as being especially elegant, but does not appear fundamentally different from the other pedestrian zones, although in the summer heat it gains its own atmosphere with the sunsail stretched crosswise high over the street. It ends at Plaza La Campana, where the tribunes for the Carerra Oficial, the grand procession during Semana Santa, Holy Week, are set up.

Tapas in Seville **Insider Tip**

The Barrio de Santa Cruz is a good place for tapas: **Cervecería Giralda** right next to the cathedral (C. Mateos Gago) **Casa Roman** on Plaza de los Venerables. But good places can also be found elsewhere in Seville. **El Rinconcillo,** founded in 1670 (C. Gerona, 50; see photo), claims to be the oldest pub in the city, and is worth a visit just to see the interior. The **Bodega Torre del Oro** (C. Scamander, 15) is a quaint cellar that fills up quickly, especially after a bullfight. The **Bodega Góngora** (C. Alvareda, 5) near C. Sierpes is well known for its fish tapas. La Lucama (C. Betis, 8) is an example of the many nice bodegas lined up along the waterfront street in La Triana quarter. Also in La Triana is the Bar **Sol y Sombra** (C. Castilla), where hams hanging from the ceiling give the place a special atmosphere.

San Salvador

C. Jovellanos Gállegos branches off to the right from C. Sierpes to the church of San Salvador. It is on the site of the only Friday mosque and was erected between 1671 and 1712. The bell tower on the base of the minaret was built in the 14th century. San Salvador is Seville's second-largest church after the cathedral, and its mighty dome over the crossing is especially impressive. Inside the huge Baroque retable, as well as works by Montañés (Ecce homo), Juan de Mesa (Cristo del Amor) and Murillo (also Ecce homo) are of particular interest.

Palacio Lebrija

In C. de la Cuna heading northward from the church house no. 8, Palacio Lebrija (16th century), is a beautiful example of a Sevillian aristocrat's house. Today a collection of Roman mosaics and archaeological finds from ▶Itálica, a nearby ruined city, are on display here.

❶ Mon–Fri 10.30am – 7.30pm, Sat 10am – 2pm, 4pm – 6pm, Sun 10am – 2pm, admission €8

Universidad Vieja	The church belonging to the old university (Universidad Vieja) – originally a Jesuit college, it became a university in 1502 – is a little to the right of Palacio Lebrija and possesses a large retable and paintings by Roelas, Alonso Cano and Pacheco, among others.

Metropol Parasol

On Plaza de la Encarnación north of the Old University remains of the Roman colony were already exavated in the 1990s. But much more spectacular is the gigantic mushroom-shaped roof over the area, designed by Jürgen H. Mayer. It covers not only the exacavtion site but also a new market hall and a shopping centre. On the mushroom-shaped roof there is a 250m/825ft-long catwalk at a height of 21–28m/70–93ft.

❶ Catwalk and observation point daily 10am – 2.30pm, 5pm – 10pm; admission: €2

**Museo de Bellas Artes

Insider Tip

The Museo de Bellas Artes can be reached by going down C. de Alfonso XII from Plaza La Campana towards the Guadalquivir. It has been housed since 1835 in the former Convento de la Merced (17th century). Its collections are the most important in Spain after those in the Prado in Madrid and encompass Spanish painting of the 17th and 18th centuries. Exhibited in a total of 14 rooms, the most magnificent being the former convent church with its decorative paintings, are Francisco de Zurbarán's *St Jerome*, Saint Bruno *Visiting Pope Urban II*, *Christ on the Cross*, *Apotheosis of St Thomas Aquinas*; Bartolomé Esteban Murillo's *St Thomas of Villanueva Distributing Alms*, *The Immaculate Conception*, *Saints Justa and Rufina* and *The Vision of St Francis*; El Greco's *Portrait of a Painter* (his son Jorge Manuel); Francisco Pacheco's *Portrait of the Orantes Couple*, *Marriage of St Ines*; Uceda's *Holy Family*; Uceda/Vázquez, *Transfiguration of St Hermengildus*; and finally Lucas Cranach's *Calvary* and *The Last Judgement* by Maerten de Vos.

❶ Tue – Sat 9am – 8.30pm, Sun 9am – 2.30pm, free admission for EU citizens, others €1.50

CASA DE PILATOS AND SURROUNDINGS

**Casa de Pilatos

About 500m/550yd east of the church of San Salvador, on Plaza de Pilatos, is the Casa de Pilatos. This palace, which belongs today to the dukes of Medinaceli, combines Mudéjar, Gothic and Renaissance elements so successfully that it can almost be put in the same class as the Alcázar. Construction of the palace began in 1492 and was completed in 1520. As the owner travelled to Palestine in 1519, it has since then been commonly believed that the building is a copy of Pontius Pilate's house in Jerusalem. The house is constructed around an extraordinary ****patio** that is entered through a gate of Carrara

Casa de Pilatos – Seville's most magnificent city palace

marble, a work of the Genoese artist d'Aprile from 1532 that resembles a triumphal arch. The patio is a two-storey quadrangle of arcades with semi-circular arches adorned with Mudéjar patterns. Coloured azulejos cover the walls; the busts of 24 Roman emperors are recessed in alcoves. Statues of Greek and Roman goddesses in the classical manner occupy the corners. The centre of the patio is taken by a dolphin fountain with a Janus head. The Golden Room in the **basement** to the right of the Salón del Pretorio is distinguished by its splendid faience decoration and its Mudéjar coffered ceiling. The entrance portal opposite leads into the private chapel and its anteroom, both furnished with artesonado ceilings. Beyond the next room, with Renaissance sculptures, is the Salón de la Fuente. A museum in the left wing has a display of Greco-Roman sculptures including a Greek statue of Dionysus, a Hermes head from the 5th century BC and, as pièce de résistance dating from the same period, a statue of Minerva/Athena, considered by some to be the work of the legendary Phidias. A magnificent stairway leads up to the **upper floor**. Art from the collections of the dukes is on display here. It includes significant archive papers including a manuscript from the time of Charles the Bald. The Apotheosis of Hercules (1609) by Pacheco stands out among the ceiling paintings.

❶ April – Oct daily 9am – 70pm, Nov – March until 6pm, admission €8

Santa Catalina and San Pedro
Santa Catalina church, a little to the north of the palace, is noteworthy for its extraordinary, skilfully rendered artesonado ceilings. The painter Diego Velázquez was baptized in the Gothic church of San Pedro west of Santa Catalina.

LA MACARENA

Parlamento de Andalucía
The northern continuation of C. Sierpes leads past Plaza del Duque de la Victoria into the working class district, La Macarena, which was noticeably upgraded when the regional parliament of Andalucía moved into the former Hospital de Cinco Llagas.

Alameda de Hércules
The centre of the quarter is the Alameda de Hércules, a large park with tall granite columns from a Roman temple and statues of Hercules and Julius Caesar that have been standing on its south side since 1574.

San Lorenzo
To the west is the Mudéjar church San Lorenzo. The beautiful high altar with the likeness of St Lawrence is by Montañés. The much revered statue of Christ, Nuestro Señor de Gran Poder, in a side chapel was done by Juan de Mesa.

Convento de Santa Clara
Montañés also created the main altar of the Convento de Santa Clara church (16th century) to the north. The artesonado ceiling, however, is more impressive. Ferdinand III founded the convent at the end of the 13th century near the palace of his son, Fadrique. A tower still remains from that building.

Convento de San Clemente
A little further north on the banks of the Guadalquivir is the Convento de San Clemente, founded in the 13th century by Ferdinand III and Alfonso X. The noteworthy items in the convent church are the frescoes by Valdés Leal, the artesonado ceiling, the azulejo plinth from 1558 and the tomb of Maria of Portugal, mother of Pedro the Cruel.

*Puente de la Barqueta
Across from the convent is the Puente de la Barqueta, which connects the city centre with the former world fair grounds. The daring sweep of the suspension bridge arch has become a **new symbol of the city**.

City wall
A considerable part of the Almohad city wall that goes back to Roman times has survived at the northern edge of the barrio between

Puerta Macarena and Puerta de Córdoba. It was 6km/3.5mi long and had twelve gates.

Near Puerta Macarena stands San Gil church, to which the new Basílica de la Macarena has been added. This is where the Virgen de la Macarena, the patron saint of bullfighters and the most venerated processional figure of the city, is preserved. The many pieces of ornately decorated apparel for the miraculous images and the processional altars (pasos) are on display.

Basílica de la Macarena

❶ Daily 9am–2pm, 5pm–9pm; Sun from 9.30am; admission: €5

It is not very far from the east end of the city wall to the Convento de Santa Paula, founded in the 15th century by the Marqueses de Montemayor and one of the most beautiful convents of the city thanks to its colourful church portal by Niculoso Pisano as well as its fresco decorations on the vault above the altar. The convent museum proudly displays paintings by Ribera (*St Jerome*, *The Adoration of the Shepherds*) and an *Immaculate Conception* by Alonso Cano.

Convento de Santa Paula

❶ Tue–Sun 10am–1pm, admission: €3

Casa-Palacio de las Dueñas (15th century), which encloses a beautiful Mudéjar-style patio, lies on the way back to the city centre just west of the main thoroughfare San Luis.

Casa-Palacio de las Dueñas

ON THE RÍO GUADALQUIVIR

Paseo de Cristóbal Colón begins at the Puente de Isabel II in the south-west of the old town. On the side towards the river a beautiful park is a fine place to take a stroll. There are many bars and restaurants in the narrow streets of the city centre. The Paseo brushes **★Plaza de Toros**, begun in 1761; with 14,000 seats, it is **Andalucía's largest** and one of Spain's most famous bullrings. It also features a bullfighting museum. The La Maestranza cultural centre beyond it is one of the many new buildings that Seville owes to the world fair.

★Paseo de Cristóbal Colón

❶ **Bullring:** tours every 20 min.: daily 9.30am–7pm, May–Oct until 8pm, on days with bullfights only until 3pm; admission: €7

Behind it is the **Hospital de la Caridad** (1661–1664), endowed by the Calatrava knight Miguel de Mañara, who, after a vision of death, completely changed his licentious lifestyle. He commissioned two of the

> **!** *Seville by boat* **Insider Tip**
>
> MARCO ⊕ POLO TIP
>
> Boats sail from the Torre del Oro daily every 30 min. between 11am and 11pm for one-hour cruises on the Guadalquivir – Seville from a completely different perspective. Price: €16 per person

During Feria, the greatest event in Andalucía, celebrities arrive with their carriages at Plaza de Toros

greatest artists of his time, Murillo and Valdés Leal, to decorate the church of the charity hospital – the ***painting collection** to be seen here is considered to be **Seville's second most important** after that of the Museo de Bellas Artes. The dome frescoes are by Valdés Leal. Pedro Roldán created the retable sculptures on the theme of the Entombment of Christ, while Valdés Leal painted the backgrounds. Murillo's *John the Baptist, The Annunciation*, and particularly *The Miracle of the Bread, Moses Striking the Rock* and *St Elizabeth of Hungary Tending the Sick* can be seen here. The two works by Valdés Leal on the theme of the transience of earthly existence are downright depressing. In the painting *In ictu oculi*, death strides over the crowns of popes and kings, knights' armour and ostentatious garments; *Finis gloriae mundi* shows the decomposed corpses of a Calatrava knight and an archbishop.

❶ Mon – Sat 9am – 1.30pm 3.30pm – 6.30pm, Sun 9am – 12.30pm; admission €5

*Torre del Oro / Museo Marítimo

The Torre del Oro, after the Giralda the **second symbol of Seville** and one of the most important Moorish structures in the city, stands on the banks of the river. The twelve-sided tower was built around 1220 under the Almohads as a watchtower and lighthouse. There used to be a matching structure on the opposite shore. A heavy chain could be stretched between the two to block the harbour. It served as a treasury and prison under Pedro the Cruel. **Originally the roof was covered with gold azulejos** – the reason for the name. The present top was built in 1760. The Museo Marítimo (maritime museum) in the tower deals with Seville's history as a port.

❶ Tue – Fri 10am – 2pm, Sat, Sun 9am – 2pm, closed August, in winter it opens 30 min. earlier.; admission €3

THE SOUTH OF THE CITY

Two places particularly worth a visit in the expansive and green southern part of Seville's city centre are the Parque de María Luisa with its museums and the Plaza de España.

? Invention of the Cigarette

MARCO POLO INSIGHT

The women whoe worked in the large Spanish tobacco factories collected the crumbs of tobacco that were produced in the process of cigarmaking. They wrapped them in paper for a relatively cheap smoke. Around the middle of the 19th cent. these »papelitos« travelled to France, where they were called »cigarettes« – the French diminutive form of »cigar«.

It is best to begin with a walk from the Puerta de Jerez at the luxury hotel Alfonso XIII to the **Palacio de San Telmo**, a large Baroque building by Leonarda de Figueroa. It was conceived as a mariners' school and serves today as a seminary (Universidad Pontífica). The high Baroque gateway from 1734 is reminiscent of an altar. Twelve statues of famous Sevillians have been placed on the side facing the hotel.

Directly neighbouring is the former tobacco factory (Fábrica de Tabacos), a huge building erected in 1757 – the only building in Spain larger at the time was the Escorial near Madrid. This is where Prosper Merimée had his **Carmen** rolling cigars – in reality up to 10,000 female workers were doing this at the peak of production in the 19th century. The factory was closed in 1965. The building belongs today to the university, which means, among other things, that there is no problem in walking around there.

*Fábrica de Tabacos

Parque de María Luisa; a broad park donated by the Infanta María Luisa Fernanda de Borbón, begins across from the tobacco factory. Designed as an English garden, it was drastically altered by the buildings of the Ibero-American Exposition held here from 1929 to 1930. Of these, the former casino, today the Teatro Lope de Vega, is still to be seen right of the entrance, then Plaza de España, the buildings around Plaza de América and a smaller pavilion on Paseo de las Delicias called Costuero de la Reina (seamstress to the queen) that is today the city information office.

*Parque de María Luisa

*Plaza de España

The semi-circular Plaza de España on the Avda. de María Luisa is definitely not a thing of beauty, but it is **original and always worth seeing**. The intention of the architect, Aníbal González, was to quote all the styles in Spanish architectural history in the immense Palacio Español. At the centre is the Palacio Central. Two galleries leading from it to the two 82m/269ft-high corner towers that are supposed to be reminiscent of the Giralda. The whole building is covered with azulejos, upon which the coats of arms of the Spanish provinces are prominently displayed. Even the Venetian bridges over the waterfall in front of the building are covered with azulejos. Hardly a Sevillian bridal couple fails to pose for the obligatory photo taken in front of the plaza and its little canals.

The Plaza de España with its benches and water fountains is a good place to rest

In the southern section there are three former exhibition pavilions around Plaza de América: Pabellón Real (Royal Pavilion), Pabellón Mudéjar and Pabellón del Renacimiento (Pavilion of the Renaissance). **The Museo de Artes y Costumbres Populares** (folklore museum) in the Pabellón Mudéjar displays regional costumes, handicraft, furniture, porcelain, all kinds of domestic utensils and tools and more from Seville's past.

Plaza de América

The **★Museo Arqueológico** in the Pabellón del Renacimiento displays archaeological finds from western Andalucía from early periods to the Moors. Prehistoric and Iberian items are exhibited on the ground floor. The prize exhibit is the **Treasure of Carambolo** (near Seville), a collection of gold coins dating back to the 8th and 7th centuries BC. The Iberian culture is primarily represented by burial objects. The focus of the exhibits on the upper floor is on finds from ►Itálica. The eye-catching exhibits include some beautiful mosaics from there, a Hermes statue, and a head of Hispania found in the Roman settlement of Flavium Munigense in Mulva in the province of Seville. Furthermore, there are attractive pieces of Roman sculpture including a head of Alexander and two statues of Aphrodite. A collection of Moorish-Arab pieces completes the exhibits.

❶ **Both museums:** Tue–Sat 9am–8.30pm, Sun 9am–2.30pm; free admission for EU citizens; others €1.50

RIGHT BANK OF THE GUADALQUIVIR

The barrio of Triana lies on the right bank of the Guadalquivir. It was named after the Roman emperor Trajan. The wharves for the ships from the New World extended on this side of the river, between today's San Telmo and Isabel II bridges.

Barrio de Triana

It was near Puente San Telmo that **Magellan set sail for his circumnavigation of the globe**. Triana was the barrio of Gitanos, sailors and potters and this tradition lives on in the many pottery shops that still exist here. The hustle and bustle in the covered market right next to Isabel II bridge is also an attraction.

Although its much-extolled original character can no longer be found in unadulterated form, Triana's nightlife and gastronomy are worth a visit. There is a very beautiful view of Seville lit up by night from many of the restaurants and bars along the river bank.

About half-way between the two bridges stands **Santa Ana** church, which Alfonso the Wise had erected around 1280 in Mudéjar style; it is the oldest church in the city. Among the church's possessions are the miraculous image of the Virgen de la Rosa, the Apparition of Saints Justa and Rufina by Alejo Fernández as well as paintings by Pedro de Campaña on the high altar.

Isla de la   In 1992 Seville was the scene of the **world fair EXPO '92**, and under
Cartuja   its **overall theme, the Age of Discovery**, everything was geared to
                  the 500th anniversary of Columbus' voyage of discovery in 1492. The
island of La Cartuja, in the Guadalquivir north of the barrio of Triana was selected as the exhibition ground. It was connected to the old city by a maglev train, cable car (Telecabina) and two new bridges, Alamillo and La Barqueta, from Santiago Calatrava. The middle point was the Royal Pavilion, the only old structure on the island. It was originally the Carthusian monastery of Santa Maria de las Cuevas founded in 1401, and it was there that Columbus planned his voyage. It was used as a ceramics factory after 1839 by an Englishman named Pickman. Its old kilns can be viewed.

The **Centro Andaluz de Arte Contemporáneo (CAAC)** is now housed there, displaying contemporary art, mainly works by 20th cent. Spanish artists.

In the meantime, many of the 70 national pavilions have been torn down. Ambitious plans to get a high-tech research park going have been considerably revised due to lack of participation. Despite that, the old

> **MARCO ⊕ POLO TIP**
>
> ! **Off to the Tablao**   *Insider Tip*
>
> Seville is one of the flamenco centres of Andalucía. The so-called tablao is the place to find dancing and performances, but all too often exorbitant prices are demanded for admission. Among the best are:
> **Los Gallos**, PLaza de Santa Cruz (tel. 954 21 69 81)
> **El Arenal**, C. Rodo, 7 (tel. 954 21 64 92)
> **Patio Sevilleno**, Paseo Cristóbal Colón, 11a (tel. 954 21 41 20)
> **El Placio Andaluz**, Avda. María Auxiliadora (tel. 954 53 47 20).
> In many bars and bodegas things happen more spontaneously but without any guarantee; try **La Sonanta**, C. San Jacinto, 31 (in Triana; Thu from 11pm), **El Mundo**, C. Siete Revueltas (Tue after 11pm) and **El Tamboril**, Plaza de Santa Cruz (almost every weekend).

Expo grounds have become one of Seville's attractions in the shape of ***Isla Mágica** (Magic Island), a high-tech amusement park. The park's theme is the discovery and conquest of America with a daring ride rushing through the waterfalls of Iguaçu, the chance to experience the world of adventure in a forgotten temple in the Movimás dome theatre or follow an (almost) real sea battle between two galleons on the artificial lake. In Puerto de Indias, actors in historic costumes show what life in Seville was like when the city was the Spain's most important port for ships laden with gold from Central and South America.

❶ CAAC: Avda. Américo Vespucio, 2; Tue – Sat 11am – 9pm, Sun 11am – 3pm; admission: €3.0; free admission: Tue – Fri 7pm – 9pm, Sat 11am – 9pm; www.caac.es

Isla Mágica: Avda. de los Decubrimientos; April – Oct daily from 11am, clsoing times vary with the season, between 7pm and midnight; admission: €29; www.islamagica.es

AROUND SEVILLE

▶ there

Itálica

Head west from Seville on the A-472 passing first Castilleja de la Cuesta, where Hernán Cortés (1485–1547), the conqueror of Mexico, died. After about 20km/12mi, the little town of Sanlúcar la Mayor can be seen on a hill. This former Moorish settlement still possesses a ruined castle. Of the three churches, the Gothic Iglesia Santa María from 1214 is interesting. It has an old minaret as bell tower and a horseshoe portal.

Sanlúcar la Mayor

20km/12mi south-west of Seville is Alcalá de Guadaira – the pasties from here are popular – with the largest Almohad fortress in Spain. The Romans already recognized the strategic importance of the location and placed a fort here. The fortress that the Moors erected on top of it became the key to Seville – however, Ferdinand the Saint was able to capture it with little effort. This is one of the places of origin of the Castilian royal family. Alfonso XI gave the fortress to his mistress, Leonora, who bore him Henry of Trastámara. Henry had his half-brother, Pedro the Cruel, murdered and so became the Castilian king and founder of the dynasty that produced Isabella the Catholic. The ring of the **✦fortress** wall fortified with battlements and eight towers stretches massively over the hill above the town. Be ready for a possible disappointment because, besides the wall, almost nothing else has survived, not even part of the huge granary in the catacombs that supplied Seville with flour. The most interesting churches of the town are Santiago (15th / 16th century), for of its tile-adorned tower, and Santa Clara with an altar relief by the 17th-century sculptor Juan Martínez Montañés.

Alcalá de Guadaira

50km/30mi north of Seville begins the solitude of the **✦Sierra Morena**. Rivers cut their way through the hilly landscape of the **Parque Natural Sierra del Norte**, in which pasture alternates with oak woods and mixed forests that are home to eagles, vultures, deer and wild boar. The **nature park information office** in Constantina – a very pretty little town on a mountain ridge with an old town (the Morería) that is worth visiting, as well as a castle ruin dating from the times of the

> **!** *Well-being through art* Insider Tip
>
> **MARCO ⊕ POLO TIP**
>
> Wonderful scenery, relaxation, regional cooking, art and music – Carmen Ladrón de Guevara y Bracho combines all this in the former Carthusian monastery of Cazalla. In 1977 she bought the buildings, converting them into a centre for artists and setting up a hotel with eight rooms in the gatehouse, which at €80 for a double room in the high season is not all that expensive (Monasterio de la Cartuja, Crta. A-455, km 2.5; tel. 954 88 45 16, www.cartujade-cazalla.com).

Moors – provides information about all the activities on offer, like hiking, horseback riding and fishing. During Roman times, Constantina was situated on an important trading route and produced wine that was even praised in Rome. West of Constantina is the idyllically rural town of **El Pedroso**, where cork is processed. The parish church stands on Roman and Moorish foundations and was remodelled from Gothic to Baroque style. The mountain site north-west of Constantina was first settled by the Iberians, then taken over by the Romans and later expanded into a fortress by the Moors, giving the place its name **Cazalla de la Sierra**, meaning fortified town. Nobles' houses line the street between the large church and the plaza. In a former Franciscan monastery there is a Baroque cloister with rounded arches to be seen. Cazalla is a good starting point for hikes in the mountains and offers a welcome refreshment afterwards in the form of good tapas bars.

** Sierra de Cazorla, Segura y Las Villas

$\rightarrow\!\!\leftarrow$ K 5/6

Province: Jaén
Altitude: 650–2107m/2132–6913ft
Population: 21,000

In the extreme north-east of Andalucía, the Sierra de Segura and the Sierra de Cazorla rise to over 2000m/6562ft above the hilly grain- and olive-growing lands of the province of Jaén, separated by the headwaters of the Guadalquivir that has its source here. Here is the watershed between the Mediterranean, into which the Río Segura flows, and the Atlantic, the destination of the Guadalquivir.

Wild and romantic mountain landscape
The national park's highest elevations are El Empañada (2107m/6913ft) and El Cabañas (2036m/ 6680ft). At more than 214,000ha combined with the Sierra de Las Villas, the two mountain ranges form **Spain's largest nature reserve**, the Parque Natural Sierra de Cazorla, Segura y Las Villas. Hiking and nature watching rank first in this wild, in places truly godforsaken mountain world. Spring and autumn are the best seasons for these activities.

Flora and fauna
The plants and animals of the nature park are equally renowned. The vast expanses of forest are unique and undoubtedly only survived the deforestation campaigns carried out throughout Iberia since ancient times because of their inaccessibility. Along with all sorts of decidu-

The Templar castle La Iruela is situated on a rocky promontory

ous trees, three types of pine primarily flourish here; Aleppo pine, maritime pine and, in the highest reaches, the black pine. The Cazorla violet is very rare and grows only here; in addition orchids, narcissus, rockroses and an endemic type of butterwort thrive here. With patience and luck, it is possible to observe Iberian ibexes, moufflons and fallow deer. Royal eagles, booted eagles, griffon vultures and Egyptian vultures circle in the heavens.

WHAT TO SEE IN THE NATURE PARK

Cazorla

Coming from Úbeda, (▶Baeza · Úbeda) Cazorla can be seen from a long way off nestled before the towering flanks of the massif. After an eight-year siege by the troops of Rodrigo Ximénez de Rada, Archbishop of Toledo, Cazorla was finally wrested away from the Moors in 1240. The pretty little town – narrow lanes, attractive plazas – is the chief town for tourism in the sierras and as such offers plentiful accommodation and sufficient restaurants and bars, the latter primarily around Plaza de la Corredera. Cazorla has two fortresses. La Yedra castle, dating back to the Moors, towers over the Plaza de Santa María from a hilltop and is home to the **Museo del Alto Guadalquivir**. It is dedicated to the history of the Sierra (exhibit in the castle keep) and shows folk art, farming implements and clothing. The plaza, by the way, is a pleasant and lively place. It takes its name

Sierra de Cazorla, Segura y Las Villas

INFORMATION
Oficina del Parque Natural
Martínez Falero, 11 E-23470 Cazorla
Tel. 953 72 01 25
www.turismoencazorla.es
The Internet site has several suggested hiking routes (clock on »Red de Senderos«).

TOUREN
Reliable organizer of guided tours with off-road vehicles: TurisNat in Cazorla
Paseo del Santo Cristo, 17 bajo
Tel. 953 72 13 51; www.turisnat.e

EVENTS
La Virgen y San Roque
From 15 to 19 August bulls are driven through Hornos de Santiago almost like in Pamplona.

WHERE TO EAT
Juan Carlos €€€€
In Cazorla, Plaza Consuelo Mendieta, 2
Tel. 953 72 12 01
Game from the forests and trout from the streams of the Sierra de Cazorla are prepared and served here.

Bar Las Vegas €
In Cazorla Plaza de la Corredera, 5
Tel. 953 72 02 77
Tasty tapas and raciones. Moderate prices, friendly service.

WHERE TO STAY
Parador de Cazorla €€ **Insider Tip**
In Cazorla, Crta. de Vadillo, Castril
Tel. 953 72 70 75
www.parador.es
32 rooms
Closed mid-Dec. – early Feb.
In the lonely, wild mountains of the Sierra de Cazorla National Park – very pleasant and just the thing for nature lovers!

Ciudad de Cazorla €
In Cazorla, Plaza de la Corredera, 9
Tel. 953 72 17 00
www.hotelciudaddecazorla.com
35 rooms
Modern building on Cazorla's central plaza, simple and good. There is also a bar and restaurant. The terrace offers a lovely mountain panorama.

from the church designed by Vandelvira and set on fire by Napoleon's soldiers. On the Plaza is an old butcher shop, which now houses the Centro Temático de Especies Amenazadas, which exhbits the endangered fauna of the Sierra. The second fortress, the Templar castle La Iruela, is on the road to the nature park, where it sits enthroned on a rock pinnacle to the right.

14km/9mi south-west of Cazorla lies **Quesada**. Quesada is a typical Andalusian village that honours its most famous son, the painter Rafael Zabaleta, in a museum.

From Cazorla to Embalse del Tranco A winding road leads from Cazorla to Burunchel, where the nature park begins. From here, the observation point at the top of the Puerta de las Palomas pass can be reached. There, with some luck (in the morning), birds of prey can be spotted. Head on to the turn-off to Embalse del Tranco reservoir; the direction to Vadillo can also be taken here, from where the parador and the **source of the Guadalquivir** can be reached. The main road – the A-319 – however, goes into the Guadalquivir valley in the direction of the reservoir, coming to the **Torre del Vinagre Information Centre** at kilometre 48.8 with its natural-history exhibition about the geology, plants and animals of the mountain range. There is also a hunting museum and a botanical garden. On the south shore of the lake is the Parque Cinegético open-air enclosure in which the larger animals of the sierra are kept. To extend the drive beyond the lake, head toward **Hornos**, which lies in a picturesque setting a bit to the right of the main road on an elevation with a castle on a Cyclopean wall towering over it.

> **MARCO ⊕ POLO TIP**
>
> ! **Safe in the wilds** _Insider Tip_
>
> If you don't feel safe roaming around the sierras on your own, then turn to the dependable **Quercus** cooperative in Cazorla, which offers guided walking tours, Land Rover treks and excursions on horseback. Adress: Pl. de la Constitución, 15, Cazorla, tel. 953 72 01 15, www.excursionesquercus.com).

In the north of the nature park lies Segura de la Sierra, once the centre of a taifa, evidenced by the castle dating back to that time. After the Christian conquest, the village was handed over to the Order of Santiago, which left the mark of its cross on many of the houses. There is an overwhelming view of the mountains from the heights of the castle. The Fuente de Carlos V, a colossal Renaissance fountain, is worth seeing.

*Segura de la Sierra

* Sierra de Grazalema

— ⊁ E 8

Province: Cádiz, Málaga
Altitude: 300m/984ft

The unique beauty of the landscape of the nature reserve is not the only attraction – right through the middle of it runs the »route of the white villages« (Ruta de los Pueblos Blancos) to such picturesque places as El Bosque, Benamahoma, Grazalema, Ubrique and Zahara de la Sierra.

At first look, it may seem surprising that the Sierra de Grazalema, the western foothills of the Serranía de Ronda, is the area with the **highest rainfall in Andalucía**. A second look reveals numerous varieties of plants, most of which are nurtured by the winter precipitation. The

Nature and the white villages

Sierra de Grazalema

INFORMATION
Centros de Visitantes
Calle Federico García Lorca, 1
E-11670 **El Bosque**
Tel. 956 70 97 33
Mon–Sat 10am–2pm, 4pm–6pm,
Sun 9am–2pm
Jacaranda, 1
E-29380 **Cortes de la Frontera**
Tel. 95 1 04 21 00
Thu–Fri 10am–2pm (May – Sept only
Fridays), Sat – Sun 10am–2pm,
4pm – 6pm

WHERE TO EAT
Venta Julián €€€€
In El Bosque
Avda. de la Diputación, 11
Tel. 956 71 60 57
www.ventajulian.com
Traditional Andalusian cooking. The
adjacent shop sells regional products like
olive oil and ham. Large parking lot.

Torreón €€€€
In Grazalema, Agua, 44
Tel. 956 13 23 13
www.restauranteeltorreongrazalema.
com
Traditional cooking, specializes in
game.

WHERE TO STAY
Villa Turistica de Grazalema €
In Grazalema, El Olivar, s/n
Tel. 956 13 21 36
Apartment complex in the regional
style, outside Grazalema. Remodeled
in 2012.

Hostal Casa de las Piedras €
In Grazalema
Las Piedras, 32
Tel. 956 13 20 14
www.casadelaspiedras.net, 30 rooms
A cosy house full of nooks and crannies
in the old village centre, with restaurant.

precipitation is the result of the relative proximity to the Atlantic. The first obstacle for clouds driven from the ocean is the sierra, whose highest elevation is Pico de Torreón (1654m/5426ft). The houses of all of the villages are covered in the same blinding whitewash. The whitewash is not only beautiful, but also reflects the rays of the sun and so keeps the interior of the houses cool. Formerly, the quicklime plaster also served as a disinfectant to prevent epidemics in the densely built Moorish settlements. **Grazalema** has the best selection of good accommodation and opportunities for hiking, and has a village centre with good bars in a most enchanting setting. **Zahara de la Sierra**, right at the north-eastern edge of the park, is truly a jewel with a picturesque village centre and a Moorish castle.

Flora and fauna Flourishing in the forests of the Sierra de Grazalema – which has been placed under protection as a nature reserve – are most notably holly oak, Portuguese oak, cork oak and carob trees. The Spanish fir, a very old species grows here, mainly on the northern slopes of the Sierra del Pinar. In addition, orchids and peonies can be found. Iberian ibex and deer gambol about in the mountains. Otters still live in many streams. Griffon vultures, royal eagles, Mediterranean wheatears and blue rock thrushes are among the species of birds living here.

Two main routes pass through the nature park: in the north-south direction, the mountain road A-374 from Grazalema through Ubrique to Alcalá de los Gazules offering wonderful vistas and, in the west-east direction, the A-372 coming from Arcos de la Frontera through El Bosque to Grazalema and on to Ronda. The park management has marked a total of eight trekking routes, four of which may only be travelled by a limited number of visitors per day. Maps, information and **hiking permits** can be obtained in the **information centres** in El Bosque and Cortes de la Frontera.

Entering the park

Those not wanting to walk can explore the prescribed routes in the nature park by vehicle. Large stands of the Sierra del Pinar's Spanish fir can be seen on the right hand of the road out of Zahara. This area

Siesta on Plaza de España in Grazalema –
public life follows the position of the sun

can only be entered with a **special permit**. A good view of the forest, and with a little luck some birdwatching as well, can be had from the Mirador del Pinsapar and Puerto de las Palomas observation points that follow. The landscape turns barren after Grazalema in the direction of Ubrique. From Ubrique head to El Bosque. This place is the starting point of the second route that leads over Puerto del Boyar Pass on the southern slopes of the Sierra del Pinar, offering once again some very nice views.

Los Alcornocales ► there

** Sierra Nevada
(Parque Nacional de la Sierra Nevada)

✳ H–K 7/8

Province: Granada
Elevation: 1000–3482m/3300–11,490ft

A massive mountain range almost 110km/70mi long, the Sierra Nevada stretches between Río Almería in the east to Valle de Lecrín in the west. The highest peaks on the Iberian peninsula tower out of its massif; Pico de Veleta (3394m/11,200ft) and the Cerro de Mulhacén (3428m/11,346ft) – which owes it name to the legend that Muley Hacen, the father of the last king of Granada, Boabdil, is supposedly buried on it.

Spain's highest mountains Since 1986, the Sierra Nevada has been a **UNESCO Biosphere Reserve**, a **nature park since 1989** and, finally, the core area has been a national park since 1999. It is **more for specialists**, who are capable of treks in high alpine regions and have an eye for rare plant life, because, although the Sierra Nevada gives the impression of being generally barren, an experienced botanist will find a rich field to work in. Over 2000 species of plants grow here, over 60 of them endemic. Animals like the Iberian ibex have withdrawn into this area. The sierra is famous for its butterflies. Hikers should first obtain maps in the visitor centres and inform themselves about mountain shelters. The southern flank of the sierra, the ►Alpujarras, is more easily accessible. Even in the times of the Moors, it supplied Granada with fruit.

Winter sports area Although a protected area, from November until into May, the Sierra Nevada is an excellent winter sports area, where even world cup ski races are held. Over 70km/45mi of ski-runs, plus cross-country courses, fun and snowboard pistes and two ski stadiums, all accessible by either cable car, chair lifts or T-bar lifts, are available in

Sierra de Nevada

INFORMATION
Centro de Visitantes El Dornajo
Crta. de la Sierra Nevada, km 23
Tel. 958 34 06 25
Sept – June Tue – Sun 10am – 2pm,
4pm – 6pm
July/Aug Tue – Sun 10am – 2pm,
5pm – 7pm
Information also in the tourist offices in
▶Granada
www.nevasport.com

WHERE TO STAY
Meliá Sierra Nevada €€€–€€€€
Plaza de Pradollano, s/n
E-18196 Sierra Nevada
Tel. 958 48 04 00
www.melia-sierra-nevada.com
221 rooms
closed May – Nov
The house was built in 1975 and is the
Number 1 for skiers. Kings of spain and
Sweden have stayed here already.

Europe's southernmost ski area. And those who come only for the
après-ski won't be disappointed. What makes it so attractive is the
proximity to the Mediterranean. Where else is it possible to schuss
down into the valley on skis in the morning and swim in the ocean
in the afternoon?
❶ Infos Tel. 902 70 80 90; www.sierranevada.com

TO THE SUMMIT REGION

An excursion to this magnificent mountain world presents no problems in the snow-free summer months and is also possible by coach
(Bonal coaches from Granada bus station). Since being declared a
national park, the trip ends below Pico de Veleta at the Albergue Universitario at an altitude of 2600m/8530ft. The A-395 climbs from
▶Granada and the heat of the Vega up into the often storm-whipped
heights. Warm clothing against the wind and cold are advisable. The
transition from the southern landscape of the green Vega of Granada
to the snow-covered summit region of the mountains is especially
impressive. Again and again there are breathtaking views at various
stopping points. Leaving Granada, travel at first over the right bank
of the Río Genil up the valley, reaching Cenes de la Vega (737m/2418ft
altitude) after 6km/3.5mi. Further up the valley, cross over the Río
Genil, passing the turn-off on the left to Pinos Genil on the Embalse
de Canales, the Canales dam. From here it is uphill (medium gradi-
ent 8–12%) with many bends in the road on the slope that is initially
still dotted with olive trees. All the while, there is a splendid view
back into the valley and, on clear days, all the way to Granada. The
1,500m/5000ft level is passed at about 20km/13mi, shortly afterwards, the tree line has been reached.

Peak experience: Piso de Velata is the second highest mountain on the Iberian Peninsula, after the Mulhacén

Sol y Nieve

After another 8km/5mi, the Sol y Nieve winter sport area (2000–2600m/ 6,600–8,500ft) is reached. It may be bearable here in winter, but in summer the **clear cutting for the ski runs** and the building frenzy are revealed by slopes already sparsely spotted with vegetation. A 4km/2.5mi-long access road connects Sol y Nieve with the **Prado-llano** resort (2100m/6900ft), from where a cable car connects to the hotel colony of Borreguiles (2600m/8500ft) to the south; chair lifts and T-bar lifts go up from there to the higher ski-runs, including Pico de Veleta.

To Pico de Veleta

The road bypasses Sol y Nieve, however, and goes past the hotel high up to the left (2500m/8,200ft), the highest hotel in Spain, and contin-ues on to Albergue Universitario (2550m/8,370ft). A little further on is the Hoya de la Mora control point. Here the trip ends, but from June to September, the park office runs minibuses to the summit re-gion of Pico de Veleta. The view is stupendous in clear weather. To the east Mulhacén, to the west the Vega of Granada and the blue sea is shimmering to the south. On the north flank of the Veleta, at an altitude of 2850m/ 9,350ft, the international Institute for Radio As-tronomy in Millimetre Wavelengths (IRAM) operates a 30m/98ft radio telescope.

Well-equipped hikers can follow the asphalt road from the bus terminal and in a good five to six hours cross the Sierra Nevada on foot. The trek ends at a minibus stop on the southern slope in the Cascajar Negro region. From here, it's on to Capileira in the Alpujarras. Naturally, the whole trip can also be done on a mountain bike.

On to Capileira

✳ Tarifa

✳ D 9

Province: Cádiz
Altitude: 7m/23ft
Population: 17,700

The sea off Tarifa at the point where the calm Mediterranean and the unpredictable Atlantic meet is Europe's best windsurfing area. Here the warmer east winds butt up against the turbulent gusts from the west that storm and blow up to 8.5m/s (20mph), which is why crack windsurfers shoot over the water here. This crowd has left its own mark on the place, not least on the nightlife.

Tarifa is a mere 14km/9mi from Africa making it the **southernmost city on the European mainland**. Over here, the last trace of Spain, already noticeably mixed with Oriental ingredients. Over there, the lights of Tangiers shining back toward Europe. Here is where the Atlantic and the Mediterranean meet, discernible mostly through the constantly blowing wind, and the weather is correspondingly erratic. Tourism profits the most because those who want to surf or engage in a similarly trendy sport (kiting is also in) come to Tarifa. Otherwise, the old city centre is certainly enjoyable. Incidentally, the constant wind was the reason why **Europe's largest wind turbine complex** went into operation here in 1993.

Europa's no. 1 surfing grounds

The Iberians and the Phoenicians settled on this **strategically important site**. The Romans called their colony Iulia Traducta. The Vandals led by Geiseric embarked from here in AD 429 to conquer the Roman province of Africa. Possession of the town as a bridgehead for the crossing from Morocco was especially important to the Moors. In 710, they sent Tarif ibn Malik to reconnoitre the area – the city owes its name to him. It was not until 1292 that the Christians retook it. In the 18th century, Tarifa was the deployment area against the British who were sitting tight in Gibraltar. Since then, Tarifa has been in the news for tragic reasons; again and again, completely exhausted or even drowned immigrants from Africa are discovered on the beach after having crossed the straits in barely seaworthy boats.

History

WHAT TO SEE IN TARIFA

Historic centre The old part of town with its maze of winding lanes was once enclosed by walls, parts of which are well-preserved today, among them Puerta del Mar and Puerta de Jerez, the latter complete with an azulejo memorial plaque in remembrance of the reconquest in 1292. This is the entrance to the historic centre with its town hall and **San Mateo** church. A late Gothic nave is hidden behind the Baroque façade. Don't miss the statue of Christ by Pedro de Mena and the Visigoth gravestone in the right aisle.

Castillo de Guzmán el Bueno The castle dates back to the time of Abd ar-Rahman III in the 10th century. It was remodelled in the 13th century. Its name commemorates Alonso Pérez de Guzmán, commandant after the conquest in 1292. The Moors immediately laid siege to the town again, took Guzmán's nine-year-old son hostage and threatened to murder him if Guzmán would not surrender. According to legend, he threw his dagger to the Moors with the challenge to use it to kill his son if they didn't have their own weapon – which they then actually did.

Africa in sight: view over the roofs of Tarifa

Tarifa

INFORMATION
Oficina de Turismo
Paseo de la Alameda, s/n
E-11380 Tarifa
Tel. 956 68 09 93
www.aytotarifa.com/turismo/index.htm

WHERE TO EAT
Souk €€€
Mar Tireno, 46
Tel. 956 62 70 65; www.souk-tarifa.es
Africa is near, so try the Moroccan dishes. They also serve Chinese and Thai food. Friendly service.

Café Central €€
Sancho VI el Bravo
Tel. 956 68 05 90
Meeting-place for surfers and locals, who also enjoy the tapas here.

Perulero €
Plaza San Hiscio
Tel. 956 68 19 97
Solid and tasty Andalusian cooking.

WHERE TO STAY
El Beaterio €€   **Insider Tip**
Plaza del Ángel, 2
Tel. 956 68 09 24; 9 rooms
Pleasant, roomy apartments in a lovingly restored Baroque convent (16th cent.) in the middle of Tarifa. Glass-covered patio, a beautiful view from the roof terrace.

Hurricane €€
Crta. Nac. 340, km 78, north of Tarifa
Tel. 956 68 49 19
www.hotelhurricane.com; 33 rooms
The Moroccan-style hotel is right on the beach. With a nice restaurant, international crowd, beautiful garden and two swimming pools.

Punta Star €€
Ctra. Nac. Cádiz, km 77
Tel. 956 68 43 26
www.hotelpuntasur.com
Directly on the surfer mile with tree-planted garden and swimming pool. There is also a bar, a terrace and a restaurant with Mediterranean and Moroccan dishes.

Misiana €€
Sancho IV El Bravo, 16
Tel. 956 62 70 83
www.misiana.com; 12 rooms
In the heart of the old part of town, tastefully furnished rooms, colourfully furnished bar, appeals to the younger crowd

Cien por Cien Fun €€
Crta. de Cádiz, km 76
Tel. 956 68 03 30
www.100x100fun.com; 22 rooms
»100% fun« says it all. Pure windsurfer scene, that means a Caribbean ambience, Mexican restaurant, colourful and flashy surfer crowd, beach, waves and wind just outside the door. 9km/6.5mi outside Tarifa.

! *Whale watching* ^{**Insider Tip**}

The strait is a passage for different species of whale – a good opportunity to observe them from a boat. A reputable organizer is the Swiss maritime research foundation FIRMM, C. Pedro Cortés, 3, Tel. 956 62 70 08, www.firmm.org.

The window recess where this all was supposed to have taken place can still be seen. Guzmán held the fortress, for which King Sancho conferred upon him the honorary title of El Bueno (the good) and presented him with ►Sanlúcar de Barrameda. He later received the title of Duke of Medina Sidonia and founded one of the most powerful noble dynasties of Spain. The restored castle is dominated by the massive **Torre de Guzmán** with the aforementioned recess, from which there is a wonderful view of the town, the fishing harbour below and the Strait of Gibraltar.

❶ Tue – Sat 10am – 2pm, 5pm – 7pm, Sun 11am – 2pm; admission: €2

*Punta Marroquí

The Tarifa lighthouse marks the southernmost point of European mainland, the **Punta Marroquí** (Punta de Tarifa), but lies within a restricted military area. On the narrowest spot of the Strait of Gibraltar, it is possible to catch sight of the 13km/8mi-distant African coast, and in clear weather even discern individual houses in the villages and towns. Morocco live offers a short excursion to Tangiers with the ferry from Tarifa (travel time 40 min.; passport necessary).

AROUND TARIFA

Beaches

Playa de los Lances and Playa de Valdevaqueros, two very beautiful beaches with fine sand and a huge sand dune rising behind them, stretch almost 10km/6mi to the north-west. The sandblaster-like wind is the only thing that can seriously dampen the beach fun.

Bolonia

Bolonia also has a wonderful beach with fantastic sand dunes. It is about 15km/9mi to the west and can be reached by taking the turn-off from the N-340. The beach alone is worth it, but Bolonia is also a **place for amateur archaeologists**, because the **ruins of the Roman city of Baelo Claudia** are being excavated on the beach there. This city was inhabited for 700 years, surrounded by a 4m/13ft-high wall, and lived from fishing and the production of garum, a paste popular as a condiment in the whole empire. Stone troughs in which the fish were salted are evidence of its production. The ruins of the Roman settlement contain all the elements of a Roman city. The forum with a semi-circular fountain, the remains of three temples, the baths and the theatre, as well as the city gate from the time of Emperor Claudius have been uncovered.

❶ Oct – May Tue – Sat 9am – 7pm; June – Sept Tue – Sat 9am – 8pm; Sun all year 9am – 2pm

The N-340 leads uphill east of Tarifa to Puerto del Cabrito summit pass in the Sierra del Algarrobo, where there is a magnificent view over the straits away to Africa.

**Puerto del Cabrito

Torremolinos

 F 8

Province: Málaga
Altitude: Sea level
Population: 67,000

If mass tourism has a home on the Costa del Sol, then in Torremolinos. This seaside resort owes its popularity to its almost 9km/5.5mi-long beach in the middle of a wide bay, its pleasant climate, and, of course, the innumerable budget-priced accommodations – 50,000-some hotel beds await the guest.

Before the hordes of tourists invaded in the 1960s, Torremolinos was a sleepy little village that had developed in the 18th century out of a settlement next to a couple of mills and the Torre de Pimentel watchtower that gave the village its name. It gained world-wide fame through the novel *The Drifters* by James A. Michener, a cult book of the hippie generation. A mile of concrete high-rises defines the image of Torremolinos today. Life around the old San Miguel Street plays a dominant role in the city centre. The two former fishing districts, La Carihuela and El Bajondilla, have largely been adapted to the needs of tourists. Since 1988, when Torremolinos gained its administrative independence from Málaga, the city council has been making some effort to improve the resort's tarnished image through building measures and by cleaning up the beaches. And the beaches really are well-kept.

Holiday machine on Costa del Sol

Water sports, sea fishing and scuba diving, sailing, bullfights, golf, tennis and horseback riding are offered as diversions.
Looking for fun and amusement? There are countless **discos and bars** to choose from.
The large **Atlantis Aquapark** is located on the N-340.

Recreation

AROUND TORREMOLINOS

The municipalities of Benalmádena Costa, ▶Fuengirola and, adjacent to the north, Málaga today comprise **one of Europe's largest tourist complexes** – with all the advantages like services of every kind

Benalmádena Costa

Torremolinos

INFORMATION
Oficina de Turismo
Plaza Blas Infante, 1 (city hall)
E-29620 Torremolinos
Tel. 952 37 95 12
www.visitetorremolinos.com

WHERE TO EAT
Frutos €€€€
Avda. de la Riviera, 80
Urb. Los Álamos
Tel. 952 38 14 50
Regular customers are Malagueños and holiday-makers who want to eat some very good fish. There are also meat dishes. Meals are served on the garden terrace on warm days.

La Paella €€€
Paseo Marítimo Bajondillo
Tel. 952 37 20 21
Right on the beach promenade with international cooking. Of course, there are paellas. Many locals come here as well. Nice service

WHERE TO STAY
Tropicana €€
Trópico, 6
Tel. 952 38 66 00
www.hoteltropicana.es
84 rooms
Very good hotel in the middle of a tropical garden with its own beach. The restaurant specializes in grilled meat and fish dishes. The rooms have a balcony and a view either of the pool or the sea.

Miami €
Aladino, 14
Tel. 952 38 52 55
www.residencia-miami.com
26 rooms
Country house-style beach hotel that stands out because of its exotic touch, which was designed by a cousin of Pablo Picasso. There is a swimming pool in the garden for relaxation.

within easy reach, but also all the drawbacks like over-crowding and noise. Benalmádena Costa has **Torrequebrada**, the first gambling casino on the Costa del Sol, the **Tívoli amusement park** in Arroyo de la Miel and a trendy yacht harbour.

Visitors like **Parque Submarino Sea Life**, where sharks can be observed in underwater tanks and **Selwo Marina**, the largest dolphinarium in Andalucía.

Situated inland, **Benalmádena Pueblo** shows what happens to the villages without tourism. It also has a pretty museum that exhibits pre-Columbian art and archaeological finds from the area.

Úbeda

▶Baeza · Úbeda

Utrera

 D 7

Province: Seville
Altitude: 49m/160ft
Population: 51,000

The small town of Utrera lies southeast of Seville in the middle of the fertile, agricultural Campiña de Seville.

WHAT TO SEE IN AND AROUND UTRERA

Utrera's churches are worth seeing, above all the church of Santa **Utrera**
María de la Asunción, consecrated in 1369. Its beautiful Renaissance
portal has figures of the patron saints and apostles. The Count of Arcos is buried in the church. The church of Santiago, built in the 15th
century, has a tower adorned with a figure of the saint. Out of town
in the direction of Seville the pilgrimage church, Nuestra Señora de
la Consolación, possesses a beautiful Renaissance portal, a Churrigueresque altar and above all a magnificent artesonado ceiling. The
miraculous Madonna is believed to have saved Utrera from being
flooded in 1962.

24km/15mi north-east of Utrera is El Arahal, once the centre of the **El Arahal**
insurgents in the farm workers movement. Very little of that is noticeable today. The sights here are La Victoria church with parts of a
Mudéjar cloister, the towers of Santa María Magdalena covered with

Utrera

INFORMATION
Oficina de Turismo
San Fernando, 2, E- 41710 Utrera
Tel. 95 4 87 33 87
www.turismoutrera.org
Daily 11am–2pm

WHERE TO EAT
Restaurante Desacuerdo €€€€
Álvarez Quintero, 15
Tel. 95 4 86 30 64
www.desacuerdo.es
One of the best addresses in town.

Excellent Spanish cooking. Good value
for money. Attentive service.

WHERE TO STAY
Hotel Vera Cruz €
Corredera, 44
Tel. 95 5 86 52 52
www.hotelveracruz.com
18 rooms
Nicely furnished rooms grouped
around a patio and inner courtyard.
Clean, friendly service. Solarium
and underground garage.

coloured azulejos, and the portal and dome of the Baroque church of Vera Cruz – don't miss the 16th and 17th century choral books on display – and, finally, the Hospital de la Misericordia.

Morón As the name says, Morón, 36km/22mile east of Utrera, was a border town on the Moorish frontier. Ruins are all that is left of the castle dating from that time, which was captured by the Christians in 1240. The entrance to the church of San Miguel is through a portal with Renaissance and Mudéjar elements; inside is a Renaissance choir screen and a retable that Montañés worked on.

✳ Vejer de la Frontera

✦ **D 9**

Province: Cádiz
Altitude: 218m/715ft
Population: 12,900

Vejer de la Frontera is one of Andalucía's most beautiful white villages, veritably clinging to a rock overlooking Río Barbate inland from Costa de la Luz. This wonderful setting is best seen when approached from the coastal road.

White village in a lovely setting The adjunct de la Frontera refers to the history of Vejer. Originally founded by the Phoenicians, it was a fort on the border of the Moorish kingdom. It was recaptured around the mid-13th century by Ferdinand the Saint. The most popular festival of the city is the Fiesta del Toro Embolao on Easter Sunday, a bull run in the narrow city streets.

Palm-lined Plaza de España in Vejer

WHAT TO SEE IN UND AROUND VEJER

Individual buildings or art treasures are not the reason to visit **Vejer**. The attraction here is the unmistakeable Moorish character of the narrow, steep lanes and the gleaming white box houses that repeatedly offer enchanting views into patios adorned with flowers, alternating with secluded squares and sections of the city wall, with four remaining city gates and three towers. Above the confusion of houses tower the ruins of the castle, which commands a view over the city, coast and hinterland. From up here, the tower of the parish church Divino Salvador stands out – it was once a mosque. The palm-lined Plaza de España radiates Andalusian tranquilly.

15km/9mi west of Vejer lies Conil de la Frontera, a popular resort on the Costa de la Luz.

Conil de la Frontera

It does not have any noteworthy sights (only the Torre Guzmán of the Moorish castle has survived) but the town lives from tourism thanks to the marvellous, long sandy beaches – Playa de Bateles, Playa del Palmar – stretching south all the way to Cabo de Trafalgar, while to the north Playa de Fontanilla runs from Fuente del Gallo on to Roche on the cliff-lined coast, where there is one beautiful cove after the other where swimmers can climb down to cool off in the sea. During the high season the place can get crowded as many camping sites are lined up one after the other in the pine woods along the coast.

> **MARCO ⊕ POLO TIP**
>
> ! *Fresh fish with anemones* **Insider Tip**
>
> Despite the ever increasing importance of the tourist industry, fishing remains one of the major sources of income for the inhabitants of Conil de la Frontera, so that fresh fish is always available in the bars and restaurants. The speciality is ortiguillas – sea anemone baked in olive oil.

The unspectacular Cabo de Trafalgar (Cape Trafalgar), 16km/10mi south of Vejer, has gone down in history because of the **famous sea battle on 21 October 1805**, in which the English fleet under Lord Nelson defeated the French-Spanish armada under Villeneuve and Gravina. Nelson was fatally wounded, and Gravina also died. Villeneuve was taken prisoner and 5,000 seamen lost their lives.

The cliffs of Caños de Meca begin east of the cape, a delightfully charming stretch of coast with bathing grottoes and fresh water streaming down from overhanging vegetation. The village of Caños de Meca itself is a bustling summer resort populated by many Sevillenos, especially the younger ones. With the exception of one hotel apartment complex, there are small, inexpensive hotels, camping sites and little holiday houses providing accommodation.

*The cliffs of Caños de Meca

A narrow coastal road out of Vejer first passes through Barbate (between 1940 and 1998 it was called Barbate de Franco – the dictator Generalíssimo Francisco Franco liked to visit the town in the summer in order to go high sea fishing) before finally reaching the village of Zahara de los Atunes. As the name already says (Span. »atún« = tuna) the place lives from **tuna fishing**. The fish are caught from May through June in the Almadraba in a traditional and seem-

Zahara de los Atunes

ingly age-old manner considered by some to be cruel. Several boats circle a school with their nets and the fishermen stick their harpoons in each and every tuna. Even if this method appears very bloody, in contrast to industrial fishing, it does not endanger the stock. But nobody is forced to watch – as an alternative Zahara de los Atunes also has wonderfully secluded beaches.

Vejer de la Frontera

INFORMATION
Oficina de Turismo
Avenida de Los Remedios, 2
E-11150 Vejer de la Frontera
Tel. 956 45 17 36
www.turismovejer.es

WHERE TO EAT
Mesón Judería €€€€
Judería, 5
Tel. 956 44 76 57
The restaurant is popular with the locals for its excellent cooking and the beautiful view of the city. They also rent out two apartments.

Mesón Pepe Julián €€€€
Juan Relinque, 7
Tel. 956 45 10 98
Good, low-priced tapas bar. Those who feel really hungry can take a seat in the restaurant.

WHERE TO STAY
Hospedaría del Convento de San Francisco €
La Plazuela, s/n
Tel. 956 45 10 01
www.tugasa.com; 25 rooms
A centrally located hotel in a 17th-century Franciscan monastery in the upper part of town with a winning combination of atmosphere and value for money. The restaurant is very popular for its good cooking.

Sol Atlanterra €€€
In Zahara de los Atunes, Bahía de Plata
Tel. 956 43 90 00
www.solmelia.com, 284 rooms
Luxury bungalow hotel with good sports facilities.

Flamenco Conil €
In Conil de la Frontera, Fuente del Gallo, s/n
Tel. 956 44 07 11
www.hotelflamencoconil.com
114 rooms
A very good, large but perfectly decent hotel 3km/2mi outside town on a cliff overlooking the beach. Indoor pool and outdoor pool. Very nice service.

Diufain €
In Conil, Avda. Fuente de Gallo
Tel. 956 44 25 51
www.hoteldiufain.com, 30 rooms
Fairly new hotel in Andalusian country house style in a quiet setting, 600m/1980ft from the beach.

Casas Karen €€–€€€
In Caños de Meca, Fuente del Madroño, 6
Tel. 956 43 70 67
www.casaskaren.com
Pretty and varied accommodation at the foot of the Pinar de Barbate nature park, and a walk away from Cabo de Trafalgar. Houses, huts, apartments – Andalusian and Moroccan furnishings.

Vélez Blanco

⬩ L 6

Province: Almería
Altitude: 1125m/3691ft
Population: 2280

In the extreme north of Almería province, in the foothills of the Sierra de María, the little village of Vélez Blanco lives from the cultivation almonds of and olives. The castle of the Margrave of Vélez is one of the most beautiful fortresses in Andalucía.

The Romans once had a fortification here and it was not until 1488 that Vélez Blanco was retaken by the Christians. In 1503, the Margrave of Vélez came into possession of the village.

WHAT TO SEE IN AND AROUND VÉLEZ BLANCO

The castle, Castillo de los Fajardo, looms high over the little white houses of the village. It is, as is also the castle of La Calahorra (▶Guadix, surrounding area), a Renaissance structure, begun in 1506 and completed in 1515; but in contrast to La Calahorra, it has a more complex and irregular ground-plan, the long rows of battlements and the ramp connecting the keep with the other parts of the castle. It was designed by Francesco Florentini. Unfortunately, practically nothing remains of its interior. Almost the entire furnishings, including a

*Castillo de Vélez Blanco

Vélez Blanco

INFORMATION
Oficina de Turismo
in Almacen del Trigo
Avenida Marqués de los Vélez, s/n
E-04830 Vélez Blanco
Tel. 950 41 53 54

WHERE TO EAT
El Molino del Reloj €€€€
Curtidores; Crta. A-317, km 163
Tel. 950 41 56 00
www.molinodelreloj.com
closed Mondays

Grilled meat is the mainstay in the old mill.

WHERE TO STAY
Casa de los Arcos €
San Francisco, 2
Tel. 950 61 48 05
www.hotelcasadelosarcos.com
14 rooms
In a palace from the 18th and 19th centuries with an arcade offering attractive views. Very pleasant rooms.

magnificent patio, were bought up by a French art dealer in 1904 and resold in 1913 to **George Blumenthal**, a New York millionaire and former president of the Metropolitan Museum of Art. He bequeathed the patio to the museum, where it has stood reconstructed since 1964 and is now accessible to the public.

Stone Age rock paintings were found barely half a mile south of the village in Cueva de los Letreros. They depict humans and animals. Named Indalo, the human figure has become the symbol of Almería province.

Vélez Rubio

Vélez Rubio, the former capital of the county of Vélez, possesses the impressive Baroque church, Santa María de la Encarnación.

Sierra de María National Park

Vélez Blanco and Vélez Rubio lie in the Sierra de María National Park. This **craggy mountain range** with a height of up to 1500m/4900 was declared a nature reserve in the 1990s. The starting point for hiking tours is the village of María 6km/ 3.5mi west of Vélez Blanco. Information about the flora and fauna and hiking can be had at the visitor centre 3km/2 mi outside María in the direction of Orce or the information centre in **Almacen del Trigo** in Vélez Blanco.

Along the cliffs of Caños de Meca

PRACTICALITIES

What is the best way to get to Andalucía? Where can you get information on the region beforehand? What public transportation is available for travelling around Andalucía? Read it here – ideally before the journey!

Arrival · Before the Journey

HOW TO GET THERE

By air   **Scheduled flights** to Málaga and Gibraltar are available from London (British Airways), but the »no-frills« airlines normally offer a better deal to destinations in the south of Spain. Flights with Iberia via Madrid are also an option. It is worth looking at the wide range of **charter flights** that are offered from many airports, in particular to Málaga and Almería, but also to Seville and Jerez.

By car   From the ferry ports at Santander (from Plymouth) and Bilbao (from Portsmouth) or from the French border crossing at Irún, it is a long but straightforward day's journey to Andalucia via Burgos and Madrid. If driving from the south of France along the Mediterranean coast, take the AP7/A7 route, leaving the A7 to take the A92N to Granada and Malaga. There are motorway tolls in France and Spain.

By train   Those who like travelling by train and don't mind the long journey may travel via Paris – Madrid – Córdoba – Seville using the high-speed train AVE from Madrid to Seville. The main lines are run by the **state railway RENFE** (Red Nacional de los Ferrocarriles Españoles). Andalucía's rail network is not very dense, making train journeys time-consuming. In compensation, the prices are fairly low. The RENFE web site indicated below gives information on many special tariffs and discounts. The **high-speed train AVE** (Tren de Alta Velocidad) runs between Madrid and Seville in a good two hours. Another high-speed train, the **Talgo 200**, services the routes Madrid – Málaga, plus Madrid – Cádiz, and Madrid – Huelva.

> **Note**
> Billable service telephone numbers are marked with an asterisk: *0180…

By bus   Eurolines **buses** leave for Málaga and Seville from Paris and many other cities in continental Europe. But for travellers from the UK and Ireland, this method of travel is normally no cheaper and definitely much slower than a low-cost flight.

ENTRY/EXIT REQUIREMENTS

Papers   Visitors from EU countries require a valid identity card or passport for entry. Children require their own passport. Those planning a **trip to Morocco** require a passport.

AIRPORTS
Aeropuertos Españoles y Navegación
Aérea; www.aena.es
Tel. +34 91 3 21 10 00

Almería
Aeropuerto de Almería
(8km/5mi to the east in the direction of Níjar)
Transport connection: bus, taxi

Jerez de la Frontera
Aeropuerto de Jerez de la Frontera
(8km/5mi to the north-east)
Transport connection: bus, taxi

Málaga
Aeropuerto Internacional de Málaga
Pablo Picasso
(8km/5mi to the south-west)
Transport connection: train service
Málaga – Fuengirola, bus, taxi

Seville
Aeropuerto de San Pablo
(12 km/7.5 mi to the east)
Transport connection: bus, taxi

AIRLINES
Ryanair
Tel. *0900 1 16 05 00
(www.ryanair.com

Easyjet
www.easyjet.com

British Airways
Tel. (UK) 0844-493-0787
www.britishairways.com

TRAIN INFORMATION IN LONDON
Rail Europe Travel Centre 178 Piccadilly
London W1V 0BA Tel. 0870 8 37 13 71
www.raileurope.co.uk

TRAIN INFORMATION IN SPAIN
RENFE
Tel. 902 24 02 02
www.renfe.es (Spanish)

GETTING THERE BY BUS
Eurolines
Bookings online, in UK through National
Express Tel. 087 05 80 80 80
www.eurolines.com
www.nationalexpress.com

The national driving licence and vehicle registration certificate of citizens of EU states are recognized and must be carried; the international green insurance card is recommended. Vehicles without an EU number plate must be marked with the sign of their nationality. **Vehicle documents**

Those planning to take pets along with them require an official EU veterinary **health certificate**, which has entries showing that the pet has been marked with a microchip as well as a valid anti-rabies inoculation. The innoculation must date back at least 21 days, yet may not be older than twelve months prior to entry. **Pets**

Movement of goods for private purposes is largely duty free within the area of the European Union, including Spain. Certain restrictions on quantities apply (800 cigarettes or 400 cigarillos or 200 cigars or **Customs regulations**

1000g tobacco, 10 litres of spirits with over 22% alcohol or 20 litres under 22% alcohol as well as 90 litres of wine and 110 litres of beer). In the case of spot checks by the authorities, confirmation is required that the commodities are truly for private use only.

HEALTH INSURANCE

Statutory health insurances   The statutory health insurances must also reimburse fees for doctors' services abroad in the EU. The precondition is that the doctor concerned with treatment is presented with the European health insurance card. (Since 01/01/2005 this has superseded the E111 form for EU citizens; a replacement certificate must be issued for those without such a card.) In many cases, a part of the medical costs or expenditures for particular medicaments must be paid by the patient, even with this card. Where applicable, the health insurance at home may reimburse the costs on production of receipts.

Private travel health insurance   The conclusion of travel health insurance is certainly recommended for travellers from non-EU countries and should also be considered by EU citizens, as costs for medical treatment and medications are paid in part by the patient, and costs for possible return transportation are not borne by the statutory health insurances.

Drugs

Spain is deemed to be one of the main channels through which hashish (»chocolate«) from North Africa and cocaine from Latin America reach the EU by the ton – the drug mafia is often faster than the police. Drug trafficking is especially prevalent in the large cities and sea ports, in particular in Málaga, Cádiz and Algeciras. Be warned: the possession of drugs is heavily penalized. Also beware of accepting »small packages for friends« from new-found acquaintances to take home, or to take from the North African exclaves Ceuta and Melilla to Spain, as there is danger of being used as a courier in this manner.

Electricity

The Spanish power supply network runs on 220 volts alternating current. The large hotels usually have usable European standard plugs; visitors from the UK or USA should bring an adapter with them (Spanish: adaptor).

Emergency

CENTRAL NUMBER
Tel. 112
Call this emergency number to reach doctors, the fire brigade, and the police around the clock in Spanish, English, French or German.

Accident emergency / emergency doctor
Tel. 061

BREAKDOWN SERVICE
RACE
(Real Automóvil Club de España)
Tel. 902 30 05 05
www.race.es

Etiquette and Customs

Cutting a fine figure is valued highly in Spain. Certain customs and ritual are a natural part of the Spaniards' everyday life and should be respected by foreign visitors as well, like the choice of wardrobe. No matter if male or female Spaniards always leave the house looking their best, even on humid summer days. Men wear long pants, knee-length Bermudas only on very hot days, a short-sleeved shirt or a fashionable T-shirt. Short shorts, muscle shirts and worn out flip-flops are not their thing. Beach clothing is just not worn in the city. People tend to cover up. Women also dress up to go to town. While they show lots of skin but they do it very fashionably and according to the latest styles. This applies especially to young people, which is very fashion-conscious and always follows the latest trends, including body piercing and daring tattoos when they are in fashion. Body hair of any kind, in the armpits or on the legs is absolutely taboo for women. Shorts and sleeveless clothing is considered inappropriate for both sexes in churches and monasteries. It is advisable to have one more elegant outfit along for going out in the evening, whether to one of the many cultural events or to enjoy the nightlife.

Clothing

> ❗ **MARCO ❂ POLO INSIGHT**
>
> *Strictly no smoking in Spain*
>
> Since 2011 there is strictly no smoking in tapas bars, restaurants, cafés, discotheques, casinos as well as public buildings like railway stations and airports. While hotels are allowed to reserve 30% of their rooms for guests who smoke many Spanish hotels do not allow smoking at all.

People embrace when greeting each other, whether man and woman or two women, even if they do not know each other well and peck

Greeting

each other on both cheeks but without too much bodily contact. Men greet each other by shaking hands firmly or thumping each other on the shoulder. Instead of using the more formal »buenos días« (»Good day!« in the morning) or »buenas tardes (»Good day!« in the afternoon or »Good evening!«) the more casual »hola« (»hello!«) is being used in the meantime.

The bar as living room **Invitations** are extended quickly and gladly, yet only very rarely to another's house. Bars or restaurants serve as an alternative. However, people do not stay long, but prefer to move on quickly to the next place. Spaniards do not like going out by themselves, preferring small or larger groups. If someone brings a friend along to the evening get-together, then he is quickly integrated and immediately belongs. This also applies to foreigners – there are few inhibitions. Yet no one who is bid farewell with a »Call me sometime« should expect a deeper friendship. It is not necessary to comply with such a request right the next day.

One for all Payment of bills in bars or restaurants is handled as follows in Spain: one person always pays for all. If a group passes through several bars, then everyone gets a turn. It is not done to sort out fussily who paid what; **generosity** is the order of the day. A foreigner may find it hard to get a turn at paying in a Spanish group, as somebody else is always faster.

»Is this seat taken?« Another rule applies in restaurants: never join a stranger at a table. A question such as **»Is this seat taken?«** is not asked. Yet guests also never sit down without asking at a free table. As a basic principle, they stop in the restaurant foyer. Within seconds, the maitre d' arrives, asks for the number of persons and suggests tables. The guests are then shown to the chosen seats and handed the menu.

Rituals when paying The **bill** is requested very casually in restaurants. It arrives on a small plate, the waiter disappears again. Someone casually picks up the bill, glances at it, and places either a credit card or a few notes onto the plate. The waiter will return equally casually and take the plate with him with a murmured »gracias«. After a while he comes again, slides the plate with change to the payer with a repeated »gracias«. The payer ignores this for a few seconds longer, pockets the change, and leaves a certain amount lying on the plate as a tip. Only once the entire table has left the restaurant does the waiter pick up the plate with the tip one last time.

Health

Pharmacies Pharmacies (Spanish: farmacias) in Spain are identified by a green cross on a white background. They are normally open Mon – Fri

9.30am – 1.30pm and 4.30 – 8pm, as well as Sat 9am – 12.30pm. Pharmacies providing emergency service are listed in each pharmacy on the sign **»Farmacia de Guardia«**, and in the newspapers.

►Arrival · Before the Journey

Health insurance

Information

IN CANADA
Spanish Tourist Office
Bloor Street West 2-Suite 3402
Toronto, Ontario M4W 3E2
Tel. (01) 416 961 3131
Fax 416 961 1992
E-Mail: toronto@tourspain.es

IN UK
Spanish Tourist Office
2nd floor, 79 New Cavendish Street
London W1W 6XB
Tel. (207) 48 68 077
Fax (207) 48 68 034
E-Mail: londres@tourspain.es

IN USA
Spanish Tourist Office
Fifth Avenue 666-35th floor
NY. 10103 New York
Tel. (212) 265 88 22
Fax 265 88 64
E-Mail: nuevayork@tourspain.es

Spanish Tourist Office
Wilshire Blvd. 8383 - Suite 960
Beverly Hills California 90211
Tel. (1323) 658 71 95, fax 658 10 61
E-Mail: losangeles@tourspain.es

CONSULATES IN ANDALUSIA
Australia
Consulate in Seville

Calle Federico Rubio 14
Tel. 954 22 09 71

Canada
Consulate in Malaga
Plaza de la Malagueta 2, 1st floor
Tel. 952 22 33 46

United Kingdom
Consulate in Malaga
Edificio Eurocom
Calle Mauricio Moro Pareto 2
Tel. 952 35 23 00

United States
Consular Agency in Seville
Paseo de las Delicias 7
Tel. 954 23 18 85

INTERNET
www.spain.info
Web site of the Spanish tourist office.

www.tourspain.es
Website of the Spanish tourist office for tourism specialists.

www.andalucia.org/en
The website of the Andalusian tourism office with lots of information places to visit, beaches, hotels, golf courses, sports harbours....

www.andalucia.com
Everything, really everything about
Andalucía, in Spanish and English.

www.juntadeandalucia.es
Website of the Andalusian government,
includes tourism information.

www.legadoandalusi.es
Beautiful tour suggestions for Andalucía,
including Route of the Caliphate.

http://cvc.cervantes.es
The online window to the Spanish
language, literature and culture.

www.parador.es
Info about paradores: Individual buildings, palaces or castles can be viewed
and booked.

www.surinenglish.com
English news site in southern Spain

Language

Vowels In Spanish the vowels a, e, i, o, u, are **pronounced** openly and distinctly. Long vowels (as in boot, path) don't exist, and a closed e and
o (as in rate, boat) equally so.

Pronuncia- c before a, o, u like »k«
tion guide c before e, i voiceless lisp, stronger than »th« (ex.: gracias)
ch as in »church«
g before a, o, u as in »good«
g before e, i as in German »ch« in Bach
gue, gui / que, qui u is always silent here, like »g«, »k«
h is always silent
j always like German »ch« in Bach
ll like »lj« or »y« (ex.: Mallorca)
ñ like »ny« in señora
z voiceless lisp, stronger than »th«

Spanish phrases

At a glance
Yes./No.   Sí./No.
Maybe.   Quizás./Tal vez.
OK!   ¡De acuerdo!/¡Está bien!
Please./Thank you.   Por favor./Gracias.
Thank you very much!   Muchas gracias.
You're welcome.   No hay de qué./De nada.
Excuse me!   ¡Perdón!

Pardon?	¿Cómo dice/dices?
I don't understand you.	No le/la/te entiendo.
I only speak a little …	Hablo sólo un poco de …
Could you help me?	¿Puede usted ayudarme, por favor?
I would like …	Quiero …/Quisiera …
I (don't) like that.	(No) me gusta.
Do you have …?	¿Tiene usted …?
How much does this cost?	¿Cuánto cuesta?
What time is it?	¿Qué hora es?

Getting acquainted

Good morning	¡Buenos días!
Good day!	¡Buenos días!/¡Buenas tardes!
Good evening!	¡Buenas tardes!/¡Buenas noches!
Hello!	¡Hola! ¿Qué tal?
My name is …	Me llamo …
What is your name, please?	¿Cómo se llama usted, por favor?
How are you?	¿Qué tal está usted?/¿Qué tal?
Fine, thanks. And you?	Bien, gracias. ¿Y usted/tú?
Good bye!	¡Hasta la vista!/¡Adiós!
See you!	¡Adiós!/¡Hasta luego!
See you soon!	¡Hasta pronto!
See you tomorrow!	¡Hasta mañana!

Travelling

left/right	a la izquierda/a la derecha
straight ahead	todo seguido/derecho
close/far	cerca/lejos
How far is it?	¿A qué distancia está?
I would like to rent … .	Quisiera alquilar …
… a car	…un coche.
… a boat	…una barca/un bote/un barco.
Excuse me, where is …?	Perdón, ¿dónde está …
… the railway station	…la estación (de trenes)?
… the bus terminal	…la estación de autobuses/ . . . .
	la terminal?
… the airport	…el aeropuerto?

Breakdown

I had a breakdown.	Tengo una avería.
Would you please send me	¿Pueden ustedes enviarme

a towtruck?	un cochegrúa, por favor?
Is there a garage here?	¿Hay algún taller por aquí cerca?
Where is the next petrol station?	¿Dónde está la estación de servicio/a gasolinera más cercana, por favor?
I would like … litres of …	Quisiera … litros de …
… normal petrol.	… gasolina normal.
… super./ …diesel.	… súper./ … diesel.
… unleaded./ …leaded.	… sin plomo./ … con plomo.
Fill it up, please.	Lleno, por favor.

Accident

Help!	¡Ayuda!, ¡Socorro!
Careful!	¡Atención!
Careful!	¡Cuidado!
Please call … quickly	Llame enseguida …
… an ambulance.	… una ambulancia.
… the police.	… a la policía.
… the fire department.	… a los bomberos.
Do you have any bandages?	¿Tiene usted botiquín de urgencia?

People eat, drink – and live in tapas bars

It was my (your) fault.   Ha sido por mi (su) culpa.
Please tell me your name   ¿Puede usted darme su nombre
and your address.   y dirección?

Going out
Where is there ...   ¿Dónde hay por aquí cerca ...
... a good restaurant?   ... un buen restaurante?
... a reasonable restaurant?   ... un restaurante no demasiado caro?
Please make a reservation for   ¿Puede reservarnos para esta
us for this evening   noche
for a table for 4 people.   una mesa para cuatro personas?
Cheers!   ¡Salud!
The bill, please!   ¡La cuenta, por favor!
Did it taste good?   ¿Le/Les ha gustado la comida?
The food was excellent.   La comida estaba écelente.

Shopping
Where can I find ... a market?   Por favor, ¿dónde hay ... un mercado?
... a pharmacy   .... una farmacia
... a shopping centre   ... un centro comercial

Accommodation
Could you please recommend ... ?   Perdón, señor/señora/señorita. . . . . . .
                                            ¿Podría usted recomendarme ...
... a hotel   ... un hotel?
... a guesthouse   ... una pensión?
I have reserved a room.   He reservado una habitación.
Do you still have ...   ¿Tienen ustedes ...?
... a single room?   ... una habitación individual?
... a double room?   ... una habitación doble?
... with shower/bath?   ... con ducha/baño?
... for one night?   ... para una noche?
... for one week?   ... para una semana?
How much does the room cost   ¿Cuánto cuesta la habitación
... with breakfast?   ... con desayuno?
... with half board?   ... media pensión?

Doctor and pharmacy
Can you recommend   ¿Puede usted indicarme
a good doctor?   un buen médico?

I have …	Tengo …
… diarrhea.	… diarrea.
… a fever.	… fiebre.
… a headache.	… dolor de cabeza.
… a toothache.	… dolor de muelas.
… a sore throat.	… dolor de garganta.

Bank

Where is …	Por favor, ¿dónde hay por aquí…?
… a bank?	… un banco?
… a currency exchange?	… una oficina/casa de cambio?
I would like to change	Quisiera cambiar …
British pounds into euros.	libras británicas

Post

How much does … cost?	¿Cuánto cuesta …
… a letter …/… a postcard …	… una carta …/… una postal …
to Great Britain/USA?	para Inglaterra/los Estados Unidos?
a stamp	sellos
a telephone card	tarjetas para el teléfono

Numbers

0	cero	19	diecinueve
1	un, uno, una	20	veinte
2	dos	21	veintiuno(a)
3	tres	22	veintidós
4	cuatro	30	treinta
5	cinco	40	cuarenta
6	seis	50	cincuenta
7	siete	60	sesenta
8	ocho	70	setenta
9	nueve	80	ochenta
10	diez	90	noventa
11	once	100	cien, ciento
12	doce	200	doscientos, -as
13	trece	1000	mil
14	catorce	2000	dos mil
15	quince	10000	diez mil
16	dieciséis		
17	diecisiete	1/2	medio
18	dieciocho	1/4	un cuatro

Relaxed everyday life makes room for a cerveza or two,
a tapa and a chat ...

Restaurant/Restaurante

desayuno	breakfast
almuerzo	lunch
cena	dinner
camarero	waiter
cubierto	setting
cuchara	spoon
cucharita	teaspoon
cuchillo	knife
lista de comida	menu
plato	plate
tenedor	fork
vaso / taza	glass / cup

Tapas

albóndigas	meatballs
boquerones en vinagre	small herring in a vinegar marinade
caracoles	snails

chipirones	small squid
chorizo	paprika sausage
jamón serrano	dried ham
morcilla	blood sausage
pulpo	squid
tortilla	potato omelette

Entremeses/Starters

aceitunas	olives
anchoas	anchovies
ensalada	salad
jamón	ham
mantequilla	butter
pan	bread
panecillo	bread roll
sardinas	sardines

Sopas/Soups

caldo	meat broth
gazpacho	cold vegetable soup
puchero canario	hearty soup
sopa de pescado	fish soup
sopa de verduras	vegetable soup

Platos de huevos/Egg dishes

huevo	egg
duro	hard-boiled
pasado por agua	soft-boiled
huevos a la flamenca	eggs with beans
huevos fritos	fried eggs
huevos revueltos	scrambled eggs
tortilla	omelette

Pescado/Fish

ahumado	smoked
a la plancha	grilled on a hot griddle
asado	fried
cocido	boiled
frito	baked
anguila	eel

atún	tuna
bacalao	cod
besugo	bream
lenguado	sole
merluza	hake
salmón	salmon
trucha	trout
almeja	river mussel
bogavante	lobster
calamar	squid
camarón	shrimp
cangrejo	crab
gamba	prawn
langosta	rock lobster
ostras	oysters

Carne/Meat

buey	beef
carnero	mutton
cerdo	pork
chuleta	chops
cochinillo, lechón	roast suckling pig
conejo	rabbit
cordero	lamb
ternera	veal
vaca	beef
asado	roast
bistec	beefsteak
carne ahumada	smoked meat
carne estofada	pot roast
carne salada	corned beef
fiambre	cold cuts
jamón	ham
lomo	loin or back
salchichón	hard sausage
tocino	bacon
pato	duck
pollo	chicken

Verduras/Vegetables

aceitunas	olives
cebollas	onions

Millions of tourists visit Andalucía every year

col de Bruselas	Brussels sprouts
coliflor	cauliflower
espárragos	asparagus
espinacas	spinach
garbanzos	chickpeas
guisantes	peas
habas, judías	beans
lechuga	lettuce
patatas	potatoes
patatas fritas	French fries
pepinos	cucumber
tomates	tomato
zanahorias	carrots

Condimentos/Condiments

vinagre / aceite	vinegar / oil
ajo	garlic
azafrán	saffron
mostaza	mustard
sal/salado / pimienta	salt/salted / pepper

Postres/Sweets

bollo	sweet bread
dulces	sweets
flan	cream caramel
helado	ice cream
mermelada / miel	jam / honey
pastel	cake
queso	cheese
tarta	tart

Frutas/Fruit

cerezas	cherries
chumbos	prickly pears
dátiles	dates
fresas	strawberries
higos	figs
mandarinas	mandarin oranges
manzana / pera	apple / pear
melocotón	peach
melones	honeydew melon
membrillo	quince
naranjas	oranges
nueces	nuts
piña	pineapple
plátano	banana
sandías	watermelon
uvas	grape

Local Foods

bocadillo	filled roll
chorizo	red paprika sausage
churros	fried dough
migas	croutons

Beverages

agua mineral	mineral water
con/sin gas	still / sparkling
aguardiente	cordial
amontillado	medium sherry
anís	anis cordial
Brandy	brandy

cerveza	beer
café con leche	coffee with milk
café solo	espresso
café cortado	with a little milk
fino	dry sherry
leche	milk
limonada	lemonade
la Manzanilla	camomile tea
oloroso	sweet sherry
té	tea
vino	wine
blanco/tinto	white/red
rosado	rosé
dry/sweet	seco/dulce
zumo	fruit juice

Literature

Novels and stories

Rafael Alberti: *Lost Grove*. University of California Press 1981. Alberti describes his youth in the port city of Cádiz in this novel.

Federico García Lorca: *Blood Wedding*. A & C Black 2006. Drama in three acts about a family tragedy on the Cabo de Gata.

Théophile Gautier: *A Romantic in Spain*. Interlink Publishing 2001. The French author's account of his journey through Andalucía in 1840 is a classic of travel literature, a book that at times is surprisingly current, sharp-tongued, and spirited.

Ernest Hemingway: *Death in the Afternoon*. Scribner Classics, 2003. Not exactly a book about Andalucía, but it is a literary standard about bullfighting from the viewpoint of the aficionados. With a narration about Ronda.

Juan Ramón Jiménez: *Platero and I*. Dover Publications; 2004. The Nobel Prize winner from Moguer, province Huelva, philosophizes with his donkey.

James A. Michener: *The Drifters*. Fawcet Books, 1986. Young people from around the world travel to Torremolinos – after all, the sun shines there all the time ... A narrative worth reading about the emotions of young people in the escapism and optimism of the hippy era, about a generation, for whom the search for the meaning of life was more important than prosperity and middle-class security.

Marianne Barrucand and Achim Bednorz: *Moorish Architecture in Andalusia.* Taschen 2002 A book that really whets the appetite for a trip to the south of Spain.

Gerald Brenan: *South of Granada.* Penguin Books, 1992. Brenan lived in the Alpujarras village Yegen from 1920 to 1934 and describes a way of life that is now lost.   History

Titus Burckhardt: *Moorish Culture in Spain.* Fons Vitae 2001. A classic account of the subject, illuminating background for a trip to the region.

Richard Fletcher: *Moorish Spain.* University of California Press, 2006. A readable book, much of it about Andalucía

Washington Irving: *Tales of the Alhambra.* Editorial Everest, 2005 Literary classic of the Alhambra literature, written by the American author Washington Irving after a long stay in the decaying Alhambra in 1832. With this work he renewed international interest in this architectural jewel.

María Rosa Menocal: *Ornament of the World.* The subtitle tells it all: *How Muslims, Jews and Christians Created a Culture of Tolerance in Medieval Spain.* Littel, Brown and Company 2003. The Yale professor writes about old Andalucía in a knowledgeable and entertaining manner.

Hugh Thomas: *The Spanish Civil War.* Penguin Books 2003. Lengthy account but a great work of historical writing and enjoyable to read

Mark Williams: *The Story of Spain.* Santana Books, 2000. Fairly concise overview of Spanish history

Media

International newspapers are available in Andalucía, in particular at   Newspapers
the tourist centres along the Costa del Sol; usually a day after publication, sometimes even on the same day. Away from the coast, and in cities such as Seville or Granada, it can be a matter of luck.

The national Spanish television (Radio Televisión Española, RTVE)   Television
offers two programmes (La primera, La 2); the commercial broadcasters include Antena 3, Telecino, and the pay-TV channel Canal Plus. Getting a taste of one these programmes in the many bars is unavoidable, as the TV often runs non-stop. A number of English-speaking channels can be received via satellite.

Money

Euro Since 1 January 2002 the **euro** has been the official currency in Spain, as in twelve other states of the European Union. **Cash machines (ATMs)** are provided with multilingual operating instructions. Withdrawals can be made from these using a bank card or established credit cards in conjunction with a PIN. Most restaurants and shops do not accept 100, 200 and 500 euro notes.

Banks, hotels, car rentals, many restaurants, and shops accept the usual **credit cards**, especially Visa and MasterCard.

In the event of **loss of credit cards**, the relevant credit card organization should be notified immediately.

Post · Telecommunications

Letter box The letter boxes in Spain are yellow with a red postal horn. Foreign mail goes into the box labelled »extranjero« (abroad).

Stamps Post offices and tobacco shops (»estancos«) sell stamps (»sellos«).

Post offices The **post and telegraph offices** (Correos y Telégrafos) are open Mon – Fri 9am – 2pm and Sat 9am – 1pm.

Telephone cards Many public telephones accept both coins and telephone cards, which can be bought in tobacco shops (»estancos«) and kiosks. Telephone calls from hotels can be up to three times as expensive as from public telephone boxes

Mobile phone When using a mobile phone (»móvil«) not registered in Spain to phone a Spanish number, the country code +34 or 00 34 must be entered before dialling a telephone number. Spanish pre-paid cards can be bought inSpanish telephone shops and shopping centres.

DIALLING CODES
To Spain from other countries:
Tel. 00 34 or +34

From Spain to other countries
International access code 00 followed by the relevant country code (44 for GB, 1 for USA, etc
When calling the above mentioned countries from Spain, the 0 of the respective local dialling code is not dialled.

Prices · Discounts

Prices in restaurants, hotels and museums are similar to the UK. Only public transport is a little cheaper. Children also benefit from discounts on admission fees, or even have **free admission** to many museums and sights. Children under four have **free rides** in Spanish trains, and children ages four to eleven pay only 60% of the standard price. There are also discounts for seniors over 60 and students on the trains.

MARCO ● POLO INSIGHT

? *What does it cost?*

Petrol: €1.41
Simple meal:
Tapas from €1.60
Cup of coffee:
€1.50 (café solo)
► Prices for restaurants p. 92
► Prices for hotels p. 108

The **table d'hôte** is usually the cheapest option when eating and drinking.

Time

During the winter half-year (end of October to end of March), Central European Time (CET) applies to Andalucía, and in the summer half-year (beginning of April to end of October) summer time applies (CET + 1 hr). This is **one hour ahead of Greenwich Mean Time**.

Transport

Use of **motorways** (autopistas) is **subject to tolls** (peaje). The autovias, **expressways** similar to motorways, can be used **free of charge**. The numbered **national routes** (Carreteras Nacionales; N-...) are also good-quality roads. Crawler lanes have normally been built for trucks on inclines, where they have not yet been extended to four lanes as autovías. The **country roads**, likewise numbered, (carreteras autonomas; A ... or abbreviation of the province), are also in good condition, provided they constitute major connections. Unnumbered secondary roads can hold surprises, however, and turn out to be **dirt roads**.

Roads

Unless absolutely necessary, **avoid driving into cities**, particularly into old town centres, where streets are often very narrow. The one-way systems make car trips into the cities complicated and lengthy.

In cities

In most cities **parking** in spaces marked in blue is **subject to fees**, and **prohibited** in spaces marked in yellow. Fees are paid to attendants, or at parking ticket machines.

Maximum speed limits
Urban: 50kmh/31mph; non-urban: 90kmh/55mph On roads with at least two lanes in each direction: 100kmh/62mph On motorways: 120kmh/74mph Cars with caravan: 70kmh/43mph; on motorways: 80kmh/49mph

Traffic regulations
Traffic in Spain **drives on the right** – as in the rest of continental Europe. The wearing of **seat belts** is compulsory for front and back seats. The **legal drink-drive limit** is 50mg of alcohol per 100ml of blood. **Using a mobile phone in the car** without a hands-free set is not allowed.

Special regulations
When **turning left** outside towns, there are separate lanes on larger roads that first veer to the right and then cross the main road (raqueta). When **overtaking**, first the left indicator, then the right one is used during the entire procedure. Overtaking is prohibited on hill brows and roads with a clear view of less than 220yd/200 m. In Spain, it is permissible to use only **parking lights** on well-lit roads (except on expressways and motorways). Replacement bulbs must be carried. **Towing** is prohibited using private vehicles.

Another kind of transport – like here in Algeciras with the rock of Gibraltar in the background

In the event of a breakdown or an accident, the vehicle must be marked with two warning triangles, one in front of the car and one behind it; cars from abroad only need one warning triangle. Reflecting warning vests must also be worn when leaving the car in case of an accident or a breakdown outside of towns (emergency breakdown number ▶Emergency).

Roadside assistance

PUBLIC TRANSPORTATION

All of Andalucía's large cities are accessible by train. High speed trains run to Córdoba, Sevilla and Málaga (▶Arrival, p. 450).

! **MARCO ◉ POLO TIP**

Al-Andalus Express **Insider Tip**

For a special treat with the atmosphere of the »good old days« of rail travel, book a 6-day trip on the luxury train Al-Andalus (between March and early December) from Seville via Córdoba and Granada to Ronda or Jerez de la Frontera or vice versa. The train has one galley car, four salon cars and seven sleeping cars from the years 1928 to 1930 for 64 passengers (starting at €2300). www.trenalandalus.com).

A close network of buses connects all of the cities and many towns in Andalucía with each other. Most cities have a bus terminal.

Bus

When to Go

Moderate temperatures and lots of sunshine make spring and autumn the **best time to go**; September and October are particularly favourable with agreeable air and water temperatures, and stable weather conditions right up to the second half of October. On the Costa del Sol the visitor is spared autumn showers the longest. July and August can only be endured to some degree right on the coast. In winter, Andalucía enjoys almost consistently pleasant day temperatures and lots of sunshine. This climate results in the early **almond blossom**, which starts as early as the end of January.

Tourists travelling in spring be warned: April is often surprisingly cool and unstable, due to frequent encroachment of cold air into the western Mediterranean. The weather is more stable in March, and also much warmer from May onwards.

Index

A

Abd ar-Rahman I 73
Abd ar-Rahman III 73
accommodation 84, 85
active holidays 110
agriculture 29
Aguadulce 145
Aguilar de la Frontera
    348
airlines 448
airports 449
Al-Andalus Express 448
Alcalá de Guadaira 423
Alcalá de los Gazules
    339
Alcalá la Real 362
Alcaudete 303
Algeciras 135
Alhama de Almería 156
Alhama de Granada 273
Alhaurín el Grande 240
Almansur 73
Almería 138
Almerímar 145
Almodóvar del Río 223
Almohads 39
Almonaster la Real 166
Almoravids 39
Almuñécar 150
Alozaina 240
Andújar 156
angling 111, 113
Antequera 158
aqua parks 90
Aqua Tropic 91
Aquopolis 90
Aracena 164
Archidona 163
Arcos de la Frontera 167
Aroche 166
art history 47
Atlantic coast 17
Averroes 73

Ayamonte 281

B

Baelo Claudia 436
Baena 350
Baeza 171
Bailén 317
Baza 276
beaches 112
Beas de Segura 182
Benalmádena Costa 437
Benalmádena Pueblo
    438
Benamahoma 427
Betic intermountain
    basin 17
biking 111
Bioparc Fuengirola 90
Boabdil 74
Bolonia 436
Bonanza 390
Bornos 170

C

Cabo de Gata 182
Cabo de Trafalgar 441
Cabo Tres Forcas 344
Cabra 349
Cádiz 186
Calar Alto 150
Caliphate of Córdoba 39
Calle Sierpes 413
Camarón de la Isla 75,
    76
Campiña 17
camping 86
Canena 182
Cano, Alonso 57
Caños de Meca 441
Carboneras 346
Carcabeuy 362
Carmona 196
Carthaginians 36, 53

Casarabonela 240
Casares 238
Castellar de la Frontera
    135
Castell de Ferro 153
Castilleja de la Cuesta
    423
Castillo de Lacalahorra
    275
Castro del Río 350
cave paintings 47
Cazalla de la Sierra 424
Cazorla 425
Ceuta 201
Chiclana de la Frontera
    195
children 89
Chipiona 391
Churriguera, José de 57
climate 19
climbing 114
Coín 240
Columbus, Christopher
    75, 281
communications 466
Cómpeta 353
Conil de la Frontera
    441
Constantina 423
consulates 453
Cordillera Penibética 13
Córdoba 204
  - Alcázar de los Reyes
    Cristianos 217
  - Judería 218
  - Mezquita Catedral
    207
  - Museo Arqueológico
    220
  - Museo Diocesano 216
  - Museo Provincial de
    Bellas Artes 220
  - Museo Taurino 219

- Museo Vivo de Al-Andalus **217**
- Palacio de los Marqueses de Viana **222**
- Plaza de los Dolores **222**
- synagogue **219**
- Torre de la Calahorra **217**
Costa Ballena **367**
Costa de Almería **145, 224**
Costa de la Luz **224**
Costa del Sol **226**
Costa Tropical **150, 227**
Coto de Doñana **227**
crafts **107**
Crocodiles Park **90**
Cueva de la Pileta **379**
Cueva de los Letreros **445**
Cueva de los Murciélagos **349**
Cueva de Menga **161**
Cueva de Viera **161**
Cuevas de Almanzora **346**
Cuevas del Tajo y de las Figuras **340**
customs regulations **449**

D
day labourers **28**
Desfiladero de los aitanes **163**
dialling codes **466**
discounts **467**
Dolmen de Soto **356**
drinks **96**
drugs **450**

E
Écija **233**
economy **28**
El Arahal **439**
El Argar culture **48**

El Bosque **427**
electricity **450**
El Greco **55**
El Pedroso **424**
El Puerto de Santa María **364**
El Rocío **367**
El Torcal **162**
emergency **451**
Emirate of Córdoba **38**
Emirate of Granada
Espera **170**
Estepa **359**
Estepona **236**
events **93**

F
Falla, Manuel de **76**
fauna **23**
feria **64**
Feria de Abril **93**
festival culture **60**
festivals **92, 93**
fishing **29**
flamenco courses **111**
flora **22**
food **96**
Frigiliana **353**
Fuengirola **238**
Fuentes de Andalucía **201**
Fuente Vaqueros **273**

G
Galera **276**
García Lorca, Federico **76**
Garganta del Chorro **163**
Garrucha **346**
getting there **448**
Gibraltar **240**
Gitanos **25**
Golden Age **55**
golf **114**

Gothic **52**
government **28**
Goya y Lucientes, Francisco de **57**
Granada 245
- Albaicín **267**
- Alhambra **250**
- Catedral Santa María de la Encarnación **262**
- Generalife **262**
- La Cartuja **271**
- Museo de la Alhambra **260**
- Museo Provincial de Bellas Artes **260**
- Nasrid Palace **254**
- Palace of Charles V **257**
- Parque de las Ciencias **272**
- Sacromonte **270**
- university quarter **271**
Grazalema **428**
Greeks **36**
Guadix **274**

H
health **452**
health insurance **450**
hiking **111, 114**
holidays **93**
Hornos **427**
hotels **85**
Huelva **276**

I
illegal immigrants **25**
industry **32**
information **453**
internet **465**
Irving, Washington **77**
Isabelline Gothic style **53**
Isidore of **77**
Isla Mágica **89**
Itálica **286**

Iznájar **349**
Iznatoraf **182**

J
Jaén **289**
Jerez de la Frontera **303**
Jiménez, Juan Ramón **77**

K
Karst de Yesos de Sorbas **147**

L
La Almadraba de Monteleva **184**
La Axarquía **353**
La Calahonda **153**
La Carolina **317**
La Cartuja **315**
La Guardia de Jaén **302**
La Herradura **152**
La Isleta del Moro **185**
La Línea de la Concepción **138**
landscape **13**
Lanjarón **155**
La Rábida **281**
Las Alpujarras **153**
Las Casas, Bartolomé de **78**
Las Ermitas **223**
Laguna de la Fuente de Piedra **163**
Laujar de Andarax **156**
Lebrija **315**
Linares **316**
literature **464**
Loja **273**
Loma de Úbeda **17**
Lorca, Federico García **273**
Los Alcornocales **134**
Los Escullos **185**
Los Millares **145**
Lower Andalucía **17**

Lucainena de las Torres **150**
Lucena **348**
Lucía, Paco de **78**

M
Maimónides, Moses **78**
Málaga **318**
Mannerism **55**
Manolete **79**, **207**
Marbella **328**
Marchena **201**
Mar de Plástico **29**
markets **107**
Martos **302**
Matalascañas **371**
Mazagón **280**
meal times **99**
Medina Azahara **335**
Medina Sidonia **337**
Megalith culture **47**
Melilla **340**
Mena, Pedro de **57**
Mengs, Anton Raphael **57**
Mijas **240**
Mini Hollywood **89**, **147**
mining **32**
Moguer **283**
Mojácar **344**
Monda **334**
money **466**
Montañés, Martínez **57**
Montefrío **363**
Montes de Málaga **328**
Montilla **346**
Montilla-Moriles **346**
Montoro **223**
Moorish-Arab bath culture **69**
Moorish science **70**
Moorish technology **70**
Moorish urban culture **65**
Morales, Luis de **55**

Morón de la Frontera **440**
Motril **153**, **155**
Mozarabic style **52**
Mudéjar style **53**
Mulhacén **430**
Murillo, Bartolomé Esteban **55**

N
nature **13**
nature reserves **24**
Navas de Tolosa **317**
Necrópolis de Trayamar **354**
Nerja **351**
Nerva **166**
newspapers **465**
Niebla **354**
Níjar **150**
Novo Sancti Petri **195**

O
Ojén **334**
Olvera **379**
Osuna **356**

P
Palos de la Frontera **283**
paradors **85**
Parque Nacional de Doñana **227**
Parque Nacional de la Sierra Nevada **430**
Parque Natural de la Sierra de Cardeña y Montoro **224**
Parque Natural de la Sierra Subbética **349**
Parque Natural del Cabo de Gata-Níjar **182**
Parque Natural Sierra de Baza **276**
Parque Natural Sierra de Cazorla, Segura y Las Villas **424**

Peña de los Gitanos **363**
pharmacies **452**
Phoenicians **35**
Picasso, Pablo **79**
Pico de Veleta **430**
Piñeda, Mariana **80**
plateresque style **54**
population **24**
post **466**
Prado Llano **432**
precipitation **21**
prices **467**
Priego de Córdoba **360**
Puerto Banús **334**
Puerto del Cabrito **437**
Punta Umbria **281**
Purullena **275**

Q

Quesada **426**

R

Rail traffic **448**
riding **114**
riding holidays **114**
Rincón de la Victoria **328**
Río Guadalquivir **18**
Río Tinto **166**
roadside assistance **469**
Rodalquilar **185**
Rodríguez Acosta **58**
Romanesque style **52**
Romans **37**
romería **64**
Ronda **371**
Ronda la Vieja **379**
Roquetas de Mar **145**
Rota **367**
Ruinas de Bobastro **163**
rural tourism **86**
Ruta Colombina **281**
Rute **348**

S

Sabiote **182**

sailing and motor boating **113**
Salobreña **153**
Sancti Petri **196**
San Fernando **195**
San Jerónimo **337**
San José **185**
San Miguel de Cabo de Gata **184**
San Pedro Alcántara **334**
Sanlúcar de Barrameda **387**
Sanlúcar la Mayor **423**
Santa Fé **273**
Santiponce **287**
Segovia, Andrés **316**
Segura de la Sierra **427**
Selwo Aventura **90**
Selwo Marina **90**
Semana Santa **60, 93**
Seneca **80**
Serranía de Ronda **386**
Setenil **386**
Sevilla 393
- Alcázar **407**
- Archivo General de Indias **407**
- Barrio de Santa Cruz **411**
- Barrio de Triana **421**
- Casa de Pilatos **414**
- Catedral de Santa María de la Sede **399**
- Gardens of Alcázar **411**
- Giralda **401**
- Hospital de la Caridad **417**
- Isla de la Cartuja **422**
- Isla Mágica **422**
- la Macarena **416**
- Museo Arqueológico **421**
- Museo de Bellas Artes **414**

- Palacio de Carlos V **410**
- Plaza de España **420**
- Plaza de Toros **417**
- Puente de la Barqueta **416**
- Real Alcázar **407**
- Torre del Oro **418**
Shopping **106, 107**
Sierra Alhamilla **146**
Sierra Bermeja **238**
Sierra Blanca **334**
Sierra de Andújar **157**
Sierra de Baza **276**
Sierra de Cazorla **424**
Sierra de Grazalema **427**
Sierra de las Nieves **386**
Sierra de Las Villas **424**
Sierra de los Filabres **150**
Sierra de María **445**
Sierra de Segura **424**
Sierra Morena **17**
Sierra Nevada **430**
skiing **114**
Solynieve **432**
Sorbas **147**
Sotogrande **238**
Souvenirs **106**
sports **111**
surfing **433**

T

Tabernas **147**
Tarifa **433**
Tartessos **35**
telecommunications **466**
temperatures **20**
tennis **114**
Texas Hollywood **147**
Tharsis **281**
theme parks **90**
time **467**
To Pico de Veleta **432**
Torremolinos **437**
Torres, Julio Romero de **58**

Torrox 353
Torrox-Costa 353
tourism 32
Tours 118
traffic 467
Trajan 80
travel documents 448
Trevélez 155
turismo rural 86

U
Úbeda 176
Ubrique 427
Upper Andalucía 13
Utrera 439

V
Vandals 37

Vega de Granada 273
Vejer de la Frontera 440
Velázquez, Diego de
  Silva y 56, 81
Vélez Blanco 443
Vélez-Málaga 354
Vélez Rubio 445
Villacarillo 182
Villamartín 170
Villanueva del Arzotopo
  182
Villanueva del Río y
  Minas 201
Visigoths 37, 49
Viznar 273

W
water 18

water shortage 18
water temperatures 21
Western Leone 147
when to go 469
Wildlife parks 90
windsurfing 113

Y
Yegen 156
youth hostels 86

Z
Zahara de la Sierra 428
Zahara de los Atunes
  441
Zuheros 349
Zurbarán, Francisco
  de 55

List of Maps and Illustrations

Sightseeing Highlights **2**
Facts and Figures Infographic **14/15**
Climate **19**
Provinces **25**
Europe's Hothouse (infographic) **30/31**
Battles between Moors and Christians **38**
Types of Arch **50**
Civilisation for Europe (infographic) **66/67**
Tours Through Andalucía **118/119**
Tour 1 **124**
Tour 2 **127**
Tour 3 **129**
Tour 4 **131**
Algeciras **137**
Almería **139**
Almería, Alcazaba **143**
The Sun's Energy (infographic) **148/149**
Baeza **175**
Úbeda **179**
Cádiz **189**
Carmona, Necrópolis romana **200**
Córdoba **206**
Córdoba, Mezquita Catedral (3D) **213**
Córdoba, Mezquita-Catedral **215**
Coto de Doñana, Lageplan **202**
Écija **235**
Gibraltar **244**

Granada **251**
Granada, Alhambra and Generalife **253**
Granada, Nasrid Palace **256**
Granada, Alhambra (3D) **259**
Granada, Cathedral **265**
Huelva **279**
Huelva, Monasterio de Santa María de la Rábida **282**
A Mistake Makes History (infographic) **284/285**
Itálica, Roman Town **287**
Jáen, Cathedral **290**
Jáen **292**
Versatile Fruit (infographic) **300/301**
The Secret of Sherry (infographic) **306/307**
Wine growing regions **310**
Jérez de la Frontera **313**
Málaga, Cathedral **323**
Málaga **324**
Marbella **332/333**
Ronda **374**
Bloody Relict (infographic) **384/385**
Sevilla **400**
Sevilla, Cathedral **403**
Sevilla, Cathedral (3D) **405**
Sevilla, Alcázar **408**

Overview **back cover inside**

Photo Credits

Publisher's Information

1st Edition 2015
Worldwide Distribution: Marco Polo
Travel Publishing Ltd
Pinewood, Chineham Business Park
Crockford Lane, Chineham
Basingstoke, Hampshire RG24 8AL,
United Kingdom.

Photos, illlustrations, maps::
173 photos, 52 maps and and illustra-
tions, one large map
Text:
Rainer Eisenschmid,Reinhard Zakr-
zewski, Martina Johnson, Wieland
Höhne, Tobias Büscher
Editing:
John Sykes, Robert Taylor
Translation: David Andersen, Barbara
Schmidt-Runkel, John Sykes, Robert
Taylor
Cartography:
Franz Huber, Munich; MAIRDUMONT
Ostfildern (large map)
3D illustrations:
jangled nerves, Stuttgart
Infographics:
Golden Section Graphics GmbH, Berlin
Design:
independent Medien-Design, Munich
Editor-in-chief:
Rainer Eisenschmid, Mairdumont
Ostfildern

Printed in China

Despite all of our authors' thorough
research, errors can creep in. The pub-
lishers do not accept any liability for thi
Whether you want to praise, alert us to
errors or give us a personal tip Please
contact us by email or post:

MARCO POLO Travel Publishing Ltd
Pinewood, Chineham Business Park
Crockford Lane, Chineham
Basingstoke, Hampshire RG24 8AL
United Kingdom
Email: sales@marcopolouk.com

FSC
www.fsc.org
MIX
Paper from
responsible sources
FSC® C011918

MARCO POLO

HANDBOOKS

MARCO POLO
TRAVEL HANDBOOK
ANDALUCÍA
INFOGRAPHICS · 3D ILLUSTRATIONS · PULL-OUT MAP
Insider Tips
NEW

MARCO POLO
TRAVEL HANDBOOK
BARCELONA
INFOGRAPHICS · 3D ILLUSTRATIONS · PULL-OUT MAP
Insider Tips
NEW

MARCO POLO
TRAVEL HANDBOOK
BERLIN
INFOGRAPHICS · 3D ILLUSTRATIONS · PULL-OUT MAP
Insider Tips
NEW

MARCO POLO
TRAVEL HANDBOOK
DRESDEN
INFOGRAPHICS · 3D ILLUSTRATIONS · PULL-OUT MAP
Insider Tips
NEW

MARCO POLO
TRAVEL HANDBOOK
FLORIDA
INFOGRAPHICS · 3D ILLUSTRATIONS · PULL-OUT MAP
Insider Tips
NEW

MARCO POLO
TRAVEL HANDBOOK
GRAN CANARIA
INFOGRAPHICS · 3D ILLUSTRATIONS · PULL-OUT MAP
Insider Tips
NEW

MARCO POLO
TRAVEL HANDBOOK
ICELAND
INFOGRAPHICS · 3D ILLUSTRATIONS · PULL-OUT MAP
Insider Tips
NEW

MARCO POLO
TRAVEL HANDBOOK
LONDON
INFOGRAPHICS · 3D ILLUSTRATIONS · PULL-OUT MAP
Insider Tips
NEW

MARCO POLO
TRAVEL HANDBOOK
NEW YORK
INFOGRAPHICS · 3D ILLUSTRATIONS · PULL-OUT MAP
Insider Tips
NEW

MARCO POLO
TRAVEL HANDBOOK
PARIS
INFOGRAPHICS · 3D ILLUSTRATIONS · PULL-OUT MAP
Insider Tips
NEW

MARCO POLO
TRAVEL HANDBOOK
ROME
INFOGRAPHICS · 3D ILLUSTRATIONS · PULL-OUT MAP
Insider Tips
NEW

MARCO POLO
TRAVEL HANDBOOK
VENICE
INFOGRAPHICS · 3D ILLUSTRATIONS · PULL-OUT MAP
Insider Tips
NEW

www.marco-polo.com

Andalusian Curiosities

Robbers, cave dwellings, a blue village – Andalucía has a few curiosities on hand.

►Robber stronghold Ronda

If the Ronia the robber's daughter had known: Ronda was once a real stronghold for robbers, namely in the 18th/19th century. The men raided and robbed in the surrounding canyons of the Sierra and stole Robin-Hood-like mainly from the rich. Incidentally, the last one was named Juan José Mingolla alias »Longstride« (Pasos Largos). He died in 1934.

►Please touch!

That doesn't happen often. The Museo Interactivo de Música in Málaga has signs that ask guests »Please touch« instead of »Please don't touch«. There you can compose melodies, beat drums and try out wind instruments.

►Blue village

The village Júzcar lies hidden between the co-called Pueblos Blancos, the white villages in the Andalusian interior. But after a long debate the villagers decided to paint their village blue. The reason: Júzcar was the site for the world premier of the film »Smurfs in 3D«Sevilla.

►Soccer City

Sevilla is famous for its buildings. A curious but hardly known fact: the city also regularly produces world-class Spanish soccer players, including David Prieto, Enrique Corrales Martin and José Angel Crespo.

►Schnaps under his robes

The hood wearers of Cuenca in Castile treat themselves to an anis schnaps during the Holy Week processions. The custom is not unknown in Grenada and as well.

►For a Fistful of Dollars!

The dusty movie set town near Almería is called Mini-Hollywood. Instead of holiday-makers, in the past stars like Clint Eastwood, and Burt Lancaster came here to shoot it out in true Western style. Filmy like »For a Fistful of Dollars« were made here because the backdrop was no less than the desert-like landscape in California – but filming was cheaper here.

►Double bed in a cave

In Andalucía there are state-owned accommodation, megalithic hotels, tiny mountain B&Bs. But in Guadix visitors sleep in caves. Not bad in this heat …

►Cuddle-macho as producer

Antonio Banderas is Spain's most successful actor. Once he was even a producer. In 2006 he made the nostalgic movie *Summer Rain* in his home town of Málaga – using only young unknown talent.